Quintessential Jack

Quintessential Jack

The Art of Jack Nicholson on Screen

SCOTT EDWARDS

McFarland & Company, Inc., Publishers
Jefferson, North Carolina

Photographs are from the collection of the author unless credited otherwise.

Library of Congress Cataloguing-in-Publication Data

Names: Edwards, Scott, 1960– author.
Title: Quintessential Jack : the art of Jack Nicholson on screen / Scott Edwards.
Description: Jefferson, North Carolina : McFarland & Company, Inc., Publishers, 2018 | Includes bibliographical references and index.
Identifiers: LCCN 2017052749 | ISBN 9781476670942 (softcover : alk. paper) ∞
Subjects: LCSH: Nicholson, Jack—Criticism and interpretation.
Classification: LCC PN2287.N5 E39 2018 | DDC 791.4302/8092—dc23
LC record available at https://lccn.loc.gov/2017052749

British Library cataloguing data are available

ISBN (print) 978-1-4766-7094-2
ISBN (ebook) 978-1-4766-3086-1

© 2018 Scott Edwards. All rights reserved

No part of this book may be reproduced or transmitted in any form or by any means, electronic or mechanical, including photocopying or recording, or by any information storage and retrieval system, without permission in writing from the publisher.

On the cover: Jack Nicholson in *Heartburn*, 1986 (Paramount Pictures/Photofest)

Printed in the United States of America

McFarland & Company, Inc., Publishers
  Box 611, Jefferson, North Carolina 28640
    www.mcfarlandpub.com

Acknowledgments

There are many people who have honored me with their inspiration, without whose contributions and assistance this book could not have been possible:

My mother and father, both of whom passed away during its writing. My older brother, Kenny, now gone for 16 years, who shared and fueled my early obsession with film. And my younger brother, Michael, who now keeps the family going with me.

Love and support from Natalie.

Encouragement and enthusiasm for the craft of writing from friend David Stuart, author of *Jane at the Fair: The Adventures of Calamity Jane at the 1901 Pan-American Exposition*. The confidence to try from Diane di Prima (directed specifically to me) and Ray Bradbury (as part of a group).

Special thanks to Mews Small for the behind-the-scenes photo shown in the Preface and to Emily Corey for permission to quote from and show her father's notes found in the Jeff Corey Collection at the Ohio State University. Appreciation to Rich Maurer for his sonic forensics to uncover additional content in recorded interviews.

Gratitude to all who took their time to provide interviews and insight, in particular Mews Small, Gary Kent, Michael Margotta and Dr. Brooke Cannon.

Table of Contents

Acknowledgments — v
Preface — 1

1. The Actor as Auteur — 5
2. Heroes and Villains — 29
3. Men on a Mission — 50
4. Pieces of Schmidt — 65
5. A More Perfect Union — 75
6. The School of Roger — 90
7. As Cuckoo as It Gets — 100
8. Hippies and Hogs and Horses — 120
9. From Ballbusters to Heart Attacks — 138
10. The Developing Delinquent — 146
11. Writers on the Storm — 155
12. Rom-Com Wonder — 176
13. Misfits and Misanthropes — 193
14. The Dicks Versus the Hoods — 204
15. Head Trips — 220
16. The Occasional Filmmaker — 248

Chapter Notes — 267
Bibliography — 275
Index — 283

Preface

"This project will be a little tough to get off the ground."[1]
—*Jack Nicholson's agent, Sandy Bressler*

Mr. Bressler was correct. But 12 years and 100,000 words later, this book belongs to you, the reader. *Quintessential Jack: The Art of Jack Nicholson on Screen* presents the most comprehensive study of the actor's career that is neither a story of the man's life nor a *Films of…* approach, but rather an in-depth examination of roles, acting style and technique, and screen persona, as well as the films' thematic links.

Every film is represented, organized into chapters that correlate the types of characters (such as disaffected youth or men trapped in a fatalistic cycle); compare and contrast movie archetypes (heroic roles vs. the villainous); examine the portrayal of the human condition (the depiction of those suffering from mental illness); and follow common messages and themes (sexual freedom and anti-consumerism).

The fluid nature of the book's structure, liberated from a film-by-film chronological format, allows for an enriching exploration of seemingly disparate men. For instance, a shared dedication to duty, honor and a higher organizational calling bring Colonel Jessep from *A Few Good Men* into the same orbit as Jimmy Hoffa from the Danny DeVito biopic and ACLU lawyer George Hanson from *Easy Rider*.

To help collect even the most incongruent characters together in this way, a literary device brings the men of a given chapter together in the same physical space at the same time to introduce them within that chapter. Jessep and Hoffa and Hanson are in one place at one time. They coexist physically just as they coexist via shared character traits.

Four or five Nicholson characters might be in the same diner or jailhouse or some other related setting. This cinematic device underscores the intersection of multiple movie worlds and provides a creative entrée to the idea that is presented in a particular chapter.

Preface

In addition to covering all of Nicholson's motion picture roles, the book also includes individual chapters devoted to his screenwriting work and his directorial efforts.

* * *

This analysis has been augmented by full interviews and "grab-and-go" comments from actors, directors and crew with whom Nicholson has worked. Interview subjects include Shirley Knight, Joe Turkel, Mews Small, the late Ed Nelson, Millie Perkins, Michael Margotta, Nancy Allen, the late Hazel Court, Gary Kent, James Hong, the late Barry Dennen, Jimmie Rodgers, Richard Kaufman and Salli Sachse. Shorter encounters have included the Monkees Michael Nesmith, Micky Dolenz and Peter Tork, as well as Veronica Cartwright, Jack Hill, Ed Begley Jr., the late Martin Landau, Marion Ross, Ve Neill, Noah Wyle, Peter Fonda and Bruce Dern.

Additional perspective has been provided by a range of experts, including

A special moment in time, captured by an unknown photographer between takes of *One Flew Over the Cuckoo's Nest* (1975) at Oregon State Hospital. Jack Nicholson treated Marya (Mews) Small "like a kid sister" (courtesy Mews Small).

several Apollo astronauts (related to the Garrett Breedlove character in *Terms of Endearment* and *The Evening Star*); original TV Batman Adam West; a reporter covering the trial of Whitey Bulger; a psychology professor specializing in the depiction of mental illness on screen; a founding member of the Oakland chapter of the Hells Angels; and the founder and president of the Institute of the American Musical.

The result is a practical viewer's guide for the actor's filmography that presents the Jack Nicholson beyond the cliché, so much more than toothy smiles and arched eyebrows and what I've called his "Jacksplosions" of explosive physical action. My hope is that *Quintessential Jack* can become a passenger as you make your personal journey through the career of one of our most acclaimed actors. Keep it handy as you watch the movies discussed and enjoy your trip through the films of Jack Nicholson.

1

The Actor as Auteur

There is a room. It is large, but sparsely furnished.

Scan the room and see only men. At least 50, maybe 60, 70. Hard to guess what they have in common or what brought them here. Young, old; strong, flabby; loudmouths and introverts; a few are leaders and famous and command attention, while more are questionable, shady, and evade eye contact.

Seating arrangements weren't exactly thought-out, with a hippie next to a military officer and a couple of cops eyeing a few obvious hoods. A drunk astronaut, a drunk ballplayer and a drunk retired detective have too much in common—leveling their differences through a corrosive commonality.

Too happy, too depressive, too goddamned obsessive, they're all here together with writers and rockers, a lawyer and a dog trainer, an insurance bean counter and a hotel caretaker. This is some group of a bunch of real characters.

What brought them together and what can they have in common?

They are all the creation of one man, one man who brought them to life through truth and effort and research and will. One man made almost 75 men come to life in collaboration with many other men and many other women.

This room is filled with Jack Nicholson, filled with his creations and his collection of characters. This one, large room is large enough to hold the career's work that breathes the essence of this actor-writer-director. That is the "quintessential Jack," all that defines Nicholson's film career.

"Jack wanted to appeal to the whole world. And he did." That's how co-star Millie Perkins put it.[1]

In a career spanning over half a century, Nicholson invented nearly 75 men, men who all reside in this one place. They coincide, not always so comfortably, yet have come together to influence each new visitor. The room always stays the same size, while the experience and insight and feelings fill it up more and more.

* * *

Traditionally, it's only the director who's been given the credit as auteur, but why not the actor as well?

Directors merit scholarly study. They are filmmakers. They shape the film. When they are big enough and important enough, we call them auteurs.

But what about the serious actor? Isn't it possible that a screen actor of import who can command exorbitant salaries can also shape his or her career choices into meaningful patterns of theme and subject matter, with formative influence over the work beyond the role itself?

If an actor has the commercial power and artistic integrity of a Jack Nicholson, it does seem likely that the stories chosen, the messages intended, the issues advanced, and the aesthetics embodied become an integral part of that actor's choices.

Nicholson admitted that "some movies can't get made without someone like me in them. You can't call yourself an auteur if you want Robert Duvall for a part but wind up with Jeff Goldblum."[2]

True, many of the movies were primarily commercial decisions and others obligations to colleagues (no other explanation than the latter can plausibly justify *How Do You Know* or *Man Trouble*). But look at this list: Films like *Carnal Knowledge*, *The King of Marvin Gardens*, *The Last Detail*, *The Passenger*, *Reds*, *The Border*, *Ironweed*, *Hoffa*, *The Crossing Guard* and *The Pledge* don't get produced—at least not on the scale they were and for wide release—without the weight of this star and the influence of this actor-artist. They could have been made, completed with difficulty on the smallest budgets and independently distributed, yet they probably would *not* have gotten the exposure, nor would they be recalled these many years or decades later, no matter how artistically successful, without the heft of a Jack.

Political and social messages are interwoven throughout the actor's career. Once established, Nicholson was able to choose his projects. Prior to the breakthroughs of *Easy Rider* and *Five Easy Pieces*, the decisions were more or less made for him, to pay rent and get credits. He didn't exactly go on *The Andy Griffith Show* (twice!) because he wanted to put the spotlight on small town America struggling to survive against big city encroachment.

His screenwriting, however, does provide clues about the man's beliefs, through patterns about sexual liberation, materialism, drug use and the Vietnam War that begin to offer a view into the artist's sensibilities.

Take another look at that list of films with this in mind and it's easier to craft an image of an influential figure who creates and chooses projects and roles in order to say something. Nicholson grew into the "actor as auteur" role, blending social commentary with box office acceptance to forge a truth as actor, writer and director.

Obviously, this use of "auteur" applies more to the French translation of "author" and a dictionary definition of "an artist whose style and practice are distinctive," rather than relating to the auteur theory, which represents the director as the "primary creative force." Calling the actor an auteur is more about formative and foundational involvement, and exercising a meaningful structural influence instead of any sort of suggestion that Nicholson takes over a production just because he's a big star (not that such a thing has never happened in the history of the movie business).

In *Reframing Screen Performance*, Cynthia Baron and Sharon Marie Carnicke posit that a film's "author" is not necessarily an individual but an abstracted personality, and that audiences create a "Jack Nicholson" persona from the characters plus the actor's personality. A "recursive process is formed between the iconic 'Nicholson' construct and the Nicholson films, wherein the two constantly shape and reshape each other," making connections between scenes and continuities among characters.[3] Dennis Bingham adds that this dynamic puts the "author" of a Nicholson film open to debate, with the actor's presence strong enough for the persona to transcend the *mise en scène*.[4]

Nicholson wrote that the "actor brings to his work the undeniable uniqueness of himself and the work takes on a personal quality that has a fabric incomparable to anyone or anything else."[5]

After over 60 motion picture credits as an actor, six as screenwriter, and three as director spanning more than 50 years, Nicholson meets the standard deserving an in-depth examination of his work, in a new way—the way ordinarily afforded solely to directors.

* * *

Sometimes, Hollywood gets it right. But it might take a while.

It took several years of small roles and experiments in script work, but Jack finally broke through in 1969 with *Easy Rider*. The following year's *Five Easy Pieces* made him a star.

Millie Perkins, who worked with him in Monte Hellman's back-to-back productions *Ride in the Whirlwind* and *The Shooting*, told me about that struggle: "He wanted to make it badly; he wanted to have a career. He wanted to *be* in the business." She recalled the moment of the breakthrough: "Jack came to New York and he needed a place to stay, and he stayed with my husband and me there. I remember him walking down to the beach and I saying to my husband, 'Poor Jack. He wants to make it so bad, but he probably never will.' And there he was, right after that—*Easy Rider* and all the rest of them started to happen and there he was. The guy made it!"[6]

The years of slow progress did get to him, as actor-stuntman Gary Kent remembered while connecting that frustration to Nicholson's forays into writing and producing. "He was quite proud that he had done Weary Reilly in *Studs Lonigan* and had been a minor hit in Europe. And he kept saying, 'In

Europe, they know who I am, but over here they don't, they don't know me yet.'" Kent felt that Nicholson's "main interest was acting, and that if he had to produce in order to do it, then he was going to."[7]

Robert Vaughn, who worked with Nicholson in acting classes in the late 1950s, recalled Jack's frustration about his career. Vaughn had become a star via TV's *The Man from U.N.C.L.E.*, while Nicholson was struggling in exploitation movies and small television roles. In the early fall of 1967, Nicholson sat on the floor of Vaughn's dressing room and declared, "Vaughnie, I'm going to give myself two more years in this business. Then I'm going to look for another way to make a living."[8]

While collaborating on the Monkees movie *Head*, Nicholson let loose to director Bob Rafelson: "I'm tired of it. I always get to play the shitty B-part, not the A-part, and it's always in conventional movies."[9]

That challenging journey began in acting classes taught by Jeff Corey and Martin Landau. Bruce Dern recollects, "Whether they'd been in the Actors Studio or not, we all basically came to California with the same desires and urges. [Nicholson] came right to Hollywood and I think he was working at Metro" and at that time "was in the acting class along with a bunch of other really terrific young actors, taught by Marty Landau."[10]

"I'm still teaching," Landau told me, not long before he passed away. When I asked him the most important thing he taught actors like Nicholson, he replied, "Everything. It would take me two years to explain." The Method teacher felt that Nicholson had "tremendous potential, but not a lot of craft."[11]

Nicholson has paid tribute to Corey's influence, but Nicholson's early notices—in the form of Corey's own class notes—aren't exactly indicative of a formative future award-winning icon. Here is one such example:

> Nicholson!—needs poetry—surge—conservative—undoing—bilious—must enthuse more. Petty childish—needs maturity and some degree of caring application. Too concerned with self—doesn't care for acting as such—Quite disappointing—Won't face his fear of acting maturely. Ought to discuss possible termination. Put up or shut up.[12]

A personal assessment provided to Jack was just as unfavorable:

> Nicholson, J
> Have to select more carefully what it is you are playing. There is a kind of undisciplined wandering. Too vague—not fixed enough. Make yourself a surer target. You move and filibuster as though to keep from committing yourself.... Just a vague impression of charm and humor.[13]

As part of my research, I had the rare privilege of accessing 23 boxes of materials relating to the acting class, thanks to the Thompson Library Special Collection at the Ohio State University. The aspiring young actor struggled at first, with feedback both direct and critical, yet ultimately invigorating and helpful:

1. The Actor as Auteur

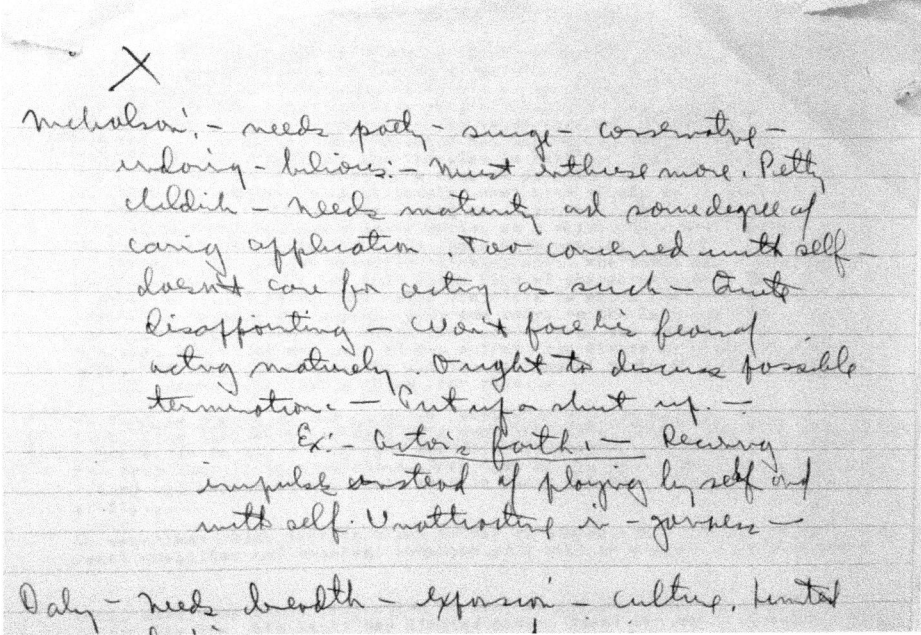

After actor Jeff Corey was blacklisted, he helped some of the biggest names in Hollywood learn the craft of acting—including Jack Nicholson. These class notes from the early 1960s, in Corey's own hand, show that Nicholson was far from obvious star material at the time (courtesy Jeff Corey Collection, Thompson Special Collection, Ohio State University).

> Jack.... Sometimes the voice is strong and authoritative and the body is rambling, uncoordinated and unsure ... sometimes the body is commanding and impressive and the voice is weak and high pitched.... Bear down on the parts that belong to you ... claim what is yours and beat the living hell out of it...[14]

Gary Kent pointed out that the LA scene at the time didn't include much in terms of stage work, so actors "belonged to what we called 'groups' and they were really intense. Jack and Harry [Dean Stanton] were in that together, and they were like acting gymnasiums. They were a great place to work out and do acting if you couldn't get a picture."[15]

Shirley Knight, who worked alongside Nicholson nearly four decades after these classes (as Helen Hunt's mother in *As Good as It Gets*), remembered, "He and I were in acting class together in 1959 ... the Jeff Corey class."[16]

Millie Perkins also studied with Corey, but after starring in *The Diary of Anne Frank*. "Jack was a working actor," she said. "He was young when he came to Hollywood. He *wanted* to be in the movie business and he was doing plays and everything he could to make it in the business."[17]

Nicholson, J
Have to select more carefully what it is you are playing. There is a kind
of undisciplined wandering. Too vague-not ~~fixe~~ enough, Make yourself a
surer target, You move a d filibuster as though to keep from committing
yourself. Try more concretely to do 'a' thing. Don't rely on chance
success. Think back on all the things you've done and its hard to get
a clear image of anything. Just a vague impression of charm and humor.

Reynolds
Exemplary effort. Loves his craft. Have to avoid too much of the excep-
tioanl. Have to make comment on the ordinary. Not intending to discourage
the poetic...Make more characterization comment. We've discussed the
tendency to overgeneralize and romanticize. M_ore silences. Act as clearly
non-verbally as verbally. Vocal dimensions extraodinarraly expressive.

V Aldridge
Immaturity. Lack of threat and motivation. Have to care more. Be larger
woman. R_eact as in crisis. Little girl devices keep conflict too petty.
Vague look in eye deny reality. Also.; play need. Sexual insulation.
There is a false security. A complacency which is not dynamic or energetic.

Varsi
Spontaneity. Use associations. Ckncentrate more on implications...

Severs
Goes well. Learned use of polarity. Movement must be more contal nes. Too

---

PERSONAL

Jack. A question of solidifying..of integrating all your qualities into
a totality. There is a diffusion of parts..a seperation of elements..
a reluctance, it would seem, to appear in one defineable quality...
Much of the work has rendered wonderful qualities and then the seperateness
would manifest itself. Sometimes the voice isstrong and autheratative and
the body is rambling, uncoordianted and unsure..sometimes the body is
commanding and impressive and thevoice is weak and high pitched. I think
that what has to be created is a concept as self as a whole..In working
on characterization to think thusly; what kind of man am I..who have I
known..how did behave..How strong am I..or weak..what wights can I
lift or manipulate..can I sew a button on a shirt..What about my amours..
what kind of women..How do I get along with men..de I think myself better
or worse..This kind of specific thinking about character can reduce random
portrayal and present the full blown kind of characterization that you're
capable of... Would suggest vocal exercises to match the man and physical
exercises to help you possess your own body. In the last analysis , that s
what it is..you need to reclaim the usex of your own organism for your
own use. Don't let any part of you suffer from disuse or neglect..bring
back, forcibly, if necessary, all the componebnt parts of your being into
useful ,productive work withinx the role...

We tend to behave as though we're borrowing our own voices, operating our
limbs like they were borrowed on a tentaive rental basis from some circulating
library. We're timid with our own devoces..loathe to work them too hard
fir fear they'll be expoloited..Bear down on the parts that belong to you
..deny all seperateness..claim what is yours and beat the living hell out
of it,...

We sometimes think that it works better on ethers..That the use of certain

Top: Acting teacher Jeff Corey's class notes about student Jack Nicholson didn't indicate the potential later realized. In contrast, Burt Reynolds was at the time highly regarded. *Bottom:* It's a testament to Jack's dedication that he continued to act, as this Jeff Corey assessment illustrates (courtesy Jeff Corey Collection, Thompson Special Collections, Ohio State University).

Despite his years of low-budget exploitation movies and forgettable TV gigs, Nicholson colleagues do look back as if his success was predetermined. Salli Sachse played a key role in the Corman-produced, Nicholson-scripted *The Trip* and recalled Jack as "pretty experienced at that time. I mean, he had done quite a few horror movies with Roger. He was talented and he was funny and there was no doubt that he was on his way. No doubt about that. And I think it was the next year that they did *Easy Rider*."[18]

Perkins makes it sound almost mystical: "Jack had a gift from the gods. Somebody blessed him and said, 'You're gonna be there and you're always gonna be there.' ... He's always a star and he will always be, and when he's on-screen you watch him and you don't watch anybody else. He's just got gold over his head or something that's magic that other people don't have."[19]

* * *

Supernaturally assisted or not, once Nicholson got his chance, he never let up. This actor effectively balanced big Hollywood turns with more artistic, small-scale projects. Commercial, yes, but also personal.

Upon the success of *Easy Rider* and *Five Easy Pieces*, Nicholson became a new star of the New Hollywood. He also started to become a force in the filmmaking itself. He's a versatile actor as well as a multifaceted professional, equally adept as a hapless hero (flawed, famous men in *Mars Attacks!*, *Broadcast News* and *Terms of Endearment*) as he is playing monstrous villains (in *The Departed*, *The Shooting* and *Batman*). He can play big and gregarious (*One Flew Over the Cuckoo's Nest*, *Easy Rider*, *Goin' South*) just as convincingly as small and uncertain (*About Schmidt*, *The King of Marvin Gardens*, *Ironweed*). He's made characters into icons (such as Bobby Dupea in *Five Easy Pieces*, Melvin Udall in *As Good as It Gets*, Jake Gittes in *Chinatown* and *The Two Jakes*) and has made real people more accessible (Jimmy Hoffa and Eugene O'Neill). Intellectuals and idiots; men who reach enlightenment and losers mired in misogyny; the monsters, the killers, the charmers, the loyals, the vindictive; chasers, poets, the disillusioned and the dedicated.

In David Mamet's AFI tribute essay about Nicholson, the playwright explained that in great performers, "we see not the characters created for the part, but the true character of the performer."[20] Nicholson said that "the actor is the litterateur of his era" who writes his inner history "through choice of roles and how he plays them."[21]

* * *

Watch the eyes. They glare, they stare, they search, beseech, betray, seduce, wrench, defile and pierce. Blaring fast when upset or lying, and staying impossibly still with intimidation or conviction. They form tears when inconsolable.

It's the eyes that get the attention when looking at a picture or studying a person. On the screen, they can be magnified and lighted and framed to carry a scene and convey every emotion more than any dialogue ever could.

Eyes are the actor's secret weapon. This is no secret to Jack Nicholson.

Without actually watching the films, it's easy to remember his eyes, most famously and most menacingly when announcing himself through a hole in a door made by an axe in *The Shining*. Or the range of emotions held by those eyes in *Cuckoo's Nest*, from the jester and the conspirator to the instigator and the victim. Recall the eyes of Melvin as he tells Carol she makes him want to be a better man in *As Good as It Gets*; the disdainful glance he throws toward the pompous elitists and the pedantic waitress in *Five Easy Pieces*; the unhinged, endless search for the same clues and the same witnesses over and over again by the retired detective in *The Pledge*; the masochist in *The Little Shop of Horrors* and the raucous in *The Witches of Eastwick, Anger Management* and *Batman*.

Compare two different Nicholson performances from 1992. When Jimmy Hoffa says that he's "gonna do what I gotta do," he is an out-of-control beast whose threat is reflected in his eyes, eyes that are glowing, wildly darting, and with the moist appearance of someone who desperately needs more sleep or less alcohol. When Colonel Jessep tells his immature inquisitor in *A Few Good Men* that he "can't handle the truth," that threat is reflected in his eyes through their steely self-control, an unblinking stare and disciplined focus that could not be distracted or impaired, the kind of a glare that is fueled by disgust and superiority.

* * *

How does one human being become so many others, and do so in a convincing enough way to draw an audience in, break them away from their own world, and impel an emotional response—whether empathy, disgust, encouragement or pity? For a Method actor such as Nicholson, preparation and connecting personally to the character each play a big part.

Amongst actors, Nicholson is famous for the depth of his preparation and research. Joseph Turkel, who played Lloyd the bartender in *The Shining*, tells of how he saw the actor reading a book in his dressing room during that production. When Turkel inquired, he was told that it was about the effects of freezing on the human body. "My character freezes and I want to know just how it happens," Nicholson explained. "I want to get it, feel it, show it, as it is."[22]

That last sentence may well best sum up the value of preparation in creating a role imbued with truth.

According to Gary Kent, much research preceded the production on *Ride in the Whirlwind*. "Jack had spent a lot of time in the library before we went up to shoot, reading about those times [the Old West] and studying those times." He said that "dedication and research and a lack of fear" were the most significant contributions to the quality of Nicholson's work.[23]

Millie Perkins remembers how she argued with Nicholson over a hat at Western Costume because Jack wanted the same one she chose for her role in their other Monte Hellman western, *The Shooting*.[24]

Kent also underscored the importance of physicality to the actor, having heard that Nicholson "always carried something in his pocket that he thought belonged to the character or fit the character that he could touch whenever he felt out of touch."[25]

Often the preparation and the physicality go together. The actor must learn to appear to have a certain vocation or master a given skill. Handling a gun, painting a picture, working on a car, riding a surfboard. No matter the activity, the actor must look natural or it distracts from the story and brings attention to a phoniness that can only undermine a performance.

When Nicholson was getting ready to play Daryl Van Horne in *The Witches of Eastwick*, he practiced every day for about three months to learn to *appear* to play the violin. His violin coach Richard Kaufman described the process as "working very hard for what on camera ended up being about 15 or 20 seconds."[26] He was also on set for the days of shooting that involved the music sequences, an experience he termed "the highest level of filmmaking.... [Y]ou don't get to work at that level unless you have a great commitment and desire to do the very best possible work."[27]

Barry Dennen, who played Bill Watson in *The Shining*, remembered Jack as "so confident in his own body, so comfortable with himself. He liked himself, which a lot of actors do not." Because of Nicholson's preparation and experience, he could slip in, do the shot and go back to editing down the hall. "They'd call him in, literally just a few minutes after they got the camera set up (with a stand-in). He just popped into place and started to work. He was very quick, and very good." Dennen, who considered working with Nicholson a great honor, called him a "fucking brilliant pro" whose magic is that he knows how to do it, and he does it. "And it's always Jack. It is always Jack, and it is always wonderful."[28]

Hells Angel Sonny Barger recalled that Jack seemed such a natural on a motorcycle in *Hells Angels on Wheels* that "every other chapter [motorcycle club] thought he was from another chapter." Sonny elaborated that it wasn't so much how Nicholson handled a bike, but "because of the way he handled himself."[29]

Perhaps a Jersey boy doesn't take to riding a horse as confidently as riding a Hog. According to Gary Kent, "When [Nicholson] used to dismount from his horse, he'd always look down at the ground." The veteran stuntmaster had to intervene and tell the actor, "You look like you're afraid you're going

From a front porch in Neptune, New Jersey, to handprints in Hollywood. Jack's childhood home on the Jersey shore hid the secrets of an unknown father and a misidentified mother.

to step in some horse shit. Step off your horse looking straight ahead like you know where you're going. And it's going to make your character stronger." Nicholson thanked Kent and did it Kent's way, "and years later, he told me, 'You know, I still use that little thing you gave me, that tip you gave me, to act like you know where you're going. I still use that.'"[30]

An actor who regularly resides at a higher level is a prepared actor. Noah Wyle, who worked on *A Few Good Men*, was still amazed a quarter century after watching Nicholson prepare for his role as Colonel Nathan Jessep. His pre-shoot table read-through was "almost identical" to what we eventually saw on the screen. "He went for it. That scene where he was, 'You can't handle the truth!'—we heard it right there for the first time in that room. He came in with a great performance already dialed in."[31]

Nancy Allen, who played the girl that Badass Buddusky tries to pick up at a party in *The Last Detail*, described Nicholson as "very well prepared, has done his homework, knows where he is going with the character, and like any good actor that's really prepared, you can be laughing and talking one minute and just slip into the character because you have done your homework."³²

Becoming the character also involves channeling, as Bruce Dern explains. "If you come to work sad and you're in some grim circumstances in your life, then find that to work into the day's work that day if that's part of your character." He further relates that process to the Method by outlining its basic principles: "You really look at something; you really listen to what they're saying; and everything comes out of that, comes out of what's really going on at the moment."³³

When you talk to a lot of actors, you hear words like "truth" and "real" and "respond" along with phrases like "in the moment" and "depth of character." When you talk to a lot of actors about Jack Nicholson, you hear those same words and those same phrases a lot. You also hear the words and phrases "dedicated," "sincere" and "conscientious"³⁴ (Robert Dix from *Rebel Rousers*); "organic"³⁵ (Allen); "extraordinarily talented"³⁶ (*Carnal Knowledge* co-star Rita Moreno); "the master actor"³⁷ (James Hong from *Chinatown* and *The Two Jakes*); "hard-working," "serious" and "always into his character"³⁸ (Kent); and "a person who wanted to grow and learn"³⁹ (Perkins). Knight concluded, "I think the work tells. Let me put it that way: The work shows, and people who know really know."⁴⁰

Nicholson's dedication to research and detail, down to his attention to wardrobe and dialect, come to life through what I call "character energy." Character energy encompasses the combinations of immediacy and action that go into a portrayal, together with all of the preparation and obsession that help shape the role and make it true. In this way, Nicholson's characters achieve their strength and lasting resonance by virtue of hard work, mental application, emotional connection and studied craft.

This is an actor who also intrinsically knows all facets of the filmmaking process, which helps give the juice to his work. He studied at what Bruce Dern called "the University of Roger Corman,"⁴¹ an apprenticeship of sorts perfect for anyone who had the desire to learn and the spirit to apply what was learned. Making do with small budgets and pitching in to fill multiple roles was never perceived as additional work without additional pay for those with enough foresight to grasp its potential.

Mews Small, who played Candy in *One Flew Over the Cuckoo's Nest*, described Nicholson's great skill and how he helped the then-inexperienced film actress, "like when I came through the window [into the mental institution], he would just pick me up, spin me around, and put me in the right place for the camera."⁴²

He knows where the camera is and what it does, and what he should do to take advantage of the actor's relationship with the lens. He has written screenplays, so he knows what makes a story work and how to advance a narrative through exposition, action and dialogue. He understands the interrelationship between characters, as well as how to create an effective characterization. He has also directed, learning to frame a story and compose a shot, along with working a Moviola and in the process gain a functional understanding of editing. Michael Margotta, whom Nicholson directed in *Drive, He Said*, passed along a lesson from Nicholson: "He said to me one day, 'If you learn film editing, you could save yourself eight years.'"[43]

Hollywood's most successful actor of the past few decades, combining box office appeal with industry accolades, earned his success through study and effort. Stardom may have been late-blooming, but hardly accidental. Taking risks and sublimating fear made—and continues to make—the difference between Nicholson's character energy and an ordinary actor just playing a part.

Ed Nelson, who worked on Jack's big screen debut *The Cry Baby Killer* in 1957, explained this essential ingredient. "Talent is important, but it's number two by a long, long way. Number one is courage. You need the courage that you can face defeat."[44]

Nancy Allen said of Nicholson, "I think that he's just fearless. I think most good actors are. And sometimes you're great and sometimes you maybe miss the mark a little bit, but at least it's a deliberate choice." Having worked alongside the actor on her first film, *The Last Detail*, she observed, "He's very specific about his choices. I think there's no safety there. I mean, he really goes full out, and no guarding against it. He usually makes his choices and goes all the way with them."[45]

Kent, who worked with the developing actor on four films, also describes this lack of fear: "Jack was not afraid to take unattractive parts and do something with them." He talks of how it never bothered Nicholson to be different. "It wasn't only dedication, but he had courage toward this business. 'Let's go for it. Let's try it. If it advances the story, let's do it, let's not play it safe.' I admired that. He wasn't afraid to take a leading man and make him into a character."[46]

Observing Nicholson work on *Terms of Endearment*, Jeff Daniels learned "to simply walk into the action of the scene and go with whatever happens." Daniels watched how the actor "set himself up with the basics of the character and the situation, and then he'll just go with it. He's not afraid of making wrong choices."[47]

Courage does not necessarily mean total dominance, as singer Tom Waits explained after working with Nicholson on *Ironweed*. "Jack makes you look good when you're with him. He's not picking your pocket, never grandstanding, not trying to eclipse the people he's with. He's trying to make himself small."[48]

Drive, He Said star Margotta, now an acting instructor in Rome, spoke from innate knowledge when he said, "Jack is a strong, courageous actor. His choices are always strong.... The career speaks for itself."[49]

Perhaps Nicholson is his most courageous and most willing to give it all, with no physical or verbal limits, with what I call his Jacksplosions, those memorable moments of explosive action for which he has become so well-known. In *Five Easy Pieces*, he attacks his own car's interior when trapped by girlfriend Rayette into taking her along on a trip to see his family. Colonel Jessep blasts at Tom Cruise's Kaffee that he "can't handle the truth," even recognizing that this outburst exposes his own complicity. Buddusky, McMurphy, *The Shining*'s Jack Torrance, Charlie Smith and Charley Partanna, the Devil and the Joker, Jimmy Hoffa and Frank Costello have all lost it, in the controlled chaos that brings Jack's character energy beyond limits many actors dare not approach. When a character's dialogue becomes incoherent; when he pushes and punches wildly and in a blur; and when a man loses the self-control and forgets his self-awareness such that drool flows (seemingly absentmindedly) and spit flies (apparently lost in the moment); when these things happen, they do not occur without control, but because of it.

Writing about *The Last Detail* in *Acting in the Cinema*, James Naramore describes Nicholson's "snarling, inarticulate rage during which he punches a lamp and smashes his fist against the wall." No longer Jack Nicholson, the actor becomes Buddusky and loses all free will as the character goes out of control. "These frightening outbursts of anger set a pattern in Nicholson's films, of definitive moments when the character becomes an embarrassment, when one would like to look away but can't."[50]

Ed Nelson talked about having control over one's being. "You give up yourself. It doesn't mean that you're not in the picture. You can't give away your physical being, you can't give away the actions of your life." He explained a key relationship that happens when making a movie that appropriately personifies the camera itself: "The camera loves you. It is your closest friend. It will never let you down. It always will see what you're thinking, and it loves you, so please remember that the camera is part of the scene and he loves you.... There are many people who are afraid of it, subconsciously afraid of it."[51]

Nicholson's knowledge of the camera and the value of expression help him command the screen and take charge of a scene. Confidence plus preparation yield results, in many cases famous and even iconic ones. A lesser-known pair of films, shot back to back in the Utah desert in the mid–'60s, provide a lesson in on-screen human potential.

Monte Hellman, who directed *Ride in the Whirlwind* and *The Shooting*, agreed with my proposition that acting students would benefit from seeing Millie Perkins and Jack Nicholson play drastically different characters, in quickly made movies made in the same place and with much of the same

It took sixteen years from Nicholson's motion picture debut to join the Grauman's Chinese Theatre forecourt of superstars.

crew.[52] In *Ride*, they are backward and awkward, uncertain and near-innocent, while in *The Shooting*, they are harsh and hardened, hell-bent on revenge and sadistic to the core.

That same knowledge of the camera and the need for the actor to engender a relationship with it also influenced his support of other actors. Acting is a collaborative art, and Nicholson became known for "sticking around off-camera, after his part of a scene was completed, and feeding his lines to other performers." For a *Carnal Knowledge* scene with Candice Bergen on the telephone, Nicholson "overacted like crazy to force her out of her reserve and raise her performance."[53]

Director Milos Forman paid tribute to Nicholson's generosity as an actor by jokingly writing that he attempted to win over the other actors by feeding them their lines so the "superstar" could rest, but it failed because Nicholson stayed to read lines himself. "It was pure selfishness on Jack's part because somehow he found out that helping the others would make him even better."[54]

* * *

1. The Actor as Auteur 19

Meryl Streep wrote, "[T]here he is, where he belongs, the outlaw icon, slipped into the culture like a letter under the door, a letter we always like when we find ourselves reading it."[55]

A classic Method actor, Nicholson uses his body as an instrument, wholly aware of himself and of his body's potential to add accents to his dialogue; depth to his characterization; power to his interplay with other actors; edge to his conflict; and pathos to his struggles.

While working, Nicholson reminds himself, "Remember, everything counts. Everything." He's led by Strasberg's definition, "Anything that works; that's the Method." Nicholson claims to be amazed that he's not considered a Method actor and that "I'm still fooling them" and considers it an accomplishment to keep fooling the experts, because "there's probably no one who understands Method acting better academically than I do, or actually uses it more in his work."[56]

Re-watch your favorite performance, or try a movie you have not yet seen, but turn the sound off. No distractions, no dialogue, no distinctive Jack voice. Pure silent cinema, with a man reaching out through the screen to touch the viewer, traveling all the way from bombast to nuance, at once a train barreling toward you propelled by mass and energy, and next a broken and bent figure of pain and vulnerability. So much more than the teeth and the eyebrows that form the caricature, Nicholson uses muscle and sinew ... or a faint flicker of a slight squint ... or a wave of the hand with a rocking on the feet. Without the sound, you see how he uses his body as an instrument, and like any instrument, the tone and volume and rhythm come from the body.

Watch McMurphy as he surveys the inmates' party and marvel at how many expressions and thoughts you can identify without sounds; watch Colonel Jessep's icy glare on the stand as he uses all of his discipline to focus perfectly forward; watch George Hanson take a belt of booze and become a bird; watch Jack Torrance in a catatonic state as he tries to comfort his son while succeeding in creeping us out; watch Garrett Breedlove, Francis Phelan, Henry Lloyd Moon, J.J. Gittes and Harry Sanborn each give in to love and convey their feelings in their own ways. Watch closely the control and intent, and you are watching someone doing rather than pretending, being instead of acting.

Author Beverly Walker saw and heard the crew applauding the actor during the shooting of *Cuckoo's Nest* (a rare honor for an actor). It happened again and again as they watched "a remarkable, spookily personal performance" during which Nicholson reached such a "Zen-like state of oneness with his character the director's voice calling 'Cut!' caught him unawares and he'd blink in surprise."[57]

Art Garfunkel described how Nicholson pushed himself "to the top of the Richter scale" on *Carnal Knowledge* in take after take of an entire scene in which Jack had to reach "the absolute top of rage and embarrassment over what he thinks [Ann-Margret's Bobbie is] doing to him.... I was just humbled and awed at the amount of work energy asked of him." Garfunkel wondered where it all came from, and Nicholson gave him a conspiratorial look as he answered, "I love to act."[58]

Like an instrument produces notes (the material provided in the script), the actor produces moments. But it's the overtones that distinguish a Jack Nicholson performance from someone doing a note-for-note reading of the same lines from the same scenes. Without overtones, all musical instruments would sound the same when producing any given note at any given pitch and any given volume. Without overtones, the same note on a clarinet and a piano sound identical. You cannot tell the instruments apart. The overtones color the tone, creating the timbre so you can tell one instrument from another. Nicholson employs an actor's version of these overtones, using voice and expression, stance and motion, to color the character and play the harmonics within a role.

Bruce Dern reduced good acting to playing a part without performing, to being what he called "publicly private."[59]

* * *

Now turn the sound on and cue up some memorable dialogue moments. Hear Nicholson and concentrate on his delivery, how he believes the words he is saying.

Listen as he orders a chicken salad sandwich in *Five Easy Pieces* as no sandwich has been ordered before or since. Concentrate on how he navigates the character energy from cool to hot to explosive, beginning neutrally until he is blocked by inanity and mindless rules that are delivered in a patronizing manner by a waitress who cares less about service than servitude. He feigns patience as he tries in vain to be helpful. Jack becomes snotty and sarcastic, the antihero attitude emerging degree by degree, his voice rising in volume, pitch and speed simultaneously. This is a battle of generations and about freedoms, a battle than cannot be won by either side. With "You see this sign?!" one of the most famous Jacksplosions clears the diner table. Having the monitor off, what you don't see is how casually he then puts on his shades, post-release in a post-coital moment of sudden calm and control.

Fast-forward almost 30 years to appreciate the subtleties in Melvin Udall's confession to Carol at a restaurant. Yes, he should have danced with her, but he never would have been driven to bare himself in such a vulnerable and touching manner. Nicholson is soft-spoken but anything but soft. He brings a dramatic control to the pathos, revealing how he's started to take his medicine because of her. He is a better man, a man whose nuanced intonation turns Melvin from a broad, near-caricature to a richly defined human. Jack sounds sincere because he feels every word, and he feels every word because the actor's craft makes him live it as he delivers it—rather than reach the words he already knows. You can tell that Udall is thinking about what he says, in measured and meaningful tones, words pushed out as if breathed, perhaps because the new direction of his life is relying on every syllable. Ed Nelson explained, "The actor knows his lines, but the character doesn't."[60]

Michael Caine wrote that a film actor is in charge of the material and in tune with his character so that he can "think his character's most private thoughts as though no one were watching—no camera spying on him."[61] To Nicholson, this is the search for the reality and how to make it real for himself.[62] "I started to develop an approach to acting which embarked on a search for the *self*" so that "all he feels is included in the life being expressed, and then the resulting emotion contains all of his own personal truth and reality." He summed up his Method, a natural process of responding to life, as one of *being*, "a state you work to achieve. To *be*, you must find out what you feel and express it totally."[63]

Next, seek out contrasts. Travel from the sneering insanity of Billy Spear in *The Shooting* to the semaphore lesson in *The Last Detail*; from the fractured naiveté in *The Border* to a determined Jimmy Hoffa; from a wedding toast by an uncertainly proud father in *About Schmidt* to a privileged eulogy to an uncommon friend in *The Bucket List*.

Nicholson has used character voices as Charley Partanna in *Prizzi's Honor*, Wilbur Force in *The Little Shop of Horrors*, Oscar in *The Fortune* and Henry Lloyd Moon in *Goin' South*. Some are broad and rowdy for comic effect and work perfectly, while others seem over the top and distracting. He's played it polished and silky, as president, network news anchor, celebrated playwright and French lieutenant without a French accent. He's played it tough and macho, as with Frank Costello, Colonel Jessep and Buddusky. Insecurity is not outside of the aural range of the famous "Jack." Witness portrayals in *The King of Marvin Gardens*, *Ride in the Whirlwind* and *Ironweed*. However, confidence overflows (sometimes to a disgusting degree) in *Carnal Knowledge*, *How Do You Know*, *One Flew Over the Cuckoo's Nest*, *Batman* and *Terms of Endearment*.

Many might think only of the nasal twang when thinking of Nicholson's voice. That Jersey twang has made 75 characters become different people. But the perception is also misleading. Jack has used his vocal instrument in the many varied ways outlined above, altering the timbre and how he plays the notes as any top-level musician expands the manner of playing. Is Miles Davis the soft and lyrical or the caustic and electric? Does Brian Wilson rock the surf or touch the soul? Nicholson emotes, using expression and meter to pour blood into a character's flesh, turning words in a script to thoughts of a person. His Method abilities do betray themselves when he pushes too hard, as if the character takes control over itself, as in *Goin' South* and moments in *Hoffa* and *The Witches of Eastwick*. However, it doesn't matter how many critics call Jack Torrance "over the top." That delivery and that attitude reflect a man who is, appropriately, not in control of his senses to the extent that he is no longer in control of his communication faculties.

In *Reframing Screen Performance*, Baron and Carnicke explain, "[A]ctors adjust the quality and energy of their gestures, voices and actions to fit their characters' shifting desires and interactions with others," contributing to the trajectory of a dramatic action.[64] That is how Nicholson can make transformations that present two distinct characters within the body of the same actor, such as the demented, extreme physicality in *The Shining* compared to the naturalistic and understated drifting in *Five Easy Pieces*.[65] This causes audiences to "make inferences about characters' temperaments and emotional states by observing the quality of the physical and vocal expression crafted into filmic representations."[66]

Gary Kent described the quintessential Jack as a combination of the famous grin and the voice that's "so hard to change. No matter what he does, accent or whatever, there's that Nicholson voice."[67] Yet that Nicholson voice *has* changed, and has changed drastically and seemingly without notice. The actor's vocal delivery has migrated from the nasally twang, even high-pitched at times, to a low and smooth tumbling of thought to speech, a fine sandpaper applied to someone's true feelings.

This transition happened in the 1980s, though it did not occur across a straight line. In *The Shining*, we hear the old Jack, in *Broadcast News*, the new one. Along the way we also hear snippets of the old and the new residing side by side in other films of the era. Confusingly, the J.J. Gittes in *Chinatown* sounds different than the J.J. Gittes in *The Two Jakes*. Perhaps the detective's increased refinement and growth in respectability (though limited) accounts for this. The occasional emergence of the original Jack twang could provide the proof (or it could simply capture an imperfect changeover).

The later Nicholson is more sophisticated, even and precise than the earlier model, with the sound coming from the chest and throat instead of the head and nose. Clearly a studied and intentional enhancement, the new Jack voice was likely the result of lessons and the kind of dedication he put into preparation—only this time the preparation continues over the long term and over the course of many different roles.

One intriguing note about the actor's voice and delivery is how he uniquely treats those most common of responses in the English language, "yes" and "no." When other people, including actors, normally say these words, they're abrupt and merely provide information. Nicholson intones the same words with care, giving them time and imbuing them with meaning.

Instead of throwaway words that typically lead directly into the next phrase, when Nicholson responds "yes," he has thought about the question and weighs his answer, imparting the significance it deserves. When he responds "no," he does so with equal deliberation so that the emotion comes through, whether regret or defiance. An actor who puts so much into two small words is a student dedicated to bringing the most out of the provided dialogue.

* * *

But what *is* a Jack Nicholson character? For some time, he was labeled an "antihero." Deficient in typical heroic traits like idealism, courage and traditional morals, the antihero appealed to art house denizens such as Nicholson, who later latched onto the alienation and countercultural slants associated with Vietnam War protests, free expression and free love, plus recreational drug use.

This dissonance, "caused by his conscious or subconscious awareness of the role [the characters] are forced to play in society ... captures the disaffection males feel from being constantly surrounded by social forces that seek to contain them within a sphere of accepted behaviors." Nicholson faces these challenges with a "dislocation technique" that embodies this inherent tension and become "a unique feature of Nicholson's acting style."[68]

Early examples stemmed more from the kind of roles that were available to young unknowns, from Corman quickies to biker exploitation. He graduated from juvenile delinquent in *The Cry Baby Killer, Too Soon to Love, The Wild Ride* and *Studs Lonigan* to gang member in *Hells Angels on Wheels* and *The Rebel Rousers*. As he gained fame and took greater control over his career, Nicholson's personal stamp—and the manifestations of "actor as auteur"—formed an impression that the man and the actor shared personalities, one that may have confused media, fandom, and even studios and filmmakers.

Nicholson became known for playing characters adrift, and not necessarily worried about it. A rocker older than most guys playing to little success in *Psych-Out*; a classically trained pianist who turns his back on his similarly talented family to go nowhere as an oil rigger in *Five Easy Pieces*; a nighttime radio personality without much personality in *The King of Marvin Gardens*; a reporter as much escaping from an undefined past as searching for a story in Antonioni's *The Passenger*; a former insurance adjuster who finds he had as little life before his forced retirement as in his less-than-golden years in *About Schmidt*; an astronaut explorer turned skirt chaser in *Terms of Endearment*; and his directorial debut *Drive, He Said* (in which he does not appear), the story of a college basketball star who questions his commitment to the game or any notion of the future.

Nicholson plays full-blown antihero J.J. Gittes in *Chinatown* and *The Two Jakes*; the morally-under-fire border agent Charlie Smith; the cynical

Navy escort Buddusky; a messed-up father of a little girl killed by a drunk driver; and a publisher who becomes a werewolf and beds his enemy's daughter. He also scripted *The Trip*, about a *Mad Man* ad exec who skips the booze in favor of acid.

Right and wrong don't motivate these Nicholson characters, who go through the motions, who live more for reaction than action, and who are pushed by no ambition and pulled by no relationships (at least of a mature nature).

Other misfits and misanthropes, such as the tragic and pathetic Jonathan in *Carnal Knowledge* and the besotted, romantic Francis Phelan in *Ironweed*, round out a group of mentally ill unfortunates in *Cuckoo's Nest*, *The Shining*, *As Good as It Gets* and *The Pledge*. Actors are drawn to the dark side, reveling in the villainous and the evil. Nicholson gave such portrayals teeth and potency, from his brief appearance in *The St. Valentine's Day Massacre*, to *The Postman Always Rings Twice* (another antihero), to *Flight to Fury* and *The Shooting*, to *Prizzi's Honor* and *Batman*, to *Blood and Wine* and *The Departed*.

More recently, as he has aged, his characters have remained young through the discovery of romance, often in unlikely ways with unlikely pairings. He doesn't deserve Diane Keaton in *Something's Gotta Give* but earns the love of Helen Hunt in *As Good as It Gets*. He's outclassed by classical singer Ellen Barkin in *Man Trouble* and prudish widow Mary Steenburgen in *Goin' South*. He also indulges

Above and opposite: Getting into show business isn't always a direct hit. This early Nicholson play (with Suzanne Sydney) made *L'il Abner* seem ultra-sophisticated (original program, c. 1956).

male fantasies with the captivating Tuesday Weld in *A Safe Place* and the supernatural trio of Michelle Pfeiffer, Cher and Susan Sarandon in *The Witches of Eastwick*.

Another Nicholson archetype has been the comic eccentric, exemplified in the Roger Corman classics *Little Shop of Horrors* and *The Raven*; meatier interpretations such as in *Easy Rider* and *Anger Management*; caricatures in *Goin' South* and *The Fortune*; along with a devil and a president in *Witches* and *Mars Attacks!* respectively.

* * *

Of course, it could very well be that a big factor in Nicholson's success in film is that he loves doing it. Kent observed, "Jack always has a zest—and I see that little boy, I see Weary Reilly [in *Studs Lonigan*] again, in a different costume, just jumping in and doing his best."

It's about loving the work and loving those who do love the work. "Jack loves film and film people. When I see him around, I think he feels that he always wanted to be in this business and I think he's really pleased that he was in it." Kent pointed out that not all the top actors shared this affinity for the endeavor or the industry, recalling that Robert Mitchum "made fun of it, 'We're just pretenders and we really aren't doing anything great.' But I think that way down deep, Jack has had a ball and I'm glad because he deserves it."[69]

Barry Dennen agrees that a key to the Nicholson success is his enjoyment of the process. "He's a lot of fun to be around. He jokes, he laughs, he tells stories, but the minute he goes into acting mode [*Dennen makes a gun-loading sound effect*], you can hear the bullets being loaded."[70]

Perkins agreed that Nicholson has this unbridled enthusiasm, calling him a "Hollywood boy who worshipped the big old movie stars. He liked knowing them and being respected by them. It was important to him."[71]

* * *

Two of Hollywood's greatest come to mind when thinking of Nicholson as an actor who created his own identity, fusing the perception of the man with the impression of his characters. They are Cagney and Cary. Not that Jack necessarily modeled himself after James Cagney and Cary Grant, nor that they on the surface have much in common aside from having attained iconic superstardom.

The Cagney connection is the more obvious. He is physical, pushing, making hitting an art and shooting an act of thrusting ahead to force the bullets out of the gun. Nicholson shared this physicality, as he does the active eyes and the toothy grin that betrays more than mere happiness or bonhomie.

Both propel themselves forward and seldom stand still. Nicholson bounces on the balls of his feet, perhaps an interpretation of "the Cagney stance," poised to act and ready for the moment, always advancing and always with purpose. This was the essence of Cagney's approach to acting. "Never settle back on your heels. Never relax. If you relax, the audience relaxes." Cagney was always on the balls of his feet, ready to spring like a bantam chicken.[72]

Cagney pushed a grapefruit in the face of Mae Clarke, while Nicholson cleared off the entire table at a diner. Cagney riles up the other independent hacks in *Taxi!* with the type of anger and true emotion we later see in Nicholson's appeals to the union in *Hoffa*. Look into Cagney's eyes as he's led toward the death chamber in *Angels with Dirty Faces* and we see the horror and anguish suffered by Jack Torrance in *The Shining*. Both Nicholson and Cagney are considered mannered in their acting styles, "so busy with stylized movement that everyone can do a reasonable imitation."[73]

Less overt is the connection between Cary Grant and Nicholson. Like Nicholson, "Grant's performances often suggested a man who was simply having fun making a movie."[74] Most bluntly, they are both movie stars often accused of playing themselves, of playing the same role over and over.

Grant had the ultimate smoothness to give the impression that he never was acting and that he was playing himself. How many critics have said this about Jack, especially after he became "Jack"? Grant good-naturedly made fun of his critics' accusation, telling Peter Bogdanovich, "Even I'd like to be Cary Grant."[75]

Grant's sophistication helped hide his Nicholson-like physicality and versatility. Both employed explosive energy and studied movement to raise their characters' blood pressure, thinking that it was not nearly enough to merely bring them to life. Beyond action sequences, this liveliness also applies to Nicholson's affectations and Grant's eccentricities, highly stylized creations "made of peculiar movements and an interesting combination of expressive codes."[76]

Like Nicholson's journey between the Grand Guignol and the understated or the farcical and the menacing, Grant shaded his roles with textures as different as tough and callous in *Only Angels Have Wings* and hardboiled in *His Girl Friday*, to heartfelt and heartbreaking in *Penny Serenade*, unpleasant in *Suspicion* and cold and manipulative in *Notorious*.

Jack and Cary transform single characters in singular roles. Nicholson grows and becomes more "human" the more time he spends with Helen Hunt in *As Good as It Gets*, just as Grant grows and becomes more "normal" in response to Katharine Hepburn in *Bringing Up Baby*. Both rom-coms dramatize a sunrise that happens to these men's personalities as the protection of their facades erode. Yet make no mistake, love can only conquer when the right actors bring the right temperament, humor and vulnerability to their roles—to make the audience forget that acting is happening.

* * *

Shirley Knight talked about how she and Nicholson progressed as actors between their early acting classes and when they reunited on *As Good as It Gets*, saying that both were more shy then, searching when very young. "We now both have a certain *joie de vivre* and confidence that we show both in our character and in our work."[77]

That skill came over time, according to Millie Perkins, who feels that Nicholson's accessibility and iconic fame is largely attributable to being a great entertainer who's very lucky and seems aware that luck played a big role in his success. "In later years, he did some fabulous work, but at the time I thought of him as someone who was an entertainer … and he became an actor later."

The "actor" part is where the study, dedication, hard work and preparation came in. Along with a little intercession from the show business gods, as Perkins sees it. "Somebody blessed him somewhere along the way and said, 'You're gonna have it all, all the time.' He did it. He got it. He did what he wanted to do."[78]

Not bad for someone whose June 18 (year not indicated) Jeff Corey acting class session notes read, "Jack rather bland and tended to be too ingratiating and kindly for its own sake."[79]

* * *

2

Heroes and Villains

You search for the little things. A bit of a flinch, a lick of the lips, a flit of the eyes, a blot of some sweat. Trying to look innocent is the quickest way to tell someone's guilty. Looking like you've done this before—been in a police lineup, or two, or ten—is another. Spotting the villains is certainly easier than finding the heroes.

Presidents, astronauts, respected newsmen. These are the ones we're taught to admire. Respect them because they are special. *Become* them because they are worthy. They walk taller, look bigger, seem stronger. You won't catch them flinching, licking, flitting or blotting. But you can ID them because you'll feel the energy you can't explain and can't ignore.

The most celebrated heroes and the most evil villains stand out from the rest of us, not only for what they've done, but also because of how they carry themselves and the aura they carry with them. So it's only natural that they can intermingle in some sort of power summit of powerful personalities.

Our hall of heroes includes a president of the United States facing his country's greatest threat. An Apollo astronaut faces life after his most momentous accomplishments. A network news anchor faces a new reality for his profession. They're all important. They're all heroes. And two out of the three are boring.

None of the villains are boring. Not even close. Two mob leaders, a hired gun and two jewel thieves menace with panache. Maybe evildoers can't coast. They can't live off their past and must maintain their edge. Admirers aren't as demanding as enemies. Plus, heroes may be reluctant, but villains seldom are. Or they've gotten over it long ago.

Actors often say they prefer playing the bad guy over the good guy. Meatier roles, more interesting characterizations. Additional freedom and extra abandon. Let's face it: Stoic dignity, control and humility can't compete with unhinged, unpredictable and uncontrollable. Leadership is necessary, but danger is tasty.

* * *

Jack Nicholson has played the president—in *Mars Attacks!*—and his commander-in-chief doesn't carry nearly as much command as his mobsters, the Joker in *Batman* and Francis Costello in *The Departed*. His supporting role as TV news icon Bill Rorish can't touch his supporting role as gunslinger Billy Spear in *The Shooting*. His only American hero that outshone his villains was *Terms of Endearment* astronaut Garrett Breedlove, more memorable and multi-dimensional than jewel heist failures Alex Gates in *Blood and Wine* and Jay Wickham in *Flight to Fury*.

The bad guy–good role vs. good guy–bad role contrast is easily seen when comparing Nicholson's two Tim Burton movies. *Mars Attacks!* is flat and unfunny, while *Batman* has depth and style. The former sports an all-star cast that's all but wasted, an attempt at a *Mad Mad Mad World* quality, without the quality. Thoroughly unenjoyable, the film is fun-deprived and laugh-free, with just about everyone unlikable and superficial.

Aside from the wonderful Sylvia Sidney, Pam Grier had the only real character and the only real feeling in the film, while Rod Steiger seemed the only one who realized this was supposed to be a comedy (or at least knew what to do about it). Many of the other players instead assumed a knowing tone and affected manner that seemingly was meant to cue the audience, "Hey—we're being comedic now!"

Much of the problem lies in the distance between the source material and its all-too-loose adaptation. Based on trading cards co-created by Wally Wood— "one of the greatest science fiction comic book artists of all time, if not the greatest," according to comic book historian Arlen Schumer,[1] the movie was slapstick and campy instead of scary and fantastical.

"It should have been like *Night of the Living Dead* meets science fiction, with horror and fear combined with aliens and technology," Schumer explained. "The movie did a disservice to the legacy of the cards. Those cards were done in the spirit of *The War of the Worlds*. That was scary, meaning that when Mars attacks, it's gonna be all-hell-breaks-loose and they have no mercy." Schumer attributes this to Burton's lack of understanding of the original source (as with *Batman*). Burton's interpretation was "a little too goofy and kind of light."[2]

Nicholson had two roles, the bland president and the broad Art Land, with the latter likely a way to make up for the former. As President Dale, he starts appropriately thoughtful and optimistic, almost a businessman-as-head-of-state before its time. His other character is all teeth and big movements, but the fun-loving ne'er-do-well feels more natural for Jack than moving into the Oval Office would. The two characters do feel like they're played by completely different people, in look, carriage, sound and attitude— a true testament to Nicholson's breadth. It's just that the role of the leader of the free world isn't interesting enough. Not bumbling enough to be hapless nor intense enough to be mock-dramatic, this character is simple and simply weak.

With tightly pursed lips, Nicholson's James Dale is self-important but empty. Preparing for the arrival of the Martians, he accordingly shows the Hollywood interpretation of a phony politician who's all style, lacking in substance, and filled with false strength. Nicholson's composed but stupid; thoughtful yet superficial; stoic yet befuddled; in some ways similar to his below-the-surface Rorish in *Broadcast News*. Even in disaster, he has his president exuding false restraint. In his "Why?" monologue to the Martians, Nicholson adopts a charming but empty politician mode, exuding a sort of smarmy leadership.

He does loosen up a bit in the bedroom scene with Lisa Marie and in bed with Glenn Close, looking less than dignified and far below sexy, the kind of personal freedom from "image" and "movie star" that's characterized many of Nicholson's performances. Jack also acts gamely and realistically when playing against the special effects, after having done so effectively when wondrously attacked by *The Witches of Eastwick*.

But it's really the Art Land character that garners his attention. Until he takes off his hat and lets his hair netting down, you might not have guessed that this was the celebrated Nicholson, though makeup artist Ve Neill contended that "everybody knew it was Jack. There was no hiding that."[3]

Additionally, he's having fun when he's Land. His presentation to the cowboys and sheiks serves as parody to Bruce Dern as Nicholson's brother in *The King of Marvin Gardens*—once again lampooning his friend and frequent partner (after having played an entire role as Dernsie in *The Fortune*). At the nuke point, Jack's Art gamely hangs on, like a drunkard holding onto his last piece of dignity.

* * *

There is more (so much more) in Burton's earlier work and his first collaboration with Nicholson, as Jack Napier in *Batman*. Like in *A Few Good Men*, Nicholson makes this movie. He gives it weight. He adds style. He creates. When Nicholson talked about what he has learned as an actor, he said, "I was particularly proud of my performance as the Joker. I considered it a piece of pop art."[4]

To *Batman* comic expert and author of *The Silver Age of Comic Book Art* Arlen Schumer, that was precisely the problem. The reference to pop art connects to the TV series, not the original comic. "The TV show is not really the 'right' version of *Batman*. And the TV show is all Tim Burton knew. He didn't know anything about the comics."[5]

Nicholson not only gives the movie its acting substance, but he reportedly played a major part in making its production possible in the first place, with part of the pitch being "and we'll get an actor like Jack Nicholson to play the Joker."[6]

This is Nicholson's application of character energy at its finest. First-billed above the title star Michael Keaton, here is an actor who ranges from tough and tenacious to fun and flamboyant to smart and salacious. When he warns that Gotham City had better wait until they got a load of him—and his new kind of unpredictable terrors—it's more menacing than cartoonish. The portrayal affirmed *Batman* creator Bob Kane's preference for Nicholson as the Joker after seeing the actor in *The Shining*.[7]

Schumer dismisses this as Kane mythmaking. "Anybody who was a *Batman* fan who saw *The Shining* would have said, 'That's the Joker!' ... It sounds like something that came out of Bob Kane's mouth in order to take credit."[8]

Perfect as Beetlejuice, Keaton remains wooden and eminently miscast as any kind of hero. The villain instead saves the day. This is perhaps Nicholson's most physical role, dancing, strutting, sashaying, parading and doing the other purple one (soundtracker Prince) proud. The pre–Joker mobster is arrogant and understated, with his only out-of-ordinary foreshadowing affectation a slight eye twitch. With the facial deformity, Jack transforms from Jack Napier to the Joker through expanded physicality that's more bodily demonstrative.

A true villain, yes. A cartoon character, no. Yet he's having fun here, shooting behind the back and over the shoulder, the Jimi Hendrix of criminals.

Jack's Joker is more than an action figure, using his voice and delivery to slither from guise to guise naturally. He does a spot-on impression of Jack Palance to sidekick and friend Tracey Walter. The vocal emphasis he adopts is Nixonesque, interesting because of his earlier play at Tricky Dick when huffing and puffing and axing down the bathroom door in *The Shining*.

Unlike so many of his contemporaries in big roles in big movies, Nicholson delivers his catchphrases with feeling and meaning, without the "Here it comes!" telegraphing associated with lesser artists. He asks about the wonderful toys with conviction, not calculation. He truly wants to know who can be trusted with all that money, employing strength laced with irony.

Sure, he was the Clown Prince of Crime, but he was also a homicidal lunatic Joker. Schumer felt that Nicholson carried the Clown Prince aspect, but without the true menace of the crazed murderer. "He was cast as the Joker based on what he did in *The Shining* in 1980, but the problem is they didn't get around to making the movie until 1988. By the time Nicholson plays the role, he was ten years older and he was ten years heavier." Jack was the obvious choice, but perhaps too obvious. "Yeah, he played Jack Nicholson—the grinning, maniacal laugh—but predictable."[9]

I had the honor and pleasure of working on an award-winning advertising campaign with iconic Batman Adam West. When I asked his opinion on Nicholson's work in the first of the modern interpretations of the character, he paused ... he breathed ... and he intoned as only Adam West can: "There appears to be a little steam in my stride....Yes, I've always enjoyed Jack's work. Yes, I love it."[10]

Said to be camp, the *Batman* TV series allowed itself to appeal to adults with irony and style, to kids with action and attitude. Though that comic antecedent became so ingrained, Nicholson shook off any temptation for over-the-top acting. This represents a significant maturing for Nicholson, and a realization that a character from the comics doesn't necessarily demand broad comedy, or even a broad caricature.

In *The Departed*, Jack plays another driven mobster. As with the Joker, Jack is always in control and never overextended in making Francis Costello a real—and really scary—person. In no ways gangsterish (and, for the love of God, in no ways like Hoffa), Nicholson stays centered and nuanced, keeping the energy always internal, so that the viciousness and treachery is contained under the skin where it can do more harm. This is a villain outside of any comic realm.

Reporter David Boeri, who has covered the Whitey Bulger case for over 25 years and currently does so for the Boston NPR station WBUR, unfavorably compared Nicholson's portrayal of the fictionalized Bulger with that of the comic villain. Before our interview, he watched the movie again; "I laughed out loud. Because what you have here is not Whitey Bulger; it is the Joker moving from Gotham City to South Boston." Boeri explained that the real Bulger was a neat and tidy control freak who despised people who drank, let alone indulged in drugs. "The idea that he was scattering coke, throwing cocaine over people, as was indicated in *The Departed*, that his hair is undone and he's going into this insane, slovenly, gluttonous behavior is out of consideration. It's over the top."[11]

Nicholson confronts Leonardo DiCaprio with his story of a rat in a *tour de force* of exposition and expression—wonderful teeth and nose of a rat and lively, animalistic eyes of someone thinking too much about too many things with too much distortion and distrust. Find the truth of the character in and behind those eyes. He unnerves Leo's character Billy, and it's real. When Costello returns to the table, sneaking back and sniffing at Billy and reaching in ostensibly because he left his cigarette behind, there's a good chance it was an ad lib. If not, it's more impressive still.

Nicholson's is the first voice you hear in this movie, in voiceover. He sounds more Irish than elsewhere in the movie, weathered and old prior to being introduced in shadow and silhouette, quietly forceful in the opening grocery scene. We are then introduced by Martin Scorsese to a guy of edges. Jack's Costello knows how to get an edge on his game, over his adversaries

Reporter David Boeri covered the Whitey Bulger case for over twenty-five years and considered Nicholson's portrayal in *The Departed* (2006) "over-the-top.... The Joker moving from Gotham City to South Boston." Nicholson is shown here with co-star Leonardo DiCaprio.

and victims and those he controls, but he is not necessarily in control of the edge on which he is delicately balanced.

That edge is the key to the character.

Nicholson is not merely playing a villain, a bad guy, a mobster or even a cold-blooded killer. He's more dangerous because he doesn't care what he says or does. He's infinitely more dangerous because he's dissociated from any kind of normal thought or rational behavior and disconnected from any concept of right or wrong. Long ago, Francis stopped recognizing any difference, stopped caring one way or another.

Amoral and psychotic, the calm Costello scares more than the explosive one. Nicholson's range imbues the character with a psychological makeup that's unbalanced and that keeps others off-balance. When he shoots a couple on the beach and observes that the woman "fell funny," he does so with a grin of true curiosity. He is disconnected from the act and from its meaning, reducing a pair of cold-blooded murders committed point blank in the open and in bright daylight to a humorous crack as if about a jump shot that caromed off the rim in an unexpected way. Boeri found the line consistent with the killer he covered. "That was something Bulger might say. He was a cold character."[12]

Add the scene where Costello matter-of-factly removes a severed hand from a plastic bag, takes off the wedding ring, and gives back the hand—all while discussing business with Billy as if doing paperwork, with no toughness, no reaction—and you're sensing a psychopath and not a characteristic bad guy.

Here, the real-life inspiration and the movie character depart from one another. "He may well have enjoyed killing people," observed Boeri, "but there's no evidence of Bulger playing in blood, of holding a severed hand, of celebrating gore. He might have liked killing people, but there's no sense of that wild-eyed bloodlust that Nicholson engages in in *The Departed*."[13]

He doesn't play it one-dimensional and obvious throughout, or even in any controlled, understandable pattern. Laughing and chummy here; threatening and intimidating there; sarcastic and cutting altogether; Frank Costello keeps you on your toes and off your guard. Berating priests to enjoy their clams but to refrain from "doing" the young boys contrasts sharply with a cocaine orgy with two young women at an opera, where he looks to be a truly wasted and out-of-control devil.

Bulger was nothing like this character, explains Boeri. He was shrewd, cold, fastidious, calculating, and not particularly interesting—in sharp contrast to engaging in "self-indulgence and debauchery in this sort of sybaritic style that you see Nicholson in, with arched eyebrows, the hair out of place, the look of dissolution, and this maniacal laugh."[14]

Scorsese's picture becomes a contest of intensity between DiCaprio, Mark Wahlberg, Matt Damon and Alec Baldwin. All that is crushed when Frank mercilessly bashes Billy's broken hand with his own boot in order to determine if Billy is still a cop.

But in another sequence, Costello croons "Mother Machree" in a parodic manner. Later, he teaches Asian microprocessor smugglers that automatic weapons don't enhance their manhood and lectures upon how a proper transaction is made "in this country," adopting a perfect tone of controlled power that seizes the upper hand through sarcasm and bigotry. Nicholson's Costello takes control. His control gives him the edge, using the type of affected familiarity that delivers the advantage, along with humor that's not meant to be funny. Always attentive to wardrobe throughout his career, Jack looks quirky and puzzling with a wonderful floppy hat and '70s-ish brown sunglasses.

Costello goes downhill quickly after a police killing that redefines his world. A fantastic shootout and Frank's escape from his car lead to a final, explosive confrontation with the ultimate rat (as played by Damon) and Frank's glorious death. He's gurgling up blood, propelled backward into the dump box of a dump truck, and finally blown back into a crucifixion pose. Amongst Nicholson' death scenes, this one is near the top, ending in a stance reminiscent of that in *The Shining*.

Through Bulger's lawyer, Boeri asked the crime boss if he saw *The Departed*. "I got an answer from him that was clever, though not what they would call dispositive": Bulger admitted that he had seen the movie, "and later says the place where he allegedly saw the movie is a nice theater."[15]

Who are *The Departed*? The dead, of course. They've departed from their background and upbringing (just about everyone) … from their honor and training and moral code (the corrupt police and compromised investigators) … and perhaps from their sanity and humanity (Jack defining Francis Costello).

* * *

Heroes can also lose their way, because they are human and because their faults flesh out their characters. Garrett Breedlove departed Earth itself, returning from space without trajectory for a life without a flight plan. In *Terms of Endearment*, he's revealed in his first scene as a drunken buffoon of a lech.

Prior to his big "Jack" entrance, the character referred to only as "The Astronaut" is discussed, setting the tone for Breedlove not as a character but as a figure. He's reduced to a celebrity object—a celebronaut—forever known only for accomplishments extremely limited in number though infinitely limitless in nature.

Astronaut Garrett Breedlove is first spied upon by Aurora (Shirley MacLaine, whose character name is an astrological reference that's relevant to a relationship with an astronaut) as he's falling out of his car in a white tux and bow tie. Breedlove resembles a suitably aged Wilbur Force, Jack's *Little Shop of Horrors* character. Nicholson uses the same across-the-hair-on-forehead sweeping gesture we've seen before and since. It's a little Zero Mostel, a little Red Skelton.

When called a "hero" and "real live astronaut" in conjunction with descriptions of disappointment and disillusionment, Nicholson intentionally overacts, indicating that this is the whole point. He is compelled to deflate the image, while doing the same to his ego, believing that image to be unattainable or at least unsustainable.

I spoke with *Apollo 9* astronaut Rusty Schweickart, who also happened to attend high school with Nicholson in Manasquan, New Jersey. Rusty encapsulates the psychology of that era's space explorers, military or test pilots whose lives changed forever when they joined NASA. Ready for adventure, check. Ready for danger, check. Ready for challenge, check. Ready for flight, check. Ready for fame, not necessarily. The first man to pilot the lunar mod-

Jack attended Manasquan High School in New Jersey with future astronaut Rusty Schweickart, yet never sought help about the Garrett Breedlove character in *Terms of Endearment*.

ule, Schweickart admitted to me, "I don't like being a hero, if you haven't noticed, and I don't like playing up to heroes. It's not something I've ever done."[16]

Apollo 11 Command Module Pilot Michael Collins agreed: "I'm not a hero. I get very irritated if people call me a hero," providing a contrast to Congressional Medal of Honor recipients who have "done something 'above and beyond the call of duty.' Astronauts, no. They're good, they're competent, they're smart (some of them), but they're not heroes, no."[17]

Nicholson becomes nuanced. This was a transitional character for the actor, who previously had been broader and bigger, actively cueing the viewer that comedy ensues. Here, though largely comedic, his range within the character is honest and complex, colored enough to provide the entertainment yet not overdone to distraction. He's subtle, with shades of humanity and vulnerability balanced against the spoiled arrogance that can be an unfortunate consequence of making history.

There's also a transition within the character that's masterful. In the first actual meeting with MacLaine, he is blustery, uncomfortably veering from lecherous to uncertainty to blindly self-confident. Then, when Aurora shows up at his door a few years later after having been driven away from her own birthday party, he proves his lack of "star" guile, once again looking unglamorous and ordinary. He lets his gut hang out, the inspiration for the line, "sexy with a belly like Jack Nicholson" in Cindy Lee Berryhill's song "Damn, I Wish I Was a Man." The singer-songwriter explained the reference to me. "Yeah, I'd say it was that film *Terms of Endearment*, that encouraged that line. I remember his character having a big belly and yet the character still had that bad boy sexiness about him."[18]

Garrett is not prepared for this approach by Aurora, so off-guard he's confused and looking and acting more like David Staebler in *The King of Marvin Gardens* than a famous astronaut. The next day on their date, however, Breedlove is back in control. He's prepared, with a manly confidence in place. Breedlove is dressed for the part, at the wheel of his fast machine—the sports car so associated with that era's pioneer astronauts. Nicholson shades another angle on the character at lunch, exhibiting uncouth and uncaring behavior that's offset by a realistic presentation of that character and the real charm of the man. Jack's clearly having fun and enjoying the role, showing it with the playful hiss on the word "ass" when he accuses MacLaine of having a bug there in need of being killed.

After this lunch, we meet another part of Garrett that's perhaps the most real of the lot. This is quintessential Jack and the quintessential image of Garrett with Aurora. Driving on the beach and steering with his feet, Nicholson shows the joy of power, the exhilaration of risk, and the spirit of adventure (and of showing off). It's reminiscent of Nicholson's ride with Captain America in *Easy Rider*, Jack's arms waving as if flying, totally free in the moment. Schweickart observed, "It was kind of wild. I remember the Corvette whipping through the surf in Galveston."[19] *Apollo 14* astronaut and fourth Moonwalker Alan Bean said, "Good stuff with the Corvette. I never heard of an astronaut driving it with his foot."[20]

Then, in the surf, Breedlove shifts from romantic to lusty to pained to angered, ultimately admitting that Aurora brings out the devil in him. Perhaps he means the devil as Jack, his womanizing persona in real life as well as a premonition of his Van Horne character in *The Witches of Eastwick* a few years later. As *Apollo 16* command module pilot Al Worden put it, "Jack Nicholson had a hell of a time getting her. Finally, he had to realize that she was a great gal and he had to change to make that relationship work."[21]

Within the family environment, Nicholson reduces Garrett to extreme discomfort as Aurora's family reunites. He retreats quietly back to his own world, shrinking as he moves away, adding another shade to the man, another phase of the Moon. When Breedlove timidly returns, he kisses Aurora with

This iconic scene with Shirley MacLaine in *Terms of Endearment* (1983) is reminiscent of Nicholson's ride with Captain America in *Easy Rider*, as the ex-astronaut comes as close to the freedom and adventure of space as he can on earth.

the knowing regret that betrays that he would be better off with her, yet cannot handle the commitment.

When he travels to Nebraska to support Aurora (her daughter, played by Debra Winger, is dying), Garrett's matured into strength—that is, until Aurora confesses her love and Garrett shows himself to be boyishly unprepared.

Finally, we see the last phase of the Moon Man's character shading. After Winger's funeral, Garrett shows a caring insight in a scene with a little girl. He's part Godfather (like Brando at the end of the first film in the trilogy) and part grandfather.

Jeff Daniels, who played Winger's scapegoated husband Flap Horton, described the veteran actor's process as an artistic exploration. Daniels saw how Nicholson struggled for his lines and for his approach in the first five takes. "But then in takes six through ten, he was able to put it all together, and each one was quite different from any of the others." Director James L. Brooks was faced with the decision which to use, with the resulting debate between actor and director inching Nicholson toward the auteur position. "It was wonderful to see Jack rehearse on film," Daniels added, "and to have the power and clout, in order to do that and to influence which take or pieces of which take will be used."[22]

I had the opportunity to ask real-life astronauts what they think of Nicholson's Garrett Breedlove character and the difficult adjustments he must make. "It's a little Hollywood, a little over-the-top, but it was entertaining … and Nicholson was great," remarked Apollo 16 moonwalker Dave Scott. As for being conflicted about having accomplished something so important but having that defining moment diminish into the past, Scott reflected, "I figured we were lucky to do it and did it, but life goes on and you gotta do other things."[23]

Dick Gordon, Bean's *Apollo 14* crewmate, added, "Your life is a book and they're full of chapters. And if you write 30, at the end of each chapter you go on and do something else. And that's life."[24] Bean talked about becoming an artist devoted to telling the space story. "I'm celebrating one of the greatest human achievements of all time. It's maybe better than Magellan, I don't know. But a thousand years from now, they may say that what we did on Apollo was more."[25]

Apollo 13 commander Jim Lovell directly addressed the challenges. "Some of us didn't work out so well…. We all faced working for a living after our space flight. You know, it's really great, you're sort of on a pedestal and then you step off the pedestal and you talk to somebody and they say, 'Well, what can you do for me now?'"[26]

Worden has become philosophical about the transition. "Why do you allow that to get to you? It's hard to explain, because once you've been in a spot where you've got the president of the United States going out of his way to do something for you, that's hard to live down."[27]

This challenge is most pointedly portrayed in the film when Aurora accuses Breedlove of pathetically using the trappings of space fame to trap women. He explodes about having "earned it" and of being one of only a small number of astronauts in the history of the world. There's partial truth and partial jealousy in her insinuation. He indeed does use it, but his accomplishments are truly special, and he is rightfully proud of that rare achievement. This hurt rage sparks another shading of the character and one which resonated with the real astronauts. As Colonel Scott explained, "Some guy's office looks like a museum; other guys you could hardly tell they had been there [the Moon]."[28] Worden summed it up dramatically by admitting, "You live the rest of your life borrowing against that three days."[29]

Michael Collins, who didn't know anything about the movie ("I'm aboriginal"), felt otherwise. "I don't feel defined. Some do, some are would-be astronauts, astronauts and all-the-rest-of-their-life astronauts. I'm not. I was an astronaut. It was the best job I ever had, but I went on to other things and I don't feel defined."[30]

Greatness was not a word to be associated with the unsatisfying, if not annoying, sequel to *Terms of Endearment*: *The Evening Star*. This is a painful movie until the latter section, when Garrett returns on the occasion of an Apollo reunion, walking into the frame in a scene mirroring his breakup with Aurora at her gazebo. In this cameo, Jack's more devilish and jokey, yet softer and more philosophical. When Aurora talks about looking for her true love, Breedlove jabs her about her diminished opportunities and punctuates his "not that many shopping days till Christmas" crack with a fun little, playful "Woo!"

Marion Ross, best known as Mrs. Cunningham on TV's *Happy Days*, portrayed Aurora's maid and friend, Rosie. She admired the interplay between Nicholson and Shirley MacLaine, saying, "They got along really great," though also contrasting the actors' respective personalities. Nicholson was a great guy and "the crew loved him," while MacLaine "was tough to get along with. She was tough on everybody."[31]

Breedlove exhibits true fondness for his old flame and older ex-lover. There is the tenderness of lovers who have become old and precious friends. They recreate the driving scene on the beach, Nicholson's primary purpose for being in the film, during which Aurora lets Rosie's ashes fly in the wind as Garrett's convertible races beside the surf. Ross was honored that her character brought the pair back to the beach to relive that iconic moment from the original film, marveling at the tribute and calling it "a really wonderful scene."[32]

* * *

Not necessarily heroes (except to those in or aspiring to journalism), newsmen of the sort played by Nicholson in *Broadcast News* were truly admired. Think Murrow and his men, Walter Cronkite, Huntley and Brinkley, Harry Reasoner and Howard K. Smith, John Chancellor and Barbara Walters, and even later reporter-anchors such as Dan Rather, Peter Jennings and CNN's Bernard Shaw. They were respected, larger than life, and heroes of the truth. Bill Rorish represents the last of his era, while William Hurt's Tom Grunick stands for a less credible, more flashy future.

Director-producer-writer James L. Brooks certainly knew his way around the newsroom—both in real life (working at CBS News) and in a fictional sense (many years on the CBS hit *The Mary Tyler Moore Show*). His concern for the credibility of television journalism can be perceived as hopelessly naïve today, but within the context of the film's time, it made sense. Nicholson portrays the veteran and the old guard, against Hurt's uninformed, blow-dried teleprompter reader. It's not much more than a cameo, not nearly a supporting role, but Jack got a New York Film Critics nomination for Best Supporting Actor. Twenty minutes into the film, he's first heard in voiceover, then seen as anchorman, following a veteran's story called *The Homecoming*. Rorish smiles, which the audience is cued happens to be a rarity, to show his admiration and appreciation for the work. Otherwise, he's proper and serious, verging on intense. But then, off-camera, we glimpse the truer man, who himself is distracted and empty.

Subtly developed and in no way called out—risking its loss to viewers—is that Nicholson's Bill Rorish is in fact the same type as Hurt's Tom Grunick. The key moment occurs when Jack fills a dead moment during the broadcast with a vapid look toward the ceiling, as if saying, "dum-de-dum" internally. Just a few seconds of screen time opens up the possibility that Rorish is the same as Grunick, differing only on the surface. Nicholson portrays the anchor as the acceptable version of the same "odious" type signified by Hurt's star reporter.

Rorish is dignified and stiffly proper as he pretends to be the solid "anchor" having alleged depth and substance, while Hurt plays Tom as a more obvious "pretty boy" who can't hide his empty head as effectively. Otherwise, they are the same, separated only by age and eras, so handing over of the anchor chair was not the dramatic lowering of the bar feared by the other characters.

Even when walking through the newsroom on layoff day, the only scene in which he is standing, Nicholson is stiff and mechanical when depicting Rorish's feelings about the firings, jutting out his lower lip in an attempt at empathy (detached as it is).

Brooks does trade newsroom reality for dramatic license in one key instance. There's a major suspension of disbelief in the service of drama when Holly Hunter's character falls for Hurt's on-camera emotional reaction during a date rape story. News professionals—particularly a producer like Hunter's Jane Craig—would know that such a reaction shot (the cutaway) is done separately and that the reporter's tears had to have been staged. For such a pivotal moment, the hero reporter need be exposed as a calculating actor. Perhaps that was where prescience overcame naiveté.

* * *

Billy Spear, however, is no hero. He may not be a villain, either, as that would necessitate some enterprise or direction. Instead, this sadistic gun for hire (and perhaps for enjoyment) in Monte Hellman's *The Shooting* is a fantastic though little-known step forward in the characterizations of Jack Nicholson.

His character takes satisfaction in incurring a psychological pain that comes from the promise of physical pain. It might even be said that Billy gets joy from this sadism, except he seems incapable of such an emotion as joy, even in the pursuit of pain. Yet it is a promise Billy is more than willing to fulfill, if not looking forward to doing so.

Where many of Jack's characters have easy, welcoming smiles, his Billy appropriates a welcoming sneer. Spear's menacing personality gets perfectly set up in a dramatic first shot for the character that's an extreme close-up of his eyes. We then see that he's dressed like a gambler who has a dangerous, quick draw. Co-star and Spear's searching partner Millie Perkins explained her interpretation of Nicholson's character to me: "My attitude was that Jack was a gun for hire and I hired him to help me find who killed my family. And I knew he was a bad man, but I didn't care. I wanted him to kill whoever it was that killed my family."

This insight, however, did not come from director Monte Hellman, for whom they shot this film and *Ride in the Whirlwind* back to back. "The truth of the matter is, Monte would never explain anything. We'd ask Monte a question, 'Monte, what are they there for?' He said, 'Oh, I don't know.' That was Monte's way, the avant garde, or Antonioni's, who knows who else."

Perkins invented a character backstory for herself: "My thought to myself was that someone killed my family and I was out to find that person and kill them. And so that's why I had that determination and unsympathetic attitude towards everything." She illustrated to me how she connected that motivation to Nicholson's character: "That was my choice. I don't know what Jack's choice was, but I felt that he was a gun for hire and he didn't give a damn about anybody. When I saw how Jack was playing it, it helped me decide how I was going to play it, that he was a bad guy I hired I didn't particularly like, but I needed him."[33]

It's a pity this movie didn't reach a larger audience, as Jack delivers some memorable dialogue with the kind of zeal that comes from playing pure villainy. He has a couple of lines that could have become Nicholson catchphrases had the movie been more widely seen. A creepy Jack sneers, "Your brain's gonna fry out here … you know that?" with a hateful, spiteful, sadistic look. He tortures Warren Oates' character and threatens that he's "gonna blow your face off" and means it.

Gary Kent compared Nicholson's approach to the two widely varied roles in the Hellman films. "He was not the tough guy associated with a gunslinger in *The Shooting*, and that totally disappeared after the film had stopped. There was just no sign of him around; it was Jack. But the second character, in *Ride in the Whirlwind*, was pretty much Jack."[34]

Perkins defines *The Shooting*, playing a "man without a name" who just happens to be a woman, relentless and letting nothing get in her way, least of all sentiment. Horses can die of exhaustion; people can be left to die of heat and thirst in the desert; and anything goes as long as it keeps the group moving. Perkins' evil personality gives license to Jack's amoral sidekick.

At times making the film precipitated serious conflict. "Jack and Monte had arguments all the time, but it was for what they thought was the right way to go in the movie." Perkins captured the atmosphere, continuing, "Jack was emotional and he was dramatic and he lost his temper a lot and he got angry. He and Monte would fight on the set, I'd hear them screaming at each other.... He wanted it badly and Monte Hellman wanted it too. And the truth was, that Monte didn't have the gods looking after him like Jack did."[35]

Despite the arguments, Nicholson and Hellman were dedicated to making the films—and to the realities the films depicted. And like the gods, Hellman also looked after Jack, giving the near-unknown the final shot in both *The Shooting* and *Ride in the Whirlwind*.

* * *

The director and the actor also worked together in the noirish and atmospheric *Flight to Fury*. The story was Hellman's and the script was Jack's. In Jay Wickham, Nicholson wrote himself a fine role of a man who's truly revealed bit by bit, from hail-fellow-well-met and busybody to opportunist and mastermind. The glad-hander becomes the villain in stages. Jack handles himself well during the first phase, playing it naturalistic and delivering his dialogue with relaxed poise, ease and casualness. Nothing is forced. After "working" Joe Gaines (Dewey Martin) by buying him Scotch, plying him for information, and tying him in with an Asian hostess, Jay murders the woman to set Joe up. When the young woman opens the drapes in her hotel room to reveal a hiding Wickham, Jack gives a slight grin as he holds out a ligature, an early preview of Jack Torrance in *The Shining* in this second phase.

In his third stage of the character's development, Nicholson shows up in Martin's room after Joe's been to the police station, and Jay betrays just enough insincerity to show his true character. Yet he holds back enough to make it plausible that Martin does not catch on. In doing so, Wickham actually dupes his mark to help arrange a plane out of the country, slyly insinuating himself even more into the intrigue when he shows up on the plane.

There's an interesting non-narrative scene on the plane, when Jay asks Hellman's then-wife Jacqueline (in her only film role) if she knows anything about death. We see a glimpse of a thoughtful but damaged man, as Nicholson's character follows with a monologue on death and how man fools himself about his ultimate demise. Wickham counters that inevitability with the idea that man could regain control and grab it fully if he makes a conscious and open decision at the age of 50 to decide to go on or go out. Remember that Nicholson wrote this scene for himself.

True, it advanced the character into a more substantial psychological space, a place where death is as much theoretical as practical, but this fourth stage fits snugly with a monologue by a swami about belief and existence in the Monkees' movie *Head*, which Nicholson also scripted.

The fifth phase of Jack's Jay Wickham character emerges after a plane crash. He's enjoying disaster! Not someone else's, but one in which he takes part. In a moment of odd disassociation, Nicholson talks about the "rush" (a term not yet in vogue at the time) and the feeling of immortality he gets from surviving the crash, while sporting a beatific yet slightly twisted glow. *Flight to Fury* is a great early role for Jack. By 1964, his ability is accomplished to a degree that would not become apparent to the general public until a few years later, because this was a small, largely unseen movie. But he had advanced greatly as an actor since *The Cry Baby Killer*.

In the sixth and final character development phase, Nicholson adopts the amoral disconnect we see many years later as Francis Costello in *The Departed*. He shoots a Japanese man because he "moves too slow" and uses Destiny Cooper (Fay Spain) as a shield and hostage to get Joe to drop his gun. When Destiny breaks free, Wickham shoots her in the back (it looks like he aimed for her buttocks) and then is himself shot.

Wickham is holding stolen diamonds. He reveals he's been in on it all along and begins a final chase with Joe Gaines. Rather than escape, they're after each other. Perhaps this, too, may seem familiar from a later Nicholson role. Once he's given up his cover story, Jack stays consistent in character as killer and heavy. With Jay's realization that he's finished after a severe hit from Joe's gun, he finally gives up—without giving in. This will seem extremely familiar. In a final move of perversion and selfishness, Jay simply tosses the diamonds into the water, and yells that Joe can't shoot him before killing himself. The final shot focuses on Nicholson's dirty shoes.

The film is taut and twisted. Nicholson uses an actor's fan dance, revealing in sequence more and more about his character until the bare truth is uncovered. Wickham is not transformed; he's found out, and the viewer finds out just as the other characters do. Nicholson's creation is an interesting character with range, engaging and inquisitive at one end and odd and manipulative at the other.

* * *

He throws the jewels. He tosses everything he's worked for and cared about into the water. He is Jay Wickham. He is also Alex Gates in *Blood and Wine*. Thirty-two years later, one failed jewel thief faces the same fate as the other. Seeing defeat, diamonds fly to freedom, sinking low ... low ... lower ... just as the men themselves have sunk. Sparkling jewels into sparkling water, nature back to nature, but for different motivations. Wickham throws his cache into the stream for spite. He could not win, so no one else should benefit. Gates jettisons his riches as surrender, an admission of the kind of defeat a deep-down loser should expect. Wickham will surely die; Gates' injuries are serious enough he very well might. If not, he will never truly live again.

It can surely be no coincidence that the ending of *Blood and Wine* mirrors that of *Flight to Fury*. Nicholson plays both roles, and co-wrote the earlier film. Strangely, Monte Hellman "never saw it," showing no curiosity about the connection with his own creation, though adding that "Nicholson owns *Flight*."[36]

It's a mystery why the 1996 film *Blood and Wine* is as little known as it is. There's a great cast (with some big names), particularly the then-hot Jennifer Lopez and perennial favorite Michael Caine. It could have been because the film was subtle or hard to classify for marketing. It is bleak, and there are no real heroes, or even particularly likable characters.

Peter Tork, who worked together with the other Monkees and Jack to develop their movie *Head*, described Bob Rafelson's works as embodying being stuck in "the black box," such as the one that trapped the band in their sole film.[37] The Monkees could not escape, with circumstance and fate leading them back inside their career trap, their black box. In Rafelson's *Five Easy Pieces*, Bobby is trapped by his family, their musical legacy and its attendant expectations, and his pregnant girlfriend Rayette. His attempt to escape, by hitching a ride with a truck driver, necessitated leaving his identity (represented by his jacket and wallet) behind. As you watch the closing scene inside the truck, you know Bobby isn't escaping a thing. The brothers in *The King of Marvin Gardens* put past differences aside to pursue the dream held by the stronger personality (played by Bruce Dern) through the exploitive pursuit of the weaker brother (portrayed by Jack). Bad plans, bad luck and bad brains turn escalating failure to violence. Nicholson returns to his box and into his radio booth as confessional monologist.

Four films, four boxes with no way out. Though tinged with an unidentified bitterness toward the *Monkees* series co-creator, Tork's evaluation of Rafelson's oeuvre is insightful and intriguing.

Rafelson called *Five Easy Pieces*, *Marvin Gardens* and *Blood and Wine* "an informal trilogy" of adversarial family dynamics. The first "was about a fundamental relationship of son to father"; the second about brothers; and the third was a result of several years of discussions between director and actor "about whether we could do a film where [Nicholson] played the father, as opposed to the son or the brother." In *Blood and Wine*, the conflict pits the father against his wife and stepson.[38]

In *Blood and Wine*, Nicholson is soft-spoken and understated when dealing with his troubled family and its troublesome undercurrent. This partly fuels Gates' attempt to break free from his mild-mannered and limited life as a wine dealer by enlisting someone named Vic. In a beautiful actor's summit with Nicholson, Caine completely inhabits the smarmy, ill, down-and-out hoodlum, making the elder thespian the true winner here.

"Movie acting is a delicate blend of careful preparation and spontaneity," Caine explained. "[T]he camera sees *everything*, especially lack of spontaneity." Success in making a character as real as Vic, of new-minting thoughts and dialogue, "comes from listening and reacting as if for the first time."[39]

Caine credits Nicholson for restoring his faith in the business and for the joy of working with such a "tremendous actor." The combination of this script, Jack and Rafelson was "very seductive and I decided to have one last shot at being a movie actor."[40]

Nondescript and unassuming, Jack as Alex sees one chance to escape from the black box of his family, his lot in life, his status as servant to the rich. Normally solicitous and polite, even bland, Gates' whole attitude and physical demeanor changes in his hotel date with Gabby (Lopez). He's in charge, he's with a catch, so he's confident and smooth, expressive and cocky, dancing with flair and moving with panache. Of course, this is yet another role of an older Nicholson paired with a much younger and fetching woman, but the required disbelief works here. Lopez plays a poor Hispanic maid, so Alex has somebody over whom he can feel superior—in class if not in looks.

Though nearly 60 during filming, Nicholson doesn't take it easy or rely on facial "Jackisms." In fact, many of Nicholson's best moments in *Blood and Wine* are physical. When Judy Davis (as his wife Suzanne) hits him with a poker, we feel the impacts; after a couple of solid blows, he hesitates, attempts to get up, and falls—a moment that comes across as genuine.

Alex reaches a point of desperation and self-disgust that is palpably real after Vic drives Suzanne and stepson Jason (Stephen Dorff) off the road and she lies dying. Here we meet a man who realizes he's gone too far, reaching beyond anything he had in his mind when deciding to give crime a chance.

Harkening back to *Five Easy Pieces*' diner scene, Nicholson has a classic moment when tossing his tray off the cafeteria table in response to Caine's complaint about there being nowhere to sit. Nicholson picks up the tray, he drops it from a distance, and he quips in sarcastic disgust, "How's that?"

There are two exquisitely violent and unrelentingly extended sequences that form a double climax to the movie, supplying the *Blood* portion of the title in much greater quantity than any emphasis on *Wine*. Purposely uncomfortable in length, both expertly turn conflict and battle into desire and revenge. Desire takes over in the form of an all-too-human lust to inflict pain on another, with revenge the pulsating and explosive force that destroys reason in favor of sadistic victory.

The first is a bloodcurdlingly exciting scene in which Vic attacks Alex with a golf club, progressing fabulously with Gates in terrific pain because of the well-placed strikes. Vic is simultaneously coughing himself to near unconsciousness, so they're both out of control in their suffering. The point of no possible return, wherein the sickest aspect of man emerges from a single, defining moment, manifests in help turned to hurt. Alex "helps" Vic to a patio chair to calm him and explain everything, only to push a pillow forcefully onto Vic's face. They struggle greatly. The stronger man defeats the weakened, ailing man. This is what passes as triumph in this particular world. Alex victoriously downs a glass of wine at the conclusion of the duel of these two older and imperfect partners-turned-rivals. Two losers struggle in battle and one lesser loser emerges in a shameful parody of success. That final gesture joins the blood with the wine.

The second climactic sequence is the final battle between stepfather and stepson, except this battle has only one participant. The younger man pummels his elder without mercy, concentrating years and decades of pain and neglect into one supersaturated campaign of pain. Alex is brutalized by stepson Jason's near execution of his stepfather, ramming Gates' legs against the pier with a fishing boat. This is finely crafted defeat, with an ironic sense of dark humor. Even in such mortal pain, lying on his stomach and unable to rise to his knees let alone his feet, Alex writhes like a fish on land. He gazes at the jewels he stole from his wine collector client, the jewels that now have robbed him of everything, if not life itself. Gates grimaces and almost laughs. This man sees the irony, can perversely appreciate the (in the literal sense) crushing defeat.

Alex Gates must release himself from the cause of his suffering. He must separate from what he wanted most to retain whatever remains of what he now needs most: his life. A disease, a cancer, is hurled into the water as a cleansing. Though scenically similar, the difference between the exact act in *Blood and Wine* vs. *Flight to Fury* is that the later movie uses the jewels as a radioactive and destructive element. Alex Gates must remove the source of his family's, his career's, his life's destruction. Jay Wickham instead retains control to the end by disposing of the valuables so they will not be found and reward anyone else, the "If I can't have it, no one else can" philosophy. Denying others becomes a twisted victory for such a man.

He wears white, but Jay is certainly a villain. As is Alex. The difference is that Jay revels in his wickedness, while Alex denies it. Alex accumulates ruthlessness, figuratively destroying his family and literally causing the death of his wife.

* * *

Villains kill. If not people, then hope. In *The Shooting*, *Batman*, *The Departed*, *Flight to Fury* and *Blood and Wine*, people die. Some are good and some are in the way of the villains, while others are the sort simplistically labeled "innocent victims." These men will not hesitate to inflict pain or exercise authority. They kill with a fixed grin or a mobster's detachment. They murder for purpose or gain. They defeat others and are defeated by themselves, perhaps the defining quality of a villain. Heroes, in contrast, must live up to an ideal often created by others or an accomplishment that transcends the time of its achievement—turning a moment into an eternity. Astronaut, president, news anchor. All are symbols. Yet all are people, living with their limitations that reality uses to restrict us all.

If we are actors, we choose the wider vistas of villainy. If we are mortals, we aspire to the lower percentage of heroism. In life, heroism can be extremely important yet totally uncelebrated. In movies, heroism can be less rich than playing the "bad guy."

Would you rather be a bland hero or an exciting villain? Jack Nicholson is not the first actor, nor the one millionth person, to answer that bad beats good … any day.

3

Men on a Mission

It's in their eyes. Always intent and never idle. Every detail scanned, each face studied, all situations evaluated. Darting, squinting, focusing, reacting, anticipating, homing, searching, narrowing, straining. Eyelids glued open in intense concentration. Or they blink with hummingbird-like rapidity, while recording and analyzing and storing, taking nothing for granted and everything as potential.

The searchers search outside, out in the open and with the widest, most grand area to cover. Sun, dust, nature, noise and reality itself all distract but do not dissuade these men from their mission. Since they seek only the quest, they do not note one another, as those outside the mission are irrelevant. One is a retired cop, still obsessed with the final case of his career, the still-unsolved murder of a child. So he will not note a radio operator, struggling to make contact with his command. Nor could he possibly care about a couple of guys crossing off another goal from their ultimate list of to-dos. Or even someone desperate and shaken, focused only on one adult male and caring nothing about anything childlike despite his prey having stolen a child away. A border guard has everything to worry about, while the labor organizer's under control and all business.

Great actors play great people. They also bring flawed people to life, dramatizing faults and obsessions and neuroses. Or psychoses. Sometimes the mission can become the psychosis, a promise can become the trap. In *The Pledge* and *The Crossing Guard*, Nicholson's promises become obsessions that imprison his characters, cornering the men until they give everything, including everything beyond reason. Both were directed and co-produced by Sean Penn, who also wrote *The Crossing Guard*, in which Nicholson makes a promise to himself to kill the drunk driver who killed his young daughter. In *The Pledge*, he makes a promise to the mother of a little girl to find the girl's killer. Yet even then, the promise was to himself, the retiring detective who had to prove his worth by solving one more case, a cold case that had implicated the wrong man.

Little girls dead. Men dead and dying inside, living off only one thing: their commitment to avenge those children, a postmortem protection too late to matter to the little girls and too little to accomplish more than merely elevate their own self-worth.

In *The Pledge*, Jerry Black becomes so fixated upon tracking one young girl's killer that he's blinded to the fact that he turns another young girl into live bait, betraying his lover and her daughter in the service of pursuing the case. His pledge is sacred, because he promises it to another mother, one who is at her most vulnerable and raw, and because the perception about his entire career—and his worth as a cop—is at stake in this last desperate effort.

Nicholson felt that his character was so driven to solve the murder as "his way of fighting back against all the shit in the world and all the meaninglessness out there. He's trying to find some purpose and vindication in a life that's become a black hole."[1]

The opening scene of *The Pledge* is a harrowing one, with a completely disassociated man, silent or near-silently ranting to himself or to imaginary others, with Jack's appearance bloated and shockingly punished.

Upon going back in time, he looks like the character in *The Border* several years on, which is fitting because he is a cop again, but retiring to an emptier future as in *About Schmidt*. Sean Penn then sets the scene, while Nicholson applies his full character energy into developing a name and a situation into a complex and multifaceted person. The low, soft voice of Jerry's hesitant promise contrasts the police veteran's normally intense demeanor. He starts to lose it, becoming more upset when seeing his own image on TV, with distress setting in as his manner becomes more fractured, confused and visibly shakier.

The investigating detective must connect with his subjects, projecting empathy and involvement to elicit essential information and engender trust. Nicholson conveys this warm, sensitive and inquisitive feeling in his scene with Vanessa Redgrave, who portrays the murdered child's grandmother. As he interviews one of the child's classmates and other possible witnesses, you can sense that this is a man thinking and discovering at that moment in time, reacting in the moment. Black is troubled and perplexed, increasingly frantic in his demeanor with a psychiatrist (Helen Mirren), exhibiting a subtle growth in distress, degree by degree. When she touches him, he looks like a man who hadn't been touched in quite some time, showing longing and unease that's tentative in its childlike uncertainty.

Jerry makes this promise to a mother, a person like so many others to whom he's had to intone, "I'm sorry for your loss." This time, he got a little too personal and went beyond the standard "do everything we can" to making a specific, definite and emotional pledge. That mission had to destroy him, as he worked against a system that wants clean, easy solutions without loose ends and inquisitive second-guessers. Turning the case into a personal quest had to be Jerry's downfall. He set the conditions. He established the rules. Without cracking the case and keeping his pledge, this retiring cop becomes a sad and sodden nobody, with one dead little girl knocking down years and decades of the finest performance as one of the town's finest.

Nicholson attributed the strength of his portrayal to his ability to identify with the character. "It was a very dark character [with] a sense of hopelessness and absurdity to his life and those are philosophical kinds of issues that have always been very close to my heart."[2]

There's a scene in a clothing store, in which Lori (Robin Wright Penn as the mother of a little girl that Jerry eventually uses as bait) and daughter Chrissy (Pauline Roberts) inquire about a red dress. We get the realization that Jerry is using that girl as a lure, a shocking reality that then ties back to a previous scene when this surrogate father, latter-day lover and manly protector purposefully places a new swing set right by the road—and we now know why.

Betrayal takes full form when he sends Chrissy toward the suspect known as the Wizard, knowing that he represents total danger and seeing that the Wizard has a telltale porcupine candy. That betrayal is shown in Jerry's cold stare at Lori, the stare of another dangerous man and sociopath, the one who was supposed to be protecting them.

On the stakeout, Jerry's eyes get unnaturally big. During Lori's attacking confrontation, as she berates Jerry for his betrayal, he breaks from reality, no longer seeing or hearing her, and becoming fully convincing as a man who believes he is alone and studying the scene of a crime not committed. Unless that crime is his own against his lover and her daughter.

The end of the film returns us to the scene introduced at the film's opening. Jack's quick transitions between expressions and among emotions—from happiness and pissed off, to searching and finding, to certainty and the shaking anger of loss—happens as if in fast motion, a compressed time. At once, Jerry becomes the cop again, yet within the body of an alcohol-addled bum. He rolls the evidence around in his head, re-interviewing witnesses not there, and accusing suspects seen but not present.

This sequence, revealing a roll call of emotional range, is reminiscent of one in *One Flew Over the Cuckoo's Nest* in which Nicholson sits down towards the end of the inmates' illicit party to show McMurphy contemplating what's happening, what's happened, and what may still happen, seamlessly transitioning between disparate emotions and expressions within mere moments.

The Pledge revolves around a crime of one dead girl and the criminal misuse of a trusting and loving relationship to bolster a retiring police detective's self-image on his final case. The other crime was that Jerry was right all along and all alone in being so. He did keep his pledge without even knowing it, and without anyone else believing it; in the end he gets no credit for sanity, let alone discernment and superior insight.

Of course, that applies to the simplified, if not "dumbed down" version that was the final release. Actor Tom Noonan, who leads the parish and was seemingly proven as the Wizard and a pedophile killer, explained to me that he was in fact not the killer. "I was in two other scenes with Jack that were never shot, because they ran out of money," Noonan explained, pointing out that this then necessitated a more ham-fisted ending that provided Jerry's character with the ultimate pyrrhic victory.[3]

* * *

Freddy Gale of *The Crossing Guard* also exists for a promise, waiting for a prisoner to be released to meet his execution at Freddy's hand. Freddy must kill the man who killed his little girl, but Freddy is no cop and resides outside of the justice system. Nicholson creates three men as one character: a boozy strip club lecher with money; a wasted, blasted, mentally disabled father; and a predatory, monstrous man on a murderer's mission.

In his initial appearance, wordless at first, Nicholson looks like a real person, thus setting the tone for the piece. Is this his most real performance? Critics talked about "underplaying" in *About Schmidt*, but this film shows him disappearing into a role as much as someone we can't help but recognize can ever hope to do.

As seen many times before, Nicholson seems to revel in looking far less than star-like. As he gets out of bed with a stripper, he's not afraid to look real and really terrible, tired and hung-over and sporting man-boobs. Without our seeing his face, Nicholson is also able to convey that this man is on a mission, with purpose and focus.

John Savage, star of *The Deer Hunter* and Bobby in *The Crossing Guard*, related to me that when director Sean Penn asked him to play another collateral victim in a scene, he gave his performance a wrenching reality by drawing upon his own recovery and his work with Mothers Against Drunk Driving.[4] The intercuts between Bobby weeping as he tells his story of personal pain to a support group, contrasted with Gale's debauchery in a strip club with his own support group of drunken losers, shows how different men deal with the same tragedy in dramatically different ways.

Later, when Freddy talks about his "job in life" with his ex-wife (Anjelica Huston), the mother of their deceased child, we believe it. Huston was affected by their scenes together, explaining that it "always broke my heart when Jack played damaged men." She hadn't seen Nicholson for a few years and "I think Sean asked me asked me to play the part of Jack's ex-wife because of our history."[5] Penn confirms that he "thought that history would be invaluable, particularly because it would just set a level of honesty to the film."[6]

The Crossing Guard **(1995) featured key scenes between former lovers Nicholson and Anjelica Huston, who had not seen the actor for a few years prior to being put together by director Sean Penn "because of our history."**

    Nicholson uses his face and body to become a uniquely powerful actor. His success in portrayal and triumph in embodiment are testament to an actor in command of his physical tools and conscious of their use, moment to moment and life to life.

    After a confrontation inside a strip club, Nicholson moves his head back and forth in a manner to provide a view inside his character's mind, navigating between extremes of disbelief, torment and menace. When he pulls out a gun and cocks it, he is not an actor, but a man concentrating on that mission, driven to a goal that's neither commendable nor condemnable. He must. Not for pleasure, not even for satisfaction, but because of the pledge made to his dead daughter. Even Freddy thinks the promise is to himself. Nevertheless, he must become the father he was not while she was alive. He must undo the hurt she can no longer feel.

    In a scene that takes place in a bathroom, Gale is on the phone with his ex-wife, Mary. We witness a man full of pain that's authentic, the cry of a man who doesn't cry much, a moment of complete agony and with no affect.

    Watching Freddy's final diner scene with Mary, you can only hurt for these people, because they cared, they loved, they lost, they suffered. Together, Nicholson and Huston's characters share tenderness and intensity—that is, until Gale spots pity. He suddenly morphs from broken parent to blind, unthinking monster, lashing out and breaking out so hard and so fast that his attack—hoping that she "fucking dies"—is shockingly real. He's dangerous and heart-wrenching at once, a seeming illogical combination that Nicholson pulls off in this essence of character energy.

Later, when Gale kisses a little girl (obviously thinking of his own), it's another piece of your heart dripping away, in a sequence reminiscent of the Nicholson-scripted *The Trip*, when Peter Fonda wanders into a home and converses with a young girl played by Caren Bernsen.

As volatile and explosive as Freddy is portrayed, there are also moments that enrich the character with lightness and vulnerability. A scene with director Sean Penn's mother and her "perfect fucking seven" ring size is comic genius of a sort that we could only wish would be more evident in some of the comedies Nicholson has made. He dances, rolls on a stripper pole with dexterity, and stretches our definition of the man in his scene with Kari Wuhrer, who called the experience "one of the greatest movie moments of my life."[7]

The final confrontation is masterful, an old, tired and broken man against a strong yet weakened, imprisoned man. They are the same while they are different. They chase and they play, but without the playfulness of any sort of game.

Freddy Gale needs only the failed vengeance of the seriocomic scene in his prey's trailer to have accomplished a full career of greatness. Fumbling and failure are associated with broad physical comedy rather than a personal psychological collapse, but Nicholson plays it so that it fits and makes sense. As the two men eventually surrender to the worthlessness of it all, one the killer (of the little girl) and the other the killed (caused by her loss), they kneel down in shared pain and join hands—making you share their moment.

Penn described the film's themes as recognition that some tenderness is always possible, and the question of how to deal with unbearable loss. The screenwriter and director explained this response as a lifelong effort to maintain sensitivity and compassion despite having it beaten out of us, every day, bit by bit.[8]

Nicholson's Freddy Gale is a complex man, a portrayal that takes character energy and turns it into deeply flawed flesh-and-blood truth. In this world, a fist's thud on a cemetery's ground signals the moment when a new life begins. Revenge is not sweet, but a self-destruction that leads to redemption and resurrection.

* * *

Charlie Smith has an entirely different promise to keep. In *The Border*, Charlie is overwhelmed by the aspirations of his wife, knowing he cannot fulfill them, but still going along because he is not in charge. Charlie is not in charge of his life at home, resulting in a loss of control over his job as border cop.

Charlie Smith is a nondescript name for a nondescript guy. It's *Five Easy Pieces* turned right and gone south, as his wife Marcy (Valerie Perrine) unfavorably compares to Bobby's lover Rayette (Karen Black) in the earlier film. Marcy fancies herself a budding TV star, but her appeal can only relate to sex. She has no talent, while Rayette was a good singer. Marcy is selfish and extremely materialistic, the opposite of Rayette's giving and loving personality. Rayette made Bobby a better person, while Marcy came close to destroying Charlie both as border agent and as a man. She spends what he does not have. Home, furniture, swimming pool, waterbed. She cannot control herself—because she doesn't want to—and he cannot control her.

Nicholson portrays Charlie as being comfortable only when he has his uniform on and his cop glasses down. This shift in the interior of the character that contrasts his home life (lacking in rules and structure) with his career life (aided by those rules and that structure) is real. Jack's demeanor changes based on Charlie's comfort with where he is and his assigned role.

To pay for a lifestyle he does not want and cannot afford, he must compromise on his promise to protect the U.S. border. Charlie becomes a dirty cop, helping an illegal immigration ring.

The Border was directed by the great Tony Richardson, interesting because a British director helms this story of Mexicans crossing into the U.S. Here, the Bureau of Naturalization & Immigration is seen as a game, a give-and-take show that's more about quotas that are just for the record rather than with any real purpose.

The film is one of social commentary, likely chosen by the star to bring attention to the plight of Mexicans seeking an honest and hard-working life, chased down by crooked cops driven to greed and materialism and to cynically play the system both ways for their own gain. In fact, it could very well be that this film could not have been made (or at least could not have been anything more than a small-scale independent and unknown production) without Nicholson's interest. Here's a "social message": One border agent asks another, "How do you spell 'illiterate'?"

Charlie's domestic life is undomesticated and his work life is spent wastefully rounding up domestics they call "the wets." Nicholson's characterization of this man's process of giving up and giving in takes him from a clean cop in a dirty system, to a dirty cop who plays the game, to one who rethinks it all.

Most comfortable in uniform and within rules, Charlie looks his most smooth and natural in a rifle formation saluting a dead partner. Duty becomes perverted by his personal home obligations. Nicholson takes the character

Tony Richardson's *The Border* (1982) may be more topical now than upon its release in 1982. This confrontation between Charlie Smith (Nicholson, right) and Cat (Harvey Keitel) presents the intensity of two powerful actors in a battle of wills.

places where Charlie himself could not have anticipated and about which he could not have been at ease. He's relaxed when on the job but pressured and trapped at home.

He has a classic Jacksplosion when unsuccessfully putting his foot down with his wife, screaming, "No more means no more!" and that he "can't afford a fucking dream house," spewing the words through his teeth to the extent that you can almost feel the spit pushing the point home.

After witnessing a gratuitous food fight at the couple's show-off-the-house-and-its-accouterments barbecue, Charlie rolls a grill right into the pool, sarcastically announcing "soup's on" in a pure Jack moment.

This transformation is not all lightness. In fact, it is painful to watch. Charlie feels trapped, so he gives in—and gives up his conscience—to join the exploitation scheme. Nicholson portrays the emptiness of full compromise, the loss of self and humanity that comes from selling out. Smith is given no choice but to face this pressure head-on, and when showing this distress, Charlie rubs the lower part of the palms of his hands on his forehead.

Nicholson takes that desperate man further, reaching the core that can slowly form a scab around indifference and covering conviction. Charlie's choice is a conviction to change, to change himself and the sick system. He starts with a confrontation with Cat (Harvey Keitel), in a scene that presents the intensity of two powerful actors battling with each other's reality, concerning the murder of drivers illegally transporting Mexicans across the border. That border, not the physical one, but the border of honor, is one that Charlie Smith cannot cross.

The actor is completely convincing and honest as a man who gives up everything to go on a crusade that takes him from looking for a baby with a pimp to busting top cop Red (Warren Oates) and taking on J.J. (Jeff Morris), the lynchpin to the entire on-the-take enterprise.

When Charlie shoots out Red's tire, it is striking that Keitel (with whom he'd reteam eight years later in *The Two Jakes*) is crushed beneath a big earthmover in a way similar to Jack's demise in *The Departed*.

Charlie's only true moment of warmth is with the Mexican woman, Maria (played by Elpidia Carrillo), who yearns to find her child. He wants nothing from her, just to "feel good about himself," the saddest commentary of all about this man.

But Charlie's smile at the film's end, when passing the baby to its mother, is priceless, and the only time in the movie we see this open, relaxed, expansive and real smile that comes from the unrestrained joy of caring.

To be on the border is to be on the edge, and Nicholson's Charlie Smith is on the edge between corrupt and clean, honest and compromised, devoted and cheated, dedicated and renegade, materialistic and magnanimous, cop-cold and humanity-warmed.

As union organizer Brimmer in *The Last Tycoon*, Nicholson has no such edge, nor a need for one. His mission is that of his business, but he doesn't allow himself to take it—or a ridiculously contemptuous and aggressive Monroe Stahr (Robert DeNiro)—too seriously.

The film itself is a slight conclusion to the monumental film career of director Elia Kazan, based on an unfinished novel by F. Scott Fitzgerald. DeNiro appreciated the director's supportiveness and technique of improvisation, not on the screen, but "improvising behind the scenes to find other colors." However, the actor saw the weaknesses in the script, to which Kazan adhered "practically word for word" to make good on a promise to screenwriter Harold Pinter.[9]

The chief miscast in *The Last Tycoon* marks the film's biggest mistake. What we don't need is a toned-down DeNiro, a thoughtful *Taxi Driver*, a reflective *Raging Bull*, or a cerebral *Cape Fear*. The choice of DeNiro at this point in his career should be a choice for intensity and power, just dangling over the dangerous edge. Instead, the actor's explosiveness gets tamped to the point of becoming nothing more than boring. Monroe Stahr is a powerful person without being a powerful character.

In what amounts to nothing more than a cameo, Nicholson plays a union organizer for screenwriters as a professional and inquisitive man. Jack is playful in this portrayal, boorishly pushing his food in and exhibiting his contempt for DeNiro's character as he discusses helping the writers. There's much irony in Brimmer's voice, while sideward glances, tics, smiles and eyebrows all punctuate his words. He's openly playing with Stahr, going after food stuck in his teeth with his lips just as he relentlessly goes at Stahr without disguising his low opinion of the studio's star producer. Brimmer shoots a happy, perky "Oh, yes!" when challenged that he's not "a Red."

To Brimmer, this is a serious game. He eats Stahr's food like a pig and with a sort of artistic flourish; he drinks his coffee; he takes his cigar; and finally, he essentially takes Stahr's girl.

In her film debut, Theresa Russell plays Cecilia Brady, the daughter of studio chief Pat Brady (Robert Mitchum). She's fresh and insouciant, both innocent and too-knowing. She becomes the reason for the next challenge, a ping pong contest between the two men. Stahr plays with an increasingly out-of-control aggressiveness that's near violence, while Brimmer handles himself with aplomb by not reacting to provocation. Then, Stahr gives up with disgust, leaving Brimmer to play a friendly game with Cecilia. Their game is just for fun, which further enrages Stahr, as does the obvious attraction between the participants. Brimmer and Cecilia are adept and flirty, until the besotted Monroe Stahr challenges Brimmer for a third time, this time to an actual fistfight.

Brimmer remains patient with Stahr's juvenilia to the point that when pushed beyond any reasonable retreat, he cleanly decks the producer—even gingerly lowering the vanquished to the ground with Cecilia's help.

This scene also served as a duel between the more experienced Nicholson and the de-energized DeNiro. Brimmer remains steady and cordial as he thanks Cecilia for the game and retreats into the shadows.

* * *

Sometimes, a man's mission is set by others, like the intel-recon mission on the Filipino island Luzon by the Americans in 1944. Even soldiers handle the same situation differently, as depicted in Monte Hellman's gritty *Back Door to Hell*, made 20 years after the actual event.

Lieutenant Craig (played by singer Jimmie Rodgers, whose biggest hits were "Honeycomb" and "Kisses Sweeter Than Wine") freezes when he needs to kill one of the Japanese occupying the island. Jersey (co-screenwriter and Nicholson pal John Hackett) has no problem with such a chore, not seeing the Japanese as humans nor caring much for people in the first place. Nicholson, as radio operator Burnett, is somewhere in the middle. He still is tugged by lingering humanity but gets through it all with sardonic jokes mixed with philosophical observations.

A Korean War veteran, Rodgers was understandably unhappy with this aspect of his character. "I was discouraged with it because I had to play a coward in the film, which I really didn't like, but I thought, 'Well, it's important for the story.'"[10]

In this role, Nicholson is approaching the *Five Easy Pieces* Jack, though a little less relaxed in his dialogue delivery. In one scene, tightrope-walking to cross a river, his high-pitched laughter is reminiscent of Wilbur Force's in *The Little Shop of Horrors*.

This American-Filipino co-production was shot together with Hellman's *Flight to Fury*. Filmed in documentary style, in black and white on location in the Baco Region of the Philippines, *Back Door to Hell* is an oddly dark choice for the exploitation of a pop star. A somewhat cynical war-antiwar story isn't the typical vehicle for crooners, particularly a narrative that involves an occupier's threat to execute one Filipino school child for every hour U.S. soldiers remain free.

Rodgers described the challenging conditions, from bugs and killer snakes to praying mantises that played catch with Nicholson and the singer using balled-up newspaper. The crew could be challenging as well, mostly due to their status differences at the time. "Nicholson was the only one who spoke to me and when I walked through the door he looked up at me and he said [*imitates Nicholson's drawl*], 'How you doin', Ro-o-o-gers?' They didn't like me there because it was their group, it was Nicholson's group, and I got the feeling that I wasn't wanted because I was the star and they didn't want a star. They wanted somebody to come in to be one of the boys."[11]

They did eventually come together, with the inevitable practical jokes that can result from being stranded in a remote location. Rodgers stills laughs about how he got back at Nicholson with Hackett's help. Nicholson had found a secluded spot where he could jump in and swim away to come out behind a rock where nobody could see him. When he didn't come out after 20 minutes, they thought he was dead. When he finally emerged, "he thought that was funny, so when we were doing that scene in the old Catholic church, Nicholson had to crawl up a wooden ladder and he was reading his script up there and Hackett and I waited and we got even with him by ringing the bell and we rocked him out of that place for 20 minutes. He came down there and he couldn't hear and he couldn't talk for two days."[12]

Much of the mission depicted in the film centers on radio access, as the trio of soldiers has been sent to establish the extent of the Japanese defense in the days leading up to MacArthur's return to liberate the island. Their radio is destroyed, necessitating a raid on a Japanese communications outpost.

3. Men on a Mission

Popular singer Jimmie Rodgers (right) never heard of Jack Nicholson (far left) before they worked together on Monte Hellman's *Back Door to Hell* (1964), along with John Hackett (middle left). However, he saw something special. Nobody knew Nicholson in those days, but Rodgers sensed his potential: Jack "was a star when I met him."

The small cast and Burnett's role as radio operator provide Nicholson a chance to explore his range. He portrays a wiseguy, joking his way through tough situations while working with dubious Filipino guerrilla partners. He is the techie geek, fixing the radio and hedging confidence with caution as he sums up, "I think it's ready." He is a thinker, examining his own reaction to war in a bar scene when he observes, "Don't even know if I'm even supposed to feel anything" in a suitably existential manner. He is educated and well-trained, not only speaking but translating Japanese quite credibly, to the point of taking the opportunity to toss "shitty" into the mix, just because he could get away with it.

Nicholson is action star and war hero (within the limitations of this story in this production), with his character performing a pivotal function by planting a grenade in the top level of a church during the main assault; serving as sniper in its bell tower; and finally succumbing to a hail of bullets while in the act of getting his reconnaissance message out. Burnett single-handedly makes certain that they complete their mission, retreating behind and nearly beneath a desk in order to communicate by Morse code while under attack.

Rodgers recalls noticing Nicholson's potential, even in a limited role in a small film. "I didn't know who he was at this time, in those days nobody did. He was a star when I met him. He didn't know it at the time but, boy, this guy was so good on-screen and I knew that he was going to make it. And I admire him a lot. He's a character, but he is very talented."[13]

Nicholson makes Burnett a real person as much as possible in a low-budget potboiler that's just over an hour in length, with a believable and understated glimpse at his abilities as a developing and aspiring actor as of 1964.

* * *

One doesn't have to be a cop or soldier or even a parent bent on revenge in order to have a mission. Sometimes it just takes dying. *The Bucket List* pairs Nicholson with Morgan Freeman as men thrown together in a hospital room and joined by the short time remaining to them (six months to a year at best). When told how long they've got, their eyes—the actor's soul—meet in a powerful and expressive way. These are two veteran actors, and they are the best you can be at this.

During the period when I was writing this book, both of my parents passed away. They had no bucket list. They lived hard lives trying to bring us something better. They never would even have considered the possibility of such personal self-indulgence as they neared their final days. Instead, they got sick, they suffered and they died. But that isn't the only reason I view this movie with skepticism.

There's a contrivance at play, with so much seemingly constructed rather than plausibly lived. The audience is manipulated into sympathizing with and projecting themselves into these main characters.

Edward Cole (Nicholson) is a billionaire hospital magnate and Carter Chambers (Freeman) a black auto mechanic. In life, they are far removed. In impending death, they become partners.

Cole's rich, so he needs the poor guy to teach him about life. Chambers is black, necessitating a false irony as much more literate and appreciative of knowledge and science and culture. Edward's successful yet estranged from his daughter, contrasted with Carter, who struggles to provide for his family while enjoying a loving life with them.

So, if you don't have Edward Cole's kind of money, you just sort of die. If you do, you can finance a feel-good adventure for yourself and another terminal case.

The actual "bucket list" part's pretty boring and lacking in emotional reality, featuring a series of vignettes of two old guys jumping out of planes, getting tattoos, racing cars and hitting some famous sites.

People adore this movie ... and the idea it represents. However, only the acting rescues the Rob Reiner film from being a complete audience-pandering confection.

In Nicholson's establishing scene, showing Cole's presentation to a hospital board, he portrays his character almost as if giving a glimpse of what he might think we envision Nicholson to be like in real life, all about personal pleasure and superior to others in an artful way. Reduced to experiencing his own hospital as an actual patient, Edward fights his physical reality, yelling, "I hate tubes!" in a struggle worthy of *Five Easy Pieces*. When Cole gives us a glimpse of himself, telling us, "I've never been sick before," we painfully witness a real moment of a real man, not a fictional hospital executive.

Nicholson plays it quite physical for a guy in bed, but then the actor's use of his body has always been an important part of his technique. Clearly, Nicholson feels that an actor shouldn't need dignity, but should pursue character energy no matter the means or the surface sacrifice.

Does the car race scene take him back to his early juvenile delinquent role in *The Wild Ride*? Was the Cole-plus-Chambers journey supposed to serve as their Wyatt-plus-Billy *Easy Rider* road trip?

In terms of contribution to the work, the acting beats the locales. In France, Nicholson's reaction shot to Freeman in a bathtub consists of doing *nothing*, yet the moment is real and human. At the pyramids, Nicholson looks worn, but builds true character energy when telling the story about his abused daughter and how he "fixed it" with his wife-beating son-in-law. When Cole mentions how she responded that he was "dead to her," we feel the father's emotion and loss.

As Nicholson describes taking care of the abusive husband, only with generalities ("Don't know what they did"), he's like Hoffa declaring "I'm gonna do what I gotta do…" but with thoughtful retrospect instead of bombastic threat.

Later, Edward cries while facing a window, alone—a solitary release that is an on-screen rarity for the actor.

The Bucket List is really Freeman's movie. Chambers is the stronger, more fully realized character, exhibiting a love for his limited life and the wonder of new experiences, while Cole's arc is a narrower one that opens the door from cold businessman to caring human being.

While the two men look at each other back at the hospital following their shared adventures (with a throwaway "pea soup still sucks"), they are actually looking at their own mortality.

Nicholson's funeral speech for the Freeman character was a moving eulogy for a friend, as well as a tribute to a real person rather than toward another actor playing a part. That is acting. And *that* is the only reason to care about *The Bucket List*, despite its entry into the vernacular and into the lives of viewers who ponder their own mortality.

* * *

Mortality becomes its own mission, one which touches us all. A parent of a senselessly killed child suffers in his own mortality; a detective desperate to fulfill a personal pledge to the parent of a murdered little girl fights the mortality of the innocent against the enduring life of the evil; another cop transcends his own mortality by bringing meaning into his own life against a system with no borders between right and wrong; soldiers and representatives serve others in a small bid for greater humanity; while mutual mortality sparks a shared humanity for a last-act odd couple.

Our mission must be humanity versus mortality, whether real cops or soldiers or billionaires or parents of lost children or parents of film book authors. Truth engenders that victory, every time, for actors or for characters.

4

Pieces of Schmidt

One long room separates two small men. Not small in stature, but in significance. At one end, the first is young and taut and straight-backed. At the other, the second is old enough for retirement and soft and slumped. The first is chiseled and angular in visage, with the furrowed brow of the thoughtful. The other is doughy both inside and outside of his head. Attentive and active eyes contrast with dead and soulless ones.

Yet they are the same person, 30 years apart.

Decades ago, Bobby Dupea effectively became Warren Schmidt and accomplish his goal of having no goals; assume the identity of someone without one; and live the life of the truly lifeless. Bobby Dupea escaped because it was easy. He severed all connection with his past, his family and his own abilities because it was easy. Like vamping on piano behind Vegas showgirls, he could fake his way through an empty career as an insurance actuary and an empty existence with a family that was barely one—because it was easy.

Nicholson played Robert Eroica Dupea to perfection in Bob Rafelson's *Five Easy Pieces*. Just over 30 years later, Nicholson artfully embodies that same character's deflated future in the form of Warren Schmidt in Alexander Payne's *About Schmidt*.

Dupea wanted to disappear (and he did) into Schmidt's meaningless corporate existence where others tell you what to do, when to do it, and how it should be done, leaving out only the whys as irrelevant and immaterial.

In *Five Easy Pieces*, Nicholson is most alive during the explosions that helped define this breakout role, while establishing the "Jacksplosions" that became so prevalent through the actor's career. He explodes in the traffic jam "dogfight," descending into an actual barking match with an equally frustrated German shepherd. He explodes in his own car upon the character's realization that he has no choice but bring Rayette (Karen Black) with him to see his family, becoming a trapped, violent and wild animal, yelping and kicking, uncontrolled and drooling. He explodes when live-in therapist Spicer (frequent Nicholson player John P. Ryan) makes the moves on his sister Partita

(Lois Smith). Most celebrated, he explodes when idiotic rules reduce the customer to powerless patsy in the famous chicken salad sandwich diner scene.

About Schmidt features such explosions, but they are less about meaningful emotion and more about reflex and reaction. He explodes upon discovering the affair between his best friend Ray (Len Cariou) and his wife Helen (June Squibb), with Nicholson adopting the same body motion, stance and action in his violent fit as Orson Welles directed toward his wife's character in *Citizen Kane*. Warren Schmidt wobbles as Charles Foster Kane wobbles. Schmidt lurches and staggers like Kane. And Schmidt robotically tosses and swipes away his wife's stuff just as Kane does with his wife's. The scene also is a nod to the "all this crap" slamming and sweeping of Catherine's (Susan Anspach) perfumes and cosmetics, her narcissistic possessions, by Bobby in *Five Easy Pieces*.

Schmidt also explodes (or breaks free) with his liberating, look-Ma-no-hands urinating on the floor, using the same technique and same flourish with which he marks his territory directly onto the shoes of James Spader in *Wolf*. When Nicholson looks in the gas station rest room mirror at the end of *Five Easy Pieces*, it's a reminder of the self-examination by the Monkees in a movie studio rest room mirror from the Nicholson-Rafelson-scripted *Head*.

Intriguingly, Karen Black's copy of the script shows that Bobby was not directed to study himself. In fact, he was "avoiding looking at himself in the mirror" and later "once more not confronting himself in the mirror."[1] It appears to be another invention by the actor, with Nicholson choosing to look at himself and look within himself to make this ultimate decision to escape into anonymity.

When Nicholson's Dupea looks at himself, only his eyes move. He searches for something as he searches for himself—in the same way Nicholson's Jack Torrance does in the mirror during *The Shining*. Dupea and Torrance find the same thing: nothing. Nicholson's eyes are all that move as Bobby makes the decision to cease to exist. Bobby's remnants of a soul empty into the mirror, only to emerge as the nothing known as Warren Schmidt.

* * *

In connecting *Five Easy Pieces* as prelude to *About Schmidt*, we see that escaping doesn't necessarily mean to a better place, or even to any place at all. Bobby had already abandoned his talent, believing he wasn't a good enough pianist. Warren completes the process, living a life totally devoid of music or *any* art. Bobby, for all intents and purposes, has left his family behind (with the exception of periodic connection with his sister Tita, played by Lois Smith). Warren negates family from within, merely existing beside a lifeless, loveless wife with no emotional or physical charm, while pathetically reaching out—no, grasping—to an unappealing, annoying ingrate of a daughter (Hope Davis, as Jeannie). Jeannie's contemptuous rejection of her parent is something normal kids grow out of in high school or early college, while her self-absorption is wholly unjustified based on her status and merits.

Bobby Dupea enters a logging truck at the conclusion of *Five Easy Pieces*, abandoning both Rayette and his identity. Cinema scholar Don Schiach believes Dupea "represents the American male in flight from commitment," reinforcing Nicholson as the eternal alienated outsider who must escape, without realizing that what's really necessary is to escape from himself.[2] Bobby is again heading elsewhere, in motion or thinking about it, a psychological dilemma called "'flight forward,' a compulsion to escape the unbearable present."[3]

Rafelson's two-shot of Nicholson beside the driver evokes the image of Dustin Hoffman and Katharine Ross in the back of the bus as they escape to uncertainty at the end of Mike Nichols' *The Graduate*. We're on the road to nowhere, indeed.

Dupea's future, on the other hand, is not uncertain because he gets exactly what he seeks: nothing. From a gas station in Washington State, he

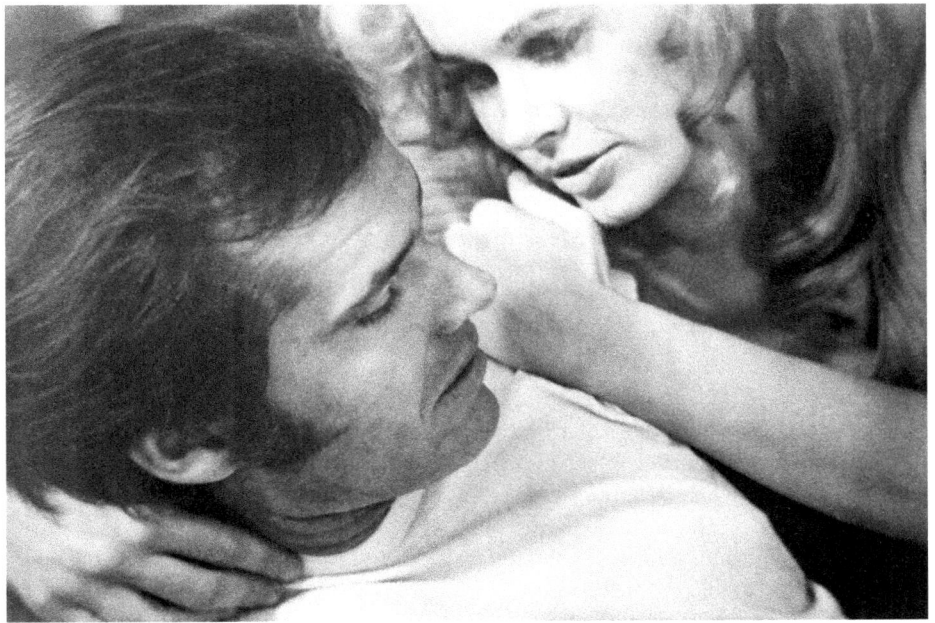

One of Nicholson's best films, *Five Easy Pieces* (1970), presents an antihero who wants to escape his upper-class roots. A highlight of the film is the interplay between Nicholson and Karen Black, pictured.

rides along to Alaska, then to who-knows-where before eventually settling on an anonymous life in clear sight in Omaha, Nebraska.

The original *Five Easy Pieces* ending had Bobby drown after his car plunged off a bridge, with Rayette emerging to search in vain for Bobby and then reducing their relationship to one final "You son of a bitch."[4] Schiach called this ending existentialist, as Dupea "is stripped of almost everything by a deliberate act of will." He sweeps his life's connections—from family and lover to identity and possessions—just as he clears the diner table and Catherine's bureau top of "crap." He runs away from responsibilities and the burden of his unfulfilled "auspicious beginnings." Schiach all but confirms the viability of disappearing in plain sight as Schmidt, noting that Bobby is "reinventing himself, not in a mood of joyful liberation, but out of miserable desperation."[5]

Bobby's life as Warren Schmidt does not even rise to the level of being empty. He works for a company that forgets about him as soon as he's out the door on his last day. His wife's most passionate acts were reserved for his own best friend and her liveliest moment was her death. His daughter is as worthless as she makes her father feel.

Schmidt appears to have no interests. He is uninteresting and disinterested. His accomplishments number not just in the single digits, but the single numeral. Bobby Dupea has escaped … life itself. He sheds his background, his family, his abilities—but he keeps going until he also sheds personality, inquisitiveness, purpose and meaning. He is too successful in his quest to avoid life and feeling.

Nicholson is as masterful inhabiting the mercurial, emptily lustful antihero Dupea as he is in sliding into the formless, mirthless poster boy for unquestioning conformity we come to know as Schmidt.

* * *

While *Easy Rider* was Jack's big break, and a break that saved his moldering acting career, *Five Easy Pieces* established him as a solid acting lead. A movie star. The sensation around the former film's success was important, as Nicholson became the proverbial "overnight success after years of struggle" and was nominated as Best Supporting Actor. But there have been plenty of those who never made the next step up and many more who never had the chance for as tasty a subsequent role.

Five Easy Pieces was reportedly written expressly for Nicholson by friend Carole Eastman (under the name Adrien Joyce). To most moviegoers, he was an unknown apart from *Easy Rider*, and *Five Easy Pieces* would establish him as the Jack Nicholson with whom audiences soon grew familiar (at least mid-period Jack, that is). He was camera-savvy enough by this point to act with more nuance, expertly controlling his face, his forehead's transverse lines, and the vertical wrinkles at the top of his nose and between his eyes produced by the corrugator supercilii muscle. Part actor, part physiologist.

In the invaluable Robert Crane–Christopher Fryer interview collection *Jack Nicholson: Face to Face* (1975), Nicholson named this his top performance, adding, "I would say that philosophically, I'm most attuned to the character in *Five Easy Pieces*."[6]

What makes this portrayal so special, aside from the freshness of seeing someone with talent take opportunity and fully seize its possibilities, is Nicholson's character energy. It's an energetic play, grabbing the character completely and immersing himself into every aspect of his being. Nicholson plays the competitor (bowling and cards); the cad; the caring brother; the womanizer; the disaffected and the disillusioned; the compassionate; and the loner. Most of all, Bobby *is* solipsism, a wandering discontent who is wandering without getting anywhere in particular and who is only focused inward, yet without any particular interest. Rayette serves as a force to escape … that is, until she becomes the catalyst for the next escape. Though Karen Black "was in heaven when I made it," the actress had to enter a hell to understand her character. Despite being the victim of Bobby's cruelty and neglect, "[s]he's open, she's not critical, she's had a lot of life force, and she's not thinking."[7]

It's a cerebral movie with a thoughtful portrayal, yet what's most striking is the actor's use of motion. *Five Easy Pieces* is an action movie, but rather than car chases and explosions, we see a character chasing himself away with full intensity and with the occasional Jacksplosion along the way.

Here, Nicholson is an actor with no physical limits. He didn't just settle for passionate sex with Sally Struthers, but fused with her while swinging violently into walls and knocking over lamps. Thirty years later, she gushed to me, "I did that naked scene with Jack!"[8] To Crane and Fryer, she was less excited but more expansive, saying that she learned to avoid pushing a scene from working with Nicholson. "He underplays so beautifully, he's so natural," explained Struthers, "a lot of the way he moves around with his head, or his hands, or doesn't always look at the person he's talking to is kind of a Marlon Brando thing." She called Nicholson's awareness of his own natural approach "a kind of studied unstudiedness."[9]

He doesn't just play cards, but turns it into a ballet of joy and flirtation, tossing in the same unusual hand-swept-across-the-neck motion he introduced in *Easy Rider*.

He's completely body-aware. Notice his use of hands and exaggerated movements at the oil rig in the scene when Bobby attacks Elton (Billy Green Bush) about getting him to work there. When Nicholson walks, he swings his arm wildly like any proud New Jerseyian would, yet adopts a whole different body language when visiting his sister in the recording studio—with hands in pockets, subdued speech and tamed expression. Nicholson's Bobby conforms to what he imagines is expected: Bombastic and aggressive on the rig; domineering and callous with Rayette; irreverent and subversive with his family. Vulnerable and out-of-place in the strict studio environment, Nicholson uses small motions, restrained movements, dampened speech, muted expression. Contrast that with the falling and flailing expansive body motion as Dupea tells Elton off about "the good life," baring teeth and spitting words in dismissive condescension over Elton's moralizing and Rayette's pregnancy trap.

This particular Jacksplosion looks like an onscreen version of an Abandonment Exercise practiced by acting teacher Eric Morris as described in his guide *No Acting, Please* (Nicholson provided the foreword). This exercise helps an enormously tense actor "blast through your barriers" to

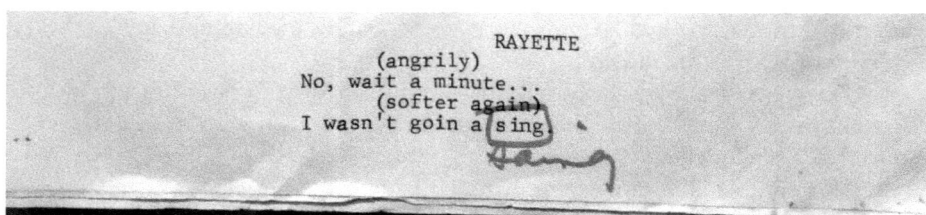

Top: A portion of a page from Karen Black's original script for her role as Rayette in *Five Easy Pieces*. *Above:* Karen Black noted Rayette's pronunciations in her *Five Easy Pieces* script.

release tension, so intensely that it requires the removal of jewelry, glasses or any other objects that could hurt the student. It requires a soft surface like a carpet and enough space to safely accommodate expansive action. Morris instructs his acting subjects to "hurl yourself into what might resemble having a physical 'fit,' kicking, flailing your body in every direction, screaming, howling and being as vocally abandoned as you are physically." Having this sort of guided fit eliminates anxiety and allows an actor to get deeper in order to free reluctant emotions until physically spent.[10]

Now, re-watching the scene as Bobby reconsiders about bringing Rayette on his trip against his deepest, inward drive to escape—and then violently reacts to his own decision—you are witnessing one of Nicholson's acting exercises in practice, though he does so trapped inside a car too small to fulfill the instructor's advice about doing so in a large, soft-surfaced space.

Most significantly, there is no indication of any of this in the script saved by Karen Black. It goes straight from the direction that Bobby throws the suitcase on the back seat of his car, gets in, "immediately starts the motor, and puts both hands on the wheel"[11]—right to the next interior setting when he pulls the needle across Rayette's record. The script reads that he "puts both hands on the wheel." Then ... nothing. No flailing, no kicking, no animalistic screams punctuated by randomly recognizable profanities. All invented by the actor himself, in a true moment as felt by his character, and nothing from the page itself.

His character energy is boundless. Watch the iconic diner scene. Nicholson moves through Dupea's journey from reasoning to patronizing to anti-authoritarian to violent punk. starts so calm, becoming clipped and demonstrative, next betraying the edge in his voice when he says "between your knees," and then putting his glasses on to give license as he takes on the attitude and bearing of a biker character.

* * *

Nicholson's performance in *About Schmidt* is smart and subdued, and notable for its acclaimed and surprising restraint, as if the actor was considered incapable of reeling it in when necessary. Shaded and deft, human and exposed, the work draws attention with finesse rather than clumsily commanding it.

Nicholson called it a film about humanity and "human problems, human aspirations and human frailties." Proud of his work and the film's rejection of pandering to the movie masses, he admitted, "If I wasn't in it myself, I'd say it was quite beautiful."[12]

While *Five Easy Pieces* shows the process of becoming empty, with Bobby emptying his life and himself of all touches, connections, responsibility and meaning, *Schmidt* provides the result: a man completely drained. Picking up

Bobby Dupea may well have hidden in plain site as Warren Schmidt. In *About Schmidt* (2002), Nicholson "underplays" as he grows from a "nobody" into an average retiree.

Bobby Dupea's story, and reconnecting with the character, Schmidt watches and waits as the clock clicks to five p.m., and as his last bit of life shrivels away (because his wife's dying doesn't quite rise to that level of significance).

Nicholson lowers his acting blood pressure, plodding along as a stuffed figure of a person, not as much without any emotion as without any need for emotion. We first see him totally immobile and unblinking, intentionally and extremely dead.

Here is an actor in command, so strong that he can be delicate and subtle. Jack's mindful that in real life, people try to hide their pain and insecurity, so he acts (or underacts as many have characterized it) accordingly.

This is seen at Warren Schmidt's retirement dinner in the near-wincing look on his face upon the mention of a meaningful life and raising a great family, betraying its complete lack of accuracy. This subtle sickness harkened back to the whole of a life that was more deserving of a bittersweet reflection, as long as it left out the sweet.

The range of emotions Nicholson displays during a phone call with Hope Davis (as his daughter) travels seamlessly from happiness to disappointment, from disgust about a lousy gift and a lousier son-in-law-to-be, all the way back to affection.

As he matured, Nicholson would not hesitate to allow himself to look unattractive, unglamorous or ridiculous. In the film, an extreme close-up titled "two weeks later" (after his wife's death) is priceless in showing his face as a distorted, puffy bloat, as on a dead body floating on the surface of a pond. More than not caring what he looks like, Nicholson is devoted to the disheveled, from the distended belly in *Terms of Endearment* and the total wreck he became in *The Witches of Eastwick* to the comical mess who suffers a losing battle with a waterbed in *About Schmidt*.

Exaggerated for effect, but never veering into the overdone, Nicholson successfully becomes Warren Schmidt. He walks old and tired, but not in the falsely stiff and caricatured way most actors "age" themselves for an elderly role. As he exits the Woodman Tower after a brush-off by his replacement, he moves as if he's wearing clothes inflated with air bladders under his trenchcoat. Cognizance and control over the body is a discipline only a truly careful and studied actor can master, and usually after many years of growth.

Nicholson described a sense of connection with Schmidt "as the man I might have become if I wasn't lucky enough to wind up in show business." The man faces a sudden sense of emptiness, "like what happens when the normal activities of your job no longer drive your day, your loved ones move away from you, your children get older."[13]

But it's the personal, emotional transformation that most remember about this film. Schmidt could not come to life without the death of his wife. He nearly joins her until his symbolic release. She had trained him to urinate seated. Warren gets pissed off and rejects her influence with his no-handspee. Perhaps missed by many is the tear in his eye, a subtle tragicomic touch that precedes this act of liberation.

The truly emotional part of the film is its set-up. "In the course of the movie," Nicholson relates, "everything is systematically taken away from him."[14] Director Alexander Payne echoed the character theme of "taking all of the man's institutions away from him. Career. Marriage. Daughter." Schmidt's journey is triggered by "suddenly learning that everything you believe is wrong—everything."[15]

Next, his Easy-RV-Riding trip allows him to emerge as an independent being. His first expression of love was at the beginning of a one-sided dialogue with Helen from the roof of the vehicle. Nicholson's Schmidt grows in self-confidence enough to make a clumsy move on his trailer park neighbor. He evolves further during his visit to his daughter's fiancé's family. He then fully blossoms during his father-of-the-bride speech. An understated *tour de force*, it was a short but significant journey from agitation and doubt, mixed with some disgust, toward acceptance and positive emotion. Plus grace. Jack transcends, all through expression, body language and voice quality. Its impact is strengthened by the coy and perhaps faux dramatic lead-in to this speech, delivered in a new voice of smooth openness.

* * *

What then of Ndugu—and Schmidt's outpouring of emotion? That too is not quite as pure as intended or interpreted. Nicholson's Schmidt and Jack's Dupea are connected once more. Both weep, not for the child in the former's case, nor for Bobby's father in the latter, but for themselves. The first clue is Nicholson's slight raise of his eyebrow as Angela Lansbury speaks the words "touch the life" in the *childreach* TV commercial. This subtly indicated that Schmidt's reaction was about himself and not about the plight of the children.

Until the end of the film, his "adoption" of Ndugu is for his own satisfaction. Schmidt's disconnection to the kid's life and economic condition is both comical and revealing. Ndugu in *About Schmidt* serves the same purpose as Bobby's wheelchair-bound father Nicholas in *Five Easy Pieces*. Following Warren Schmidt's realization that he is weak and a failure, and having made no difference to anyone, he opens the Ndugu letter containing the boy's painting.

Warren's tears circle back to those shed by Bobby when alone with his father in the earlier film. Dupea's monologue with the old man, first a straightforward expression about his own life, causes him to cry as he opens up in confessional. His final breakdown is about Bobby's understanding of himself and his life. The son then recovers as he sums up the situation with his father. Oddly, the overall trajectory is almost as with a lover, like a sexual act of foreplay to excitement to climax to parting.

And so it is "About" Bobby, just as it is "About" Schmidt, rather than being about the father or the boy. Both cry in self-pity. There is one difference, one that signaled ultimate redemption. Nicholson mixes seemingly opposing emotions to wrench all he can from the final scene. He rises from excruciating sobbing to smiling tears. This cues the viewer that the meaning behind the tears had suddenly shifted from self-pity to self-realization, thus redirecting his emotion toward the boy. The emotional journey that brings about Warren's final emergence into the world of the living happens through an actor's expressions.

5

A More Perfect Union

Duty. Honor. Country.

Awaiting their separate testimonies in unrelated cases sat an imperfect pair of imperfect men who shared this credo. Both were leaders of men (a few good, tough men at that), one of Teamsters, another of Marines. Neither was above using physical persuasion as a means to an end, even if that meant killing. The two were totally dedicated to their respective organizations, nearing the point of obsession. Each had defining moments in a courtroom, with varied results.

Colonel Nathan R. Jessep never knew James R. Hoffa, and if he did he might not admit it. Since one was fictional and one was real, that had a lot to do with it. Testifying represented a defining turning point for each.

Jessep's duty was to protect the United States of America while Hoffa's was to grow and protect the Teamsters Union. They both honored their particular unions. Their country made such freedom possible.

In Rob Reiner's *A Few Good Men*, Nicholson lectures Tom Cruise about guarding walls, saving lives and following orders, doing what he has to do—or people die. He was nominated for an Academy Award for Best Supporting Actor. As Teamsters boss Jimmy Hoffa, Nicholson will riot, burn, fight, use muscle and use political pressure—doing what he has to do—at first to get the union in and later to get his union back. He was nominated for a Razzie Award as Worst Actor.

They are two officers, though of a different sort, who do what they have to do. To them, loyalty means everything, whether demanding it or extending it.

These two films were consecutive roles for Nicholson, a supporting player in only four scenes in *A Few Good Men* and then in the title role and in nearly every scene as *Hoffa*.

In his four *Few Good Men* scenes, Nicholson adds weight to the movie, elevating the piece. Otherwise there is no film, not of this caliber, not to be remembered or quoted or admired. Without Nicholson's contributions, the story and the main players are too superficial and the acting too cute. J.T. Walsh, Kiefer Sutherland, Kevin Bacon and Jack Nicholson—supporting players all—bolster *A Few Good Men* up from the slightness supplied by Cruise and Demi Moore.

Noah Wyle, who played Corporal Jeffrey Barnes, related to me how Nicholson raised the level of the entire production, starting at the table read-through. Just prior to the start of shooting, the actors were brought together with the director and a few key crew members. "You sit around a big table and you read the screenplay out loud," Wyle explained. "Everybody is watching to see what everybody else is gonna do ... whether they're gonna really go for it or they're going to hold something back. Most of the time you hold back. You service the script, but you don't really go for a performance level." But Nicholson showed the likes of Bacon, Moore, Cruise and Kevin Pollak—professionals all—that even a table read-through could become something else entirely. "He gave the performance you see in the film, that day in that room. He dialed it in and it was like, 'Oh, we're doing it for real.'" Wyle remembers how everybody's energy level went up "and the room became electric. But he lit the spark."[1]

Nicholson's first scene is 16 minutes into the film and five minutes long, but he establishes the tough and superior character of the Marine colonel, with nostrils flaring in intensity while employing a smooth, clipped manner of speech (a juxtaposed combination that is not easy). His controlled sarcasm with Walsh and Sutherland is both convincing and commanding in making the case for the unfortunate, harassed Marine to stay. While irony is not a quality civilians might associate with the military, Nicholson is devilish within his character when he suggests the whole squadron should be reassigned because Private Santiago has a problem. He is masterful at being soft and smoldering at the same time. In the short office meeting scene with Cruise, Moore and Pollak, Nicholson plays embarrassed, but in an in-charge and proper sort of way.

The crucial third scene, starting at the 40-minute mark, is an outdoor lunch—a contentious debate that turns into a sermon about honor, code and loyalty. He diminishes Demi Moore's character and dances with Cruise, accepting the necessity of instructing, in the ways of his military, those to whom enlightenment is impossible. He goes through the motions, certain the act is a waste, and so is disingenuous and appropriately patronizing to those outside his rank and beyond his insight.

He foreshadows the tremendous discipline that will be so striking in the later courtroom scene when he gets square-jawed in response to Galloway (Moore) pushing him. Jessep is confident in his superiority and in being absolutely right, and Nicholson shows it. His head does not move in position while his maw independently opens and closes in broad-mouthed expression.

5. A More Perfect Union

As Colonel Jessep in *A Few Good Men* (1992), Jack Nicholson assumes the stone solid, perfect stance he will hold throughout the court interrogation scene. In the movie, Nicholson's head remains nearly as motionless as it is in this film still.

He demands courtesy be extended. He exhibits snotty affability with a dismissive air. And he is as solid and immobile as the Marines on that wall.

Watch this scene, and look on as intently as Nicholson looks, and notice that his eyes do not move at all for about two minutes of screen time. Not only is this amazing control, but also a perfect embodiment of what the character would do and how he would think. A classic instance of Nicholson's character energy, Jack breathes as Jessep, sees as Jessep, reacts as Jessep, and refuses to budge to inferiors as Jessep. Nicholson's eyes lock—perfectly centered—and remain there, something physically challenging to endure but necessary as a key character physical trait, created by the actor to symbolize discipline.

Jack's fourth and final scene is the climactic courtroom scene in which he skillfully plays with Cruise's Kaffee and willfully impeaches himself because it is the honorable thing to do. Again, Nicholson's head does not move at all, not to either side in order to react or notice, and not up or down to reflect or dissemble. He keeps his head stationary, resolutely staying at attention in service to his country. Right before this iconic scene, and perhaps as a contrasting set-up and lighter moment, there's a wonderful transition. First, Jessep is upset because he's not called "colonel" or "sir" by presiding Judge Randolph (J.A. Preston). He is soon thereafter put in his place by that same judge for neglecting the same protocol ("your honor" or "judge"). As Nicholson sits back down, he cricks his head side to side, displaying discomfort—which he then instantly wills away for his battle with Cruise.

Jessep is stone-solid in his perfect stance. He wants to make himself clear, to educate the lawyer, and to demonstrate his contempt without any possible misinterpretation. The colonel builds the confrontation, raising the temperature dramatically on his inferior with a deliberate rhetorical dare about wanting answers.

Jessep knows Kaffee cannot handle the truth and even though it means an admission of complicity, he unveils that truth, he spits out that truth, he triumphs with that truth, following his screamed flourish with disdain and disgust for his adversary. As Nicholson takes Jessep from chastised to lecturing to garrulous to incredulous, the undercurrent of condescension stays constant. Jessep advances on his enemy with aggression and strength, not flanking but directly, going in for the kill with the confidence of a commander who has right on his side. Along the way, he instructs—or tries to instruct—the glib officer who does not hold any of the qualities Jessep demands (no dignity, no courage, no honor, no significance) nor embodies any notion of honor that would qualify for being one of "a few good men."

Nicholson expert Dennis Bingham suggests that the actor and the character are intrinsically connected. "The performance's fascination comes from the fact that this is 'Jack Nicholson,' whose persona cannot be held in by social strictures, as a character who represents those strictures at their most rigid." It's as if the impact of Jessep's downfall can only work because he's played by the former antihero and anti-establishment symbol, and that "the performance strongly etches the character while emphasizing once again a clear space between character and actor," while "Jessep is in the Nicholson self-destructive mode."[2]

James Marshall, best known as Laura Palmer's boyfriend on the TV series *Twin Peaks*, played one of the court-martial defendants, Pfc. Louden Downey. He told me that the filming of this scene was "definitely surrealistic and definitely fun." Nicholson the actor was as disciplined as his character, as Marshall explains. "Jack got it right the first couple of takes. You could tell he does one or two takes and moves on…. He pretty much nailed it. It was a neat day, very neat."[3]

5. A More Perfect Union

Nicholson's performance carries the intensity and mastery of Miles Davis on the title track from his landmark album *Bitches Brew*. Potency trumps convention in this celebration of reaching beyond comfortable limits. Muscular bleats and stings create patterns at once controlled and unsettling. As in the music, this courtroom explosion carries true emotion, true because it was true to Jessep and his credo. As someone known to belong to the anti-war and anti-establishment '60s generation, Nicholson succeeds in capturing a character seemingly diametrically in opposition to his own sensibilities, not only realistically and convincingly, but also compellingly and beautifully.

Much of it happens in that posture, head straight ahead and forcing away distraction as it avoids movement. It happens in those eyes, sturdily centered and perfectly fixed, through extraordinary discipline made formidably effective. Yet, throughout the entire sequence, the viewer may not even specifically register or realize the work behind the effect.

* * *

As Jessep's eyes tell a story, so too do those of Jimmy Hoffa. The eyes of Hoffa sear—glowing, monstrous and poisoned—never leaving their target in the "I'm gonna do what I gotta do" confrontation with Armand Assante's character, D'Allesandro. At this point in the film, Nicholson has shifted Jimmy Hoffa from in-charge to out-of-control. Now desperate and wild, Hoffa is unrestrained as he paces and blasts at D'Allesandro, his eyes dead and black underneath.

Just like with Jessep, watch those eyes and see that they rarely stray from where we know the Assante character to be positioned, showing terrific concentration—particularly given his body's uncontrolled motion. Nicholson portrays the intent and intensity that Hoffa must have actually felt in this situation, as his life and his union were being pulled away from him. He shows that Hoffa feels the meaning of betrayal. The actor again shows he's not worried about how he looks, letting saliva build and pool on his bottom lip on the left side. The more upset, the more truthful and open, the more it was allowed to accumulate.

This is the key scene to Nicholson's capturing of Hoffa the character and Hoffa the man, especially in contrast to the two other opposing views he offers us. At one end, the bombastic leader filled with optimism about his future, his success, and his certainty about being right. At the other, the broken, bloated caricature, driven only by the quixotic hope to take back his dream while waiting in the back of a sedan at a nothing diner. As the younger man, Nicholson keeps Jimmy always pushing forward, bouncing with heel lifts and speaking with head nods, always moving—like a boxer—using head motion and body language as if making a speech all the time. As the older man, he croaks nasally and ages believably as the thick, tired, out-of-shape, out-of-power has-been Hoffa. Nicholson ages Hoffa like a bug, like a lizard or snake or some other cold-blooded creature, brows low and eyes darting and always searching.

Balancing the real person with the recognizable actor was crucial to establishing *Hoffa* and telling his story without distraction. "We didn't really want to cover Jack's face," Academy Award–winning supervising makeup artist Ve Neill told me. "We thought that if we just altered his nose, that would probably be a good start to it." Neill spent about an hour each day on this transformation, through the use of a prosthetic nose and different hair pieces.[4]

The first biographer of Hoffa who suggests ties between the union leader and the mob in the assassination of John F. Kennedy, investigative reporter Dan E. Moldea referred to Nicholson's portrayal as "fairly flamboyant" and "essentially a caricature." The author of 1978's *The Hoffa Wars: Teamsters, Rebels, Politicians and the Mob* believed that Robert Conrad should have played the ex–Teamster boss, but the deal—though considered—was not consummated. Moldea told me that the best film representation of Hoffa was provided by Robert Blake in *Blood Feud*,[5] made nine years earlier; Blake was nominated for Emmy and Golden Globe awards.

Following Jimmy Hoffa's rise and fall, woven around his set-up and betrayal as he attempts to rise again, involved a journey through decades with many of the same actors spanning that time. Neill described her role in makeup as helping Nicholson, Danny DeVito and other cast members "look younger and then aging them with the times." The process was quite ambitious. "It was intensive as far as keeping continuity, because I had to know what year it was and what look they had. They had probably five different looks, each one of them."[6] His appearance may have changed, but the personality of Hoffa seldom strayed from hardnosed and driven.

There are two breaks of tenderness between those two extremes. At the mass funeral after a strike ambush, Jack's Hoffa opens up slightly with a light trace of a smile upon seeing a boy's mother show up to bring food to her son after having thought the youngster lost. The clean, economical dialogue is not what we'd associate with David Mamet, nor is Nicholson's characterization of Hoffa in the scene with the widow what we'd associate with Mamet's Hoffa. This is a real moment of intimacy, taken down to a human level that contrasts the otherwise larger-than-life persona.

Nicholson uses a similar sincere understatement when Hoffa gives his speech to the Teamsters on the stairs prior to leaving for jail. He becomes more real, later touched by true warmth and sweetness upon the truckers' sendoff, with thousands of trucks lined up on both sides of the road like an honor guard. Otherwise, his portrayal lacks subtlety and humanity, likely because Hoffa himself never was less than full-on.

Mamet described his script as "a paean (and, sad to state, but true, a requiem) to two complex organisms: the American Labor movement, and one of its members, my father." Though he went to see the film with reservations, Mamet felt it brought the mission to life and captured the spirit of the movement through a "genius performance of a great actor...."[7]

Perhaps James R. Hoffa could never stray from his mission or rest from his vigilance, just like Colonel Nathan R. Jessep. Hoffa lives and dies for his union. Jessep lives and would sacrifice his life to protect the union.

* * *

A man of another sort approaches the pair, also preparing to enter a court of law. He's there to take testimony rather than give it. George Hanson's union, to which he's taken an oath of duty and honor, is the American Civil Liberties Union. And because he lives in the Deep South, that's one serious pledge. Hanson's struggling through his hangover—one of two things he shares with Billy "Badass" Buddusky. The other is a peculiar interpretation of duty, honor and country.

Easy Rider and *The Last Detail* were released only four years apart, but for the actor, much had changed. Supporting actor to lead actor. Journeyman to star. Looking for breaks to making them for others. Without *Easy Rider*, Nicholson's career could not take off. But without Nicholson, *The Last Detail* might not have taken shape.

More than his belated break, the George Hanson role was believed by many to have saved Nicholson's acting career. Ed Nelson, who worked on Nicholson's first movie *The Cry Baby Killer*, told me, "He became a great actor but, boy, when he started, you know he quit he was so bad." Nelson continued:

> He went off to Seattle, I came back with him on a flight to San Francisco and we sat together quite accidentally. He was going off to do a little motorcycle picture with a friend of his, the other crazy guy, Dennis Hopper ... and yeah, Peter [Fonda], that was his closest friend. And I said, "What kind of picture?" and he said it was a motorcycle picture. And he named them, but they were nobodies. You know, I recognized their names only because of their fathers and I said, "Good luck with that, Jack." And he didn't know whether or not he was gonna do it or not and he did it and it made him.[8]

Bruce Dern described the early struggles—and how the young actors handled it. "Jack had trouble getting in big films and so he went off and made his own films. Dennis kind of the same way ... we took a lot of bad raps early on because of [being] a kind of Method-type actor."[9]

Stuntman-actor Gary Kent described a long drive from Bakersfield back to Los Angeles together with Nicholson while working on *Hells Angels on Wheels*, in response to my question about whether Nicholson had voiced any disappointment about the lack of success of their earlier collaborations (*Ride in the Whirlwind* and *The Shooting*):

We both smoked something very strange and so he was quite talkative and quite expressive on the way back. He kind of went into what a hard business film was and what a difficult thing it was.... I thought it rankled him a bit that he was more or less ignored, because he worked so hard on his parts and on the film, telling me how big he was in Europe for Weary Reilly [in *Studs Lonigan*], like, "You don't know me, Gary, but I played Weary Reilly."[10]

Without *Easy Rider*, Nicholson may very well have taken a career turn similar to Henry Jaglom and concentrated on making films of his own devisement rather than struggling with television roles and exploitation movies in order to perpetuate his acting career.

Shirley Knight, who attended Jeff Corey classes with Nicholson and later played Helen Hunt's mother in *As Good as It Gets*, said that luck and chance made all the difference. "If Rip Torn and Peter Fonda and Dennis Hopper hadn't quarreled, Rip Torn would have been doing that part in *Easy Rider*.... So, sometimes careers become accidental. I think Jack, he was doing Roger Corman movies, and he got that break because Rip and Dennis and Peter quarreled. Life is so bizarre!"[11]

Odd as the comparison may seem, Nicholson's portrayal of the ACLU lawyer seems a refinement of his Wilbur Force invention (*Little Shop of Horrors*). Though less broad in general, mannerisms like the big smile, eyebrow lifts and hand-circling around his elongated neck are quite similar in both roles. Even the voice and accent have a character connection. The later film introduced some new Nicholson "business," like lots of tongue action and expanded open mouth, furrowed brows and yawns, along with the signature drinking ritual of flapping his winged arm as he grimaces and recites a nonsensical blurt picked up from the movie's motorcycle wrangler.

In her excellent study of ten key roles, *Jack Nicholson: Anatomy of an Actor*, Beverly Walker writes that Hanson is loosely modeled on a recurring figure in William Faulkner novels, progressive lawyer Gavin Stevens. They both live among people whom they are unlike, yet get along with on the surface, all in the service of aiding those who most need it. They were *in* the South (Stevens in Mississippi, Hanson in Louisiana) but not *of* it, getting along while exercising a courage that had to carry risk. Faulkner biographer Jay Parini acknowledged the plausibility of the connection, that of the insider whose conscience resides outside their culture.[12] Walker credits screenwriter Terry Southern for the literary antecedent: "Southern conceived George as more conventional than the two hippies, yet capable of articulating their melancholia about America—'a mouthpiece,' Southern called him."[13]

The then 32-year-old Jack Nicholson only appears in the film for a half-hour of running time, yet he seizes the screen as only a superstar can. His best "acting" probably was feigning innocence about marijuana, but his most precious scene is that entire campfire sequence, particularly when he can't

5. A More Perfect Union

keep it together during his "Venusians" monologue. Jack loses it, breaking up, and repeats part of it (something that normally would have been cut out, but was instead kept in to fit the stoned behavior).

Fonda explained that he purposely pushed Nicholson to get more and more stoned before shooting the master of the campfire scene. "Jack began his UFO speech. He was letter-perfect, and very stoned, a pro. As we got deeper into the scene, I began to feel a strange energy from the other side of the camera." Medicinally fueled laughter spread from actor-director Dennis Hopper to sidekick Fonda and toward storyteller Nicholson. They all struggle to stifle and muffle and deflect the laughter. "Jack's speech and character were doing just fine, but the absurdity of the speech's content was almost too much to handle, even for The Pro. When Jack got to the words 'meeting with people from all walks of life,' it all went over the edge." The most important scene in the most important film at the most important moment in Nicholson's final shot at acting was seemingly ruined. He pleaded with Hopper to start

On a weed-fueled campout, we learn about how Venusians are among us, meeting with people from all walks of life—and that this used to be a helluva country. Peter Fonda plays Captain America to Nicholson's ACLU lawyer, George Hanson in *Easy Rider* (1969), the film that made Jack a star.

at the top, close to tears, but Hopper moved on. The screw-up, the breaking of character, the place that "went haywire" was instead the happy accident that made Jack a star. Perfection in the moment outplays perfection in the technical sense.[14]

Two images from *Easy Rider* have other Nicholson connections. First, Hanson's gold football helmet—the lawyer's substitute for a proper motorcycle helmet—looks very similar to that used by Ray Nitschke in *Head*. The way Nicholson examines it is quite like the manner in which William Tepper studied an enigmatic orange in Nicholson's *Drive, He Said*. Second, Nicholson's freedom ride on the back of Fonda's Captain America bike had to inspire his motions during a similar freedom ride when racing his convertible on the beach in *Terms of Endearment*. Arms outstretched, these two images of pure joy in travel also seem a possible inspiration for Maria Schneider's free-flying passenger ride in the convertible driven by Nicholson in Antonioni's *The Passenger*.

While Jessep informs Kaffee that he can't handle the truth, Hanson reveals that none of us can. Around a campfire, Fonda and Hopper serve as his apparent listeners, but we are all the true targets of his eternal truths. The freedom Jessep provides is just a sham. You can talk about it, but just try being it—and don't tell anybody because they'll use violence to prove their freedom. When Nicholson gives the campfire speech, it's as if he's spontaneously speaking what he thinks and believes and wants to share rather than delivering words from a script.

Another truth we could not handle is Hanson's assertion that Venusians live amongst us, seemingly natural and completely unnoticed in every part of society. Yet this clearly is not the reason the USA was no longer a "helluva good country." America was scared of the image of freedom the bikers (and freaks and hippies) represented, a truth that simply could not be handled. Hanson lived the code of defending civil liberties to protect those unprotected misfits, while Jessep's code was to defend the nation and protect an unprotectable freedom—whether it was real or delusional.

* * *

Ostensibly, Badass Buddusky also defends the country, though he was unable to see how that could possibly be the case. Without getting his orders for more meaningful service, he was left with details like transferring prisoners. In *The Last Detail*, Buddusky is introduced the same way as Hanson is in *Easy Rider*, hung over and hard to stir. Though summoned to report on-the-double, Jack takes his time to smooth his hair, swill and spit his beer, slowly study his flat hat, and leisurely create his character before our eyes.

Nicholson has cultivated a look that suits the nickname "Badass," with the cop mustache, gum, cigar and attitude of disgust. Dennis Bingham wrote that Nicholson's visualization of Buddusky, as represented in the bare-chested pose seen in the film's advertisements, "suggests something a bit off balance, since the signs of masculinity are so overdetermined as to suggest parody."[15] When Badass first presents the name to his detail's partner, Mule, he does so with a classic Jack grin and repeats it with varied meanings and emphases. His hair sweep gesture, seen before in *Little Shop* and later in *Terms*, is part of this characterization. At this point in his career, Nicholson's voice is in transition from the nasally hyper-pitched drawl of his earlier years toward the lower registered and softer delivery used in his later roles.

This is an experienced actor at work, with true moments and authentic emotions on display. After Meadows (Randy Quaid) falls asleep on a train and his shoplifted candy bars fall from his sleeve, he bolts, is subdued by Buddusky and Mulhall (Otis Young), and is brought back to his seat. Nicholson's complex emotion of revulsion mixed with sympathy and apprehension is real in his reaction to Meadows' pathetic blubbering.

Film historian Don Schiach called this "an aware, true performance," emphasizing that it was not a middle-class actor impersonating a working-class character but that Nicholson had obviously "known, observed and empathized with men like this in his own life."[16]

He shows flair when demonstrating hand signals to Meadows in a hotel room, followed by a nice scene in which he quietly and patiently teaches the procedure. Nicholson's arm motions are disciplined, with his trunk and body remaining stationary and erect.

As Quaid's character reminisces about his high school on the way to a doomed trip to see his mother, Jack reacts wordlessly, with a look conveying Buddusky's disappointment in life; a dismay and sadness that's tinged with loathing; plus a compassion that's marked with bitterness. It is an eloquent moment, a reaction shot to what the character actually sees, how it triggers personal feelings, and how it culminates in a spontaneous generation of new thoughts. One face, one moment in time, several true emotions.

The actor was considered something of a "subversive force" in his 1970s films, full of criticism of the dominant order. Bingham called *The Last Detail* "a convincing example of Nicholson's deconstruction of character and the masculinity that determines it." His performance dominates nearly every scene, thus derailing "the naturalistic character motivation perfunctorily present in the script."[17]

Nicholson masters the use of his body and masters his character energy, with motion and gesture that makes Buddusky a dimensional swabbie. There's even a Jacksplosion in full bloom, the victim a bartender who learns the hard way that Badass *is* the shore patrol who'll pull his sidearm to prove it. He encourages Meadows to romp and stomp with great animalistic demeanor and expansive, explosive gestures that shoot out and get pulled right back in.

Trying to get Meadows to fight, Badass gets apoplectic, with bursts of inarticulate compressions of many words into smaller strings of nonsense.

Bingham contrasts Buddusky's public side, "an expression of bravado and toughness that he has internalized to the point where there is no interior," with his private side that bursts forth as "uncontrolled, debilitating rage."[18]

When Nicholson strolls into a train station rest room to confront rival Marines, it's with a relaxed swagger and physical assurance that's true Badass attitude that pays off in a punch-up and triumphant escape to the streets and into a cab.

There are fun, comical and warm moments, such as when Buddusky's hustling other gamblers with the same wacky tongue push used as George Hanson in *Easy Rider*; putting on Meadows with a story about a whore with a glass eye who would "wink off" men for a dollar; and both MPs delighting in Quaid's transformation. Like proud parents, they relish watching Meadows ice-skate; they smile, encourage and talk it up with each other.

At a get-together at Donna's (Luana Anders) pad where Nicholson hits on Nancy (Nancy Allen), he talks to and mostly impresses himself while going through his inventory of stories about the power of the uniform and the Navy as a man's job. She looks bored and snootily unimpressed.

Carrie and *Blow-Out* actress Allen told me about the three days of her motion picture debut in freezing Toronto after years of commercial work in New York. "I think that she was supposed to be bored with him and not interested in him. I will admit that I was really kind of terrified [*laughs*]. And I think that that terror, that natural feeling that came up, was just feeling almost like free-falling in that atmosphere, because I didn't have anything to ground me. I'd never been on a movie set before and I didn't have time to sit and talk to the director about what I was to do." She explained that her defensiveness "appeared naturally, which helped fuel the character. So I think part of it was intrinsically in the script, but it was my own discomfort in the situation that really supported the character."[19]

Her first exposure to film acting revealed a different atmosphere and a different process. But her director and star made it more natural: "Hal Ashby, what he did was create a very safe atmosphere for people to create." Allen was nervous because it was her first time in an environment like that. They did a little bit of improv and started shooting. "The first thing we shot was where Jack was telling the tale of the sea," she recounted, "but we kind of improvised, we did a rehearsal, and then Hal Ashby liked it and we just started shooting."[20]

Nicholson biographer Patrick McGilligan described Ashby's method toward actors as *laissez-faire* ("the kind of method Jack preferred"), setting up the environment and letting the actors do their job.[21]

Nicholson has a nice moment when he accidently knocks into a hanging bulb and starts it to swing, then follows its motion before launching into his hand signals display. He's seen things, he dramatically intones, but Nancy mocks him with restrained irony about seeing all that it's done for him. He's so true in Buddusky's exaggerated and clumsy build-up of his own significance, so centered on himself that she barely exists even though she is his quest.

Jack's second scene with Allen starts with his yodeling (of all things) as Meadows goes upstairs with Donna. Then he turns his yodeling into a tongue flick toward Nancy, likely an ad lib. Allen said, "It really was more free-form than I was used to, a lot of improvisation, and just sort of letting things roll."

Allen was amazed at Nicholson's ability to start the scene without any signs of doing so. "I remember sitting at a table with Jack and we were just kind of talking and the next thing you know, we were in the scene. I couldn't see him slip into the character. It was just so organic in that moment that at first it disarmed me. I thought, 'Aren't we just talking here?' And 'What is he doing?' And 'I don't get it,' which is fine. I was really knocked out by how he just rolled into the scene and I couldn't even see that he was doing it."[22]

Nicholson's *Last Detail* performance is to film what Jimmy Forrest's 1951 instrumental single "Night Train" is to music. Bump and grind, atmosphere and attitude, they both tease and wink, riffing on a basic groove with panache and bravado. Bingham calls this "Nicholson's first strongly Brechtian performance, or what Brecht called 'acting in quotation marks' in which 'the character who is being shown and the actor who demonstrates him remain clearly differentiated.'"[23]

In the film's climax, Jack passes from poignant to pissed off. He absorbs Meadows' fate more than the kid himself. At their final "picnic," Badass gets agitated, then upset, then teary and regretful. Gulping his Schlitz, Nicholson's face becomes distorted in disgusted sadness at how Quaid's character doesn't stand a chance in the military prison, presenting a more painful bookend to the ennui he shows in the scene when they travel on the train to the kid's mother's home.

Nicholson feels for Quaid's character. His empathy becomes real, to the point that his uncontrolled rage at Meadows' attempted escape in the snowy park is more about the personal affront and betrayal than the act itself. Parenthood severed is personal; a prisoner's escape is not.

That is why there is no goodbye at the prison and no last look. But it didn't take long for the nonconformist among the most conformed of careers to rebel against authority (in the form of Michael Moriarty's Marine OD). Afterwards, Nicholson harangues Young about it, combining hatred with pride, bombast with triumph. Badass has a problem with authority. He rails against the man in charge of a system that's in charge of him and his destiny, represented by the long walk with Mule into the distance at the end of the

What happens when your last detail is a chickenshit one? Director Hal Ashby seeks the answer, a more complex and probing one than might be expected, in *The Last Detail* (1973). Badass Buddusky (Nicholson, center) subdues prisoner Meadows (Randy Quaid) after he is recaptured by Buddusky and partner Mulhall, played by Otis Young.

film. Their last shot, grainy and lifelike, shows two men wracked with uncertainty about getting their orders or a more likely continuation of more "chickenshit" details.

Schiach categorized *The Last Detail* as "a discourse on class in American society," with the Navy lifers representing the working man valued only for the menial tasks they perform, "in this case the escorting of one of their own to a punitive establishment where he will be treated with cruelty and contempt." And they know it.[24]

Nicholson should have gotten the Oscar. Reportedly, he felt so. Nancy Allen summarized his actor's strength, explaining the "quintessential Jack" by saying that he is "specific about his choices. No safety. Goes all the way with his choices and is fearless. All great actors are."

That is the actor's code. Duty to his character ... to truth ... and to the emotion of the moment. For a simple swabbie, Badass Buddusky is a pretty complex character. He does defend freedom, even while taking it from a kid named Meadows. He is not in the position to decide. He cannot judge. He can only follow the orders to support his union—like Colonel Jessep, like Jimmy Hoffa, like George Hanson. In the service of duty, honor and country, together they show us that liberty does not involve interpretation and that freedom does not invite individualism, let alone scrutiny.

6

The School of Roger

The Cry Baby Killer did not cry, nor was he a killer. In his haste to escape, Jimmy bumps into Wilbur, who not only doesn't cry but laughs and delights at pain. The juvenile gunslinger could have hit the west, at first an innocent in a gang traveling under the name of Brocious or Wes and later hardened into a frontier hit man working for a vengeful and heartless woman, and finally as a big city mobster.

All the while, a promising up-and-coming actor grasps for the opportunity to learn the movie business, whether as actor or writer or director.

Paying dues never paid off so well. Whether Francis Ford Coppola, Martin Scorsese, Robert DeNiro, Ron Howard, Sylvester Stallone, Peter Bogdanovich, Talia Shire, Jonathan Demme, James Cameron, Sandra Bullock, John Sayles, Peter Fonda, Dennis Hopper, Bruce Dern or Jack Nicholson, much of the later 20th century's filmmaking owe a huge debt to Roger Corman.

Bruce Dern explained, "Different guys came from different routes, but in the early- to mid-60s, we got to go to 'The University of Roger Corman,' which I call it, which was the luckiest experience of our lives for us."[1]

* * *

In Nicholson's first film, he played the title role: *The Cry Baby Killer*. Corman executive produced it (and played a bit part). In the opening of the film, Nicholson's Jimmy Wallace backs away in fear as four guys corner and beat him unconscious. Today, we would consider this bullying a prelude to the victim's antisocial behavior. As expected with a newcomer, Nicholson has his good moments and his bad. In an argument with Fred, Jimmy's all about fast eye-blinks with his head jabbed forward, too earnest to emote and project. After his character accidentally shoots his attacker and backs his way into a storage shed with a woman with her baby and an African-American cook, Nicholson becomes mercurial—distraught and explosive, playing his role big with wild hand gestures, carrying an ultra–Anthony Perkins aura.

6. The School of Roger

At times, Nicholson becomes overblown and over-the-top, but then shows promise when he gets very quiet and exhibits subtlety when talking about the baby being hungry. This wide balance can be seen as the premiere precursor of the classic Jack, bursting from Jacksplosion to soft-spoken and thoughtful.

Mostly, however, Nicholson portrays Jimmy with jugular-popping yelling, as the highest of the high-strung. He holds his gun so tightly, you can see his forearm muscles straining. Many years later, the actor called it an insane film, but one that helped him learn, because "you get a chance to see what you're doing that is horrible and then you eliminate it."[2]

At the end, though, when soda shop girl Carole talks to him, Jimmy softens, loses his way and comes out. He finally relaxes as he's taken away, the first in a mini-trend of Nicholson being taken into custody to conclude a film, just as with the other J.D. in *The Wild Ride*.

In a curious sidelight, the film foreshadows reality TV, when a news truck shows up to capture the real-life drama. Ed Nelson plays the frenzy-whipping reporter, cheerleading viewers to "witness as it happens," while a crowd forms to watch the stand-off unfold. Called a "public service," the live coverage was nothing more than an exploitive play-by-play spectacular.

Nelson recounted, "Jack had never done any films at all. I saw this just last week.... I wanted to see what Jack did and remember it. He was hated, you know. A lot of the great stars when they started out were really hated. And he was really hated."

After Nelson did a nasally, indiscernible impression of Nicholson, he continued: "He talks like this ... 'Can you talk up a little bit, we can't get that.' [*more mumbling*] He became a great actor, but boy, when he started..."[3] *Cry Baby Killer* co-star Brett Halsey agreed, describing Jack as just one of the young kids starting out with "nothing outstanding about him."[4]

The movie's trailer was a lie, showing Nicholson violently breaking the storeroom window and shooting three times, hugely dramatic action that never happens in the movie. Perhaps this sequence was originally intended to be included, but deemed too intense for a general audience with a youthful bent.

* * *

Promotion played a large part in the Corman magic. Another part of that magic was giving young talent a chance to explore and get exposure in (low-budget) Hollywood films ones. Dern explained the draw best: "It was a chance for us, not knowing it, to be in a college of how to make a movie; how to get star billing in a movie; how to get big parts in a movie; and how to learn how to make a movie for $195,000. And that stood pretty well for us through the years."[5]

Nicholson: "I was originally drawn to films by a creative drive, so I really did almost any film."[6]

I asked Roger Corman if he ever tried asking Nicholson or the others to whom he gave their first break for "a favor" later and work in one of his films, but he said he never did and never would have considered it.[7]

* * *

Today, Nicholson's most famous appearance in a Corman film is one of his briefest. He plays a true masochist—not so much because he loves pain as much as because he enjoys going to the dentist. Thirty-four minutes into *The Little Shop of Horrors*, a high-pitched and giggly Wilbur Force enters the dentist's office and proceeds with some good character business involving a magazine called *Pain*.

When Nicholson enters the dentist's office, he walks closed-in with a slight hunch and taking small steps as his knees and feet are narrowly held together. His vocal delivery sounds somewhat like a higher registered lampoon of Peter Lorre (a coincidence given that he later plays Lorre's son in Corman's *The Raven*). Expression comes from extra-active eyes and eyebrows. He shows a widened smile and emits a nervous, excited laugh combined with a needy air intake, as Nicholson pulls in air when he laughs.

In a panel discussion at the Ohio convention Cinema Wasteland in 2007, *Little Shop* screenwriter Charles B. Griffith and stars Jonathan Haze and Jackie Joseph told me about Nicholson's contribution and answered moderator and audience questions. Griffith described the dentist scene: "Jack was fantastic in that scene. He followed every word in the script, but he came up with all the business; pricking his finger and tasting the blood was all his. Jack dazzled everybody on that day."[8]

Haze added his own perspective on that same scene with a view inside the world of Corman as director and producer: "Roger borrowed the dentist chair from his dentist. He didn't pay anything and he was concerned about not damaging it. Instead of saying, 'Cut!' he ran to get the dentist chair."[9]

Griffith's insight into the low-budget, compressed schedule was that they "rehearsed the whole thing in one afternoon and started shooting the next day. A special leading lady [Joseph]; a special leading man [Haze]; and a helluva script [by Griffith himself]."[10]

Haze had known Nicholson for years as a regular at Schwab's Drug Store, but *Little Shop* "was the first time I worked with Jack. Jack was in the same acting class as Roger, who took it to direct actors. [Jack] was fantastic, so much fun."[11]

Much of the fun was in the goofily inventive character energy and the actor's business such as putting on his own patients' smock to get ready for the drilling in ecstatic anticipation. Part of it was the delicious lines, turning down Novocain because it "dulls the senses," his "goody-goody" amusement park excitement, and the exhortation of innuendo: "Don't stop now!"

At the end of his first triumphant scene and first comedic breakthrough (brief as it was), Nicholson leaves the dentist office looking like Alfalfa, complete with a gap in his teeth and slicked-down hair. Haze, who played the iconic role of Seymour, stated that they hadn't aimed to make a cult movie, except that it was "touched by magic. Because it was shot so fast, it had wonderful spontaneity and we weren't playing it for laughs much, but straight."[12]

Nicholson remembered, "I went into the shoot knowing I had to be very quirky because Roger originally hadn't wanted me.... I just did a lot of weird shit that I thought would make it funny."[13]

* * *

A few years later, Nicholson played in back-to-back productions starring Boris Karloff for producer-director Corman. In *The Raven*, he plays Peter Lorre's son and doesn't show up until a half-hour into the show, which is also the first time on-screen that we really see the teeth that have become so famous. After his character's fidgety introduction, Nicholson drives a coach as if completely possessed in a nice transformation for a young, inexperienced actor. Yelling and baring his teeth maniacally, Nicholson then comes out from under the spell and becomes more like Dennis Weaver as "the night man" in Orson Welles' *Touch of Evil*. At this point, the youth injects the first sign of life in the movie. Hazel Court told me, "We shot the coach scene in the studio with back projection and it was quite a lot of fun as Jack Nicholson was driving the stagecoach going crazy."[14]

Mostly, Nicholson had lots of reaction shots and "Yes, father"'s, more physical than verbal and using quick eye-blinks. He's not necessarily sweating, but shiny under the lights (perhaps a sign of youthful discomfort). There is a sign of the Jack we later came to know, attacking with "Scarabus, you maniac!" full-on with teeth and sneer working together. Otherwise, he most notably engages with some wonderfully playful action against the raven (meant to be his father, on his shoulder), with light, amusing interplay.

There's also an interesting and effective recurring comic physical bit with Lorre, featuring some business of fussing with his dad's collar, coat, and more as a way to make contact—yet always rebuffed with disgust by Lorre.

Corman described it as a Method-type subtext worked out on the set, with Nicholson wanting nothing more than his father's love and approval while Peter wants nothing more than to be left alone by his son. "The business with Peter's cloak was just actors' devices," Nicholson explained. "I grabbed his cloak—actually I grabbed a lot of other things that aren't visible in the frame—just to keep him alive to the fact that I was trying to get him out of

When Jack played Peter Lorre's son in Roger Corman's *The Raven* (1963), unfounded charges of nepotism and unfounded rumors that producer James H. Nicholson was his father followed him around the shoot. From right: Olive Sturgess serves as a distraction from that problem for Vincent Price, Lorre, and Nicholson.

there. Of course, the good actor that he is, he just reacted to it spontaneously, slapped me and lashed out."[15]

Court reminisced, "It was my favorite film to work on because of all the great actors in it. A lot of it was improvisation. [Karloff, Price and Lorre] were such naughty boys. They laughed and giggled and we just had tremendous fun. It was a memorable film working with the three of them. They never gave up teasing me, all day long!"[16]

One might guess that Nicholson, the aspiring actor, would go out of his way to learn from these accomplished men to the point of becoming a pest. Court described it more as an early indication of Nicholson's ambitions beyond merely acting, and a sign to his period of work as screenwriter and sometime director. "Unbelievable. He would say every night he was going home to write, and I think he did, he wrote several pictures. He was working on the first big success he had. He would write when he was on the film. He kept saying, 'I want to go to write.' He wanted to do his thing."[17]

Perhaps some of his aversion to socializing could be attributed to the veteran actors' misapprehension that Jack was the son of producer James H. Nicholson. Corman encouraged the young actor to learn from the professionals in order to complement his comedic improvisational strength. Vincent Price's daughter Victoria (who coincidentally attended high school with Jack Nicholson's daughter, Jennifer) told me that Price and Karloff were not too happy with this, particularly since they felt Nicholson was "kind of bad."[18] Producer Samuel Z. Arkoff remembered, "Vincent and Boris used to joke amongst themselves, 'Nepotism! Nepotism!' and roar with laughter."[19]

Less entertaining is the companion film *The Terror*, an odd combination of horror movie and period piece. Most curiously, Nicholson plays Lt. André Duvalier, seen for the first time in the film on a horse, familiar from his early westerns, yet in Napoleonic garb. He co-stars with then-wife Sandra Knight, then pregnant, with whom he has a powerful interplay upon their meeting.

Another Corman alum, director Peter Bogdanovich, called the "very young and callow Jack Nicholson ... a pretty unlikely Legionnaire." Bogdanovich used footage from this "fairly lame Victorian-style horror film" in his Charles Whitman–inspired debut, *Targets*.[20]

Nicholson is mostly stiff and smaller than the part would dictate, as co-screenwriter Jack Hill pointed out forcefully and more than once. Nicholson doesn't sound particularly French (unless they spoke very differently back then). Hill, who later became a cult figure admired by Quentin Tarantino for directing *Spider Baby* and the Pam Grier Blaxploitation vehicles *Foxy Brown* and *Coffy*, wasn't exactly a Nicholson acolyte—at least then: "He wasn't really happy being in the movie and made jokes about everything. I thought he was totally miscast. I didn't think he was a very good actor until I saw him in *Little Shop of Horrors* and then I realized what his quality was." Hill co-wrote the *Terror* script and had a vision for the characters, and apparently Nicholson did not fit that vision as Hill re-emphasized, "He was kind of miscast."[21]

Miscast as he may have been, Nicholson comes off as very intent, with his brow suitably furrowed. In a confrontational scene with character actor extraordinaire Dick Miller (playing Boris Karloff's manservant Stefan), Nicholson instills dominance and superiority vs. Miller's anger and abruptness. Against Boris, Nicholson insinuates himself into the castle with an arrogance that's indicated through his clipped, impatient manner of speech. Karloff is nuanced and poignant, emoting naturally, while Nicholson is stiff, one-note and flat throughout. It's as if Nicholson decided to purposely underplay the role in order to reach the status of the person he is portraying. The thought may have been sensible, but the result lies there, dull and stiff.

In his last scene with Miller, Duvalier takes a physically superior stance for the first time. After Stefan escorts the lieutenant from the castle at gunpoint, Duvalier punches Stefan and they fight with convincing rolling around and struggling before Duvalier knocks him out. This leads to the single "Jack"

In *The Terror* (1963), Nicholson is unlikely as a French military officer, shown here with then-wife and co-star Sandra Knight. She was pregnant with their daughter Jennifer Nicholson during filming.

moment in the entire film, when he threatens an old woman to call off an attacking bird and threatens that she answer him "or I'll break your neck!"

It's action that brings him to life, throwing Dick Miller against the castle wall or attacking an old woman. Finally, though, his acting chops must be tested by a denouement reaction shot. Jack reassures his real-life wife and on-screen lover Sandra Knight that she is finally safe, just before he kisses her and lightning strikes, after which she becomes the decaying dead, degree by degree, causing him to look increasingly sickened and shocked until only a bloody skeleton remains.

* * *

A year earlier, Corman was uncredited producer on the short studio feature *The Broken Land*, a weird oater, because the lead is a bad and unlikable sheriff, while a gang of four bandits (one of whom is Nicholson's boyish and principled character Will Brocious) is far from perfect yet choose to defend against the attack on a simple-minded character named Billy (Gary Sneed).

6. The School of Roger

The role was small, but Nicholson was able to show a range of emotions, from anger and sarcasm to empathetic and flirty, handling dialogue with aplomb and his horse with skill. Jack was said to have won the job over Burt Reynolds because of his riding ability. Preparation for acting paid off. B.J. Merholz, John Herman Shaner and Nicholson "decided they had better learn to ride horses ... and took lessons at Sam's Rocking Horse Stables at the edge of Griffith Park in Burbank."[22]

* * *

The Raven and *The Terror* seem worlds away from a pair of Monte Hellman westerns from only a few years later. Roger Corman was uncredited producer on *Ride in the Whirlwind* and uncredited executive producer on *The Shooting*, and despite the uncredited connections both films share the Corman trademark of piggybacking productions in order to maximize product and save money.

The Hellman movies, shot back-to-back in Utah, represent a different kind of western that are markedly distinct from one another. *Whirlwind* is more conventional, but deals with injustice against a black man (Nicholson friend Rupert Crosse), along with a duo of mismatched outlaws, Jack and star Cameron Mitchell, who—to put it simply—aren't all that bad. Nicholson plays a naïf, with subtlety and grace, in his interaction with a charming and socially unaware Millie Perkins.

In *The Shooting*, Perkins becomes an amoral, vengeful monster, enlisting a sociopath and killer-for-hire (as well as for pleasure) disturbingly brought to life by Nicholson. Where *Whirlwind* has strong and evocative moments, *The Shooting* serves as a delicious celebration of frontier terrorists Perkins and Nicholson, along with virtual hostage and eventual victim Warren Oates.

* * *

The year 1967 found Nicholson playing an uncredited role as a hit man in Corman's major-studio debut *The St. Valentine's Day Massacre* and writing a sexy, psychedelic visual stunner called *The Trip* that featured everyone from future *Easy Rider* co-stars Peter Fonda and Dennis Hopper to Nicholson regulars Bruce Dern and Luana Anders.

In the former, it's painful to watch Jason Robards lumbering around as Al Capone, witnessing an actor so celebrated for his interpretations of Eugene O'Neill murder this murderer through overplaying, overacting and overemoting. What should be simple gestures become broad enough to help guide a plane to a safe landing.

Nicholson is Gino, a hood who's perhaps the guy in *Studs Lonigan* a little down the line, out of prison and qualified for nothing but two-bit robberies and anonymous hits. Jack does employ an interesting vocal delivery that's either based on Jonathan Haze's Gustaf in *The Terror* or forerunner to future neighbor, co-star and original inspiration, Marlon Brando, when playing Don Corleone in *The Godfather*. Nicholson delivers his one line of dialogue about dipping his bullets in garlic (because you die of blood poisoning if the bullets don't kill you) as if punched in the throat, a pushed half-whisper that instantly conveys a gangster who's seen some bad scrapes.

This minuscule role could now be seen as an interesting novelty, a favor done with harm undone, for Corman. Reportedly turning down a larger part, Nicholson likely foresaw the value of a small profile in this bloated melodrama, playing an uncredited role of a one-line hoodlum with a gun nine years after playing the title role of a confused kid with a gun in Corman's *The Cry Baby Killer*.

* * *

The same year as this *Massacre*, Nicholson wrote his fourth script that reached the screen. *The Trip* sees LSD as exploration and advertising as assault. Part Fellini and part Bergman, complete with a dwarf, a witch, a blonde with a painted face and two hooded riders in black on a horse, his script is a kaleidoscope of emotional and experiential images with innovative and colorful effects.

Salli Sachse (the distorted image on the film's poster) abruptly went from Beach Party movies to this counterculture cult classic. "The script? Well, it was a lot of visuals," she told me. "It was very different, a smaller cast with a lot of location shooting in Big Sur. It wasn't the big crowds and all the older actors like Keenan Wynn and Vincent Price and Buster Keaton, Dorothy Malone, Mickey Rooney. It was not as refined as those movies."[23]

Definitely no *Ski Party* (on which she worked with Corman's brother Gene) or *Beach Blanket Bingo*, Nicholson's vision of *The Trip* stood out as a moviemaking trip for Salli. "The scenes were kind of vignettes of fantasies. There was this merry-go-round scene and it was hard to piece it all together just from the script, but then you got to the set. It was just very, very different."[24]

The movie was an avant garde commentary about drug mores, sexuality, class and militarism, beautifully and insightfully directed by Roger Corman, with fantastic editing and futuristic special effects sequences. According to Sachse, the vision was compromised, hacked and mistranslated. "Close buddies, Peter [Fonda] and Dennis [Hopper] were raving about this movie. They thought it was going to be the best thing in the world, and then they were so disappointed the way it was cut, and the way it was put together, and what was left, the deeper meaning of things. I mean, Peter thought this was going to be the movie that was going to change the world [*laughs*]."[25]

* * *

6. The School of Roger

Instead, that film had to wait a couple of years. It was *Easy Rider* that changed the world, that being the world of filmmaking as well as the world of Fonda, Hopper and Nicholson. *The Trip* didn't change the world, nor did it advance the careers of that trio any more than their other motorcycle movies, westerns, youth culture exploitation flicks or anything else they had done to that point.

But all three benefitted from attending the School of Roger, or fellow alum Bruce Dern's University of Roger Corman. Corman's low-budget, high-margin whirlwind moviemaking and legacy of giving chances to future stars was honored in 2009 with a Lifetime Achievement Academy Award. His lifetime achievement was largely their career lifetime achievements, like a Jersey kid waving a pistol can eventually become a psychedelic screenwriter. Novocain may dull the senses, but garlic poisons the blood.

A naïf of the west on one day can become a sadistic enigma on a horse the next day. All because of getting a big chance, an opportunity to learn the movie business by growing into new characters, inventing ways to keep a production moving, and trying many aspects of their craft, from acting to writing to directing. Look at the films and you'll see that there's a little bit of Wilbur Force in Garrett Breedlove, though there's not that much in common between *The Little Shop of Horrors* and *Terms of Endearment*.

7

As Cuckoo as It Gets

The voices kept getting worse. They told him to do things. Ugly things, hurtful things. To himself ... to his family ... to strangers ... and to all of those, those people, those people who have done him wrong.

He washed and scrubbed and scraped, over and over again. He sings and he throws his breakfast if the eggs aren't over easy. He kidnaps a newspaper reporter, leaves a man to die in the desert, and throws a cop off a roof. He breaks into song without warning or need; yells at dead people; relives the case over and over again. He is also someone who lives without life, pretends he's watching the World Series, and plans on correcting his wife and child at the edge of an axe.

The voices don't help a bit. They don't remind you to floss or file your taxes early. They confuse and confound, building frustration and hatred and despair with each whisper. Voices in the head push, and push, and keep on pushing.

These are the voices of dramatized mental illness, based on some real aspects of psychological conditions, yet heightened and stylized for effect. The cuckoos, the crazies, the psychos, nutcases—those are the Hollywood characters who represent most of what stands for diseases of the mind. No matter if from degeneration, injury or trauma, these unbalanced characters bring a crooked smile to a studio's balance sheet.

Characters with mental illness have long been a staple of the movies, and these parts offer actors an explosive range, from a raging psychopath to a mumbling introvert. They also offer meaty roles and payoffs in the form of awards. Both of Nicholson's Best Actor Oscar performances are in films with psychological and sociological conditions at their center, *One Flew Over the Cuckoo's Nest* and *As Good as It Gets*. He has played characters suffering from a mental illness or exhibiting symptoms of such in many other movies, including *About Schmidt, Anger Management, Batman, The Departed, Ironweed, The King of Marvin Gardens, The Pledge, The Shining* and *The Shooting*.

In examining the conditions depicted and the degree of accuracy of their portrayals, I owe a tremendous degree of gratitude to Dr. Brooke Cannon, who holds a Ph.D. in Clinical Psychology and serves as Professor of Psychology and Counseling at Marywood University in Scranton, Pennsylvania. Dr. Cannon also teaches a course in Psychology in Film, has published extensively on the topic, and has created a website on the subject (www.psychmovies.com).

* * *

In *As Good as It Gets*, Nicholson plays Melvin Udall, a writer of romance novels (an issue he knows nothing about), and whose life is controlled by Obsessive-Compulsive Disorder (OCD). Dr. Cannon also points out that it's necessary to separate the OCD from Melvin's less attractive personality traits, because of course "all people with OCD are not hostile, homophobic jerks!" His symptoms and behaviors were deemed true to the condition. "Although Melvin was still able to function as a writer, the degree of impairment from his disorder was evident in how his symptoms interfered with his social functioning (long shower, borrowed dinner jacket, etc.)."[1]

Nicholson plays Melvin the jerk, overlaid with Melvin the victim.

He does suffer. Someone with OCD feels the need to check and double-check and check again (routines and rituals called compulsions) to try to control upsetting thoughts (worries called obsessions). Udall's obsessions include fear of contamination, so he compulsively washes, using a new bar of soap for each application, and brings his own silverware to the diner with each visit. He worries about injury, thinking bad things will happen if he steps on a crack or if things are out of order. He gives in to superstition and locks, locks, locks, locks, locks himself in his apartment and away from others.

Melvin's condition reflects those with multiple obsessions and compulsions and who have a family background of such. "OCD has a strong genetic component," Dr. Cannon points out. "In the movie, he suggests that his father had some sort of disorder, that he did not leave his room for 11 years."[2]

The actor accurately portrays the disorder in a natural and unforced manner, showing his legendary research and preparation. Without much exposition, the viewer understands OCD and how it impacts a real person's life. You believe that the character is someone going through these rituals and dealing with these fears every minute of every day rather than seeing a few parts of scenes as representative of something bigger. This is essential, as the non-stop serial nature of the condition has to control Melvin in order for the film to work. We have to believe in the truth of the condition, or the story and the arc are not possible.

Nicholson explained that as a Studio Method actor, "I was prone to give some kind of clinical presentation of the disorder. But [director] Jim Brooks never wanted it up front, and I understood that." He studied obsessive-compulsives and found that they are adept at hiding their disorder. "I like to kind of hide the performance, just to make it different. A lot of my performance of the disease is simply not written. I might be wriggling my fingers where the cameras can't see, but it energizes what I'm doing."[3]

Shirley Knight played the mother of Helen Hunt's character, and explained the importance of this "depth of character" and the difference between "really being in the moment" versus "acting the moment."[4]

"I think what Jack was saying is that he and I both are very instinctive actors, so you won't see a scene between the two of us where we're not really connected, and listening, and being. It's all about being. It's difficult to explain, but you just need to be in the moment."[5]

Nicholson exists as a man with OCD. More important, "being" this man rather than playing a part, means that Jack can seamlessly weave the condition with the exaggeration of comedy and with the warmth of romance. His obsessions and compulsions become part of the story to show why Melvin is such a jerk, and do so comically. It's important that the audience not hate or even dislike Udall. The OCD brings some empathy, but the comedic nuance disarms the viewer with just the right balance of self-deprecation and vulnerability.

Melvin's bad and he can't help himself. Okay, he can. But he knows that we know it, and that opens him up to a truth that allows the narrative to come to life.

Udall's comfort with this disorder of discomfort makes it possible that a little dog can come to mean so much to the man. This opens the door, both figuratively and literally, to Melvin caring about Simon (Greg Kinnear) and Carol (Hunt). He changes so meaningfully and dramatically, perfect in tone and presentation for the character and the story. When Shirley Knight's character comes out of the apartment she shares with her daughter, into the stairway after Carol exclaims, "Why can't I have a normal boyfriend?," the mother is the only one in control and with sense. Melvin goes from out-of-control mental illness to out-of-control in love. After all the touching and kissing with Carol (remember that this is a germaphobe), he loses a main compulsion. "I forgot to lock the door?" What's most curious is whether someone can "get better" as he does, with the Helen Hunt character not only changing him into a more likable man, but also reducing the effects of his condition to the point of functioning as a near-normal person.

Dr. Cannon sees this as another example of how "love cures all" is so typical of the movies, though not so in real life. "Melvin states that his love for Carol motivated him to 'be a better man' and that was what pushed him to finally agree to take medications for his OCD," she explains. However, behavior therapy is the standard approach, usually coupled with medication.[6]

It is necessary to break the continued association between the compulsive behavior and the negative reinforcement that reduces the anxiety. "That is, Melvin would have to confront his feared situations and not be allowed to engage in his compulsive response." The psychology-in-movies expert sums things up: "It is unrealistic to think that the 'cure' could happen so quickly ... or that the symptoms would be completely gone, rather than just diminished or controlled. He could be 'a better man,' but not a 'different man.' Overall, though, I think *As Good as It Gets* has more right than wrong."[7]

* * *

Randall Patrick McMurphy is a better man than many, but a different man than society desires, or demands. *One Flew Over the Cuckoo's Nest* could be the quintessential role for the quintessential Jack, deftly combining the devilish with the destroyed; the gregarious with the hapless; and the streetwise with the dangerously naïve.

"Mac" may be his most beloved and revered part. There is a complexity that belies the stereotype of a simple man, against the typical notion that someone must be educated or accomplished to be multifaceted.

McMurphy is duped by the system. What hurts most is that McMurphy is duped by himself. He chooses the mental ward because he reasons that it'll be easier than prison, not knowing that prisons have sentences that end and mental facilities have a beginning, but not necessarily an end (at least not a good one).

Ken Kesey's novel is understood as commentary on conformity, particularly as its writing so closely followed the white-bread, man-in-the-gray-flannel-suit, McCarthy era. Dr. Cannon unequivocally states that McMurphy did not have a mental illness. "He was a crafty individual looking to avoid jail. [The character] showed some signs of narcissism, but not to the level of a diagnosable personality disorder. As he developed relationships with the other patients, it was clear that he cared about them and that he did not expect special treatment."[8]

Michael Berryman, who played inmate Ellis, confirmed my theory that McMurphy was a J.D. past his prime (recall that Jack played several troubled youths). "He was actually a grown-up juvenile delinquent taking advantage of the system. And then he realized that some of us were not committed and we stayed because we were broken."[9]

Mews Small (then billed as Marya), who played Candy, never discussed that aspect with Nicholson, but saw Mac as "just a regular old rebellious guy. You put him in a circumstance like that, you never know what's going to happen to a person." She felt the situation pushed his behavior to a place it never had gone before. "You know, people are complicated."[10]

McMurphy may not have had a mental illness, but he certainly exhibited sociological issues. A juvenile delinquent who never grew up, Mac had a stunted personality, as if he stopped maturing at about 15 years of age. He delights in showing Dr. Spivey pornographic playing cards during his induction interview. He displays a false chumminess with the guards who bring him to the institution. He has problems with authority and problems with women in authority (the "party girls" offer no such threats to his adolescent manhood), which makes his clashes with Nurse Ratched inevitable.

Berryman provides some background about the difficult transition from book to screenplay that initially involved the author: "Ken Kesey could not write a screenplay. He wrote 500 pages. Michael Douglas told them finally to take control of it and make their version. And we thought Ken would visit the set, and he never did."[11]

The author's son, Zane Kesey, corrects that assertion by declaring that the producers were looking to avoid paying Kesey for his screenplay. He sued; they settled. "Dad never saw the movie," Zane wrote to me. "During deposition under oath, the lawyers said he was probably flattered and would be the first in line to see it. Dad got pissed and said he would never see it." His father simply wanted his contract honored, as the family was "flat broke and in deep debt and the movie had broken records in box office."[12]

According to Mews, "We used the book as our guide, almost like it was a script." She described taking "all the character stuff" from the book, while the script itself was very well-written, "and I had those wonderful lines to say from Lawrence Hauben and Bo Goldman."[13] Likely, the seeming contradiction is easily solved by considering the novel more as guide to theme and sensibility rather than content and structure.

Of course, the most dramatic—and cinematically necessary—shift was from a first-person interior narrative to a third-person neutral one, a change that also more commercially placed the focus on Nicholson's character. Berryman explained that Kesey "always thought it was through the eyes of the Chief, and the star was truly Jack as McMurphy, so that's how it happened," resulting in this "incredible film!"[14]

Nicholson established his character at once as juvenile glad-hander, class wisecracker and ingratiating schemer. Just after being led into the facility, he performs a pretend "crazy" jig and kisses a guard. During his processing with Dr. Spivey (played by Dr. Dean Brooks, the real-life head of the Oregon State Hospital, where much of the film was shot), McMurphy adopts a conspiratorial "just between us" manner when explaining his grand plan to avoid work detail at jail by faking mental problems. Mac's ensuing confusion when opening up about this to the facility director comes across as part genuine, part contrived, culminating in a nice, probably unscripted moment when he reaches to squash a bug and Dr. Brooks reacts with delayed raised eyebrows.

Jack Nicholson: Anatomy of an Actor author Beverly Walker watched the interview sequences being filmed, witnessing how they "evolved from extensive improvisations between Nicholson and Dr. Dean R. Brooks, the hospital's game psychiatrist." She perceived Nicholson as "playfully devilish" in his attempts to shock the doctor (an ironic turnaround of sorts). "Every take was hilarious. Nicholson—adept at playing overlapping actions within a scene—presents McMurphy as both impudent and clueless."[15]

McMurphy immediately asserts himself in group sessions and effortlessly grabs the unopposed leadership position over a bunch of dope-placated, introverted inmates. While his first session devolves into madness and anarchy, you witness the first realization that Mac's scheme wasn't such a good idea.

These scenes took place in an actual mental institution environment to enhance the disassociation from the outside world and the claustrophobic effects of confinement, while adding realism no set could replicate.

Vincent Schiavelli (Fredrickson) reported that the confinement went beyond a mere visit, as the inmate actors arrived on location a week before filming began and "allowed ourselves to be locked up in the ward" each afternoon, choosing their own beds and collecting their own personal items, "so we essentially became the characters whom we played." The actors visited inmates and attended group sessions. "In *Cuckoo's Nest*," the *Amadeus* and *Fast Times at Ridgemont High* actor explained, "it became clear that you had to reach inside yourself to find your own insanity and its manifestation."[16]

Of course, the cast must not have been totally closed off from the outside world, as Josip Elic, who played Bancini joked to me that Jack was "a pain in the ass!" because he always wanted to finish in order to watch the Lakers games.[17]

Small described the hospital as an eerie place, with 150 patients on the film's payroll who were there because they didn't understand what was going on in their lives. "In the shock treatment ward," she explained, "all of those people except for Sydney [Lassick], Jack and Will [Sampson, who played Chief], they're all the real deal—the real doctors, the real nurses." She told me how director Milos Forman used the reality to set a mood, such as when he "pans around so you can see the faces. The first picture you see in the film, you look in that doorway and there's a person looking out of the doorway. That is a patient, not an actor."[18]

Berryman set the scene by explaining, "It was 127 days and we had two weeks of rehearsal with camera for the major scenes, blocking for two weeks, and then we started rolling principal photography. And it was a real hospital with real doctors, with Dean Brooks, and some of the patients upstairs were real patients, and they performed a lobotomy while we were there. And we knew it was us or them."[19]

That feeling of "us or them" permeated the atmosphere. McMurphy increasingly views Nurse Ratched as an enemy who is there not to help the patients, but keep them under a system of rules and procedures more about control and conformity than treatment and care for the individual. "Us" represent people; "them" is the system—or, applied more broadly, the individual vs. society.

McMurphy can't help but become upset at what he views as the squashing of the inmates' personalities and needs, manifesting itself in mistrust and rebellion. He plots in ways that matter and can make a difference, yet he also plots about things that simply betray his own inner conflict and ingrained tendency to stir things up.

These natural tendencies are showcased in the initial scene on the basketball yard, as McMurphy tries to teach the massive Chief the fundamentals of the game (something he knows about from having directed *Drive, He Said* as well as from all those Los Angeles Laker games) in order to take advantage of it later.

Mac's hopefulness combines with his scheming and his personal strength at "mixing." The J.D. who never grew up always has a game going, whether the metaphorical game against the system or literal games such as hoops, cards or watching the World Series. The games are not always fun or satisfying. In his first card game, his impatience with the other patients foreshadows a trouble in socializing. McMurphy can only fit in so much, misfits as they all are. Some are simply beyond being reached, because of their mental condition and because of the institution's conditioning.

The vote on whether to watch the World Series stands as pivotal to McMurphy's mental state, as well as his attitude toward the facility. Nicholson is coquettish and even a little boyishly seductive with Louise Fletcher's Nurse Ratched. At first.

When the door to opportunity begins to close, we see his change. When that door is closed for good, locked and bolted as compulsively as if by Melvin Udall himself, Nicholson moves his character's nature from boy Randall to leader Mac to troublemaker McMurphy.

During the first World Series vote, Jack ranges from helpful to hopeful to confused, then from dismay to disgust to disappointment. All one man, all one scene, yet embodying three aspects of Randall Patrick McMurphy's personality—not a split personality, but a splintering away of his necessary buoyancy to reveal his underlying authority problems and anti-feminist core.

On the second World Series vote, McMurphy loses on a technicality, with men unable to comprehend what's going on, let alone take a position on it, counted among the total to defeat the motion. Nicholson shows how the man is thoroughly shattered, first with a classic Jacksplosion and then through denial, by pantomiming his own play-by-play as if watching the game in triumph.

The choice of the words "henhouse shit" (as in "You're not going to pull that now...") gives away McMurphy's attitude about strong females making the rules. Creating a fantasy response falsely put the man in charge, with Mac pretending he won against Nurse Ratched and her system. In his temporary world, which he probably knew was not real even as he was enjoying it, the men get to watch the ballgame despite what the women say.

As Dr. Cannon pointed out, Randall did not have a mental illness. He was in touch with reality. He just didn't like it.[20]

Berryman reflects that this "was the major question. 'What is reality?' 'What is real life?' We were being medicated constantly, [while] the humanity came from Jack's character, which Louise had to crush because of her issue of control and rigid thinking."[21]

R.P. McMurphy responds to the control by building up his own pressure. He actually believes that extra pressure could give him superhuman strength, and he gives it all he's got when he attempts to pick up a huge bathroom fixture. He believes. And he is not showing off to the other inmates.

Try watching this one scene without the sound distracting you. Nicholson is in the bathing area with this imposing porcelain sink structure. Watch his eyes for the range of emotion and expression that reaches beyond his eyes to his feelings. Then, switch the sound back on and hear the groans and gurgles and wordless—yet completely understood—utterances, as he off-camera starts his struggle to lift it. Having seen the concentration and exertion without sound, and then having heard the accompanying full-on intent and physical strain, we now feel the actor's total energy, his intensity in the moment and focus toward the action, as it happens.

It's entirely credible that he could have succeeded, as impossible as the task was. He believed. And he nearly burst in order to make it happen. McMurphy sums it up to the spectators, but Mac might just as well be summing up the film's message of rebellion against a mindlessly controlling society. He does so even with the rational knowledge that only total failure can result, stating forcefully that giving up is not an option. Mac spits it out in disgust about the reality of a guy getting beat down by the system, throwing out the words as if the words themselves are the enemies: "I tried, goddamn it, at least I did that." Let this serve as Randall Patrick McMurphy's epitaph, and the epitaph of generations of those who could only abhor conformity, yet were ineffective in combatting it.

The pressure is relieved by the presence of Candy (Small) and Rose (Louisa Moritz), introduced when a jubilant Candy is pulled onto the bus from her trailer for the inmates' escape trip. Small reminded me that the film had been shot in order, "so when the girls showed up, the guys didn't have to act excited," describing the fishing sequence as "four days of fun ... except for those who were sick."[22]

Even cinematographer William Fraker, who took over for Haskell Wexler and Bill Butler, was seasick the whole time. Mews remembered that money was running out and staff was cut, so that this final shot sequence used a skeleton crew in a place where the water is usually very rough. "We only had four days to film, and we had to finish the film in four days," with luck intervening for those four days, before conditions returned to storminess. "Out there, we're all free on the boat. I was one of those who didn't get seasick, and Jack didn't. All of the actors were wonderful," including Christopher Lloyd, who passed the time reading Shakespeare while so many colleagues dealt with seasickness.[23]

There's joy in this independence, and Randall shows leadership outside in contrast to his bossiness inside. As mentor, he encourages participation and what today would be called empowerment. All respond favorably and all seem normal, or at least their own versions of normalcy.

This Mac is a different man than the one imprisoned as much by the helplessness as by the institution's walls and fences. When he finds out, from a guard who enjoys destroying Randall's hope far too much, that he's in to stay (unless those in charge deem him fit to leave), the life drains from Mac's face in a way that foreshadows the electroshock scene.

With all the hope in his mind wiped out, McMurphy's reaction is to put his body into the fight. He twists it and stretches it, burying his head into his fist, all leading to his ultimate attack on the facility itself. His frustration explosively escalates from a battle over cigarettes to beatings, from breaking the glass on the nurses' station to a fight with an attendant.

This is where everything gets serious. *Cuckoo's Nest*'s matter-of-fact use of shock therapy and lobotomizing has contributed to a lasting negative view of mental health treatment and its practitioners, according to Dr. Cannon, but that image has improved over the years. "Since earlier movies such as *Bedlam* and *The Snake Pit*, there has been a gradual shift toward portraying characters with mental illness and mental health treatment more accurately and in a way that is less stigmatizing, with recent examples including *It's Kind of a Funny Story, Lars and the Real Girl* and *Silver Linings Playbook*."[24]

Here, however, the stereotype and its dramatic possibilities burn intensely. When Cheswick is dragged away for shock treatment, Mac's confusion and horror is real, just as real as his joyous and surprised reaction when the Chief thanks him for a stick of gum. Mac delights that they have something in common, something still meaningful to him, even in this moment of frustration and defeat, that they both can still put one over on the system, Mac and this "sly son of a bitch."

Facing his own electroshock experience, Nicholson's false bravado and chumminess with the staff heightens the terror and inhumanity of this medical "treatment." Cringingly photographed in close-up by director Forman and cinematographer Haskell Wexler, McMurphy's punishment is harrowing and stark, that is until his braced and distorted body gives in, and he becomes infant-like in his breathing and jellied in his structure.

But this is not the end of R.P. McMurphy. Nicholson introduces additional facets to his character, nearer to developmental adulthood than the juvenile delinquent has come before. He's tender and caring with the Chief, showing a depth and maturing that society does not want him to possess and which he himself would likely deny. McMurphy also becomes big brother to Billy (Brad Dourif). Upon recognizing Billy's interest in Candy, he sets up the stuttering and shy young man with his sometime girl, an act about which he later explodes in guilt when it violently backfires.

In these intimate scenes between Candy and McMurphy, Jack "treated me just like a younger sister," Mews fondly remembers. "He really spent some time helping to calm me down, because I was nervous." There is a behind-the-scenes snapshot that shows Nicholson conversing with Small between takes on a bench, not noticing the camera, a moment captured that she calls "magic."[25]

Small says that the scenes were not rehearsed, but that "we would block, set up and shoot." Light rehearsal protected the reality, and everybody knew their lines and knew their part, "and sometimes we'd run it once and sometimes we'd just shoot it." She believed that Forman's approach was to spend significant time casting and therefore didn't feel the need to provide much direction. "Milos is very interested in people being real," looking for performances after he cast actors he thought could do what he wanted them to do. Mews recalled that he mostly let the actors be and that he didn't say much to her unless necessary. "One day, Jack and I were a little lazy and he said, 'Just pick up, just pick it up a little bit.'"[26]

After sending Billy in with Candy, Mac retreats from the melee of the party and sits down, showing for just this one time Nicholson's devilish triangled eyebrows. Then, in an extended medium close-up free of words, McMurphy travels through an amazing array of emotion. McMurphy tires ... becomes concerned ... uncomfortable ... pleased ... reflective ... disturbed ... morose ... happy ... calmly content ... sleepy. One man, one unadorned and uninterrupted study in acting fundamentals, a nuanced impression that's perhaps his character's sole glimpse into the possibility of having a mental illness. Mews described this as "that moment in your life when you decide to do something and you know your life might end and you do it anyway."

When Nurse Ratched and the staff return the next morning, the party turns into a nightmare. She knows Billy's mother and threatens to tell her that her son had been with Candy. The actress who portrayed Candy still feels the scene when seeing it many years later, almost as if it is real and is happening. "Poor Billy. Louise [Fletcher] says she's going to tell his mother. It was just devastating."[27]

Nurse Ratched (Louise Fletcher) pushes Randall Patrick McMurphy (Nicholson) over the edge in *One Flew Over the Cuckoo's Nest* (1975) as Martini (Danny DeVito) and Col. Matterson (Peter Brocco, in wheelchair) look on. Mews Small, who played Candy, explained that producer Michael Douglas showed Jack the choking technique used in this brutal attack: "It looks like you're pulling in, and you're pulling out."

Nicholson watches with revulsion and true empathy as Dourif's Billy reverts to a sniveling child, begging and animalistic, becoming a creature destroyed. Once that destruction is complete, Ratched must be destroyed.

As with Cheswick and his cigarettes, McMurphy loses control only when it is on behalf of the other inmates, most dramatically when he rightfully blames the head nurse for Billy's suicide. Clinically or functionally, Nurse Ratched does drive Randall insane. He attacks her with such force and abandon that Nicholson must have hurt Fletcher, until he is struck on the back of the head, causing him to fall forward on her as if in sexual release. This serves as the ultimate comment on their twisted feelings and distorted relationship.

Mews recalled that it was producer Michael Douglas who showed Nicholson the choking technique. "It's the reverse. You pull out. It looks like you're pulling in, and you're pulling out. She did get red, but she was not injured." Small also mentioned that the only times she saw the real patients react were when Mac strangles Nurse Ratched ("That was unbelievable and they all applauded afterwards") and when Chief breaks the window to escape.[28]

Michael Berryman explains that Nicholson "played it the way it was written, which was that he was just taking advantage of the system. Just like when Nurse Ratched says, 'You're a con artist,' and he was fine with that until he realized what happened with Billy, and that's when the whole story changes."[29]

Again, more punishment than therapy, a more extended and extensive procedure is deemed necessary to render McMurphy safe. He is destroyed by lobotomy, reduced to a vegetative state. This time it's no act, as Randall Patrick McMurphy is no more, having been defeated as a person; made devoid of his humanity; rendered inert and harmless the way society always wanted him to be. The con man is out-conned.

The slightest smile welcomes the pillow that releases him when the Chief smothers him, an act of love that gives Randall more than the system ever did. That escape precedes the Chief's great escape, finishing what McMurphy could only aspire about, as the giant man lifts the huge porcelain bathroom fixture and tosses it through the chained windows. Chief becomes one Native American who frees himself, an achievement triumphantly celebrated by Christopher Lloyd's ecstatic yelping salute.

Humanity makes R.P. McMurphy's story a tragedy. When that man loses his humanity, he must be released from the very society that held him down, ironically enough by an Indian—himself a victim of that society.

Mews Small looked into the heart of Chief, understanding that keeping Mac alive after they destroyed his brain was "torturing the soul." Chief's act of release was the right thing to do for his friend, in that "sometimes, someone fulfills a request even though you can't speak the request. The soul speaks it or the other person understands it."[30]

* * *

Twenty-eight years later, Nicholson again addresses the subject of mental health treatment, this time with a much lighter touch and from the perspective of the practitioner rather than the patient.

Dr. Buddy Rydell is as far from Nurse Ratched as *Anger Management* is from *Cuckoo's Nest*. And nobody's as far away from McMurphy as Adam Sandler is as Dave Buznik.

How anyone can be as angry as Buznik when in a relationship with Marisa Tomei is a suspension of disbelief that's a good first sign that this movie isn't going to be a serious treatise on the subject of personality disorders.

Dr. Rydell has an anger group with misfits such as Luis Guzmán and the deliciously over-the-top John Turturro. He also appears to have issues of his own. Hilarity ensues, at least as far as the moviemakers' theory holds.

Though not a fan of the flick, psychmovies professor Dr. Brooke Cannon agrees that much of the character conflict between the leads arises because of the irony that Dr. Rydell has the condition that he treats. "Yes, I believe that the humor in the movie arises from the fact that Nicholson also has anger management issues. This would be diagnosed as an 'Impulse Control Disorder.'"[31]

Dr. Rydell goes beyond a typical doctor-patient relationship with Buznik, moving in with him and going on a road trip reminiscent of that in *As Good as It Gets*, putting a good deal of the comedic situations into *Odd Couple* territory. Sandler isn't as annoying as usual, while Nicholson deftly swings from crafty to crazy and psychobabbling to soft-hearted. It's an enlarged supporting role, with Nicholson exaggerating the doctor's non-traditional method of immersive home therapy to great effect. Dr. Cannon observes that Rydell's "behavior and methods would be considered unethical, particularly when the client did not provide informed consent to engage in the different activities."[32]

* * *

Warren Schmidt, in the previous year's *About Schmidt*, has no connection to his wife, in some ways similar to Bobby's occasional distance from girlfriend Rayette in *Five Easy Pieces*. For this reason, as well as the other empty aspects of his life, when Warren returns from his nothing job he's left with less than nothing.

The death of his wife then seems to trigger a type of freedom that eventually leads to an exploration and ultimately to a newfound ability to experience full emotion. Dr. Cannon cautions that if that interpretation is based on the dictionary definition of "freedom" as "being without necessity or any constraints over choice or action," then Schmidt is technically free. But he's more like "an untethered balloon."[33]

She explains that this is a man with no direction, having "never really had to make decisions regarding his life" as the company man and dutiful husband. "Now, without his wife, he is taking stock of his life and finding it empty." She contextualizes Schmidt by placing him in the last position in Eric Erickson's stages of Psychological Development known as "Integrity vs. Despair."[34]

He asks if he has made a difference with his life. He does not like the answer. What's worse is that his negative assessment is accurate. Dr. Cannon comments, "There is some great dialogue in the movie that perfectly captures this life review."[35]

Dealing with this unfavorable internal conflict, Warren Schmidt strives to make his life "about" something. He starts by trying to make a difference in his daughter's life, as if her snotty and ungrateful attitude—not to mention her questionable choice in husband—deserves anything more than dismissal. "His adventures along the way highlighted his 'untethered' state," continues Dr. Cannon, "as he careened from one situation to the next."[36]

He returns home. He returns to nothingness, realizing that he still has not influenced the lives of others, most notably his own daughter and son-in-law. That's why sending some money to African foster child Ndugu mattered, even if a manufactured connection or making a difference made through marketing. Warren Schmidt gets appreciation, the type that's mere recognition as a living being, an acknowledgment from a stranger (if an actual Ndugu exists) that he never felt from his own so-called loved ones.

Dr. Cannon says of Schmidt's life culmination, "The most powerful scene in the movie is when he reads the letter [from Ndugu] and realizes that his life matters, that he *has* made a difference." She also points out that the Japanese movie *Ikiru* has a similar story, one that focuses on a bureaucrat who discovers that he has cancer, and also realizes that his life has made no difference.[37] Akira Kurosawa's 1952 existentialist masterpiece follows a man who finds the meaning of life only when dying, and who dedicates himself passionately to building a playground for neighborhood children.

Kurosawa's character Watanabe finds solace as he sits on a swing, in the snow in the park, the same not-too-late meaningfulness that causes Schmidt to weep in gladness about the boy he may have saved.

The word "ikiru" means ... to live.

* * *

In *Wolf*, Will Randall turns any depression he experiences about losing his job into a desire for revenge against those who did him in (Christopher Plummer as Raymond Alden, the publishing house's owner, and James Spader as the protégé who plotted to replace him). Randall's werewolf transformation could in part have a less than supernatural explanation, as suppression that had built up and was suddenly and violently released.

The former chief editor's vengeance, based on his frustration with the duplicity of Alden, ultimately escapes through his alter ego and by his freed libido (courtesy of Alden's daughter, played by Michelle Pfeiffer). The question raised by this Mike Nichols film is whether such an assumed identity can be used as an excuse for extreme behavior that is not under the control of the person. After all, the wolf is not human, taking Randall's change beyond the transformation of good human Dr. Jekyll to the bad human Mr. Hyde.

* * *

Another depressive character is David Staebler, the radio host in *The King of Marvin Gardens*. Based on samples from his show and what we glimpse of his personality, this is a guy who in the vernacular would be termed "a downer." Even Staebler refers to his life as a "tragedy that isn't exactly Top 40," while the closest he can get to a punchline is a story about his grandfather choking on fish.

Monkee Peter Tork has criticized director Bob Rafelson for trapping his characters in a black box (a reference to the literal and figurative black box prominently figuring in the Nicholson-Rafelson-penned *Head*).[38] Here, the radio studio staging and dark lighting suggest this sense of place, just as it represents the embodiment of David's life.

When David's brother Jason contacts him out of the blue to basically force him to take part in a questionable business venture in dormant Atlantic City, David goes along reluctantly and flaccidly. When the situation gets more bizarre, David emerges from his downbeat and introverted non-personality, and it's no coincidence that this occurs when David takes on assumed personalities. He's a boardwalk huckster, a Miss America pageant master of ceremonies, a business hustler to Japanese investors. He's everything but David, and often less than a partner or a brother.

When insane violence takes Jason, David retreats back to his Philadelphia prison of an apartment and shrivels back to his nothing self, only a weeping and pathetic voice on the radio.

Significantly, the opening and closing radio monologues are shot to give the appearance of someone opening up about his thoughts to a psychiatrist. Unfortunately, no such professional is actually present, and David's self-therapy does nothing to help his condition.

* * *

In *The Shining*, Jack Torrance's job also gets him down, but not as much as does his family and his fatal bout of writer's block. Nicholson attributed his character's state to what he brought to the Overlook, rather than what he found there, saying that "the most volatile element in our culture is the pressure inside the family unit."[39] *The Shining* is considered a descent into madness, yet there are signs of the character's mental imbalance from the beginning of the film, such as his odd countenance on the drive to the hotel and his strange reaction to the mention of cannibalism and the Donner Party. In fact, his backstory shows more serious signs, most notably having broken his son's arm while drunk.

Diane Johnson, who co-wrote the script with director Stanley Kubrick, admitted, "Nicholson was very much crazier from the outset of his performance than in the book, and very much crazier than Kubrick envisioned, I think."[40]

Dr. Cannon agrees that Torrance was already suffering from undiagnosed mental illness prior to going to the Overlook, with "a predisposition to schizophrenia, but it required significant environmental stress to trigger the disease. Once triggered, though, it follows its course. This is consistent with the 'diathesis-stress model' of schizophrenia (*diathesis* meaning genetic predisposition)."[41]

In a 1980 interview with Michel Ciment, Kubrick described his intention to "strike an extraordinary balance between the psychological and the supernatural in such a way as to lead you to think that the supernatural would eventually be explained by the psychological: 'Jack must be imagining these things because he's crazy.'"[42]

Torrance withdraws into his "writing" and into an isolated condition, not solely because of the remote, snowbound condition of the hotel, but also a self-imposed distancing from his family. The more he stays away from them, the more he (seemingly) hallucinates, and the stranger his disassociated state becomes. Dr. Cannon explains, "People with depression or anxiety (maybe what might happen in writer's block) can develop psychosis," in response to environmental stress or sensory deprivation.

As a mental health professional who has put a good deal of effort into surfacing and refuting falsehoods about psychological conditions depicted in films, Dr. Cannon also emphasizes that *The Shining* "once again perpetuates the myth that people with mental illness are more dangerous than others," pointing out that statistics show otherwise. However, "whenever someone commits a heinous crime and happens to also be mentally 'ill,' such as the Unabomber, that makes news."[43]

* * *

Nicholson has portrayed other men whose substance abuse contributes to social dysfunction, seriously in *Carnal Knowledge* and to more comic effect in *Terms of Endearment* and *Easy Rider*. He becomes a dangerous drunk in *Studs Lonigan* (committing rape at a wild party) and most dramatically in 1987's *Ironweed* and 2001's *The Pledge*.

Ironweed is based on William Kennedy's novel of the same name. Nicholson plays Francis Phelan, whose life and baseball career ended when he dropped his infant to his death while intoxicated (shades of breaking son Danny's arm while drunk in *The Shining*). He lives a Skid Row existence and has dropped out of his family's life (a route Jack Torrance was traveling prior to his total break with reality and the resulting murderous attacks).

This man clearly suffers due to the accidental death of his baby. Francis reacts to this traumatic event by shutting himself off from society and building his life around abusing the substance that led to the tragedy in the first place. Phelan also sees "ghosts" from his past, something that increasingly interferes with his life, such as it is.

Jerry Black also gets to the point where he hallucinates and relives his final, failed case about a murdered child. In Sean Penn's *The Pledge*, Black's

In Sean Penn's *The Pledge* (2001), Jerry Black's (Nicholson) failure to keep his promise to parents (Michael O'Keefe and Patricia Clarkson, lower left) of a murdered child, coupled with his guilt about betraying his lover when he uses her daughter as bait, pushes him over the edge of reality and into a world of hallucinations.

failure to keep his pledge to parents of the victim, along with his guilt about betraying his lover (Robin Wright Penn) by using her young daughter as bait for the suspected killer, pushes him into a muttering, bitter world of constantly recreating each detail.

The retired detective becomes so obsessed with the case that he puts another child in danger—one he truly loves—no longer having the discernment to see that what he is doing is wrong and dangerous. The beginning and the end of the film bookend harrowing studies of a drunken and broken man, a man who cracks under the pressure that he himself has built up.

* * *

In Tim Burton's *Batman*, Nicholson carries a mystique and creates a persona that makes the film. When I asked Dr. Cannon if a trauma such as the disfiguring and life-changing injuries suffered by Jack Napier would cause someone to first desert society and then attack it, as some sort of revenge

7. As Cuckoo as It Gets

based on a feeling of victimization that "life isn't fair," she asserted that it would not. Otherwise, "we'd have a society overrun with homicidal maniacs." She does draw attention to "correlations between childhood trauma and the development of Antisocial Personality Disorder (sociopathy, psychopathy, etc.)" as perhaps applicable to the character.

The psychmovies professor also noted that depicting a villain as disfigured in some way ("pirates with eye patches and peg legs and hooks for hands, the Phantom of the Opera with a disfigured face, etc.") is a standard movie convention. "The disfigurement in the Joker could be used as an excuse to follow his otherwise natural tendencies. There is a genetic component to criminality and psychopathy." She tantalizingly adds, "If the story was true that his father caused his injuries, then that suggests a genetic contribution as well."[44]

* * *

Two Nicholson characters who are most fearsome because of their nonchalance about killing, are Billy Spear in Monte Hellman's *The Shooting* (1966) and Frank Costello in Martin Scorsese's *The Departed* (2006). Three decades separate these performances—but no logic, no rational thought, no principle of humanity or earthly emotion can explain the abject disregard and viciousness that joins them.

Spear is a hired killer riding with a nameless Millie Perkins character. Costello is a gangster and murderer based on Whitey Bulger. While Spear helps Perkins on her relentless ride for revenge, Costello's killings are entirely his own choice and not always for business.

Billy likes to torture others psychologically and physically. His words add a sick sting to his acts. He threatens, "I'm gonna blow your face off." He promises, "Your brain's gonna fry out here, you know that?" He says "Leave him" about abandoning someone in the desert with no horse and no provisions. Billy is sadism personified.

Costello loses his temper easily, screaming at a group of priests to "enjoy your clams, cocksuckers" when one dares direct a comment that "pride comes before the fall" in Frank's direction. He's coked out and on the edge. He, too, takes pleasure in unnerving and intimidating, shaking up Leonardo DiCaprio's character by acting out a story about a rat who got what he deserved. He handles body parts like toys and stands bemused after a point-blank shooting victim "fell funny." Frank makes the mob look bad.

Millie Perkins considered Billy Spear a "gun for hire who didn't give a damn about anybody," while her character "knew he was a bad man, but I didn't care."[45] Frank Costello seems to enjoy the violence and depersonalized it to the extreme point far beyond the need even required of a murderous criminal. This may well be a manifestation of an individual's defense mechanism at work, similar to the way a soldier must do so in war.

Dr. Cannon illuminates non-professionals about this, revealing that both physiological and brain functioning differences exist for psychopaths. Their body's resting state, such as heart rate and blood pressure, is much lower than normal subjects, allowing them to "stay cool and calm in situations or when engaging in deviant behaviors, because the activities simply bring their psychological state up to the level of normals at rest."[46]

David Boeri, who has reported on the James "Whitey" Bulger case for 28 years in Boston, explained that the real man was consistent with this assessment. "The reports were that he kills and then he likes to take a nap, that there was some sort of release when he kills people."[47]

Method Actor that he is, it's unlikely that Nicholson went so far as hearing and listening to voices to prepare for a role, unless there were voices telling him to take the points on *Batman* to forever reap the formidable benefit from his percentage of profits. The Joker himself didn't need voices to push him toward vengeance, and Dr. Buddy Rydell was enough of a maverick that he didn't need any encouragement either.

David Staebler tried to be a king of Marvin Gardens, a king of nothing. His own voice kept reminding him of regret and sadness and loneliness and failure. Psychologically sourced interior voices would have been superfluous and would not have done as good a job in keeping David down.

R.P. McMurphy wasn't even mentally ill. Warren Schmidt was left adrift. And Melvin Udall had a condition that controlled him, but didn't require any voices in order to do so. Psychotic killers in *The Shooting* and *The Departed* may have given in to the evil voice, no doubt having slain the good voice long ago, long enough ago to not recognize the sound of that voice should it ever return.

Francis Phelan heard voices. He saw people who weren't supposed to be there. But ultimately, the most important voice in his head was the beautiful, lilting singing voice in the idealized vision he shared with his beloved Helen (Meryl Streep) in *Ironweed*.

The detective Jerry Black was left with black thoughts, an endless dialogue with countless voices because he held a guilt about betraying a woman and a child he loved, and because he could not keep a pledge—no matter how far he was willing to go to honor it.

That leaves Jack Torrance. Always suffering through the present caused by a relentless past. Always the caretaker who had to "take care of" his family. Always driven to roam the halls; sit and stare; seek memories he could not nor should ever connect; and retype the same sentence just as he relives the same insane tragedy.

Here's Johnny, again and again, hearing his own voice in disturbing concert with those of other Overlook staff members and with who-knows-how-many other voices, telling him and begging him to "correct" his son and bash his wife's brains in. He told Danny he would never do anything to hurt him. He didn't try to hurt Danny, but he did try to kill him. He told Wendy, "I'm not gonna hurt ya. I'm just gonna bash your brains in. I'm gonna bash 'em right the fuck in!" as he laughs at what his own voice has said.

Little Danny also hears a voice, the voice of Tony, a little boy that lives inside his mouth and tells him things.

Do you ... hear any voices?

What do they tell you ... to do?

8

Hippies and Hogs and Horses

There are hippie dives, biker bars and cowboy saloons, with little mixing between them despite there being only little differences between them. They're rough and unwelcoming to strangers, more about the atmosphere—the kind that's only comfortable to the hippies, bikers and cowboys who spend more time inside there than in any other kind of "home"—than about the amenities.

The three habitués wouldn't be too eager to issue an invitation to either of the others, but they too have more in common than they'd want to admit. Often outlaws, always outsiders. Open to action and closed to interference. Moving boundaries and restricting membership. Conformity is rejected, while codes regulate behavior.

Jack Nicholson has played his share of hippies and ridden his quota of Hogs and horses, particularly during the early portion of his career. *Psych-Out* was his more notable counterculture role (though he seemed a little old to be trying to make it with a psychedelic rock band); *Easy Rider* was his biggest biker flick (but he didn't play a biker in that one); and *The Missouri Breaks* was his highest profile western (despite the movie having been stolen by Marlon Brando with his bewildering array of getups and accents).

* * *

In *Psych-Out*, a Dick Clark production originally titled *The Love Children,* Nicholson plays a rock guitarist subtly named Stoney and is third-billed to Susan Strasberg and Dean Stockwell even though he is on screen more than anyone. Director Richard Rush made the film when he was in love with the hippie scene in San Francisco. In a heavy-handed fashion, a product not of Rush's direction but of American International's intention, the movie reflected how the glory was receding as "the drug culture had flourished to a point where it became troublesome."[1]

8. Hippies and Hogs and Horses

Psych-Out (1968) features Nicholson (left) as a rocker named Stoney. He looked a little old to be playing in clubs, a bit stiff to be a pro on the axe, yet comfortable enough in the settings to be enjoying himself. He's shown here with fellow Haight-Ashbury hippie Dave, portrayed by Dean Stockwell.

Nicholson is a main subject of director of photography László Kovács' rack focus handheld opening, though San Francisco is its true star. Nicholson has the first line, using a giggly and high-pitched tone, while his overall performance belies the hippie exploitation purpose of the release. He's been said to be careful and attentive to the point of obsession about costume. In this film, he wears a vest from a three-piece suit with no shirt underneath—possibly as commentary on the emptiness beneath the "capitalist pig" of the time or possibly because it looked interesting—with beads and medallions, black jeans, Beatle boots and an unfortunate ponytail.

He looks the part. Clothes may help define the character, but the eyes define the soul, and at this point in his career, Nicholson has learned that his eyes can be suitably expressive, showing a true understanding of his reality and his character's understanding. This is an actor moving through a lengthy transition who's become more assured of his screen presence.

Nicholson's Stoney is a man pulled between standard ("bourgeois") morality and hippie sensibility. He's a cool creator in his psych-rock band, yet a strict and authoritarian leader of that band. He's into free love, with deaf runaway Jenny (Strasberg). Jack also foreshadows his devil character in *The Witches of Eastwick* with a dirty flirty look and reaction as the group's blonde flautist invites him to bed. He has a nice, tender post-gig bed scene where he's slow and sweet with Jenny, changing attitude entirely the next morning when he dismisses her with more than the expected brushoff, but with a physicality that's like flicking away something small.

This character has more depth than an exploitation movie deserves, as Nicholson perceptively portrays a guy who is on planet Earth in a scene with Strasberg and Dean Stockwell (Dave)—who is anything but an Earthling in this story. Later, Stoney moves from hipster to sanctimonious square at his pad in a big, dramatic scene that foretells his '70s *Five Easy Pieces* mode with a pissed and pinched putdown of Jenny and Dave.

Nicholson secured future indie director Henry Jaglom a role in the film as "the guy who *psyched out*," a friend whose bad trip leads to hallucination and an attempted attack on himself with a circular saw. As Jaglom described it, "I was the moral of the film, which was if you take bad LSD—get your hand cut off ... [*laughs*]."[2]

Gary Kent, who created the innovative special effects and gaffed all the stunts, said that Nicholson particularly identified with this character.

> He was beginning to be a leader ... not of hippies, but peace people, and Jack was into that and you could feel it in the role of Stoney. He didn't have to push so hard or ask many questions, he just knew Stoney, knew the guy, knew his buddies on the Sunset Strip. And Jack at that time knew many of them and was already starting to get a reputation among that street crowd of being someone who had earned their props, so to speak.[3]

In a scene inside an art gallery with Bruce Dern as a Jesus figure and brother of Jenny, Stoney becomes the semi-square voice of reason, providing a true character study that's based on caricatures and clichés just as it represents an unfolding of Stoney from hippie musician to a man who's hip to this crisis of life. Stoney assumes the role of the sensible adult, shaking Dave and scolding him that Jenny "does not understand" the drug he's given her, his '60s version of "can't handle the truth."

After a stylish, *House of Usher* destruction of Dern's character, we're taken through a melodramatic battle between a deaf Jenny and a drug-addled Dave through the busy and oblivious San Francisco traffic. There's a terrible reaction shot by Nicholson after Dave is mortally slammed by a car (a stunt by Kent). Nicholson also had a weak and contrived reaction to a motorcycle mishap death in *Hells Angels on Wheels*. They both looked like what they were: shots made separately to simulate a person's fake reaction to an event that never actually occurred.

8. Hippies and Hogs and Horses 123

Garry Marshall was best known as the executive producer of the TV classics *The Odd Couple, Happy Days* and *Laverne & Shirley*, as well as director on the movie hits *Pretty Woman* and *The Princess Diaries*. When I showed him an original one-sheet poster for *Psych-Out*, he yelled, "*Psych-Out*! Oh, that's the truth!" and reminisced further, "I wasn't even billed here. I was unknown." It's interesting how, over four decades later, an actor who's become more known as a director and writer and producer would be concerned about credits. But then he exclaimed, "I arrested Jack Nicholson!" Marshall played a narc—"the fuzz" as he put it—and that "it was my own suit" he wore when hassling Stoney and Ben (Adam Roarke) because "that's what Richard Rush told me to do."[4]

* * *

Paying the bills had to be what told Nicholson to take part in *On a Clear Day You Can See Forever*. One of the last gasp productions of the classic-style movie musicals, this Broadway reworking uncomfortably tries to be "hip" and relevant within the familiar vernacular of that genre. They don't mix.

The Institute of the American Musical founder and president Miles Kreuger called the film adaptation "a complete catastrophe. I thought Barbra Streisand was, as usual, hopelessly overacting and that it was one of the worst movies she ever made. The casting of Yves Montand, I thought, was disgraceful. He's old enough to be her father."[5]

Nicholson's first scene is 42 minutes into the movie, revealing the near-future countercultur008al star playing sitar and dressed in hippie cool, complete with ascot. His demeanor is relaxed in his first scene with star Streisand (Daisy), playing her stepbrother Tad. He's also at ease and natural in his second scene, using a light touch and wearing a yellow turtleneck in a scene with Larry Blyden that begins an hour and 46 minutes into the film. What could, potentially, have been his most impactful scene in the movie was a musical interlude in which he sings an Alan Jay Lerner–Burton Lane piece, "Who Is There Among Us Who Knows?" with Babs joining in toward the end.

Nicholson's musical debut was not to be, which very well might have done him a favor given the overall outcome. Lyricist Lerner (who wrote its screenplay!) also "hated the movie" according to the Broadway and Hollywood musical historian. "It's not possible to like it. It's a terrible, terrible movie," declared Kreuger, who largely blames director Vincente Minnelli, whom he felt lost his way over the years.

"He became so affective. Minnelli starts out so well. *Meet Me In St Louis* is undoubtedly the best musical film of the 1940s and some of his other films in that period are so good. But then, he begins to get carried away with his own brilliance, and I think defeats himself."

What might have been his most significant scene in *On a Clear Day You Can See Forever* (1970) was a musical interlude in which Nicholson sings an Alan Jay Lerner/Burton Lane piece, "Who Is There Among Us Who Knows?" with Barbra Streisand joining in toward the end. It wound up on the cutting room floor.

As one of the country's foremost experts on musicals, Miles shared his observation that Minnelli was "a very peculiar man, very eccentric. I don't think he could have been very eccentric at the beginning. I think he just kept getting more and more peculiar."[6]

When the hopelessly dated and painfully un-mod Minnelli film faced the reality of the marketplace, Nicholson's big singing scene was amongst the material cut as the original roadshow format was scrapped (thus allowing audiences to escape the theater earlier). Oh, but what might have been....

* * *

Oddly, this uneasy combination of anachronistic musical and forced coolness was in production at the same time that the legitimate hippie masterpiece *Easy Rider* was mired in its protracted editing process. Unusual in its synthesis of the hippie exploitation with the biker exploitation, yet transcending any identification with genre pictures, *Easy Rider* is the film that delivered the counterculture into the culture. A biker movie becomes an art film. A hippie flick becomes a festival darling. Director Dennis Hopper and lead Peter Fonda become names in their own right, while supporting actor Nicholson *finally* breaks through as an overnight star over a decade after he began trying.

Yet it's a world of contradictions. Hippies are driven by the capitalist need to strike it rich and retire. Bikers don't belong to gangs, but remain unaffiliated. Wyatt's sidekick Billy the Kid isn't a gunslinging outlaw, but a cocaine smuggler.

The pair are alert and thoughtful and caring and mature. Sure, they smoke weed and don't punch a clock, but these longhairs are no revolutionaries. In fact, their Southern lawyer might just be the most liberal, activist and suspicious out of the bunch. Nicholson's George Hanson is gregarious, a glad-hander who thoughtfully questions the notion of freedom. He's a good old boy who's paranoid about outer space beings living among us. He's happy and despondent, spontaneous and vigilant, rambunctious and reserved. Hanson is a complex character. Nicholson portrays him with an intricacy of personality that displays these contradictions realistically and with full force. Fonda admired Nicholson's dedication to getting a handle on his character. "He studied the scene every day. There are photos of Jack sitting in a field with a script in his hands. He told me he was ready, and he must have told Hopper the same thing."[7]

Nicholson doesn't just talk about freedom, he embodies it. Hopper and Fonda, Billy and Wyatt, ride in tandem, Hopper alone and performing stunts and Fonda together with Nicholson—who performs a more poetic and meaningful stunt. He waves his hands like a happy and leisurely bird. Jack *is* the easy rider (note the singular form of the noun used in a film title about two characters).

In these moments, he lives freedom, contradicting the fact that the scene was filmed the day after freedom died a little more when Bobby Kennedy was shot.

For Nicholson the actor, he is flying free ... free from dead-end roles such as *On a Clear Day* or any further TV work like *Bronco* and *The Andy Griffith Show*. When rednecks pound his character to death after the second campfire scene (with his murder played out stylized, with the cutting reminiscent of the *Psycho* shower scene) each blow—"THWUMP!"—kills a paycheck like *Ensign Pulver* and—"THWACK!"—finishes off the dreaded reliance on television as career filler. The Nicholson who was ready to give up acting and pursue producing, directing and writing, was violently put out of his misery. The Jack who was ready to become "Jack" had been freed from George Hanson's corpse, the dead making way for the rise of a vigorous and living career.

* * *

Before this decade-in-the-making overnight success, however, there were more biker flicks to be made. In this tale of two motorcycle movies, *Hells Angels on Wheels* represents one of the best of the genre and *Rebel Rouser* among the worst.

Richard Rush used an active, in-motion direction with real people in the street and a *lot* of bikers, courtesy of his genius decision to enlist actual MCs (Motorcycle Clubs) for the film. Using the Hells Angels provided P.R., realism and credibility, quantity, plus a much tougher looking biker than supplied by Central Casting.

Perhaps the most famous of Angels, Sonny Barger, told me that the club voted to do it after having been offered work on other films and turning them down. He recalled the filming as fun and commented that Nicholson seemed a natural. "It was really funny, because everybody from every other chapter thought he was from another chapter. He was that good." Asked if that was due to how he handled a bike, Barger firmly corrected, "It was because of how he handled himself. He fit right into the program."[8]

There's an immediacy and a closeness to the shooting style, so you become part of the MC, involved rather than simply viewing. For instance, Leslie Kovacs shoots from in front of a car, creating some shots similar to what he later did on *Easy Rider*, traveling past a three-quarter camera view while in motion.

Rush called it "the first picture that was really representative of me … when I finally caught on to what it is that I had to do to make my pictures unique and mine." Making the film personal started with liberating himself from the script and using a good deal of improvisation.[9]

Though second billed to Adam Roarke (Buddy), Nicholson has the strongest role as Poet, with the greatest dramatic range and situational opportunities. He's the explosive Jack in his first scene when he pushes and yells at his boss at the gas station. He shows intensity in an introductory confrontation scene with Bull (Richard Anders) and the Angels. More instinctive in this set-up than in the fight itself, his natural acting strength recovers when Buddy breaks up the fight. He's part-sensitive, part-heel, in a nice moment with Sabrina Scharf (Shill). As she plays nurse to his injuries after the fight, Nicholson betrays the character's self-conscious, true reaction to his own vulnerability. He transitions from a high-pitched, seemingly spontaneous laugh—catches himself—then plays it down to a tougher persona while going straight into pickup mode. Met with a less than enthusiastic response, Poet remains tough as the sneering, drawling, ambivalent antihero.

Three overlapping emotions in one sequence makes sense for a character named Poet, but is not necessarily an expectation for such a low-budget exploitation flick.

A later scene with Scharf features another dance from emotion to emotion.

Intensely erotic in its intimate depiction of their kissing, lovemaking at Shill's place becomes playful as Poet asserts his brighter, smiling self when interrupted by her roommate. He's good at playing it coy and embarrassed in front of the intruding woman. Then he rejects Shill because he's square and can't do it in front of someone else.

Complex relationship scenes like those with Sabrina Scharf anticipate a much later strength as mature romantic comedy lead in films such as *Something's Gotta Give* and *As Good as It Gets*.

Gary Kent, who was stunt coordinator and played a small part in the film, doubled Nicholson in his fight scenes (which Kent also staged). He observed Nicholson work on his character. "I became aware of how really dedicated he was, because he spent a lot of time on Poet to make that work, and when I watch it and see that's tough to do, knowing so many tough guys and not a lot of them are really poetic, but Jack pulled that off."

The vantage point of an important member of the crew, yet one with certain, isolated responsibilities, gave Kent a special insight into the process. Over 30 years later, he still marveled when relating to me, "It was a different type of approach and it surprised me because it was a totally different character and a hard character to play because he had to be a biker and he had to be sensitive and tough at the same time and make it work. That was the first time I became aware that Jack had no fear about taking difficult situations and playing someone who wasn't the handsome lead but someone who was almost a character actor."

The three- to four-week shoot gave Gary the chance to work with one of his favorite people, director Richard Rush. "They just loved him, including Jack, and so it made it all worthwhile. Dick was so into it and trying so hard to make it something other than just a biker flick and we all knew that."[10]

"I overlaid a Faustian theme," Rush revealed. "My hero was quoting spontaneous lines like, 'Better to rule in hell than serve in heaven.'"[11]

Kent and Hells Angel Barger did remember Nicholson's skill with a bike differently. When asked if he and the club worked with Nicholson beforehand to study riding, Sonny tossed that aside, saying, "Absolutely not, he just fell into it and done it. He seemed like he could ride it. You gotta remember, he's a good actor and the guy was good at what he does."[12] Nicholson favorably impressed the Angels, especially when compared to *The Wild Angels* star Peter Fonda. Likely, the bias against Peter, a rich kid and son of big star Henry Fonda, worked against the future Captain America, about whom Barger shrugged, "The guys never liked him and thought he didn't know what he was doing on a bike."[13] According to Kent, "Jack was not that experienced with a bike … and he never did look like he owned the bike instead of the bike owning him."

Kent summed up Jack's nuanced work on *Hells Angels on Wheels* by commenting on his "absolute dedication and seriousness to the film, not his career. He was very much into the film and the authenticity of his part."[14]

Nicholson has another impressive sequence in which he moves from victimized to vengeful and then to regret and fear. A punch-up by mateys and swabbies oddly anticipates *The Last Detail*. After being beat up by four Navy grunts, he returns shamed. When he's helped by the MC after the beating, he looks down a lot—serious, thoughtful, conflicted. He again is the sensitive Poet. Later he gets his revenge in beating up a sailor who dies of his injuries ("I cooked one of them"). It is not a triumphant act. Poet's face goes slack at an Angel after-party, as we witness reality and real morals kicking in. Poet remains clearly troubled through the climactic fight scene between Poet and Buddy against cowboys in a drained pool. When the police come to break it up, the outmanned but triumphant pair climb out of the pool and Poet has a precious moment shaking hands with a cop and gesturing in victory, fingers a-wiggling (likely an ad-libbed touch).

The ending blows it, however, as Buddy is upset at Poet for dropping his weapon during their own confrontation. Poet walks away, so Buddy flies his bike through a window to literally crash and burn, leaving Jack with a quizzical and lost look, as if thinking, "How can a movie this lively and good, real and unforced, end this way—so deflated, poor, faked, and pushed?" There's something of a parallel between this ending (sudden and unexpected, resulting in a violent death of a main character) and that of *Chinatown*. Both shockers left Nicholson abandoned and alone, the conflicted survivor. The difference is that by the time he portrayed J.J. Gittes, Nicholson could master the reaction to unbelievable disaster, no longer dazed and confused but torn between being the witness and the victim.

Overall, *Hells Angels on Wheels* remains a satisfying filmic piece of work. Gritty characters, real Hells Angels, innovative cinematography, energetic direction and a rich story elevate this film out of its genre. Not famous, yet an achievement, this low-budget gem owes its enduring quality to three men and one woman: Richard Rush, László Kovács, Jack Nicholson and Sabrina Scharf.

Gary Kent remembered Jack

> asking questions of the stunt guys like, "Is this phony if I throw the punch this way?" or "Would it be phony if I did this?" He was always looking for something that would make what he was doing authentic. He would ask about himself, not that he was insecure, but he was always reaching to make it more authentic. That was what impressed me about Jack and made me think that he's gonna go somewhere, because he seemed more serious about acting and the project than he did about being a star.[15]

This film is the qualitative opposite of *Rebel Rousers*, filmed the same year but only released three years later to cash in on Nicholson's *Easy Rider* fame. In *Hells Angels on Wheels*, the violence and sex seem real; the happen-

8. Hippies and Hogs and Horses

Rebel Rousers (1970) has more talent than it deserves, a contrived bikesploitation rip-off of Brando's *The Wild One*. Jack, center, is shown with Diane Ladd (then pregnant with actress Laura Dern) and frequent Nicholson collaborator Bruce Dern.

ings, body paintings, drugs, effects from the drugs, the color and action, movement and character associations—are all real. None of this would be true of *Rebel Rousers*.

Rebel Rousers is a contrivance, true only as an exploitation of the biker stereotype in order to present an overcooked morality play. The establishing premise is directly ripped off from *The Wild One*. Since they are bikers, of course they're going to terrorize a small town, with action centered around a diner. So far, so lifted. Bruce Dern is the Brando gang-leader J.J. Weston, so it's only natural that Jack homage Lee Marvin's *Wild One* outfit with wide, horizontal black and white stripes along with a Michael Nesmith–style wool hat.

There's so much talent for so little movie. In retrospect, it's amazing that this nothing low-budget flick offers Academy Award winner Jack Nicholson and nominees Bruce Dern and Diane Ladd; notable character actors Cameron Mitchell and (Harry) Dean Stanton; legendary cinematographer László Kovács (credited as Leslie); and even Laura Dern (also an Oscar nominee), who makes an in-the-womb cameo with mom Ladd and dad Dern.

Pushing the obvious moralizing further, it seems cause-and-effect that since the gang smokes pot that they would attack a pregnant woman (Ladd) and her companion (Mitchell) for no reason. The action-heavy emphasis and character proneness for violence lends a heavy-handed, overstated tone that rings hollow and false. In contrast to *Hells Angels* pro Dick Rush, this movie was the sole directorial effort of Martin B. Cohen, who also co-scripted.

Some isolated flashes of character truth break through. In the first scene at The Cantina, Nicholson's in the background playing to a buxom blonde until he suddenly brushes her off as if she's a bug. When a fight breaks out between bikers on the beach, it has a feel of spontaneity and truth, while Nicholson (as Bunny) fits in as expert on his bike, just as Sonny Barger related.

A believable moment occurs when Bunny tells J.J., "Don't look at me with that grin on your face," before they both break character. Later in that same sequence, Nicholson comes close to introducing his *Five Easy Pieces* dog bark as he performs a little of the out-of-control Jack.

Actor Robert Dix explained that Dern and Nicholson "did an awful lot of ad libbing on this movie. They kind of rewrote the script because it wasn't much of a script in the first place, and what they did was better than what was there."[16] One such likely ad lib was when Bunny performs a mock wedding ceremony using a Harley-Davidson manual as the Bible while he has his cap completely covering his face.

Bunny's death was a dramatic highlight, and a fine touch of visual style. He died like an animal, shown from behind and dropping from a crouch to fully lying on the ground, with his striped pants from that perspective making him look like a dying tiger. The last shot of Bruce Dern as J.J., defeated and kneeling in the sand in front of the ocean surf, somewhat foreshadows the actor's climactic scene in *Coming Home*.

Dern explained the early struggle he shared with Nicholson and Dennis Hopper. They were reviled as Method types, "but whether we were in the [Actors] Studio or not, we all basically had the same principles, which were: You really look at somebody, you really listen to what they're saying, and everything comes out of that—comes out of what's really going on at the moment."[17]

Dix underscored Nicholson's commitment to such a weak show, recalling, "Jack was an interesting guy, but what some people may not know is that he was a very dedicated actor. He was most sincere, very conscientious of his work.... He was one of the reasons that the *esprit de corps* was good and how we stayed in the groove as a production team had a lot to do with Jack and Bruce Dern."[18]

* * *

Nicholson's most important westerns were the back-to-back collaborations with Monte Hellman, though his most famous was the Brando oddity

8. Hippies and Hogs and Horses 131

The Missouri Breaks. Nicholson co-produced the two Hellman existential classics and wrote *Ride in the Whirlwind* while Adrien Joyce (aka Carole Eastman) wrote *The Shooting*.

The relationships started early, in acting class with Jeff Corey. Millie Perkins was there after her debut in the title role of *The Diary of Anne Frank*, several years before they worked together on these westerns:

> I worked a lot with Jack on exercises because I was a strong person and Jack needed a female opposite. He needed somebody that was not intimidated by him, as I was not.
> Monte and Jack had history together somehow with Roger Corman and AIP ... and when they sat down and decided to make a couple movies, they had a meeting with Carole when she wrote *The Shooting* and Jack was going to write the other one, and I think it was a secret that Roger financed it.[19]

Corman financed two features with much of the same crew on the same location in Utah. When *The Shooting* finished, *Ride in the Whirlwind* began. Stuntman extraordinaire Kent recalled,

> Jack impressed me because most of the problems that a producer would run into on a really low-budget film, a disgruntled crew, airplanes when you need silence, Jack handled and he handled very well. He and Monte did it with grace and diplomacy because we had some pretty cranky people, although basically it was a fairly happy set—but is was Jack who would represent the company as producer and then he would turn around and be an actor.[20]

The *Shooting* features Nicholson as a creepy sociopath who sees killing as a job, but a job to be relished. Perkins portrays a relentless Woman with No Name who cares only about vengeance for her murdered family and becomes evil herself. She told me, "I just instinctively knew what the right thing to do was and I felt I knew who the characters were and I went out and did it. I didn't have any artistic plan other than just instinct. We finished the one film and we immediately started on the next film."[21]

The next film was scripted by Nicholson, who wrote or co-wrote five films released between 1963 and 1968, yet wrote only one other throughout the subsequent decades. He's third above the title in the credits and plays unwitting young outlaw sidekick Wes with a relaxed and understated style, using his *Easy Rider* accent a couple of years before that production. Twenty-five minutes into the movie, he's shown in close-up as shots ring out, though he looks pretty calm for somebody being shot at.

The early scenes between Wes and cohort Vern (Cameron Mitchell) seem like a Method standoff. Rupert Crosse, another member of the cowboy gang who is apprehended, is shown with a rope around his neck, an interesting social commentary in Nicholson's script given the context of 1965. Perkins is not seen until that era's version of a home invasion, during which Vern and Wes break into her family's cabin for refuge.

They're outlaws, but he's really an innocent, kid-like when Millie's character Abigail brings them food and when Wes shows his obvious delight in eating it. Jack plays it wide-eye and exclaims, "That's good!" with an open expression like an overgrown kid.

After they eat in the family cabin, Wes leaves Vern to accompany Abigail on her chores in a charming courtin' scene that combines horses, flirting, vigilantes, father and hanging.

They together depict backwardness and awkwardness, but without overdoing it. "I thought he did really well," Millie said. "I really liked the way he did that. Neither of them [the characters] were too bright and Jack was a guy who wanted out of there. He did a very good job of bringing a nice, balanced performance to what was required of him, and that was somebody who was in the right place at the wrong time."[22]

Gary Kent talked about the extensive preparation. "I thought they'd done their homework and these were tough times and they were true to that and Jack spent a lot of time in the library before we went up to shoot, reading about those times and studying those times."

Low-budget as the films were, the filmmakers truly cared about the reality they brought to the screen. Kent said, "Monte and Jack both cared a lot about this film, that it be authentic and that impressed me with the bleakness of it, of the surroundings and the location, that little valley that the family lived in, and I just thought when we were filming, 'These are really honest films.'"[23]

Talk about honest: Who would write a scene in which the only thing that happens over an extended period of time, an honest and real depiction of nothing happening—is a game of checkers while hearing somebody hitting the same tree stump over and over and over? Nicholson did, on this film, and it's not a fleeting transitional moment but a true, human scene that's given enough time (non-narrative time at that) to illustrate the type of life people experienced at that time in that place. We see a slow and uncluttered life, devoid of all of the activities and distractions of modern times, and without the need to fill every nanosecond with three things at once.

Another departure from the ordinary in Nicholson's screenplay was a dream sequence. That's not something ordinarily considered western material and certainly not common to the genre, but it nevertheless helps expand on the character psychology.

Because the members of the family become real people, it's all the more shocking when Abigail's father is killed. Yet she shows no visible reaction aside from subtly drooping eyes, a nuanced touch that comments on the uncertainty of the times while diverging from an expected melodramatic flair that would have undermined the truth Nicholson was seeking.

Perkins embodies that reality by appropriating the walk of her chickens for her character. She's out in the middle of nowhere, seen by no one, and judged by nobody. This young woman has no need for the type of affectation afforded people who need to make an impression. There is no impression to be made, so her most direct influence were her chickens. "I started thinking about the fact that what does she have to identify with—her mother, her father or the animals?" explained Perkins. "She probably loved the chickens as a little girl and identifies with them. There was no affectation. There was no idea about how she was supposed to be; she just was."[24]

Identifying with, and walking like, chickens was an adept interpretation to see on a pair of quickie westerns. But immersion and character energy were hallmarks of the shoot for Perkins and Nicholson, as Kent remembers. "Jack was so serious into this character, that when he was on camera, he was not only believable, but I could tell he was really inhabiting the guy, and I think Cameron fell into that and they worked well together." The legendary stuntman saw Nicholson as "an extremely confident guy, on- or off-camera. The second film, *Ride in the Whirlwind*, was much closer in character to the real Jack. That person was half naïve, but he wasn't going to be pushed around by anybody and was able to wisecrack on his own and come back at you with a good answer." He described the relationship on the set between Jack and Cameron Mitchell: "I'm sure there was some improvisation going on between them, which just made it better as far as I was concerned."[25]

Overall, *Ride in the Whirlwind* has a narrow plot, but there are moments of life that involve the viewer. When Abigail enters the farmhouse in which the pursued pair are hiding, Wes places his hand over her mouth to silence any possible scream. The way he lets go is quite unusual. Rather than the typical, casual lift of the hand, it's almost peeled back, systematically pulling it away with care.

Kent remembered the Nicholson-Mitchell relationship as spontaneous rather than the result of much rehearsal and "primarily just a rapport."[26] Ride with the buddy and save the buddy becomes the principle that's a theme of the movie. They don't always have to get along or even have primary motivations, but that's the way of their world. Ultimately, Vern convinces Wes to leave him behind, leading to an ambiguous getaway at the end, giving Jack the last shot in this film just as he had in its companion, *The Shooting*.

Time after time, those who have worked with Nicholson talk about the research, the intense study and the meticulous attention to details such as living conditions, manner of speaking and especially (as Perkins remembers with good humor and abiding wonder) a near obsession with wardrobe. "Before we went over to Utah, we both went together to Western Costumes and picked out our costumes and even argued over the hat. I think one of us had a hat the other wanted. I said, 'I want that hat,' and he said, 'I want that hat.' But we argued about the costumes while were there and finally ended up choosing them and went to Utah with our costumes and our suitcase."[27]

The importance of wardrobe in creating a character is perhaps no better illustrated than by Charlie Chaplin, who sought contradiction (baggy pants-tight coat, small hat-large shoes) when devising his Little Tramp. "I had no idea of the character," Chaplin remembered. "But the moment I was dressed, the clothes and the makeup made me feel the person he was. I began to know him, and by the time I walked onto the stage he was fully born."[28]

* * *

Hats and wardrobe play an important part in how we react to Nicholson's western with Marlon Brando, *The Missouri Breaks*. Much was made at the time about Brando's broad Irish accent and strange, ever-changing clothing. From handkerchief headgear to frock and bonnet, the former Sky Masterson appeared to be playing around in another genre—a *Guys and Dolls* around the campfire—shifting from Irish revenuer to western priest seemingly at whim. Critics lambasted him for not caring, for not taking the role seriously while accepting the paycheck. Audiences were bewildered, shaken by what was perceived as Brando's breaking the fourth wall as part of some bored actor's insider joke. Randy Quaid related to me that the shoot featured many strange experiences, not least of which was "Marlon Brando in a field by himself doing a 'rain dance' for an hour."[29] Director Arthur Penn called the character ephemeral, a chameleon in permanent disguise, so "he's got to be different every time we see him."[30]

However, taken without the coloring of expectation or the context of movie "realism," it makes sense. Brando's Lee Clayton is a mystery, enigmatic and effective. Clayton keeps Nicholson's Tom Logan (and everyone else in the film) off-balance thanks to this idiosyncratic behavior.

Jack underplays to counterprogram Brando's overplaying, going for real life against Clayton as bigger than life. That intended contrast makes sense.

Brando was somewhat insensitive when discussing the film. "Poor Jack Nicholson," began his sarcastic assessment of how Nicholson remained low-key to concede to Brando the bigger impression. "He's right at the center, cranking the whole thing out while I'm zipping around like a firefly."[31]

The Missouri Breaks presents a more matured Nicholson approach to comedy within the western idiom, toned down, with a more natural yet guttural and nasally voice compared with *Goin' South* from two years later. Against John Belushi, Danny DeVito, Christopher Lloyd and Veronica Cartwright in *Goin' South*, he chooses to play it big and loose, while against the *Wild One* rebel and the *Streetcar* Kowalski, he knows he must pull it down and draw it in tighter.

Marlon is mannered, with much "business" beyond the physical. In the first meeting on film of Nicholson and Brando, Nicholson wins the acting battle, using subtlety and range vs. personality and force. When Logan talks

8. Hippies and Hogs and Horses

The Missouri Breaks is most famous for its pairing of the bizarre Marlon Brando with acolyte Nicholson. Director Arthur Penn admired the latter's reality in the setting, commenting that Jack "had a very real sense of look and feel (for Westerns)."

about not having a chance when shooting at 500 feet and not looking in the eyes of his target, his character knows what he's talking about. The actor shows he knows and that he cares, employing a human restraint.

Brando is billed first, but Nicholson was clearly the lead, entering on a horse and riding toward the camera just as he did in *Goin' South*. Jack's heroines in both films were new to the screen, introducing Kathleen Lloyd here and Mary Steenburgen two years later.

Without Brando, Nicholson allows himself to open up. He fakes a laugh and becomes animated in an active push to choke back tears when told a gang member "kinda strangled for a while" being hanged. He's mercurial and emotional in response to Calvin's (Harry Dean Stanton) resolute seriousness when delivering a great monologue about a dog and his dream about moving to Canada.

Director Penn admired Nicholson's reality in the setting, amazed at how well the actor rode and the comfort he embodied. "He had a very real sense of look and feel [for westerns]. There is a degree of authenticity about Jack that just belongs to that earth."³²

Nicholson's range under Penn is quite revelatory given the circumstances and the superstar showdown. He breaks down with true touching emotion after Little Tod (Randy Quaid) is dragged by rope through the raging Missouri River. He's also vulnerable reacting to the sexual forwardness of Kathleen Lloyd as Jane Braxton, like someone pointing a gun at him. When she cries in rejection, Tom softens and lets down his guard, a nice transition of character feeling. Later, he loses his musculature when he sees the shot-up face and figure of Calvin, reflecting a real event as it in the actors' true-life friendship.

But it's the interplay with Brando that gets the attention. Their final confrontation, as the Brogue Brando takes a bath, creates a reversal of roles and an intriguing switch of styles. Brando shrinks. He becomes vulnerable and underplays. Nicholson grows. He becomes tough and blustery because he's finally in charge. Logan kills Clayton with such calm, steady of eye and safe from interfering emotion, completely on task to the degree that pushing his tongue firmly between his teeth is the only sign of effort expended and strength applied.

Critic Richard Schickel provided an alternative viewpoint about his fellow reviewers' disapproval. Yes, they couldn't believe that heavyweights Brando, Nicholson and Arthur Penn "indulged" themselves "in such a looseygoosey way." The break with the western convention was the break too far, with this subversion justified if viewed as converted into another genre entirely. "*The Missouri Breaks* may play weirdly as a Western, but it makes perfect sense as a horror picture…. [T]hink of the prairie as a big haunted house … of Brando as a monster haunting it, popping out of the shadows periodically, to bump off one of the innocents who have invaded his domain," making the picture both coherent and enjoyable.³³

Penn saw it as "convoluted … away from the flat-out face-to-face shoot-out," with a boldness to change expectations, something that ultimately disappointed the studio and the audience.³⁴

* * *

This accomplished but little-remembered film is many dusty and parched miles from Jack's first film western, 13 years before as Will Brocious in *The Broken Land*. In *Broken Land*, he has a small but solid role as an outlaw who's first seen being fed by and flirting with a girl while in jail.

Though a minor character in a minor role, this early Nicholson has a nice way with his lines, shifting from irony and sarcasm to persuasive and personable. With lots of teeth and loads of accent, the actor still looks good in close-up and delivers dialogue convincingly.

8. Hippies and Hogs and Horses

He shows understanding and tenderness to a simple-minded character who's beaten and thrown into jail for stealing a necklace to give as a gift. Brocious makes for a sympathetic character, urging the others to band together and break out of jail.

Jack's relaxed and not forced, looking natural on his horse and holding his rifle, then gentle and big-brotherish with the simpleton. Inexperienced as he is, Nicholson comes across as helpful without being condescending, and then youthfully powerful when the bad sheriff knifes the man in the back.

* * *

"The Law" is bad. The outlaws are not. They're only doing their job, just as Nicholson and Cameron Mitchell's outlaws meant no harm when invading Millie Perkins' family farm in *Ride in the Whirlwind*. Captain America and Billy the Kid weren't evil in *Easy Rider*, but they blew it because they just didn't fit in and upset some squares who blew them away. ACLU lawyer George Hanson could protect them against "The Law," but he couldn't protect them nor himself against the locals. Violent death also ends *Psych-Out*, *Hells Angels on Wheels*, *Rebel Rousers*, *The Shooting* and *The Missouri Breaks*.

Living outside the law is living with danger. Living outside of straight society is even more dangerous. Nicholson lives inside the roles of outsiders, the disaffected and out-of-place. It's hard to imagine now, but hippies were hated when these films were made. Longhairs were outlaws and outsiders, deserving only of contempt and attack. "They had it coming" was an oft-repeated chorus, referring to DNC protesters or Kent State innocents. Bikers weren't yet yuppies and certainly weren't hippies. They were feared as violent gangs of thugs and drug dealers. Western outlaws were horse thieves and held up stagecoaches. The quintessential Jack is the quintessential outlaw, outside of society and inside the biker bar, the hippie club or the broken-down saloon.

9

From Ballbusters to Heart Attacks

They are mutually flaccid. They seek assistance, Jonathan from coaxing and role play and Harry from chemistry and Viagra. They are two men who take opposite routes in their relationships with the opposite sex. Jonathan slides into a pathetic parody of sex while Harry grows into a mature manifestation of love.

In Mike Nichols' *Carnal Knowledge,* Jonathan encourages his best friend and roomie Sandy to pursue Susan—only to steal her for himself. In Nancy Meyers' *Something's Gotta Give,* Harry is a hip-hop mogul who pursues Marin—only to be rejected as he decides to go after her mother instead. The contrast of ballbuster victim to heart attack victim presents a contrasting direction in which one man descends into an impotent hell while another is elevated into an enlightened heaven.

First, Jonathan (Nicholson) is established in voiceover during the opening credits as the more sensitive compared with Sandy (Art Garfunkel). The first time we see him at a college mixer (in the 1940s), Jack looks like the guy we first saw in the Corman movie *The Raven* and on TV's *The Andy Griffith Show,* his simulation both bright-eyed and bewigged. Somehow, in the early shots, Nicholson (whose tallest reported height is 5' 9½" and Garfunkel (only a six-footer though believed much taller due to his towering over partner Paul Simon's 5' 3") appear to be the same height. No matter, they both look young and convince as young.

More important than appearing young is Nicholson's portrayal of Jonathan's naiveté as college chums after Sandy's first date with Candice Bergen in the role of ultimate WASP Susan. This sets up the emotional downfall and psychological decay. Jonathan turns devious when turning on his friend with Susan, appearing more edged and angular while acting less open and relaxed toward his friend.

There's a classic screen composition and inspired direction when Susan is humped in a field. Only when Jonathan dismounts and turns over on his back is it revealed that *he* is the rival who "gets in" first. From "tell-me-everything" friends to deceive-at-all-costs rivals: Jonathan treats Sandy with patronizing distance, becoming the *Five Easy Pieces*, furrowed-brow Jack as he pressures Susan to break up with Sandy. He then has his first Jacksplosion as he yells at Bergen to tell him his thoughts—an emotional put-down with emphatic physical overtones.

Our introduction to Harry Sanborn in *Something's Gotta Give* presents a rich mix of similarity and distinction. Harry is an older man, yet he shares Jonathan's single-minded pursuit of the young and attractive female, as much for the psychology and triumph as for the physical pleasure. With convertible, chick, cigar and sunglasses, Nicholson's opening-scene drive with Amanda Peet (as Marin Barry) is clearly a winking play at our perception of the real man. As the lithe and playful Peet strips off her clothes on the way into her mother's summer house, Nicholson does not necessarily have to stretch his acting muscles to appear to enjoy the attention and the prospects.

The get ... the game ... both men live for the temporal win, showing off to other men and showing themselves they still have what it takes to make it with women who get noticed. Harry is different from Jonathan, however. Harry doesn't take it all too seriously, in it for fun and frolic, while Jonathan sees the dark side of the conquest. Obsession is different from attraction, and Jonathan's *Carnal Knowledge* is—as the title indicates—more legalistic and clinical than Harry's frisky, dirty older man.

Harry's obscene swirling of tongue on his ice cream and devilish leer in the town's grocery store is pure Jack, a fun inside joke about the actor's image, and the type of light playfulness of which Jonathan could never have been capable.

When Jonathan becomes involved with Bobbie, introduced at an ice rink with Ann-Margret displaying her native Swedish talents, Nicholson presents his character's second phase, pinched and cynical with all openness and brightness extinguished and all emotion and expression tamped. Still young, this man has been deadened. In an office reaction shot, Jonathan looks like what we later see as the Warren Schmidt who waits and waits to leave on his last day of his job.

Wooing Bobbie reveals Jonathan as a guy going through the motions when making his moves, calculating as a tax attorney should be. For the first and only time in the movie, Nicholson's voice becomes forced and phony after Ann-Margret's character suggests they shack up. He cannot handle it, but he also cannot handle the betting odds against this relationship.

Nichols uses striking back and forth POV monologues that peer intently and unblinkingly into the characters as the best way to reveal the contrasts between what the two friends say and what they truly feel. When Jonathan

Jonathan wanted to get Bobbie into bed. He just didn't want her to stay there all the time. In *Carnal Knowledge*, Nicholson shows Jonathan's increasing anger and frustration in response to Bobbie (Ann-Margret) and her lazy, slovenly ways.

tells Sandy that Bobbie's a lot of fun, his dead look and total lack of expression betray a more foreboding future and the dissipating soul of the man.

Nicholson portrays the slide of this man, into his own emptiness, a place where nothing exists but conquest that becomes less victorious as it becomes less frequent, and sex that becomes less sexy as it becomes less successfully attainable.

Is this solipsism? Has Jonathan descended into a narrowing, echoed interior? Or is this merely the period's awakening to the "male chauvinist pig" syndrome? Screenwriter Jules Feiffer told playwright Lillian Hellman that *Carnal Knowledge* was a "picture about men's hatred of women," adding that "all heterosexual men hate women."[1] Nichols revealed that the film reflected his own "disastrous second marriage" and that it portrays the relationships between men and women with "only three types of scenes—fights, seductions and negotiations."[2]

Two scenes show Jonathan's anger and frustration at Bobbie's do-nothing lifestyle (feeding his stereotype of women) brought to life. The first is an extended confrontation scene with Ann-Margret as he tries to dress to go out, that is classic Nicholson—big and raucous, physical and loud, emotional and powerful. It's huge but not over-the-top, a "rave-up" worthy of Clapton-era Yardbirds, building in pace and intensity to a fever pitch that is released, only to build again to a torrid blast of pure energy and abandon. The second is her suicide attempt, where his reaction was over-the-top, forced yet unrealized. Completely lacking in empathy, Jonathan's response centers only on how the act affects himself. Bobbie is not the subject of concern, but the object of derision.

Ann-Margret referred to her character as "this pitiful woman, this doormat for abuse, who'd spent her life attracted to the wrong kind of man." The actress became Bobbie through the process of rehearsal during three weeks of experimenting on scenes, "reading them one way, then another" with Nicholson, Garfunkel, Bergen, Nichols and Feiffer.[3]

Both Jonathan and Harry experience defining moments, points in their respective lives that direct their destinies. Jonathan's moment is a "ballbuster" while Harry's is a heart attack.

Jonathan's defining moment is pathetic. His braggadocio in presenting a slide show called "Ballbusters on Parade" to Sandy and his girlfriend Jennifer (Carol Kane) makes the self-pitying victimhood of feminine guile more about himself than about his purported abusers. Jonathan remains oblivious to the notion that others could not sympathize with his failures (or even care about them, for that matter), and that the choice of "ballbusters" as his theme would serve as a naked commentary on his own blind illusions as well as a cue to his intractable bigotry. Jonathan's impassive slug of whiskey underscores appropriate detachment, and an arc to nothingness.

He doesn't even realize that Jennifer, let alone his friend Sandy, might find "ballbusters" offensive. Jonathan has sunken so far into his own world that he cannot consider that anyone else would be put off by such an affront. In fact, he's as triumphant about "ballbusters" as they are turned off. Interestingly this incident was staged and shot, spare and stilted like a Kubrick scene from *2001* or *A Clockwork Orange*.

Harry's defining moment is in the immediate sense life-threatening, and in the ultimate sense life-changing. It is also funny. Jack's heart attack scene represents another example of how he not only doesn't care that about being the attractive movie star, but actually goes out of his way to look terrible. He's slimy, resembling a beached whale, and his hair is everywhere but where it should be. As he is wheeled in and viewed on a gurney from above, Nicholson's eyes go back under the lids and he appears almost a parody of his electroshock portrayal in *Cuckoo's Nest*.

Stumbling and flopping around on his feet, bare-assed in his hospital gown, Jack is classic comedy. He's very "giving" and performs a breastfeeding piece of business with Diane Keaton that's like an in-control drunk—not too broad, but just right in this comedic piece. They play it like they are about to waltz as she moves to hold him up from falling. The "little boy" look he gives while lowering his head and then looking up to announce he has to pee is precious.

As Jonathan sinks, Harry rises. Jonathan becomes heavy and burdensome and tiresome, while Harry becomes light, vulnerable and engaging. Jonathan closes himself inward, especially more distant from women. This, in clear contrast to how Harry opens himself beyond his glamorous world and young beauties to appreciate people more and appreciate (perhaps for the first time) the special appeal of a woman as mature as himself.

Nicholson has attained a comfortable state with comic action, reaching only just enough instead of wildly grabbing for too much. Funny moments no longer have to be telegraphed, signaled like a pitcher who unknowingly indicates an oncoming curveball to the watchful batter; a quarterback giving away a pass play; or a boxer cueing his opponent about a left hook.

There's a small moment, as he prepares to leave the hospital, when he's truly hurt because Amanda Peet only kisses him on the cheek ("Down to the cheek," as Harry interprets it). Another more celebrated juncture occurs when Keaton strips, mirroring the scene of her daughter at the beginning of the movie. Jack accidentally sees her naked and flops around, struggling to cover his eyes while bouncing off the wall. His use of his flitting hands plays a strong part of his business in the role, as he flicks and flitters and waves and weaves in a dance of deft physical comedy.

Sometimes, comparisons can be constructive and enlightening. Other times, they can be hurtful and pain-inducing. The contrasting destinies of the male lead characters in *Carnal Knowledge* and *Something's Gotta Give* are of the sort that invite a wince and provoke a difficult swallow. There is no shining of a sunny and hopeful light on Jonathan's future. He shrinks into the darkness while Harry grows in the sunshine.

Compare the charming scene when Nicholson and Keaton walk on the beach and talk about each other with the troubling scene when Louise the prostitute (Rita Moreno) attempts to bring the flaccid Jonathan to life. Jack and Diane have a great interplay that is smooth and casual, unforced and with a little healthy sarcasm that's underscored by their grudgingly growing affection.

In shocking counterpoint, Nicholson looks like Jack Torrance at his worst upon entering Louise's apartment. An actor has to be willing to give all to the role and be a man who's confident enough in his manliness to dive into the final, ritualistic and pathetic scene in *Carnal Knowledge*.

Moreno told me that the best performers with whom she has worked were, in order, Marlon Brando in *The Night of the Following Day* and Nicholson in this film—calling him "extraordinarily talented."[4]

Louise had to go through elaborate playacting, carefully devised to help Jonathan feel confident and manly and capable. Instead, Diane and Nicholson have lunch on the beach in a scene without audible dialogue, looking beautiful together, both all in white and both desirable and desiring of each other. Louise and Jonathan play roles of sexual potency; Erica and Harry are spirited and mature, beyond the need to play games yet playful enough to flirt and be romantic. Their beauty belies the Hollywood cliché of sexiness as equal to youth and perfection.

There is nothing romantic going on in Louise's flat. Everything is base and sad (except for the performances). Louise is knowing and calculating, yet she supplies a tinge of care and concern about Jonathan. There is complete power in Jonathan's weakness, and fulfillment in his emptiness. He is slumped back, inert, and only receiving. He cannot feel, externally or internally, letting Louise do all the surface work. She shows just what a fully realized reaction shot can become, when it's in reaction to the true failure of a real life.

Nichols called *Carnal Knowledge* "the darkest movie I ever made," and a mannerist film that without planning was reminiscent of Jules Feiffer's cartoon panels.[5]

In this sick, staged pantomime of an intimate relationship, Nicholson shows the void, with the most subtle of external clues to Jonathan's inner struggle—a struggle to be alive. Sex was all the character had left, and now he no longer even has that, replaced by an *Invasion of the Body Snatchers*-like pod people of plastic, teleprompted sex play. She's fierce and feeling. He's needy and gasping for the oxygen of emotional life, masterfully rendered in nuanced detail.

The couple in *Something's Gotta Give* could not be further from the transaction depicted in *Carnal Knowledge*. While Erica has a late night dinner in the kitchen after a date with Dr. Julian Mercer (Keanu Reeves), she shares a look with Harry that's touching and priceless, with true depth and feeling. Louise and Jonathan don't even portray a real relationship, with everything surface artifice.

The actor's journey between living as Jonathan and becoming Harry is as interesting as the contrast between the relationships in the films themselves. His transformation in *Carnal Knowledge* is not growth or development but decay and descent. Nicholson's range, successfully playing Jonathan's dark and lost character as well as Harry's enlightened character of self-discovery, is remarkable. His transformation as Harry, from overgrown playboy to sentimental boyfriend, shows a realistic and restrained seemingly casual side to the intense and studied actor. Both roles take a character energy equally vital, but with the energy pointed in different directions and with widely varied styles.

As an actor—romantic or comic or otherwise—he has grown, at times

Harry and Erica are the antithesis of *Carnal Knowledge*'s Jonathan and Bobbie. Jack Nicholson and Diane Keaton portray a healthy, mature relationship through their smooth and casual interplay in *Something's Gotta Give* (2003).

seeming Bogartesque (interesting because of Keaton's co-starring role in Woody Allen's *Play It Again, Sam*) and at others cute and coy, such as when he returns to Keaton's bed after they make love for the first time so he could try "sleeping with her." In another Woody Allen connection, Erica's play about their relationship is very *Annie Hall*.

Nicholson portrays warmth when Harry visits Marin and meets her husband, and even cries in Dr. Mercer's office in a fittingly complex manner that's both softly comic in its misery and touchingly vulnerable in its dramatic tenderness.

All this is so far removed from his on-screen destruction of a bright, appealing young man 32 years earlier. Nicholson drags Jonathan from an open and lively college student to a defeated and deflated clown in a way so painful yet so beautiful in its ugly truth. Disillusionment decays his character completely, as physically as Jonathan's spine seems to disappear when he slides down on Louise's couch. That couch is no place for psychoanalysis, but one for psychosis. In portraying a feeling that's less than nothing, Nicholson makes us feel everything.

His Harry shows a different kind of connection in a different kind of relationship. When he parts with Erica, as Keaton leaves La Grand Colbert restaurant with Keanu Reeves, it is sweet … and bittersweet. He cries as he laughs in regret and self-reflection on the Pont d'Arcole bridge over the Seine. When Erica returns, you believe it's true that he's 63 years old and in love for the first time in his life.

Harry comes alive after a heart attack. He feels more and feels more deeply, allowing himself to love and to make love, and without retreating afterwards. Jonathan cannot feel, he has no depth, and he cannot perform as a man. His balls were not only busted, but tossed to piranhas. By himself.

10

The Developing Delinquent

A malt shop, night club, drive-in and race track can mean burgers, dancing, double features and competition. Or it can mean hostages, rape, attempted rape and manslaughter. The difference is the difference between the "good kids" and the J.D.s.

Names like Jimmy and Weary and Buddy and Johnny sound wholesome enough. But what about Randall P.? Where does the juvenile delinquent go when he is no longer juvenile? You do not want to know.

Like many young actors from the mid–'50s to the early '60s, Nicholson started his career with teens-in-trouble exploitation quickies, B-movies short enough to need another feature to make a legit night of it. A troubled youth, who strays because of the wrong circumstances or the wrong friends, could have gone either way. That youth could have delivered papers and joined the debating team ... or he could have drifted from pranks and scuffles to light shoplifting and heavy gang action and finally to crime and violence, jail and asylum.

What happened to Jimmy Wallace after *The Cry Baby Killer* ends the standoff and gives himself up? Do Weary Reilly and Buddy ever realize what they've done and change how they view and treat women? And does Johnny Varron get out of jail to go back for clean competition and race for all the right reasons?

If the answers aren't positive; if true progress has not been made; if the chip on the shoulder remains firmly in place and attitudes against society, women and authority stay steadfastly counter to the culture, these troubled kids can be rejected, dejected and suspected. They can become Randall Patrick McMurphy.

Nicholson's first Hollywood role was the title character in Roger Corman's production *The Cry Baby Killer*. Jimmy Wallace is beat up by four guys, bullying that sets him on a path from good kid to troubled teen who turns to a gun. Jimmy was cornered by his attackers, and eventually allows himself to be cornered in a storage shed with hostages. Nicholson is intense in this early role, broad and overwrought, as likely to be so due to the nerves of a young and inexperienced actor as it is due to a conscious effort to portray a high-strung kid.

Ed Nelson, who played the TV reporter covering the incident, explained, "It's a big advantage to know what's going on around the set and Jack had never done any films at all." Nelson was less than impressed at the time, adding, "I just found him to be different, he was very inside of himself and I'm not used to that."[1]

Jimmy becomes an unintended J.D., more juvenile than delinquent. He is driven to desperation and Jack plays him in a desperate manner, pushing the explosiveness perhaps more than necessary, but in the end the character just doesn't have killing in him (the movie title is a misnomer) and gives up. Only when ending the standoff does Nicholson let Jimmy Wallace truly relax, an essentially good kid doing the right thing after making a mistake.

His second J.D. character, Johnny Varron, also gives himself up to custody, but only after it's too late.

In less than two years, Nicholson shows so much more poise and personality in *The Wild Ride*, creating a true character rather than simply playing at acting. We also get our first glimpse at the "Jack" we've become accustomed to over the years. The twang, the sneer, the smile, swagger and explosiveness are all there in this early incarnation. Nicholson successfully swings from happy-go-lucky party boy who's also a domineering gang leader to an overconfident womanizer who occasionally betrays vulnerability with other men.

A classic J.D., Johnny has a bad attitude, a chip on his shoulder when it comes to adults and authority. He's snotty to cops and cocky and mercurial with his peers. Though *The Wild Ride* was a quickie teensploitation flick of only 61 minutes, Nicholson's Johnny is fully formed. He's a hot roddin' gang leader with a serious, broodin' 'tude.

The film's Beat attitude and hipster slang feel familiar coming from Nicholson. Overall, the film is a rather tame '50s view of the SoCal beach and racing scene, with a dig-those-crazy-cats vibe that's a few years behind the times.

With most of the crew and cast novices and Hollywood one-timers, it largely rests on Nicholson to inject some legitimacy as a veteran of two prior films and two previous television credits. More importantly, he was studying. As Shirley Knight told me, "We took acting classes together. It was in 1959 to 1960, around that time. It was Jack Nicholson, Robert Blake, Bobby Driscoll, Dean Stockwell, Sally Kellerman, Millie Perkins, me—and Sandra Knight, who of course Jack Nicholson married." This was the Jeff Corey class, in his garage where he had chairs set up with a little stage.

Shirley recalled, "Jack was an interesting character ... at the time, I thought it would be hard for him to get work because he had such a baby

The Wild Ride (1960) is a J.D. second feature that just happens to spotlight a future film superstar as a juvenile delinquent. Nicholson's characterization of Johnny is a fully formed depiction of a cocky gang leader with a penchant for trouble and a weakness for mindless violence; here he attacks co-star Georgianna Carter.

face, kind of a round baby face when he was younger. He didn't have that leading man aspect he got later."[2]

Millie Perkins studied acting with Nicholson after a starring role in the celebrated adaptation of *The Diary of Anne Frank*. She recalled, "He wanted to be there to learn. He was a person who wanted to grow and learn. He wasn't the same as everyone else." Though no more important than anyone in the group, "Jack was a very dominating, dominant person who didn't let anything go by if he didn't want to. He wasn't shy."[3]

Johnny Varron was anything but shy in *The Wild Ride*. Jack enters dancing in a light gray sweatshirt, exhibiting more style dancing than acting at this point, at first playing the character flat and humorless. When brought in by the cops, he sits with style in the police station, slumping and rolling his eyes, bringing the J.D. attitude with plenty of dismissiveness as he grins and cracks himself up. Nicholson has a mostly physical embodiment of the character, strutting and gliding with wings outstretched. His brow furrows and his eyes blink fast when delivering annoyed dialogue.

10. The Developing Delinquent

With his first Jack-ish explosion in a beach party scene, he swigs his beer and then violently throws the bottle while yelling to the gang to get going. There's a nice bit of business as he bellows at his gang members for chickening out, forcefully pushing his cigarette into the beach sand and continuing to work it in until he ends the conversation and tosses sand to show his talk is officially over.

He mentally attacks them by claiming that it's only a matter of time before they would be sitting on the sofa watching TV "and that's the end, you might as well be dead," as if he had written the lines himself.

The depth of Nicholson's portrayal is most manifest in his relationship with his friend Dave. Johnny is undoubtedly the tough stud and leader of the gang, but there's an undercurrent of an undefined tension that could be seen as a conflicted attraction to the other male. In a confrontation with Dave over a chick, Jack first blows up and then swiftly calms himself and becomes nice, even raising his arms in a bird stance to compose himself and "cool down."

He is still a true J.D. through his attitude toward women, deliberately hurtful and arrogant with his older lover as well as simply mean with friend Dave's girlfriend. When Dave shows up, Jack reacts too strongly for the situation or the scene, blasting an extended yell of "I did it for *youuuu!*"

The older woman isn't the only trophy that matters to Johnny. He's a race car driver willing to use any dirty trick to win. Like Johnny Strabler and his motorcycle in *The Wild One* (get it?), wild rider Johnny Varron ties a trophy to the front of his car.

Number 5, "the new boy" in the big race, shows a big Nicholson smile to the crowd as he waves during the lineup introductions, but this boy is anything but a sportsman. Jack is an amoral juvenile delinquent who killed a cop earlier in the film through recklessness and disregard, without looking back and with no remorse. He cheats his way to the win, a dirty racer and "top stud" who proceeds to alienate the crowd, his racing team, his gang and even the track PA announcer. Later, he causes Dave ("the chicken") to fatally crash, in a repeat of his cop killing. Only this time, Johnny sees the evil of his way—though all too late—getting out of his car for the last time to kneel by his so-called friend and react to the crash death in a manner quite similar to that toward co-conspirator Cora (Jessica Lange) 20 years later in *The Postman Always Rings Twice*. Now Johnny gives himself up to the law, while Frank Chambers (for all intents and purposes a J.D. who just didn't progress enough) suffered the bad choices and flaunting of laws and societal values enough for the both of them.

Most J.D.s are against law enforcement. Others take their frustrations out on women. Some lash out at both, like Buddy and Weary. In *Too Soon to Love*, Nicholson is pushy in his establishing scene at an amusement park and later when way too aggressive at a drive-in with leading lady Jennifer West (as Cathy) until she is rescued by leading man Richard Evans (playing Jim) who punches out Jack and sparks a big brawl. Jack at this age quite convincingly comes across as a brash, sexually forceful type, a J.D. with a chip on his shoulder. His heavy-handed move on Cathy was edging toward what today would be recognized as date (or acquaintance) rape.

Nicholson appears in only two scenes, first yelling "Get the show on the road" at an amusement park, and later driving two other guys to the drive-in while displaying his toothsome sneer.

Cathy and Jim are the ones loving too soon, though this is pretty tame stuff, with "kids in trouble" merely staying out too late and making out. *Too Soon to Love* was an early credit for director Richard Rush (who also wrote the script); he later helmed *Hells Angels on Wheels* and *Psych-Out*, both of which featured Nicholson. Rush reminisced that he met Jack while casting the movie, giving him the role of the drive-in theater villain, and "once I had seen him work, I fell in love and he was starring in all of my pictures from then on."[4]

The morals of the time (1960) appear bizarre if not quaint today. Apparently, if you wanted to find out where to get an abortion, ask your barber. But the woman performing the abortion is in a dirty and rundown apartment she calls a respectable place. She sends Cathy to a really seedy side of town, past a "GIRLESK" theater and into a ghetto (or what passes for one in this white world) to a decayed, filthy and broken-down building. The young couple in trouble encounter a woman coming down the steps after having had her abortion, but she looks like a zombie movie victim, scaring the young couple away.

Back then, the subject of abortion was worse than the attempted date rape by Buddy. A true rape, a violent and public attack by a juvenile delinquent named Weary Reilly, was a different story entirely. Buddy suffers nothing but a hangover and some ribbing by his pals. Weary is grabbed and brought in by the cops, as an out-of-control and gangsterish nobody.

Based on a James T. Farrell book from a trilogy that was important at the time but largely forgotten today, *Studs Lonigan* presented a socially aware study of the tough South Side of Chicago and its Irish youth in 1920. The film introduced Christopher Knight (who made only one more movie) in the title role. His gang included Nicholson and Frank Gorshin, who later played the classic villain The Riddler in the *Batman* TV series, coincident that Nicholson subsequently portrayed the Joker in its franchise reboot. Upon showing Gorshin an original *Studs Lonigan* lobby card at the Chiller Theatre convention, he proudly displayed it to all in the area while exclaiming, "That's me with Jack!"[5] (The Riddler and the Joker together.)

Nicholson is first seen in a pool hall wearing a reverse flat cap (also rem-

10. The Developing Delinquent

His acclaimed performance as Weary Reilly meant a lot to the then-struggling Nicholson, according to Gary Kent. *Studs Lonigan* (1960) portrayed 1920s Chicago juvenile delinquents in an adaptation of the James T. Farrell trilogy made topical to the youth crisis of the early 1960s (reproduction lobby card signed by Nicholson's fellow gang member Frank Gorshin).

iniscent of the Joker), bearing the bright, sarcastic tone of youth. He exhibits what we would later see as "Jack," the derisive attitude with what we would hear as the classic Jack voiced in the late '60s and early '70s.

Reportedly, Nicholson coveted this role. He expressed his pride in having played the part a few years later to fellow actor and master stuntman Gary Kent. Kent related that Nicholson seemed a bit rankled that "he was more or less ignored.... He kind of felt that people should maybe pay a little attention to him and weren't doing it yet."[6]

In contrast, star Christopher Knight is extraordinarily terrible, so laughably overwrought and comically over-emotive that he's almost a throwback to the worst of the early silent cinema "photo players," twisted up and contorted, suffering as if he's about to void himself.

Nicholson instead makes the most of his well-gained opportunity. In a close-up with an aging party girl at a speakeasy, he has a suitably snarky, sneering attitude that's accompanied by a quick, clipped delivery of impatient superiority. Weary is smart and smart-assed. After cracking a joke to the sad, sodden hustler (unfortunately, the joke was on her), he busts out laughing—laughing the joy of someone who has hurt the helpless, the kind who lays it on thick only to pull the rug out.

In a burlesque club scene, Jack goes out of control watching the womanly entertainment. He bounces in his seat; taps a booze bottle on his head; grabs the guys in the row in front of him and next to him; hoots, hollers, yells, whoops, becoming more like a monkey than a boyish gang member. He's too excited and worked up to handle himself, perhaps a foreshadowing of his forthcoming sexual assault and downfall, and perhaps his best early acting sequence next to the brief *Little Shop of Horrors* dentist scene.

Reilly and the gang attend a political party, not the kind that elects candidates, but the type that brings men and booze and women together and the kind where a politician makes the ultimate campaign promise by proclaiming, "The drinks are on me!"

Weary gets crazy drunk, with Nicholson convincingly so, and grabs a showgirl to drag her up the steps, forcing and practically carrying her to a room for the purpose of forcible sexual congress. Afterward, he is grabbed by two police officers and struggles to break free, accented by a strong Jackish "You ain't got nothing on me!"

The character destroyed himself, a juvenile delinquent who took it too far like cop killer Johnny Varron in *The Wild Ride*. But Gary Kent drew the comparison of the quintessential Jack with the *Studs Lonigan* gang member before he descended from bad boy to convict. "One of the things I remember was the Weary Reilly part, because *Studs Lonigan* was one of my favorite books and Weary was one of my favorite characters. And every time I see Jack on screen, I see a little bit of Weary Reilly, that tough little guy who's out there jumping on the sidewalk and playing stickball and going through life with some kind of smile even though his coat is too long and his pants don't quite fit or whatever. Like he didn't need that, he was gonna go on balls and zest for life."[7]

Fifteen years later, Nicholson improbably played another Weary Reilly, a more world-weary post-juvenile J.D. by the name of Randall Patrick McMurphy in Milos Forman's *One Flew Over the Cuckoo's Nest*. Insane or not, McMurphy's basically a juvenile delinquent who never grew out of it, straight from *The Wild Ride* to the wild house. Like all classic J.D. gang leaders, he comes into the ward all attitude, already looking for his angle, a natural con man and manipulator.

He delights in the childish and the dirty, gleefully showing the facility director a pornographic set of playing cards. He schemes and shows off, full of bravado and cheer, insinuating himself first into the group and then assuming its leadership. Nicholson embodies a full, complex character, one who plays a joyful scene where McMurphy's guidance and encouragement take his fellow inmates to an afternoon of temporary sanity and momentary normalcy on a fishing boat. But the juvenile dreams of freedom are defeated when his delinquency—and that of his nuthouse colleagues—defines him and defeats them. His act of generosity and mentoring is dashed as the group of escapees is apprehended, re-labeling big-heartedness and coaching as rebellion and "dangerous."

Overgrown as he might be, R.P. displays all of the symptoms of the late–1950s and early–'60s J.D. He hates authority and rebels against conformity. He collects compliant and fun "girls" but bristles at the strength and pressure from a strong woman. Here that assertive woman is represented by one rigid and frigid, by-the-book, dictatorial female, forever to remain a symbol easily conjured by the name Nurse Ratched.

Louise Fletcher completely lives this role and her character gets under the skin of McMurphy in one of Jack's most powerful and revered parts. She signifies the parent, a nagging mother with her rules and her tyrannical ways, just the kind a J.D. would resent. She simultaneously characterizes an official authority figure—certainly not the police but close to it—and someone with legal and living oversight.

The Academy Award winner gave Ratched "a rigidity that never wavers," making the character "the person in power who thinks they have power because of who they are and how they do their job, and they're 'right'" in the belief that there is no other way but her way.[8]

Cop, teach, shrink, mom and doc all in one immobile and rule book–waving foe, Nurse Ratched was a juvenile's nightmare (because she held complete authority) and a delinquent's destiny (since she lived to make "Mac" and his fellow inmates *know* what they do wrong *and* make them pay for it).

Nicholson revealed his secret subtext to their conflict as "one long, unsuccessful seduction which the guy was so pathologically sure of." He discussed this "secret design" only with Fletcher, that "this guy's a scamp who knows he's irresistible to women and in reality he expects Nurse Ratched to be seduced by him. This is his tragic flaw. This is why he ultimately fails."[9]

Fletcher gave the reverse perspective, that when Nurse Ratched "figures out that she's losing control and everything's been in control until this guy shows up and starts undermining her position, she begins to lose it and does lose it."[10]

She loses it to a juvenile delinquent. Though a little old for the label, Jack's McMurphy shows his juvenile side often enough to betray the character's immaturity over his insanity. He's first seen in cuffs, being led inside and looking more like a criminal than anything else, dressed all in black. Then he mischievously pretends to be nutso, doing a monkey dance and kissing a guard. He's harmless; he's having fun with a deck of cards that displays naked women; he plays hard at cards and basketball; he flirts; and he serves as big brother to Billy (Brad Dourif) when the shy younger man shows an interest in Candy (Mews Small).

Mac's juvenilia are not appreciated, but his delinquent character ultimately does him in. Society can handle a little nonsense, but not when the outsider acquires a little power, in growth from teen troublemaker to adult agitator. Jimmy Wallace in *The Cry Baby Killer* could take a few hostages (even a baby!) and face some discipline and punishment toward rehabilitation. Buddy could slip out of a near–date rape and move on to another day, while Weary Reilly took the rap but likely got out of the clink to an uncertain future.

Johnny Varron killed a cop on his *Wild Ride*. But he just never got it. He was obnoxious and openly contemptuous of the law. He was bad. He became what the system thought about Randall. But Randall ... he may have been the purest of the bunch, oblivious to any harm he might have caused. McMurphy was a gang leader, just like Varron. And we don't like that. Leaders for good, or what the majority views as good, are fine and dandy. But leaders for unrest, taking on social conventions and orthodoxy—especially along with other misfits and rabble-rousers—that is not to be tolerated.

Nurse Ratched will see to that.

11

Writers on the Storm

Where did Kafka come from? A mind met a piece of paper. The mind either accomplishes exquisite beauty or misses with excruciating emptiness. The paper either becomes a work of triumph or a symbol of abject failure. Writing is a pursuit that can result in something good and satisfying ... something useless and disappointing ... or nothing at all. The writer can become Kafka and the paper can become history; the writer can remain unknown or labeled a hack and the paper can produce piles of rejection or derision; or the aspiring writer cannot bring anything to fruition and the paper becomes garbage.

Each of these—the real writer, the pretend writer and the failed writer—pass one another as they wander bookstores in search of themselves or their rivals or their unrealized dreams. Given their heightened sense about the production and dissemination of the written word, they look and touch and judge and dismiss and imagine and pine not in chains or mass market stores, but in America's great independent book paradises.

Melvin Udall examines the displays for his newest romance novel, for symmetry and perfection, though he touches nothing. Jack Torrance randomly studies the work of others, searching for a beginning and for any inspiration, just so he can start (any start will do). Will Randall inventories the store's support for his authors, not entirely businesslike and not altogether detached. Eugene O'Neill doesn't haunt these stores as much as bless them, subtly expanding the Drama section each evening after closing. David Locke wants space, pushing from the beyond for political reporting and original documentaries. And Mark Forman is there more in the hope of being noticed than anything else, except possibly encountering a young female admirer.

All of these characters inhabit all of the great bookstores. All of these characters have been portrayed by Jack Nicholson. Nicholson has played an unusual number of writers in his movies, since a writer is not necessarily a strong potential cinematic subject. Nicholson has also been a writer for film, with screenplays for *Thunder Island*, *Flight to Fury*, *Ride in the Whirlwind*,

The Trip, Head and *Drive, He Said*. In a career of over 50 years, all six writing credits took place over only eight years, with the last occurring over 40 years ago. Though he knows of writers and has been a writer, Nicholson now clearly prefers playing them than serving as one.

He's portrayed writers four times: a novelist in *As Good as It Gets*; one who suffers from the ultimate in writer's block in *The Shining*; a celebrated real-life playwright in *Reds*; and a writer-journalist based on another real person in *Heartburn*. He's also played a book editor for a major publishing house in *Wolf* and a documentarian-journalist writer in *The Passenger*.

That's six actual writing jobs and six roles as writer-related figures. And, even considering 75 roles over 50 years, that's a good number of literary characters given the action-oriented slant of the Hollywood movie. Considering Nicholson's position in the industry, these choices are likely based more on personal interest than box office potential.

* * *

For any writer, established or novice, proven or delusional, the nightmarish meeting of the blank mind with the blank page can possess and strangle. Frustration leads to panic, which elevates stress and accelerates worry. Self-doubt is deadly. An emptiness depresses and deadens the afflicted. This so-called writer's block can turn a best seller by a promising first-timer into a flop by a wannabe, a mental mess.

Jack Torrance wants to be a writer. He thinks it'll help to get a nice, quiet job away from it all so he can concentrate on his work and spend quality time with his family. Jack was dead wrong. He was no writer, no family man, no hotelier. He was trapped by his inability, by his inadequacy, and perhaps even by time and place.

Stuck in a rut? Here's a guy who's been in the same caretaker job since the Roaring '20s. He's such a prolific writer that he's come up with a grand total of one sentence over the span of months—and has repeated it hundreds and hundreds of times.

Yet Jack Torrance is the milder, gentler George Bailey, the hero of the holiday favorite *It's a Wonderful Life*. With Jack there were signs and incidents, looks and reactions. Something about breaking Danny's arm (an accident, they said) and a drinking problem, but of course he's quit the booze. George, on the other hand, drank too much (on Christmas Eve of all days) and came home only to ruin his family's holiday. "That silly tune," as he spits out in attack, referring to a song that happens to be a celebration of the birth of their Lord. He yells at a hard-working schoolteacher, overturns tables and throws heavy objects inside their home. Imagine if Jack Torrance had said something approaching, "Why do we have all these kids?" on Christmas Eve. Can anything be more horrid other than actually attacking them physically?

11. Writers on the Storm

Sight & Sound called Nicholson's performance "a splendidly Gothic reworking of Ray Milland's in *The Lost Weekend*," explaining that alcoholics see things not there, say things not meant, and become people not themselves.[1]

Look into the dead eyes of Jack Nicholson as he sits alone on a bed in his bathrobe, robotically pretending to care, with everything forced and overspoken, in a monotonic declaration that he'd never do anything to hurt his son. Who would say anything like this unless the opposite was true? Nicholson uses such a menacingly sarcastic tone, more Bruce Dern than Nicholson, that it becomes true irony, the opposite meaning of what in fact is said.

Compare this with James Stewart as he holds his young son on his lap, destroyed and unhinged, a look of desperation and fractured reality, and betraying a dangerous insanity that could easily lead to an axe-wielding incident. Stewart looks more beaten than Nicholson, wet with sweat and shining with the drink-sodden tears of a failure. Nicholson is detached, but Jimmy is fully in charge, yet in charge of something that clearly no longer works.

As Jack Torrance descends from sanity, he becomes a nightmare, a scared animal bleating non-verbal growls before he falls out of his chair, and awakens with saliva falling from his mouth, as he collapses into a tearful state while retaining enough self-awareness to wonder if he is losing his mind.

The actor's interpretation, in my belief, is that he doesn't become uncontrolled or insane, but rather an actual monster. When he races toward the bar, his flailing, super–"Jack" body language includes hyper-shrugs, breast strokes and shoulder flings as he propels himself "down the hall," as Jim Morrison warned in The Doors' epic *The End*. He must escape to a safe, more tranquil place, the calming and closeted space of the bar of yesteryear.

Jack is big, from handshakes and laughs to looks and head turns, with teeth, hands and snaps—a proto–Joker in the bar scene—in contrast to Lloyd the bartender, who is more constrained, controlled and inscrutable. Kubrick veteran Joseph Turkel (from *The Killing* and *Paths of Glory* as well as Ridley Scott's *Blade Runner*) is impassive, with a low, staccato intonation from another world. This contrast was intentional, but Turkel explained to me that Nicholson had warned him he was "taking it all the way" due to his frustration of shooting that first bar scene for four straight, grueling and repetitive days. Nicholson became big and bigger and bigger still, with "fuck this and fuck that," as Turkel put it, purposely overdone to make the point about being tired of doing the same scene over and over.

When Nicholson completed his most over-emoted "I'll show you" take, Kubrick calmly stated, "Jack, I see that you've opened up a whole new can of corn with this approach. Tell you what. That's the one I'll put in the picture—and that'll be the end of your career."[2]

Message received. Joke got.

"Nobody did things like Stanley," Turkel told me.³ "I adored watching Stanley," says actor Barry Dennen. "He was so interesting, and the more I found out about him, the more I liked him. I liked him a lot. He was very phobic. He was very loath to shake your hand, so I didn't offer my hand."⁴ Pointing to his temple, actor Shane Rimmer, one of Slim Pickens' crew in *Dr. Strangelove*, said that Kubrick "was like a walking camera." Rimmer added, "Anybody could go in to see him. If there was a problem, he would find a way to solve it."⁵

Kubrick's exacting approach to shooting is legendary. He's known for seemingly endless retakes, perhaps executed to exhaust the players and take out the "acting." Shelley Duvall explained that a scene could take hours to shoot, "and by the end of the day you just don't have anything more to give."⁶

Music supervisor and assistant editor Gordon Stainforth acknowledged that Nicholson paced himself and that around take 12, "Jack would really go for it." Aware of Kubrick's working methods, Nicholson would get annoyed in some takes and go wildly over the top, "because he wanted to give Stanley a huge selection when it came time to edit. Jack turned in many, many great takes."⁷

"Stanley shot millions of feet of film and he did scenes over and over and over again, and I never knew why," Dennen said to me. "Nobody knew why, we didn't know what we'd done right, or what we'd done wrong, but we'd do it again." Barry compared Kubrick's approach to that of Alfred Hitchcock, "because Hitchcock never gave notes. He figured it's all in the casting. If he cast the right people and they were good, you leave them alone." Kubrick was the same way. "Stanley trusted the people he cast because he looked at a lot of auditions and he went for the one that he knew would be right and he didn't need to do anything."

Dennen didn't recall Kubrick giving direction, but hired good people and let them do their job. As sensible as that sounds, the shoot was hardly an ordinary one with ordinary talents. "My main memories and my main experiences from *The Shining* are not Jack's, so much as they are of Stanley Kubrick, who was not like Earth people [*laughs*]. He was really wonderful; strange, marvelous, and wonderful."⁸

From the beginning of *The Shining*, Nicholson and Kubrick create an atmosphere of disquiet. The disassociating opening scene uses visual distortion and deep electronic musical sounds, while the interview session with Barry Nelson seems like a 45° turn on the admittance interrogation with Dr. Spivey in *Cuckoo's Nest*. You see a hint of an odd look on Nicholson's face, not just foreshadowing, but a small glimmer of his thinking, "Why am I here? What am I doing?" to himself. In this sense, the film really becomes an allegory on the trap of family and commitment, similar in ways to *Five Easy Pieces* and *About Schmidt*.

Torrance is not a person looking forward, but someone already troubled. There's no better indication than his sole moment of true enjoyment on the drive to the hotel with Wendy (Duvall) and Danny (Danny Lloyd in a miraculous performance), when he noticeably brightens at the discussion of the Donner Party. In a cute moment of subtext, Jack rationalizes it as okay because Danny saw it "on the television"—as if cannibalism and TV were equivalent.

This character has no George Bailey worries about a "drafty old barn." Though isolated and soon to be snowbound, the hotel is huge but well-appointed, with every need accommodated and every detail planned out. But George was better at playing the part of the dutiful and involved dad (except Christmas Eve, natch) than Jack Torrance, who obviously only feigns interest during the family's initial tour of the hotel given by Nelson. Torrance throws out dead grins and robotic nods, punctuated by inanities like "cozy" to pretend he's engaged. He's only going through the motions about anything related to his family and his job. He makes them the source of all his problems and the eventual target of all his frustrations as a failed—and more damaging still, failing—writer.

Kubrick effectively sets up the monster Nicholson becomes by keeping him out of a good amount of the opening scenes. We see Duvall and Danny, without Nicholson. We see Duvall and Anne Jackson, with no Nicholson. We see Danny and Scatman Crothers, but no Nicholson. As with any thriller, the less we see of the menace, the more effective the attack.

The director explained, "Jack comes to the hotel psychologically prepared to do its murderous bidding. He doesn't have much further to go for his anger and frustration to become completely uncontrollable." Kubrick calls Torrance a failure as a writer and contemptuous of his wife, with hatred toward his son, such that once he is at the mercy of the hotel's powerful evil, he "is quickly ready to fulfill his dark role."[9]

The turning point of Nicholson's portrayal of the father takes place 44 minutes into *The Shining*. This is when a disturbed and troubled man becomes a tortured and dangerous animal. This is the transition point, with an unsettling scene of a man who hits his head and rips his typing paper in anguish and frustration. The moment is physical, as it must be for someone whose intellect has failed him, leaving only the body to find if it can perform where the mind did not. Nicholson's character energy takes full control of a man losing control. Hands, eyelashes, eyebrows, all in furious motion. He slaps his head, summons a fake smile, moves his brows more—motions and expressions that create the Jack Torrance we remember. Toward the end of this sequence, there's even a little of Nicholson's Bruce Dern riff creeping in, with a get-the-fuck-out-of-here look and a certain way of positioning his eyebrows to exude added snottiness.

Suddenly, abruptly, a ghostly Jack Torrance appears. We see a deadened man, unshaven, with a gray appearance and neglect accentuated by a black turtleneck. He appears frozen, a glimpse of the figure we see physically frozen at the film's conclusion. His eyes are upraised and stuck, with no signs of blood circulating or any existence as a sentient being. Is he already dead, excusing his later actions as those of some uncontrollable zombie or a ghost amongst ghosts?

For a break in his go-nowhere novel, Torrance has a one-time fling with a cancerous, drooping old hag. When a beautiful, bountiful young woman emerges from her bath to embrace the father, whose wife and son are within walking distance of this scene, he lustily kisses her until he sees what she's become or what she was all along. This can be taken as another comment on real marriage and real life (i.e., "That's what happens when you get married!"), a foretelling of Warren Schmidt's view of his wife, not in actual expression but in attitude and sentiment.

Torrance visits Lloyd the bartender again, adding an encounter with Grady in the lounge's rest room. As Grady "cor-rrrects" Jack, retorting that Torrance has always been the caretaker, Nicholson reacts like an old-time western sidekick, with much eye motion and thick-tongued, statically wide-open mouth. Nicholson's approach to the destructive arc of the character perfectly constitutes the notion of character energy. Many have accused Nicholson of overacting, but his approach is appropriately varied and entirely fitting.

Kubrick wanted Nicholson for the role from the start, calling him "one of the best actors in Hollywood, perhaps on a par with the greatest stars of the past like Spencer Tracy and Jimmy Cagney." The director needed the audience to believe that Torrance was a writer, even a failed one. "[Nicholson] is particularly suited for roles which require intelligence. He is an intelligent and literate man, and those are qualities almost impossible to act."[10]

Nicholson is big, yes. He plays it big because the actor does not view insanity as a subtlety. There is no subtlety to being insane. He veers from gregarious with Lloyd to befuddlement with Grady to milquetoast with his employer to dismissive with Wendy to weirdly threatening to Danny. He catapults from the kind of husband and father who can make a move and cause a flinch and a grimace to a true physical menace—all because of a terminal case of writer's block that's exacerbated with a serious dose of cabin fever.

Torrance famously types page after page after page of a single line that indeed proves himself to be a dull boy. And a duller writer. Of course he has to flip out. When wife Wendy confronts him after discovering his all-too-efficient wordplay, economizing to only eight words repeated over hundreds of pages, he starts calmly in voice. Then Jack the actor imbues Jack the character with deadly sarcasm when asking what could be "done with Danny." Oddly, and perhaps obscurely, Nicholson uses a Paul Lynde voice to push the strangeness quotient and incongruity factor beyond any sensible level—

A famous film moment (or at least one of the scores of times that moment was redone at the behest of director Stanley Kubrick), shown as it happens in *The Shining* (1980). Jack Torrance (Nicholson) tells Wendy (Shelley Duvall, at top) that he does not want to hurt her. He is not convincing in making his case.

because *that* is insanity. He then goes from Paul Lynde to Jack to Jack tinged with some Bruce Dern. He's not exactly soothing when he promises not to hurt Wendy, but to merely bash her brains in.

Nicholson centers his intense character energy in his head and body, with his hands emotive, active and alive, and his tongue expressive and physical in ways only Gene Simmons could replicate. Barry Dennen explained how Nicholson feeds that character energy through everything around him: "Jack uses all the other actors on the set. He uses the words he has to say. He uses the lighting to make you see it. And he's really good at that." However, Dennen believes that Nicholson will never tell you his tricks like the wise magician he is. "Jack is a master. He's wonderful, and what he does he makes seem so simple and easy. It also comes out of a lot of experience. He's a very experienced actor and a lot comes out of his own experience. I admire him deeply."[11]

Though the atmosphere on the shoot could be quite intense, Nicholson (and against stereotype, even Kubrick) helped lighten the set when around the child actors. Danny Lloyd told me that his best memory of working with Nicholson was when "he was clowning around, with the axe, acting like an Indian one day between takes. He was a really good guy."[12]

There are catchphrases everyone remembers, such as an *I Love Lucy*-type announcement that he's arrived home to his honey. The iconic *Tonight Show* opening line is recreated with an axe swing in place of the original pantomimed golf swing. Nicholson apes Ed McMahon with a sick and twisted grin, but what most forget were the moments that made these overplayed moments so effective. To build to this climax, his methodical and purposeful axe swings calmly advance Torrance from door to door, using a quizzical and comically insane look, invoking President Richard Nixon. When Jack does Tricky Dick as the Big Bad Wolf and warns the little pigs to let him in ("by the hair of my chinny-chin-chin"), he's referencing the unshaven 1960 debater and the drunken monster trapped in the White House with his own cabin fever and with his own enemies.

Nicholson uses his body to great effect, later adapting a strange, striding limp to attack Dick Hallorann (Crothers) with an axe, and later still when pursuing Danny through the maze. Jack said, "For the limp, I don't recall if it was [Stanley's] idea or mine, but I thought about Charles Laughton running in *The Hunchback of Notre Dame*."[13]

Nicholson's so-called "overacting" is in fact just right, yet not realistic. The situation and his character's frame of mind would not work if treated as realistic, but instead must be heightened beyond normal comprehension. This was part of Kubrick's vision for the actor.

Disappearing into the icy, snowy maze, Torrance pursues Danny, systematically devolving into a guttural, yelping, unthinking animal. Logic fails him as his son's tracks in the snow somehow appear to suddenly stop. This man, this animal, this psychologically attuned actor reacts with maximum physicality and minimum awareness. Torrance pushes his chin out, he protrudes his lower teeth like a predatory lower creature, and he trains his eyes on his prey so that the whites of his eyes dominate like the snow itself and the eerie light of this doomed evening.

He stumbles on. The blood flow in his brain slows down at his brain freezes. He replaces words with mere grunts as he shuts down his mind and his mouth, howling incoherently. These screams become louder and less lucid as instinct replaces thought. Then, the fatal cut, the murderous edit in the film, reveals Torrance as a frozen, up-staring statue harking back to the earlier scene of the mentally frozen character in his black turtleneck. That alive man had too much in common with this dead one.

Joseph Turkel provided me with invaluable insight into the oft-noted obsessive degree of Nicholson's preparation, this time for the freezing chase scene. "I had the dressing room next to Jack," he recounted. "He's recumbent on the sofa—sideways, not quite laying with his feet propped up on the coffee table." Turkel spied a book open across the actor's chest and asks what it is. "Jack says it's about the effect of freezing on the human body. I say, 'What the fuck are you reading that for?' Jack answers, 'Look: For the last scene, my character freezes and I want to know just how it happens.'" Over 35 years later, Turkel still marvels at this attention to reality and Nicholson's dedication to his craft, explaining, "Anybody else would have just winged it, but not Jack. He had to get it true. That's the kind of actor he is." Nicholson himself provided the distinction to Turkel, saying, "I want to get it … feel it … show it … as it is."[14]

Jack Torrance oversees the Overlook forevermore. His endeavor as a writer met frustration and trouble, just as George Bailey's efforts with Bedford Falls' Building and Loan suffered a run on its assets (even within his supposedly close-knit community of friends). Torrance took his frustrations out on his family and to Lloyd's bar. Bailey tortured his family when the pressure became too much, then took his frustrations to Martini's bar. They both stagger to their fates. George chooses suicide. Jack chooses murder. One act mirrors the other, with the former an introverted manifestation of the latter's extraverted outburst.

For Jack Torrance in *The Shining*, it certainly is a wonderful life indeed. For George Bailey, Frank Capra and family and friends intervene to transform that "wonderful life" from Torrance's ironic meaning to George's literal one.

* * *

Will Randall doesn't represent one of life's "monsters" (like an abusive, self-destructive dad), but actually becomes one. In Mike Nichols' *Wolf*, the unassuming and erudite book editor turns into a ferocious and vindictive werewolf. He's a mind that wakes up as a body. Nicholson forms the character first, with a stiff-backed gait, a smooth and mannered disposition, and a superior and disgusted attitude about society's cultural slide. When he semitransforms for the first time, it's also the first time the character has been at all physical, and so he struggles as he forms. Some aspects of the change are big and dramatic, while others are small sniffs and postures.

The most supernatural aspect of the production may well have been its inspiration. Screenwriter Jim Harrison visited the *Missouri Breaks* set and told Nicholson about an eerie experience he'd had in his Michigan cabin that would lead to their collaboration more than ten years later. "I rubbed my hand over my face and felt fur on it and it felt like a snout." For his part, Jack called it "neither the most nor the least outlandish thing Jim has ever said to me." Harrison felt he had been invaded by a spirit and turned the experience into *Wolf*. Jack became that oddly transformed man.[15]

When he threatens upstart Stewart (James Spader) for the first time, Nicholson shows much satisfaction in pursuing vengeance, with vigor and hate, against the perfectly slimy shit.

In the major transformation scene, before chasing down deer, Nicholson looks much like Ray Wise as the demonic version of Leland Palmer in *Twin Peaks*, using a severe upwards eye-gaze while heaving through his lower teeth (though the bushy sideburns and rough hair, unfortunately and unintentionally, make Nicholson look like an old British rocker out of place in the punk era).

Nicholson has every right to be a little playful with this role, what with romancing the younger, beautiful woman exemplar that Michelle Pfeiffer, playing Laura, represents; his delight in delivering a Hair Club for Men ad lib; and his no-hands-urinating to mark his territory against Stewart. This action foreshadows Nicholson's liberating scene in *About Schmidt* in which he stands proud, masculine and defiant—hands on his hips and peeing freely as a fluid message of control.

There are a few threatening, animalistic moments as the bookworm becomes the werewolf, most meaningfully when his wife Charlotte (Kate Nelligan) begs to come back after betraying her husband with Stewart, and he becomes frightening because it meant something to him. Upon being told of her murder, Randall is battered and ashen, as if struck to the body and staked through the mind.

The ultimate battle pits the wolf Randall has become against the predatory animal Stewart always was. Jack *becomes* the animal; they both do, in realistic action, makeup and a persuasive use of close shots and evocative cutting.

Director Mike Nichols ultimately saw the film as flawed, mostly due to a central shortcoming in the werewolf myth. "I realized very early in *Wolf* that the metaphor of vampires is very powerful, it speaks to all of us, we all know a great deal about it, but the metaphor of werewolves is not—it never has worked, never will work, because it doesn't echo anything that happens to people."[16]

* * *

Nicholson has portrayed two real-life writers in his career, one openly and the other a thinly veiled "fictionalized" version. In friend Warren Beatty's *Reds*, he is playwright Eugene O'Neill, while in Mike Nichols' *Heartburn*, he is Carl Bernstein substitute Mark Forman. *Reds* also represents the first of only two times he plays a biographical character, the second being Jimmy Hoffa. (I'm not counting *The Departed*'s Francis Costello, who was based on Whitey Bulger.)

11. Writers on the Storm 165

Beatty is actor, producer, director and writer on the epic about John Reed and the Russian Revolution. His film is structurally interesting, melding a documentary, using interview segments of *The Witnesses*, plus a portrayed drama.

Beatty friend and actor Paul Sorvino, who played American Communist Party founding member Louis Fraina, told me he considers Beatty a "great director." When I inquired as to why he doesn't get enough credit as director, Sorvino replied, "Because he doesn't direct enough, but he's terrific. He's one of the best."[17] The Academy of Motion Picture Arts and Sciences agreed, and awarded Warren Beatty the 1981 Best Director Oscar.

Nicholson starts serious and intense as O'Neill, using measured speech that's slow and low, and holding one hand in his pocket to evoke discomfort in his first scene, over whisky with Diane Keaton (playing Louise Bryant). Nicholson knows how to play it down, using restraint effectively in a short scene upon Beatty's return. Beatty and Keaton sit together on a sofa while Nicholson is seated on a chair across from them holding a wine glass. He declines another drink, calmly gets up, looks down, raises his eyebrows just slightly to acknowledge leaving and walks off.

Professor Robert M. Dowling, author of *Eugene O'Neill: A Life in Four Acts* and co-editor of a critical anthology on the playwright, loved Nicholson's performance but points out that O'Neill "was a very, very shy person, especially in the summer of '16, and not really the 'Where's the whisky?' badass Nicholson portrays (unless O'Neill was extremely drunk, which of course he was often)."[18]

Re-watching this film so many years after its release, I was not sure what made Nicholson's an Academy Award–winning performance. Then I absorbed his cumulative three-phase approach to the character. In the first phase, he establishes O'Neill the man in a serious, low-key vein. The second phase covers his romance with Keaton's Louise Bryant. Here, he employs a higher register voice to signify this more uplifting situation. In their breakup scene, he employs deliberate intensity, looking great and with more confidence in a black turtleneck with gray jacket. He carries all his "Jackness," but toned down to professional levels and in perfect distinction from Beatty's carefully cultivated impression of confusion, clumsiness, hesitancy, vulnerability and impossible ordinariness.

"The love triangle was not overly done," according to Professor Dowling. "O'Neill and Bryant were definitely lovers right under Reed's nose, and by all accounts Reed was fine with it, being no poser when it came to free love."[19]

In the aftermath of his loss, Nicholson's O'Neill becomes visibly and internally older and impaired. He is more physical and broader, with greater emphasis on his words and puffiness in his eyes. He even throws in his only forehead-raise in the whole movie to strong, ironic effect.

These contrasts in delivery, attitude and appearance show why he won the Oscar. Not makeup or obvious aging affectations, but truly direct translations of inward emotions and feelings into sight and sound. The differences are more shaded than pushed, yet the impacts are dramatic.

His third phase reveals an older man who's cleaned up. Mature and philosophical in tone, this O'Neill speaks in a subdued way again, but more due to growth than self-seriousness. His vocal expression is muted and steady, underneath the line of dialogue like the way singer kd lang winds her way just below the line of melody for effect. Her legato style, smooth and connected, reminds me of the easy, measured timbre of Nicholson's dialogue style during this phase.

Nicholson explained how he found a key that unlocked O'Neill for him to show this progression: "the fact that [O'Neill] couldn't write with anything but a pencil." This seemingly small point mattered to the characterization that Nicholson created. "He couldn't adapt to the typewriter. He couldn't dictate," which became essential when the playwright came down with a degenerative disease and was unable to hold that pencil.[20]

On *Reds*, Nicholson earned an Academy Award by taking us through three acts of an author's life, as represented in subtle tonality. People grow, they change, they get knocked down and learn; reflecting, reaching, relaxing. Character energy doesn't have to be broad and attention-grabbing. Instead, it can be as small as a person's daring; as vulnerable as an unloved lover; and as wise and weary as we all become.

* * *

Less rich and fulfilled is Nicholson's assignment, for want of a more attractive word, as Bernstein—oh sorry, make that Forman. *Heartburn* is a case of major talent and minor result. Mike Nichols (*Carnal Knowledge, The Fortune, Wolf*); Meryl Streep (*Ironweed*); Stockard Channing (*The Fortune*); Milos Forman (*One Flew Over the Cuckoo's Nest*); Jeff Daniels (*Terms of Endearment*); Maureen Stapleton (*Reds*); cinematographer Néstor Almendros (*Goin' South*); editor Sam O'Steen (*Carnal Knowledge, Chinatown, Wolf*) and others all worked on far superior productions with Nicholson than this.

What is unclear is the audience the film was intended for. Not involving enough to be pure drama, nor funny enough to be a comedy, and not likely to be considered a romantic comedy, this dour, inessential film is just not satisfying or worth all of the talent poured into it.

At least writer Nora Ephron didn't make herself out to be a princess compared to a surrogate ogre husband. Both characters often are unlikable and thus theoretically suited for one another. As for the *Washington Post* reporter and Watergate hero, Nicholson makes him appealing in a mechanical, practiced manner when courting Streep's Rachel, an appropriate portrayal of a womanizer blessed with less personal aplomb and élan than Nicholson himself.

On their wedding day, he becomes sweet and light while she devolves into a whiny "Bridezilla" before the title had been coined. The pair then become very convincing as bickering spouses, disgusted at each other and about everything else, until their warm reconciliation and joy when Rachel lets out the news of a baby on the way. Jack's "ooh, baby" is charming and provides depth to his character, as does the couple's best scene together when celebrating by eating pizza and singing duets of songs featuring the word "baby."

Nicholson, of course, likes to croon on film and presents his most lively and winsome moment as Forman when performing "My Boy Bill" in full Broadway style and mock-melodramatics. Streep considered the moment "so wonderful—never keeping what other men might consider his customary cool." He sings again when the baby is born, addressing "I Sing to You" with contentment and tenderness. His co-star recounted how she had to turn away in response to "all the emotion that came pouring out of him" and his willingness to show it all "as if he had nothing to lose."[21]

There are two other warm highlights. In a reconciliation scene at a fountain, Nicholson chokes up and harkens back to his earlier courtship mode. Later, he helps Streep as she prepares to give birth again, recounting the story of the chancy delivery of their first child. His character is back in that original moment, feeling the same feelings as they were experienced at the time. This is sentiment, not sentimentality. He completely breaks down, in shame and in love, reminiscent of the *Five Easy Pieces* monologue with his character's father.

There is one Jacksplosion, as Nicholson blows up at contractors (one of whom is comedian Yakov Smirnoff) who forget to make a door from the kitchen into the house. Otherwise, you can't help thinking about how Streep and Nicholson's characters in *Ironweed* were so much more rich and endearing, with range and empathy. That couple had nothing, yet were happier and more fulfilling as people than this couple, who possess everything—except interest.

* * *

A reporter of another sort is found in a film that's certainly of another sort, that being David Locke in Michelangelo Antonioni's *The Passenger*. Originally titled *Professione: reporter*, this existential study of identity and responsibility features one of Nicholson's most naturalistic portrayals, reacting to the moment as it happens and the situation as it emerges.

The opening places the character in the Saharan North African location of his documentary and with native peoples in just as careful and leisurely a

This self-crucifixion from *The Passenger* follows the film's sole "Jacksplosion," a result of a losing battle between man and machine that leads Nicholson's character, Locke, to beat an inanimate object—his jeep—with a shovel to the point of exhaustion.

manner as did Tony Richardson's opening of *The Border*, both of which did so without the intrusion of narrative dialogue.

Nicholson looks like he belongs in this setting and is part of what transpires, even as an outsider. This sense of true place provides a key to his clarity and success as an actor. There is a Nicholson moment, a Jacksplosion, early in the film when he throws a fit at his vehicle, mirroring man against machine of transport as in *Five Easy Pieces* and *The Border*, and by Micky Dolenz in Nicholson's co-written Monkees cult favorite *Head*. Here, his Jeep gets caught in the sand and Nicholson flings himself fully into beating the inanimate object with a shovel to the point of exhaustion, the kind of exhaustion that's from defeat rather than fatigue. He crouches down, plunging his fists into the sand like Charlton Heston at the end of *Planet of the Apes* and unconvincingly spits that he does not care.

A political documentary journalist, Locke trades identity with a dead man—a man he had just met—seemingly as a result of a spontaneous decision with no need and no rationale. When Locke stares down at the body of David

Robertson, who died in his hotel room after the pair make their acquaintance, it's as if Locke is looking at a version of himself, so intent and tender, not because of any interpersonal connection but because of an internal, inner bond. Nicholson's character decides that he instead will be the one to die, but without the responsibility of dying.

He exchanges photos on passports, changes clothes and rooms. He doesn't know why. He doesn't know what the man does and can't know what he will have to do in order to take Robertson's place.

The common wording for this act is "assuming the identity" of another. Here, the word "assuming" takes on further meanings. Locke is assuming he can pull this off without being discovered in the first few minutes. He's assuming that he can improvise some sort of reasonable simulation of a stranger's life based on the scant agenda from a calendar of appointments. Most essential, he's assuming, in order to make it possible, no one else will care any more than he does.

A colleague, interviewed about Locke's death, noted that the reporter had a "great detachment," an ironic choice of phrase given that the subject had just detached himself from his own life, his identity, his connections and his responsibilities (as in *Five Easy Pieces*).

As the switch takes place, Antonioni's pans span time as well as space, setting the tone for memory as foreshadowing and for effect as cause. It's also a masterful moviemaking technique. The director uses the full width of the screen, depicting the outdoors as landscape and people often as part of that landscape rather than foreground to it.

In a circular conversation with co-star Maria Schneider, the characters touch upon memory, relationships and the nature of reality. Does it matter if you can remember something or can stay connected with other people? If people disappear whenever they leave a room, do they matter and do they still exist? Can you exchange yourself for another with no consequences—or, more harrowingly, with no notice?

With his subtle performance, Nicholson portrays Locke as somewhat more engaged in his new persona, not because he's more interested in gun-running than reporting or more purposeful as Robertson than Locke. Uncertainty makes this inevitable. Locke can no longer merely play by the rules because he doesn't know what's supposed to happen next, let alone what the rules might be.

Aside from the attack on his Jeep, there is another more physical scene to complement this more understated and more cerebral portrayal. Locke rides in a cable car, like Orson Welles and Joseph Cotten in *The Third Man*, traveling over water. Nicholson waves his arms like wings, which gives the appearance of graceful flight from the perspective directly above. In 1975, we are seeing a more artful precursor to a later scene on the bow of the *Titanic* that featured Kate Winslet and Leonardo DiCaprio, or a more stylized reenactment of Nicholson riding with Captain America in *Easy Rider*. This transported illusion of flight is echoed later in the film when Maria Schneider rides in the back of a white convertible with red leather interior through a green-treed forest, a living part of the living beauty, a moving aspect of a stationary tree-lined road. At this moment, the otherwise understated Nicholson doesn't have to pretend to be happy and buoyant. Upon meeting the "Girl," he loses a few years and appears to become a more joyful and youthfully energetic Nicholson.

She is fresh, voluptuous and spontaneous. As he waits in a bar for Maria's character (she is never given a name), Nicholson *is* waiting, not pretending to wait, and not knowing that the waiting will be over at a defined, scripted point. He spins a glass on the bar as if his character can remain there for hours or be interrupted in just a moment. The glass is not a prop but an object of his attention, just as an orange becomes one in a post-intimacy scene with Schneider. He toys with the orange throughout their conversation. It is always handled but never eaten. It is not opened or peeled, nor is there any intention to use the orange as an orange. Similar imagery of meaningful orange manipulation occurs in Nicholson's directorial debut *Drive, He Said* and in his scripted LSD exploration *The Trip*.

Antonioni found it difficult working with Nicholson and Schneider at the same time because they were such completely different actors, "natural in opposite ways: Nicholson knows where the camera is and acts accordingly," while Maria "just lives the scene" with a gift for improvisation. "I see the film in its unity whereas the actor sees a film through his character."[22]

Nicholson provides another glimpse into a real, living man beneath the resignation in the reporter's footage when a witch doctor turns the camera around on the interviewer, revealing an embarrassed, abashed, surprised and schoolboyish response, as real as a documentary moment should be. He is natural in his unnatural reaction and its attendant feeling, providing the only point in the film that we see the celebrated Jack Nicholson smile.

The most notable part of *The Passenger* is seven minutes in duration. A single, historic and masterful shot worthy of Welles himself (*The Magnificent Ambersons* and *Touch of Evil*), this extremely slow zoom (an anti-zoom?) is the ultimate penultimate shot in the history of cinema. This is not a movie scene as much as a physical construction of life and death, action and negation, everything and nothing, denouement and ambiguity. These seven minutes took 11 days to shoot, because the wind made it difficult to keep the camera steady.

Simultaneously detached and removed (because we are seeing, yet missing the real action) while intrusive and probing (because we enter Locke's room to reveal his fate), the shot pits motion against entropy. The director wanted him "part of the landscape ... [b]ut not specifically on him."[23] Locke does become Robertson, an unglamorous and unimportant death in a remote hotel room bed. This time, a person *enters* a room in order to disappear. His true identity is revealed after the point it can ever matter to him. Meanwhile, the landscape provides the form, as cars pass, people walk by, and a lifeless life concludes.

In *Becoming Jack Nicholson*, Shaun Karli explains that the quest for authentic choices dominates the actor's performance: "Nicholson's personal understanding of existentialism informs both his choice of roles and his acting technique." Locke's change of identity is therefore based on the existentialist notion that individuals create their identities through their choices.[24]

Like a werewolf, the original identity of a man returns at the point of death. David Locke is David Locke again, after having assumed the dead form of another, as an empty form haunting the life of David Robertson. "He's a witness, not a protagonist," Antonioni explained.[25] In a tripled connection, Robertson's character in the film was played not by an actor, but by an associate producer on *The Last Detail* and later producer on *The Postman Always Rings Twice*, because of his supposed resemblance to Nicholson. Charles Mulvehill also provided the name (though misspelled as Mulvihill) for the hated detective who becomes Polanski's sidekick when performing a little nose surgery on J.J. Gittes in *Chinatown*.

* * *

Another reconnection happened on the film *As Good as It Gets* with actress Shirley Knight, who plays Helen Hunt's mother Beverly Connelly.

Best-known for her Oscar-nominated supporting performance in *The Dark at the Top of the Stairs*, Tennessee Williams' *Sweet Bird of Youth* and more recently *The Divine Secrets of the Ya-Ya Sisterhood*, this accomplished stage and screen actress studied her art together with Nicholson nearly 40 years before they appeared together in this James L. Brooks award-magnet.

Thirteen years after that triumph, Knight spoke to me at length about her career, the craft of acting and Jack Nicholson:

> I've known Jack, he and I were in acting class together in 1959. So I've known him for so long. And he married a girl in the class, her name was Sandra Knight—and over the years, everybody thinks we were married, because Shirley Knight, Sandra Knight. And so we were doing the movie, and Jack as a joke says, "You know, Shirley, people think that we were married." And I said, "Yes, I know, Jack." And he said, "You know, I really miss our marriage." Helen [Hunt] was standing right there and Helen said, "You guys were married?" and I was like, "I give up, I give up." But that's him, he's a joker.[26]

Nicholson plays Melvin Udall, a successful writer, but one whose storms are internal. Cripplingly obsessive-compulsive, he can work, but he cannot truly live. His first breakthrough is not another human being, but a dog. The iconic poster didn't depict him holding up Simon's Brussels Griffon, Verdell, because the dog was cute (though it was), but because it represented the bridge between aloneness—being alone with his writing, his piano and his clean isolation—and togetherness.

Yet even that was a rough transition. In his first scene with Verdell (Jill the Dog), Jack uses his harshest voice and attitude aside from his first confrontation with Simon (Greg Kinnear) and Frank (Cuba Gooding, Jr.).

This is a film of many Jacks. We see the exploring and expressive Nicholson, who holds up the dog as she pees with the same freedom and in the same fashion as Jack himself in *Wolf* (raining on James Spader's loafers) and *About Schmidt*. We see the rom-com lead, though romantically alone in this case, reading his own work aloud in a voice so soft and with an expression so relaxed and open that he could just as easily be David in *The King of Marvin Gardens*.

There's a hard and hurtful Jack, who is compelled to chide Simon about his plight and appearance after being brutally attacked. He does wrong, as when observing that Carol's (Hunt) son might die soon, in the same tone and significance as if describing an oncoming storm or the tough pitcher taking on the home team. This is when the subtlety of meaning takes over.

You glimpse a sudden but brief understanding that he's done wrong, a slow absorption into a being who is there but is at this point still mostly dormant. Hunt attacks Nicholson and berates him for an acknowledgment, but he takes forever to answer with his longest and most meaningful "Yes" response, a stuttered affirmative that's delicate and genuine. "Yes" may well be Jack Nicholson's favorite word as an actor, possibly because so few use it importantly, yet alone take it seriously, while this actor has consciously decided to give it the attention and intent it actually and truly deserves.

Shirley Knight delved inside the actor's mind, as only a true acolyte of the profession could. "Jack is so comfortable in his own skin. You know, he's one of these people who really knows who he is and doesn't censor himself. People say to me, 'What's Jack Nicholson like?' And I say, 'You know what you see? That's what you get. That's him.'"[27]

There's the classic Jack, during his "don't come knocking" speech at his apartment door, wherein he employs his arsenal of expressions, heel-rises, speech patterns and accents, his motion and countenance clipped and pushed forward, aggressively delivering shot after shot after shot to Lupe Ontiveros (also from *The Border*).

Nicholson sings to his canine friend, using the *Monty Python's Life of Brian* theme song as bookend to their relationship. He purposefully adds "your" when giving a message for the dog and himself to "Always Look on the Bright Side of Your Life," perhaps a strange sentiment for such a cheerless and

Storm-filled in life, Melvin is an easy writer. He writes romance novels yet lacks romance, or *any* meaningful relationship, in his life. Thus, the ironically titled *As Good as It Gets* (1997).

antisocial personage. But, after Verdell leaves, Nicholson plays a sadder version of the tune as he laughs and cries in the same moment. This is when he starts to become a man, joining humanity rather than merely writing about it.

Storm-filled in life, Melvin is an easy writer. Finishing his latest romance novel, Nicholson uses the voice of aged velvet, not pristinely shiny or perfectly smoothed, but showing some of the roughness that can come from use and life's reality.

Nicholson has fun with a nice piece of business with his sunglasses on the drive to Simon's parents. Upon the mention of Simon's mother having modeled for the young artist, the shades start down in place and move up via Melvin's raised eyebrows at the moment it is revealed that the mother posed nude for her son; then pushed up on the forehead before letting them fall down; when reacting to the story of Simon's father's beating, Melvin raises them slightly with his gloved hands to wipe his eyes. Once again, he leaves the glasses up on his forehead, only to let them drop down once again into place.

During the big date scene with Carol, Melvin reaches another turning point when a new jacket and tie he bought to meet the Baltimore restaurant's dress code seems to actually calm him down and make him more normal, more desirable and more desired. The clothes do make the man. His cute sideways wave and big triangle-shaped-eyebrows grin signals a new man.

Melvin's breakthrough does not come easy. He touches his face a lot and builds to the ultimate "compliment" with a wipe across the brow, rubbed hands and rubbed fingertips. As he recounts the story of having taken his pills for the first time and Carol challenges him as to how that could be a compliment to her, the actor goes to work. He briefly reacts and puts his hands together and intertwines the fingers. He lowers them and looks down. He smiles, bites the right side of his lips and lifts his eyes to declare that it's a compliment because she makes him want to be better, accentuating the point with a slight eyebrow raise toward the end and after enriching the statement with fast but subtle eye-blinks.

This compliment, this declaration of a devotion that truly touches his life, expands eight seconds of screen time, eight magic seconds made special because he uses six of the eight seconds for the set-up. That's why it works and creates such an emotional impact: the import of the statement, yes; the transformation of the character, yes; but the manner of pulling you into the emotional moment. Nicholson masterfully pulls you in by putting much more emphasis on the air before the spoken line and more on the preparation for the line than its delivery. That is what counts and that is what an actor who has learned and has reached a level that allows him to take such "valuable" screen time with silence and gestures to make the line so exquisite. His smooth, beautiful delivery was embodied with authentic meaning, not just acted meaning.

His sweetest, most emotionally open moment was sealed by Hunt's reaction shot, as a slow zoom follows her subtle read with slow, partial eye-closes, for a completely wonderful conveyance of feeling.

In this restaurant scene, Jack uses so many small movements and slight reactions—his eyes and the starts and stops of his speech—when Hunt moves over to his side of the table, we benefit from the luxury of an actor at the top of his game who is given the opportunity to expand the scene and elaborate on the feeling he gets when romance finally enters his character's life.

At this point in his career, Nicholson has become more adept at the comedic portion of his performances, no longer forced or awkwardly broad. When Carol calls Simon on the phone after Melvin takes him in, he uses some nice little business, wiping his brow in distress here and there, on the sides and then across, before joining the call with a romantic cough.

The conversation leads to his second emotionally staggering line when he painfully reveals his regret that he did not dance with her at the Baltimore restaurant. Nicholson even pulls in a bit of his *Prizzi's Honor* character, Charley Partanna, when reacting to Simon's lament that Melvin is luckier because he knows what he wants. Wordlessly, Nicholson beckons some Partanna in his slit eyes and slow thought.

In his final transformative scene, as Melvin and Carol go to her neighborhood bakery at four in the morning, he tells her how he's the only guy who sees how special she is. Taking such a defining stance with such certainty and strength, Nicholson transitions the character's style of speaking from realistically halting to flowing, forceful and confident. His clear delivery and tone carry attitude and manner to move through three or four modes of expression within that one section of dialogue. Nicholson brings such nuance and range of true character energy to the moment that we can almost feel his growth. Then, in the middle of this big speech, Melvin completely stops shaking and becomes precise and direct, focusing his entire being on his life and his love instead of his obsessions with cleanliness, sidewalk cracks and numbers. His obsessive-compulsive disorder made Melvin count locks and switch the lights on and off in two rooms. He does each five times. His number is five. Is this a reference to *Five Easy Pieces*, his breakthrough role 27 years earlier? Who knows? And who's counting?

* * *

Melvin Udall is. He finishes his 62nd book in *As Good as It Gets*. Jack Torrance can't start, let alone finish, his first book in *The Shining*. Eugene O'Neill and Carl Bernstein each won a Pulitzer Prize. *Wolf* Will Randall takes on the form of a werewolf while *Passenger* David Locke takes on the identity of a dead man. Writers, editors, reporters, obsessing about their own rituals or on wrongs done by others; terrorizing their wives in a remote hotel or in a new home in need of major repairs; a playwright out of his time or a political documentarian who runs out of time. They all live to put one word in front of the other and one idea as prelude to the next.

12

Rom-Com Wonder

Harry thinks he loves Marin, but he really loves her mother Erica. The astronaut loves the Southern belle and the hit man loves the other hit man until she tries to hit him. Melvin the writer has to learn how to live before he can learn how to love the waitress Carol. A devilish guy loves a trio of hot, young friends. And a fake Carl Bernstein loves himself more than he does a fake Nora Ephron. It's not *The Love Boat* or Oprah or Dr. Buddy Rydell's next encounter group.

No, it's the wonderful world of the rom-com, a world of mostly beautiful people and largely unamusing comic talents.

Think Jennifer Aniston, Matthew McConaughey, Kate Hudson, Ashton Kutcher, Julia Roberts, Vince Vaughn, Drew Barrymore, Katherine Heigl, Paul Rudd ... and Jack Nicholson?

Late in his career, the actor best known for the huge roles, the big personalities, the memorable moments of *Batman*, *The Shining*, *Cuckoo's Nest*, *A Few Good Men* and *The Last Detail*, became something of a rom-com wonder. A genre associated with the young and the pretty (both men and women) has embraced senior citizen Jack and has been rewarded with box office and awards.

There was no announcement, no press conference, no news release. But without fanfare, the antihero became a major romantic comedy star for the AARP crowd. Since he turned 60, eight Nicholson movies have been released and half of them have been rom-coms.

With a little help, even casual moviegoers can see the latter comedy tendencies of Nicholson. Alongside Helen Hunt in *As Good as It Gets* and Diane Keaton in *Something's Gotta Give*; paired with Kathleen Turner in *Prizzi's Honor* and quadrupled with Cher, Susan Sarandon and Michelle Pfeiffer in *The Witches of Eastwick*; plus the regrettable romances *Man Trouble* and *How Do You Know*.

As Nicholson has matured, so have his comic instincts. He no longer pushes, letting humor emerge naturally from character and conflict, action and reaction. Forced, broad, near-caricatures such as *Goin' South*'s Henry Moon and *The Fortune*'s Oscar smoothen to somewhat overblown treatments that feature shades of humanity, such as Charley Partanna in *Prizzi's Honor*, Daryl Van Horne in *The Witches of Eastwick* and the dual role of President James Dale and developer Art Land in *Mars Attacks!* The progression is complete with *As Good as It Gets*, the successive trio of *About Schmidt*, *Anger Management* and *Something's Gotta Give*, along with the later dramedy *The Bucket List*.

Appropriately, Nicholson's most nuanced comic performances come to life in the romantic comedies. His movements are slight and subtle except when it suits the situation to become bigger and more "Jack-like." As Melvin, his OCD provides latitude for occasional outbursts and thoughtless acts. Elsewhere, the character and the actor are both under perfect control, earning sympathy for a man who could have remained a one-dimensional bully in the hands of a lesser performer. Pauses say more than words. A wipe of the brow and a nervous rub of the fingertips endear. When shaking is replaced by level precision, we know he is a changed man because he thinks more about another than himself.

* * *

Dr. Buddy Rydell presents Nicholson the opportunity to seesaw from boisterous and rambunctious to ironic and mock-sensitive. In his introductory scene on a plane with Adam Sandler, he's all about "the stuff" that establishes comedy and character. Soon thereafter, he shifts to soft and calming, coming across as if he believes in the claptrap of "getting in touch" with ourselves. He's in charge, but not pushy, using controlled intensity as his defining character energy. At one point, he approaches a judge in command and with *Saturday Night Fever*–Travolta slickness, insincere and smooth as faux fur. At another, he's the explosive Jack who blows up over eggs (not over easy, ironically, as requested) and promptly calms down to regain his role of therapist. Is the good doctor crazy? The ongoing ambiguity could very well be a McMurphy *Cuckoo's Nest* reference.

Nicholson plays Rydell as mischievous; as spontaneous (singing "I Feel Pretty" with *basso profundo* confidence); as mercurial, when he betrays confusion about his mother in surgery and leaps from berserk to happy to suspicious, all within only a couple of actor-ranged minutes; and as demonic, with a slo-mo phony encouraging nod that boosts Sandler toward his "exploding Mr. Pants" come-on to Heather Graham.

Nicholson admitted that though he's "not that into farting and vomit jokes," Sandler interested him. "It's all a learning experience, as far as I'm concerned."[1] Director Peter Segal had been concerned that his two leads would overshadow one another, but that the reality of the concept would make the journey sufficiently believable. "Some of our first discussions with Jack were about the tone, and the balance, and how real we were going to be."[2]

* * *

In *Anger Management*, Nicholson seems to have become more comfortable in his role as comic actor—perhaps in part due to his supporting position—without feeling the pressure to be as overly energetic in carrying the show. Nicholson is feeling it without ramming it and living without pressing, sliding from aspect to aspect rather than carrying the burden to push from action to action as if doing so singlehandedly.

Harry Sanborn represented a further step in Nicholson's perfection of the comic transformation, made more difficult because it could not have been as dramatic as was Melvin's. He didn't have a condition. He was just a cad, in the minds of many Jack playing Jack. In *Something's Gotta Give*, the something was Harry's tendency toward young women. He had to mature in order to find a woman closer to his age attractive. Erica (Diane Keaton) had to give by looking beyond her self-absorption and career obsession to let someone into her life. They both had to give in order to meet in the middle.

It should be no surprise, when seeing their interaction, to find that director Nancy Meyers felt that Diane and Jack "were really the only actors I wanted for this movie."[3]

You can see that Jack enjoyed playing the rakes and playing with his own image, a delightful inside joke shared with the other actors and with the audience. He likes to shock and leer and be the dirty boy. He lampoons himself with relish, yet to the benefit of the character arc rather than any sort of comic grab for attention that could have served as detriment to the story.

Harry's career isn't exactly the drive of his life, as it is for Erica. For a hip-hop label mogul, he never mentions or listens to music. It does provide access to parties, glamour, money and babes. A heart attack shows he is no longer as young as the women he dates. He needs to be taken care of. He can't even chance having sex, which leads to a beautiful scene of comic pathos that's both a test of his will and a chance for some subtle physical comedy. Harry must climb a flight of stairs to prove he is ready for sex, with the character struggling and failing, grasping and gasping, and nearly losing (all while the audience enjoys the nice touch of using Jimmy Cliff's "You Can Get It If You Really Want It" to underscore his toil and eventual triumph).

Nicholson makes pieces of life real. We feel for a man who has become vulnerable for the first time in his life (something that is neither said nor implied, though somehow we know) when Marin (Amanda Peet) kisses him like she would an older uncle instead of a vital lover. He's hurt, he's ashamed, and he realizes the kiss-off as he gazes without focus and intones that "It's down to the cheek." In the tradition of the sad clown greats, Harry Sanborn becomes Harry Langdon, a man-child who's a striking contrast to the slain lady-killer.

The comic actor in Nicholson delivers lines with a naturalness that makes the situations connect so that the laughs come naturally. "I think there's something about the way Jack uses language," Keaton explained. "It's like he's a master of the word, and the love of the word."[4]

Nicholson also has a sense for his physical being to use his body, his hands and his expressions as instruments of humanity and humor. After all, Harry isn't a bad man. He is flawed, as he gives in to his temptations toward much younger women. Is it Harry's fault that his money and position in the music biz help him get exactly what he desires?

Jack's hospital gown scene and his accidental encounter with a naked Diane Keaton give him full license for delicious slapstick, seeming to fight his own body. He struggles to remain upright in a dance against gravity up and down a hospital corridor and he fights a wall, trying to escape a situation he cannot handle, which is remaining in the presence of a nude woman who is old enough to be his ex-girlfriend's mother (because she is).

Through his transitional period, Nicholson's Harry reprises his character's fast eye-blinks to represent moments of doubt. It's a slight movement, betraying weakness by flitting his eyes in a toned-down version of his earlier self. This is a comic actor in complete control. When Erica writes and produces a play about their relationship as revenge against Sanborn, he reacts to hearing a young actress describe his thinly veiled parody having a heart attack while messing around with a younger lover in a way that's physical and smart, not broad or overdone. He knows the temperature of the character and always keeps it in balance with that of the world in which that character resides. Critics talk about heightened reality in films, but there's less to it than that. In real life, people tend to overreact. Unexpected situations and emotional drama shock and stun, with an equal and opposite reaction the result. Should an actor be that "true" on-screen, the magnification would make every gesture and expression so large that it would overwhelm the scene. We see this on TV, where it's more accepted due to the smaller scale and even smaller expectations. In movies, the thinking actor must be true to reality while dialing it down to make the overall presentation palatable. Ninety-plus minutes of mugging and overreacting can wear an audience down and break down any connection to the narrative worth than if the story itself were full of holes.

By the time of *Something's Gotta Give*, Nicholson had perfected his comic touch, a lightness and maturity much like the hard-earned destiny of his character. Even his wardrobe comes into play. More than for appearance or for his character to inhabit, Jack uses their physicality. For instance, Harry tugs his jacket closed while in the theater when watching the scene that makes fun of his heart attack, in a pathetically inadequate attempt to hide himself. Earlier in the film, the actor uses a similar gesture when pulling his robe closed to cover himself through his embarrassment, exposed as a man coming to terms with his weakness and vulnerability.

* * *

The romantic actor in Nicholson retains this strength of portrayal in *As Good as It Gets*, though six years had passed. Both films focus on a man's transformation as necessary admission price for a mature romantic relationship. In *As Good as It Gets*, his character energy is imposing, traveling through the character with physical devotion and emotional range. Gestures and moves accent thought and feeling, yet never distract.

The motion of his eyes and action of his eyelids take us toward the man, while line delivery brings us all the way inside him. When Melvin tells Carol he stopped taking his pills in tribute to her and reveals he should have danced with her, we respond with true emotion and feel a little of what each of them feels. These are fictional characters, yet people we do not know (the actors Jack Nicholson and Helen Hunt) find a way to fuse us with these characters, making us part of them rather than merely close enough to overhear them. Here, he is sweet and emotionally open.

In *Something's Gotta Give*, he learns to become charming and casual, a more grownup version of what had made the predatory Harry so successful with the ladies. His conversion lies bare his inner emotions in ways unnecessary for Melvin. Melvin had to become aware of his faults, face them and find a way to defeat or at least subdue them. Harry had to feel his faults, having them turned against him by former conquests and through the public humiliation from Erica's play. Melvin stopped taking his pills so he could feel, but Harry needed a taste of his own medicine in order to empathize and feel how others feel.

As Harry grows up, he gets younger, playful and coy, rather than lecherous and commanding. Nicholson and Keaton become a couple when they walk on the beach and picnic together, attaining a quality sadly unattainable by so many rom-com combinations who too often only reach the point in the story where they are in love but rarely reach the place within their characters where they exude the glow of love.

* * *

Nicholson had to feel a special connection to Melvin and Harry, while much weaker films like *Heartburn* and *The Evening Star* provided only glimpses of the Nicholson who would later become so accomplished in romantic comedy. In *Heartburn*, a film that largely lives up to its name, the otherwise unsympathetic Mark Forman reconciles with Meryl Streep's Rachel in an emotionally bare and charming scene when the estranged husband and wife (stand-ins for real-life Carl Bernstein and Nora Ephron) meet at a fountain. Here, Nicholson closes up when opening up, and later breaks down entirely in the movie's other palpably true and impactful scene, when he brings himself back to how he felt during the risky birth of their first child.

In *The Evening Star*, he returns as astronaut Garrett Breedlove for a charming reunion with Shirley MacLaine as Aurora Greenway. Like Melvin Udall and Harry Sanborn, this man has grown by opening himself to those around him instead of focusing solely on his own immediate needs. He's caring and thoughtful, but not at the sacrifice of humor and personality.

The movie may have been an unnecessary and annoying sequel to *Terms of Endearment*, but Nicholson and MacLaine's time together on-screen provided a few moments as precious as those shared by the characters in life. As with Nicholson's other strong romantic comedies, moviegoers get to see the interplay between people older than the typical rom-com pairings, and in ways neither "icky" nor cloying.

Nicholson has also had his share of less refined takes on the genre, playing more for the comedy than the romantic in mid-period examples *Goin' South* (1978), *Prizzi's Honor* (1985) and *The Witches of Eastwick* (1987). Nicholson directed himself as Henry Lloyd Moon in the first title, a western farce released seven years after his official directorial debut, *Drive, He Said*.

Perhaps to make himself more comfortable, he surrounded himself with plenty of friends: Christopher Lloyd and Danny DeVito from *Cuckoo's Nest*, Jeff Morris, Luana Anders, B.J. Merholz, producer Harry Gittes and screenwriter John Herman Shaner. He even wrote the part of Whitey for Ed Begley Jr. when the young actor asked if there was a part for him. "Beg, I'll see what I can do."[5]

Tracey Walter, who later worked on *The Two Jakes* and *Batman* (again, as in this film, playing a member of Nicholson's gang), was "overwhelmed by being part of a film like that with people like that." He called it "a great film, a great experience. Me, Veronica [Cartwright] and Danny DeVito—we played the Moon Gang."[6]

Nicholson's portrayal of Moon is quite broad (as is John Belushi's debut as one of Moon's gang members). Moon has an odd vocal affectation that sounds like Alfalfa with cotton in each nostril or suffering from a permanent stuffed head. Begley fondly recalled that "we partied every night," pointing out that it was the '70s and that sort of thing was pretty common, though "no matter what we did, we showed up on time and we knew our lines."[7]

Nicholson plays a nice comedic false sincerity in the gallows speech pleading for a wife in order to secure his freedom from a hanging fate. He establishes the character with big gestures, expansive movement and exaggerated expressions. As the film progresses, in certain sequences you have the overdone and mugging Jack—delivering what he is so often accused of—but in this film it seems to make an odd sense. The bombast isn't so much overacting as it is a true representation of Moon himself. He plays it true when he plays over-the-Moon.

Later, in a scene with his savior-wife-boss, played beautifully by Mary Steenburgen in her film debut, Jack deftly softens his characterization as he moves toward and away from the camera on a porch swing. As if that action itself helps calm Henry down, he opens up tenderly and talks about how he knows about dreams, revealing the failure of his own. His eyes are wide and alive. His eyes make the character and define the man.

Henry must court Steenburgen's Julia after they are already married. At first, Julia takes advantage of saving Henry from hanging by turning him into a virtual slave, mining for gold. As the marriage of convenience and the marriage of forced labor become a marriage of admiration and then of love, the two are shown more in-frame, together (as directed by Nicholson) and the pace of the film slows.

Henry Moon becomes a romantic action hero of a different sort, a working man and outlaw who is honest as both. He has a surface truth, earnest and "just tryin' to impress" Julia. He even adds a sweetness to an escape scene. After having been trapped in a collapsed mine, Moon discovers an opening into a field, yet takes the time to notice wildflowers and pick a bouquet to present to his wife as a way to break the surprise of freedom.

Moon is a big character, yet Nicholson keeps him in just enough control without limiting the man's range. Henry navigates from insincere charmer and failed outlaw to dedicated worker and romantic pursuer. He explodes with personality at one end of the scale, then pulls inward with intimacy at the other. Henry's relationship to Julia travels from a cold employer-employee status through partnership all the way to genuine love. This juxtaposes his movement away from the old gang, from playful camaraderie (and in the case of Veronica Cartwright, a romance of sorts) to the kind of uncomfortable distance experienced by old schoolmates who meet at reunions only to find they no longer have anything in common.

Beyond the physicality of his portrayal, accented with moments of tenderness, Nicholson also displays superior riding ability. His training and prior experience in westerns shows in the opening chase scene as well as a stunt later in the movie when he jumps onto his horse from the ground in one smooth move.

When Henry and Julia get back together after the escape, their transformation of each other is complete, a symbolic embodiment of the spirit of romance. In the beginning, he was dirty and she pristine. At the end, he is clean and she is filthy and happy about it, though it didn't hurt that they are now both filthy rich and "goin' south" to Mexico.

* * *

Another romantic comedy featuring an oddly nasal accent from Nicholson and a non-traditional romance was *Prizzi's Honor*, directed by John Huston (who last worked with Jack as a fellow actor in *Chinatown*). Similar in characterization, Charley Partanna was a 600-mile trip from Jimmy Hoffa, Detroit to Brooklyn. Through the film, Nicholson never has his mouth fully closed, a mouth-breather who pronounces "ask" as "axe." His mouth was also often downturned, a bit like Bogart and a bit like he's always getting ready to whistle. His top lip was pulled out, a big upper lip with a thick philtrum for a Brando's *Godfather* in reverse.

The first time we see Nicholson, he looks like a young hood as in *Studs Lonigan*. He plays the character with an active, scrunchy face of the Italian gangster from Brooklyn, the made guy who always has to look out for enemies and friends. Perhaps Nicholson's New Jersey roots and his New York City birth come to life in this character, inherited by Charley Partanna.

As with other later comedic efforts, Nicholson here is more successful

The soul of *Prizzi's Honor* (1985) is the relationship between Nicholson as Charley Partanna and Kathleen Turner as Irene Walker. A mob parody, this John Huston film relies on its comedic-romantic core to connect with audiences.

when light rather than pushing too much or grasping for comedic attention. Always slow, always low, his mannerisms and speech underscore instead of undercut. He exhibits confidence and style. One nice recurring touch of character energy is how his use of body language shows Charley to be more relaxed when in the role of hit man. He's in his element, comfortably killing while awkward with everyday sociability.

The soul of the film is the relationship with Kathleen Turner as Irene Walker. He convincingly plays it smitten in their introductory scene at a church wedding. In a cute touch, he does a slow motion version of the Jack hair wipe before approaching her the first time to dance. In a late night call with Irene, he's flustered like a little boy (a moment now indelibly distracted by a wonderful view of the World Trade Center in the background).

In Nicholson's most powerful scene, he confronts Turner after the killing of her character's husband. He fuses voice, body and expression to create the real man. When Charley is yelling, it is real and the anger is authentic. Then a classic Jack look upward, through narrowed eyelids while his arms shake out to his sides, reveal his secret acting weapon. He uses his eyes. They move, darting as she informs him that she had been at the wedding to make a hit.

Many actors, even the great ones, do not necessarily realize what Nicholson does with the use of his eyes. They are physical and their motion serves as a sort of body language to express the state of mind of the character. They are not there to see but to reflect. In *A Few Good Men*, he is able to keep them immobile to show Jessep's obsessive self-control, while here they travel wildly both in response to betrayal and as emblematic of Charley's discomfort with a confrontation that doesn't involve firing a gun. He also partly defines the character by looking up to expose the bottom of the whites of his eyes as a recurring expression.

Nicholson's portrayal of uneasiness is the most richly detailed aspect of his Charley Partanna. When Anjelica Huston sarcastically thanks him for being "a lotta help," he shows confusion with a fast eye blink. After being found out by The Family, he's ill at ease and overly animated at dinner with William Hickey. After Irene confesses her role as hit woman, Nicholson adopts the same look and the same body hump as in his Hoffa "I'm gonna do what I gotta do" scene.

Later in the film, Nicholson rounds out the character in his "nothing but bodyguards and money" speech, in which he talks about being alone like the three older men he addresses—father, lawyer and Don—displaying a passion for life in opposition of their perverse passion for death. This depth of emotion belies the dramedy approach of the film, taking it beyond the movie itself.

His work in *The Witches of Eastwick* doesn't include any such transcendent moments, but one key sequence toward the end justifies its preceding bombastic majority. Nicholson is the perfect actor for the role of Daryl Van

Richard Kaufman served as Nicholson's violin coach on *The Witches of Eastwick* (1987). He worked with the actor for three months, not to teach him to play the instrument, but to teach him to look like he plays.

Horne in this chick flick with a devilish twist, but it wasn't necessarily the perfect role for the actor. That is, aside from having fun and working with a trio of glamorous actresses: Michelle Pfeiffer, Cher and Susan Sarandon.

John Updike, who wrote the novel on which the film was based, snuck into an afternoon showing at a local mall with his wife, Martha. Updike biographer Adam Begley related to me how she loathed it, but that he was less bothered. The special effects distracted him from the screenplay's deviation from the book, "leaving him free to enjoy the three witches, each lovable in her own way."[8]

The movie seems trite until a transitional seduction scene with Cher that snaps it tighter when she violently rejects his advances and *him*. Van Horne then becomes the insightful, sensitive drill to the truth that allows him to disarm the woman.

With Susan Sarandon, he doesn't sweet-talk her, he soft-talks her, using tenderness to breathe out song and righteousness.

Conductor and violinist Richard Kaufman, who served for 18 years as an MGM music supervisor, explained to me the amount of effort that went into training for the musical sequences. Credited as Nicholson's violin coach on *The Witches of Eastwick* (though he also coached Jack on piano and Sarandon as conductor), Kaufman worked with the actor for three months, just about every day. "The idea is to not teach an actor to play the instrument," he said, "but to teach them to look like they play, and to look like they've been playing it for most of their life" as realistically and as comfortably as possible.[9]

Nicholson's legendary dedication to research and Method-like preparation is evident on-screen, despite the brevity of his appearance. Kaufman related,

> I think that being the consummate actor that he is, Jack wanted to look absolutely realistic in every part of his performance. He devoted a great deal of time and energy to the idea that he would look like he was really playing the instruments. The music that they chose was part of a Paganini "Caprice," which is not an easy piece to play, even if you're a great violinist.[10]

Despite this dedication, he mainly plays a caricature of "Jack," the actor's name in quotes rather than the actor in control. Even Nicholson hinted as such when telling an interviewer prior to filming, "I've been studying to play the Devil. Of course, a lot of people think I've been preparing for it all my life."[11]

While Updike had been careful to keep Van Horne from stealing the show as the Devil tends to do, Begley pointed out that Nicholson, "who had no such scruple, gave an outrageously exuberant performance."[12] Nicholson's face is puffy and fleshy, yet he succeeds in coming across as unnaturally sexual as "just your average horny little devil" who repeats the invitation to "have another cherry" in a completely purulent manner.

He becomes less "Jack" and more Nicholson when he is the victim rather than the lech. When he blows up and slams his phone down after Cher hangs up on him, it's not enough to throw it down; so he peers at it with vile hatred. When abandoned by his ladies, Van Horne experiences witch withdrawal, reducing him to a slobbering, blubbery mess whose hair is out of control and all over the place. With his eyes forced upward and defocused, the actor resembles Patrick Magee as attacked and damaged in *A Clockwork Orange*. Though nonplussed by some of Jack's excesses, author Updike was pleased that the filmmakers conveyed that his story was about women.[13]

As in many others of his films, Nicholson seemingly doesn't care how he looks, vanquishing vanity in favor of character. Instead, this student of the visual actually does care and care very much how he looks, purposely destroying the "star" in favor of the rare shock of seeing a Hollywood star in the most unglamorous fashion.

As victim, Nicholson also becomes more physical, such as when he blows up at Cher while ironing, pleading for "a little respect, a little trust" as he marches maniacally with posturing and bluster. This palpable movement erupts when the witches escalate their attacks from emotional hurt to bodily harm. Nicholson has to be having fun doing the climactic, solo voodoo scene, as he's stuck and feathered, Marcel Marceau-ing while slipping and sliding.

Through pantomime and physical comedy, the trademark messed-up Jack is wet and disheveled when disgusted and disgusting, running the gamut from boorish to sensitive, hurt to befuddled, sarcastic to sympathetic.

He rants and pleads, just serious enough to portray power and invite empathy, and just exaggerated enough to evoke laughs and welcome the audience to play along. Nicholson's "Do you think God knew what He was doing when He created women?" speech perfectly encapsulates the actor's character energy. He delivers the words with sound and fury.

His physical prowess tracks the emotions of the words along with the emotions themselves. Nothing else matters during these moments. The overdone, pushing attitude of much of the preceding film is forgotten. The Jackisms have slicked down to a polished portrayal. And the punch of the words themself create an emotional momentum with verbal stabs that pierce the screen and enter your consciousness to stay.

Van Horne truly wants to know if women were a mistake or a "plot." The Devil has been hurt! He asks the churchgoers whether anything can be done, be it vaccine, immunity or exercise. What matters is that we believe Van Horne, we believe that for these genuine pained moments that one hell of a playboy has been left helpless, struggling and grasping for answers by his true loves. That's what hurts most, and we feel his pain with just enough comic subtlety more in search of a knowing grin rather than an understanding tear.

To complete the moment, Nicholson retreats from the church to a limo, walking toward the witches in a limp-run parody of Jack Torrance's race after Danny and race against freezing in *The Shining*. Jack sometimes likes these self-referential moments. We do as well.

* * *

Nicholson seduces three witches here, but was seducing the camera 16 years earlier in Henry Jaglom's *A Safe Place*. Genreless, this BBS production featured Nicholson in a cameo that was purely romantic with no comedy. Shown 14 minutes in, this fleeting foreshadowing of a later love scene with Tuesday Weld does not appear in full form until the 33-minute mark.

In an entirely improvised scene on a rooftop, Mitch (Jack) flirts with

Susan (Tuesday) and with the camera, encircling her in a POV shot as he walks and eats, all the while looking at the camera and at us. A throwaway as it might seem, done as a favor to writer-director Jaglom, Nicholson fully connects in motion, using suggestive raised eyebrows, a winsome and toothsome smile to charm Weld's character and the audience.

Jaglom and Jack had made a deal to act in each other's directorial debuts; Henry was featured in *Drive, He Said* and Nicholson kept his word, even after achieving stardom. Jaglom said, "He did my first movie for a color television set that he really liked."[14]

Mitch is simultaneously natural and good-naturedly putting her on. *A Safe Place* may very well mark our first view of Nicholson as the star ladies' man, introducing his trademark eyebrows and smile.

Weld is stunningly beautiful and fresh, yet she also shows an emotional range from joyous and innocent to lustful and intense to reflective and pensive. She goes from playful to tearful. Her eyes are the star of the movie.

Nicholson's scant screen time belies his impact. His second appearance, a love scene in which he employs plenty of tongue on Weld's neck, is intercut with pieces featuring Tuesday and Orson Welles until Welles' "Magician" makes Mitch disappear with triumphant laughter—taking up a total of seven minutes of screen time.

After a brief blink in a darker love scene at the 51-minute mark, Nicholson returns again 63 minutes into the film at 4:00 a.m. in film time, taking Fred's (Philip Proctor) place with Susan using a natural physicality that combines discomfort with desire. In such a small and parceled role, Nicholson still delivers an emotional reality. After their newest coupling, Mitch levels a disturbed intensity, using clipped speech in his lower register, until he and Tuesday's character return to cuddling and kissing.

Nicholson was seen on screen only 27 minutes in *A Safe Place*. But he became a real person, even though he had no story outside of an unseen wife named Rita, becoming fully established and fully formed. The actor was not filling a narrative or playing a character; he was a person. We just don't know who he is or why he is there. In Jaglom's world of emotional truth, that would never matter.

The director defended critical opinion that the film made no sense by countering, "I was trying to play with conventional film structure ... playing with daydream and fact, illusion and reality, and the emotions of past, present and future." Nicholson played the role and got a color TV out of it.

* * *

On a Clear Day You Can See Forever was not Nicholson's only musical. Ken Russell's adaptation of the Who's rock opera *Tommy* was more successful and much more fun, featuring Ann-Margret in an all-star cast that combines actors, Nicholson included, with musicians such as Tina Turner, Elton John and Eric Clapton.

Russell presented the story like a moving comic strip crossed with an opera, a silent movie that dramatizes the trauma of World War II. A proto–Tim Burton, Russell emphasizes color and exaggerated action, with no fear of the cartoonish or grandiose. Ann-Margret called the film "as wild and exaggerated as a hallucination" and called Russell "wild, indulgent, kind and funny, always pushing for more."[15]

Nicholson plays "The Specialist," a doctor who's first seen examining Roger Daltrey's title character from the Who singer's point of view. Nicholson then sports a pince-nez and warbles the Pete Townshend composition "Go to the Mirror" in proper British-ish accent and with plenty of vibrato.

The filmmakers had been worried about Nicholson's singing, but Townshend wrote that Nicholson "sang beautifully" and was stunned "when he began to croon like a world-class Fifties club singer."[16] Nicholson appears more concerned with appearing to properly "sing," though he does add a pleasant final look as Ann-Margret leaves him, a glance that is part knowing and emotionally touched, part academic and romantically deprived. The actor is at once sly, yet nerdy. And his whole sequence is only three and a half minutes, including off-screen cuts.

Some small roles are smaller than others. Nicholson's in *Ensign Pulver* was the smallest among the small. Title character Robert Walker Jr.'s love interest, Millie Perkins, felt that "he didn't have much of a part in that movie and didn't enjoy it at all, as far as I know … he just wanted to work."[17]

In his first speaking scene, he delivers a message that "maybe we got a liberty" with eyebrow-raised irony and suitable snottiness. Nicholson's trim and serious as the radio operator, but not great at the comedy, pushing his admittedly weak jokes and telegraphing that he's about to say something "funny."

The romance of the romantic comedy is between Walker's title character and Millie Perkins, who is adorable and cute as a nurse—natural, relaxed and flirty in an understated way. Unfortunately, Walker plays the role earnestly without any relief, pushy and yelling, over-projecting so much that it wears you down. Walker yells even when delivering lines intended for just a little intensity. Nicholson, on the other hand, plays it charming and upbeat in a light and giggly scene when he gives a happy report that sailor "John X" (played by Tommy Sands) was "gonna have a baby!"

Nicholson does not even show up in the end credits despite having a decent speaking part. It must have seemed a cruel joke to play a scene in which the crew objects to watching a Boris Karloff movie that the captain (an irritating Burl Ives) insists they view. After all, just a few years before, Nicholson had been Karloff's co-star, but now was reduced to this uncredited role in a bad sequel. It's no wonder that Gary Kent and Ed Nelson both reported to me that he was on the verge of quitting.[18]

Ensign Pulver has no shortage of talent: It was written and directed by Joshua Logan and the cast included Ives, Walter Matthau, Perkins, Larry Hagman, Peter Marshall, Dick Gautier, James Farentino, James Coco and Kay Medford. Gautier said the film was enjoyable to make, but that the director wasn't always as agreeable. "Josh Logan was a strange man. Very strange guy. I mean, I liked him, but you never knew where you were. One morning he'd say, 'You got any good dirty jokes for me?' And we'd say, 'Yeah!' The next morning I'd say, 'Hello Josh,' and he'd say, 'Get over there and shut up!' Hot and cold, you know. So we were always on tenterhooks."[19]

The promise of the many notable newcomers in the cast and the pedigree to *Mister Roberts* not only did not pay off for Nicholson, but it also resulted in a mostly painful waste of the viewers' life. According to Perkins, "I don't think he wanted to make that movie, but he needed the money."[20]

* * *

Small roles taken for needed cash by young aspirants can be excused. Terrible roles by movie stars, even if done as favors or in appreciation, cannot. It says much about the person, but does not placate the moviegoers' damage as inflicted by celluloid sewage such as *Man Trouble* and *How Do You Know*.

In the one indispensible biography of Nicholson, *Jack's Life* by Patrick McGilligan, the author noted that Nicholson had pledged to do any movie with Bob Rafelson without even seeing a script. A movie called *Man Trouble* is proof that this is true. The worst starring role in the actor's career (after all, you can forgive *The Cry Baby Killer* as his first film, but this was 34 years and 45 films later, for the love of Pete!), this story of dog trainer Harry Bliss ended up delivering the opposite of the meaning of the character's last name.

Man Trouble was made by the same team responsible for *Five Easy Pieces*, the director Rafelson, the writer Carole Eastman, the star Nicholson, along with ever-reliable Jack regulars Veronica Cartwright and Harry Dean Stanton. Cartwright saved me the embarrassment of pointing out the weakness of the film by exclaiming, "That was a horrible movie! Horrible," and also volunteering without further comment, "Well ... Bob Rafelson is a piece of work himself."[21]

Nicholson is all heels and eyebrows, sneers and teeth and wrinkled nose in the stock-and-trade tradition of the most elementary Jack impersonators. Meaning that he was playing the role of Nicholson impersonator in this movie.

Nicholson has one nice and tender moment when offering to buy a drink for Ellen Barkin's crying character. However, in a diner breakfast scene following her drunken Japanese restaurant display, Nicholson looks ashen and almost sick.

12. Rom-Com Wonder 191

The one, most true emotional moment in the film is Harry's sad and regretful goodbye to Duke as his dog is being taken away by Paul Mazursky. The dog had it lucky.

* * *

Cineplex zombies were not so fortunate 18 years later when they became unsuspecting victims of a "film" known as *How Do You Know*. Inexplicably, this rom-com-by-the-numbers was directed, produced and written by the man who performed the same duties admirably on *Terms of Endearment, Broadcast News* and *As Good as It Gets*, James L. Brooks.

The first sign of trouble was the lack of a question mark at the end of the title. It is a question, after all, as in "How do you know this movie is an loser?" Perhaps the studio omitted the punctuation as a cost-cutting measure to put more into marketing. We will never know.

Every scene, every visual, every aspect is fake and "in a movie." Absolutely nothing is realistic, let alone real. The idea of Owen Wilson as a professional baseball player works okay in a *Saturday Night Live* skit. Reese Witherspoon as an Olympic softball player is somewhat more believable. Then we get to the point where they happen to cross paths in a preposterous plot that is always hurt by Wilson's egregious miscasting.

Witherspoon's softball team lacks authenticity and the father-son relationship between Nicholson and Paul Rudd carries no sense of truth.

Nicholson plays a security company big shot who, supposedly ironically, is a crook who actually tries to set up his own son to take the fall. He plays it corporate and explosive, as the garrulous boss who clearly is pretending to be a warm father. He spends a lot of his acting time on the phone, which probably means something about the production and the limitation of the role. He does have one good scene in which he moves from exploding about working in the Middle East and paying off an Egyptian, from pushing and yelling to emotional and falsely crying on his own behalf rather than for his son, this in spite of having put his son in this precarious legal position instead of taking the consequences himself.

There's also a nice deleted sequence: In "The Office Scene," he introduces some nice business with his reading glasses (shades of the road trip scene in *As Good as It Gets*) and some good fake corporate intimacy with a kiss. He does a lower quality Jacksplosion, as if he's lost the power of his voice, but makes up for it with much better comedic balance between the real and the exaggerated.

Nicholson's best and biggest scene has been excised, though it was a sound filmic choice, because the company's backstory would have added too much exposition and distracted from the main romantic comedy. Viewing the DVD extras reveals that many of the deletions involved Nicholson. They made sense, however, not in the sense of the actor's strengths but in regards to the already threadbare plot. These cuts represented the right decisions yet proved that Nicholson's involvement was ill-planned and that he was wasted on this project.

Nicholson appeared in this debacle because of his loyalty to Brooks and appreciation for the significant earlier award-winning roles. Brooks has directed six films and Nicholson has appeared in four of them. But he's really only "Jack" once, when he uses his familiar vocal style to (perhaps self-referentially) point out that he needs to "work my voice until you get them," referring to goosebumps.

The one true revelation of *How Do You Know* is that Nicholson's voice is gone! In singer's parlance, his instrument is seemingly damaged. He was not able to propel, emote and overpower to the degree a character of this nature requires. His explosiveness was tamped, which perhaps explains why years later this stands as Nicholson's last role. It would certainly be a pity if this remains the final film for an actor as exceptional as Jack Nicholson.

Also unfortunate is the tarnished effect of *Man Trouble* and *How Do You Know* to Nicholson's triumph as latter day rom-com wonder in films as emotionally beautiful and stirring as *As Good as It Gets* and *Something's Gotta Give*.

*   *   *

Romance is alive and flourishing, more deeply and more meaningfully with the reflective and mature. Harry has to grow to love Erica. He grew beyond a life filled with pretty young things—such as Erica's daughter. He had to experience the jealousy of Erica's attention to a younger man; the hurt of public humiliation from her play; and he then had to resolve himself to "going for it" in Paris with all his hopes based on how entrancing the story of Harry and Erica had become.

Melvin learned how to love (and to like other people and to like himself) when he came to love Carol. He grew from a self-centered and hateful loner, slowly understanding that he was lonely by choice. Melvin opened himself to others, to their feelings and needs, and bit by bit conquered his obsessive-compulsive disorder because it was worth it to be with Carol.

Romance knows no age when Jack Nicholson grows for Diane Keaton and changes his life for Helen Hunt. They become human and breathe real air, in pursuit of a new life based on that love.

The characters become real, and so is their love. Their stories feel true, and so does their romance. The emotions run deeply ... and they become ours.

13

Misfits and Misanthropes

The fly is relentless, landing and re-landing on the wheat toast next to the plain omelet. Bobby Dupea waves and waves, but he's already left one diner after waving much too hard while violently clearing everything off the table because he couldn't get what he wanted. Now, he has exactly what he wants, except for the interference of the fly.

Finally, it dances and flits, bounces and twirls, moving from Bobby to David Staebler. Now, the fly alternately buzzes off and then onto David's microphone as the host tries to concentrate on his show. He's live, on radio, so cannot react or attack. David timidly ducks and dodges while he deliberates a way to persuade the fly to at least temporarily grant him enough peace to work without distraction.

Perhaps bored, the fly makes the mistake of approaching Jonathan, who will not take this interruption. He swears and jumps and swats and yells. Jonathan hates this fly. But, then again, Jonathan hates just about everything—especially himself.

Francis Phelan doesn't hate himself, but he wishes he wasn't drunk that day so many years ago. Francis may be hallucinating the fly. Francis notices he's being circled, but isn't quite sure what to do. He freezes and retreats into himself, as the fly is reminded of Norman Bates and how that Mama's boy put all of his remaining energy into a similar restraint. Norman would protect himself by pretending he didn't see and wouldn't harm the fly. Francis certainly wouldn't harm anything, if he could help it.

Warren Schmidt's final minutes of his ineffectual career at his thankless job were only slightly sidetracked by the fly. Dr. Buddy Rydell viewed the fly as an intentional slight; Melvin Udall could not believe a fly could invade his masterfully controlled apartment. The Joker welcomed the fly as a way to further unnerve his targets; Alex Gates knew wine but couldn't handle the unexpected; R.P. McMurphy and Daryl Van Horne viewed its intrusion as part of "the plan"; and Wilbur Force welcomed the foreplay of annoyance as playful prelude to the main event of pain.

* * *

I don't know Jack Nicholson's attitude toward flies, but I do know he's specialized in portraying characters who might have a range of irrational reactions to common house insects. Often called an antihero, Nicholson more commonly plays a guy who just does not fit in with others—or even sees society and other people as objects of distrust and sources of distress.

The title character in *About Schmidt* lacks emotional connections to his family or any meaningful relationships with co-workers or friends-in-title-only. In *Anger Management*, Dr. Rydell's lucky to be in a position to guide others from a detached position of authority, as he has some serious issues of his own. It's a good thing Melvin is a writer so he can get away with locking himself away from people because it wouldn't otherwise get very good for him at all. The Joker is a villain exacting revenge and Van Horne is a devil seeking souls and young women. McMurphy has his own issues with women and with authority, while *Little Shop of Horrors* masochist Wilbur actually enjoys going to the dentist—making him perhaps the most perverted character in a Nicholson canon that also includes Jack Torrance (*The Shining*) and Frank Costello (*The Departed*).

So many characters with such problems with people. They don't trust others; they remove themselves from the human race as much as possible; they run from their past and avoid creating a future. Melvin and Jonathan hurt other people mentally and emotionally. Costello and the Joker hurt them physically. Phelan, McMurphy and Gates can't seem but help to bring pain to others and themselves, while Schmidt, Dupea and Staebler can't seem to or don't want to feel. Force and Van Horne meet a cartoonish fate of being drilled and poked for the pleasure of pain and the pleasure of vengeance, respectively.

Nearly half of Nicholson's film roles can be viewed as being misfits or misanthropes, from juvenile delinquents (*The Cry Baby Killer, The Wild Ride, Studs Lonigan*) and amoral (*Flight to Fury, The Shooting, How Do You Know*) to maladjusted (*Chinatown, The Passenger, Heartburn*) and damaged (*The Two Jakes, The Pledge, The Crossing Guard*). He's been lost, searching and antisocial (*Hells Angels on Wheels, The Postman Always Rings Twice*); fighting authority or conformity (*The Last Detail, Easy Rider, Chinatown*); and a downright criminal or outlaw (*The Broken Land, Ride in the Whirlwind, The St. Valentine's Day Massacre, The Fortune, Goin' South, The Postman Always Rings Twice, Prizzi's Honor, Batman, Blood and Wine, The Departed, How Do You Know*). Even his screenplays skew toward the "antisocial" elements of drugs (*The Trip, Head*), crime (*Flight to Fury, Ride in the Whirlwind*) and rebelliousness (*Drive, He Said*), while all of his official directorial efforts deal with the oddballs and outsiders (*Goin' South, The Two Jakes* and *Drive, He Said*).

The man who eventually became the symbol of Hollywood stardom

13. Misfits and Misanthropes

struggled for many years to come in from the outside, and now his many roles as the ultimate outsider endure most.

* * *

Bobby Dupea wants to become an outsider, seeking escape from his background, his family, his calling as pianist and, more than anything, from responsibility. He seems happy and relaxed in an environment most foreign to his own. On the rig, playing cards, going bowling, drinking beer, chasing local talent. With his family and their upper class, artistic trappings, he's stiff and sarcastic and distant. Instead of fitting in with his family, he pursues his brother's fiancée.

The first sign of the real person is his look of ennui when left alone at a bowling alley. While preparing to leave Rayette behind to visit his dying father, he examines himself in the mirror with a look that's similar to his self-study in *The Shining*.

At the end of *Five Easy Pieces*, the character looks in another mirror to examine who he is and where he is going one more time before abandoning

Bobby Dupea has isolated himself from his family and his talent. He is trapped by his girlfriend and threatened by any kind of authority. *Five Easy Pieces* (1970) takes an unflattering look at a main character by no means a hero and too unmotivated to succeed as antihero. Also pictured is Billy "Green" Bush, who played Bobby's pal Elton.

Rayette at the gas station. As he looks at himself, only his eyes move, again like in *The Shining*.

Bobby is trapped by his family and he's trapped by Rayette when she becomes pregnant. He can't handle authority, whether his father, his boss or even a diner waitress—against whom he feels triumphant by battling a simple "no substitutions" ordering rule. Dupea is for nothing and against everything. He is only truly free when he rides away, first when he hops on a truck with an upright piano, in a sequence reminiscent of his *Easy Rider* bird flight on a motorcycle and his beach convertible race with Shirley MacLaine in *Terms of Endearment*—and finally when he hitchhikes to Alaska with a trucker.

Dupea's disaffected sense gets clarified by his explanation to Rayette about how he and Elton lost their job, in an excised scene set at the diner where she worked. Perhaps it was cut because Bobby spelled out his alienation in too obvious a fashion, rather than depicting its manifestations. Bobby complains "Everything worth anything is lost," of how the system is "thwarting the natural instincts of a man," which results in "the total loss of spirit."[1] This neatly sums up Bobby Dupea's instinct to separate himself, to disconnect from everything and everyone.

In several instances, Nicholson's portrayal of Bobby serves as antecedent to his characterization of Jack Torrance in *The Shining*. The two mirror scenes mentioned above are similar to those in the Kubrick film. He looks without emotion, without admiration, without interest or ego, or even without disappointment or disgust. Bobby looks at himself and feels nothing and looks for himself and finds nothing. He is as detached from himself and his surroundings as is Torrance.

After Rayette shows up at his family's Washington State home, Bobby escapes the collision of his two worlds and gets self-destructively drunk. Here we see the same disconnected and dangerous expression we later see in Jack Torrance.

Dialogue edited out of the scene in which Dupea plays piano for Catherine once again explained too much. Bobby laments having entered "this predetermined [musical] heritage" last among the family and how he "worked at it every day ... from the age of three to the age of 28, hating it."[2] The boy and the man never felt anything, never connected to it, and never experienced satisfaction, so that his family's approval and enthusiasm "does not mean a crap to me." He feels the same way about Catherine's reaction. The deleted words filled in more than was necessary. When Bobby sums up his attitude toward music, he might well be summing up his life: "I don't feel it!"

Later, as he drives back from his family's home with Rayette, she sings and she kisses, but he pushes her away. Bobby looks truly dead, in the car with his significant and only other, in the same way he looked dead as Torrance during his drive to the hotel with his family at the beginning of *The*

Shining. In the former, Jack depicts how trapped his character feels right before his final getaway, while in the latter his character is just as trapped, only to escape, first mentally and ultimately with violence.

In *Five Easy Pieces*' final sequence, Nicholson sits next to the truck driver and lets his mouth open without expression in a troubling, problematic look. This countenance reflects one of his most foreboding moments in *The Shining*, one in which Torrance sits on a bed and contemplates hurting Danny.

* * *

While Dupea and Torrance cannot handle the structure, responsibility—and most of all the emotional investments—of family and meaningful relationships, David Staebler in *The King of Marvin Gardens* doesn't avoid his family but just does not connect with them, while appearing to have no meaningful relationships from which to escape.

Nicholson plays a radio monologist on a show entitled *Etcetera*, a strange and wholly uncommercial program of personal observations and anecdotes that are more unloading than involving. He's not reliving memories because he didn't live in the first place. Again, Nicholson portrays a man who does not fit, who converses with a microphone rather than with people. He observes rather than participates; notes rather than reacts; reports rather than connects. Staebler talks of his family as he would describe the weather, detached and distant. The actor referred to his character as Kafkaesque.[3]

Director Bob Rafelson and Nicholson followed their breakthrough and breakout collaboration on *Five Easy Pieces* with this dour and non-affirming family drama about a non-family. The Staebler brothers weren't the clichéd dysfunctional family because they usually didn't function at all.

In the film's opening story, with Nicholson's face isolated on black with *Meet the Beatles*–like half-shadow, it's not clear that a radio broadcast is depicted. It appears more like a one-sided conversation or confession to a psychiatrist, because the shot's composition uses dramatic license. Given his position, had David really been doing a radio show, he would have been off-mic for much of the speech. Only when the studio's red light flashes five minutes into the movie do we get the first hint of what is actually happening.

He's looking to his right, off-screen, as if toward someone. The slow Nicholson drawl fits the character's lack of emotion, while the use of his hands is exquisitely expressive. Watching this odd monologue, the question arises, "Who would listen to such a show?" A story about a grandfather choking on fish or family tragedies described non-tragically don't make for radio ratings winners.

I asked Boston and New York radio legend Dick Summer if he had any impressions about the character and the film, given Summer's own style as monologist and storyteller (though decidedly in a more romantic and openly sensitive manner). "I tried to do what I think Nicholson did so well. Whatever you heard on the air was pretty much what I am. It's surprisingly hard to get out of the way of really being yourself on the air." The secret wasn't a gimmick, but an indirect connection:

> When I was on the air, I considered my listeners to be part of my "huddle." I was the quarterback, and we were all gathered around for mutual protection, with the singular goal of making it through the dawn together. It was real.... I think Nicholson managed to get the "real" into every character he ever played. Not a PR fiction. The real guy.[4]

Unlike Summer, Staebler is a lost soul and not one to seek what could be recovered. They are alike in avoiding sensationalized call-ins or calculated posturing in favor of a personal and human perspective. The difference: Summer delivered the human feeling while Staebler couldn't find it and couldn't fit in.

However, he did grow—only to fall when all the life and hope and dreams were destroyed. Nicholson moves Staebler from a talker to a doer, slowly and convincingly. When Bruce Dern, as brother Jason, gives him a big welcoming hug, David's discomfort (displayed by a slight backward recoil) is priceless. Jack is aware of his body. He accentuates his character's uneasiness with receiving such open affection and physical intimacy by pulling away his neck to draw attention to its flesh folds.

As the brothers work together on their hapless dream, David is drawn out bit by bit. Jack first breaks out his own bigness after a sprint run on the Atlantic City beach, ending up doubled over and practically dying through wide open mouth breaths and a stance like a penguin. To underscore the pain, he spits up something into his handkerchief. Of course, just having a handkerchief in the early '70s says something about the character.

David comes to life when selling junk to some ladies on the boardwalk … and his transformation begins. Jack's character becomes more physical and more demonstrative compared to his earlier subdued self, who was never more emotive than when showing a half-smile.

Even at his most open and spontaneous, he remains his brother's opposite. Dern is huge, loud and boisterous—ever the optimist and always the schemer. Relationships in *The King of Marvin Gardens* are atypical and awkward. The one between the brothers is strained. They have nothing in common, a point which was symbolized when they are shown opposite one another on different colored horses. The relationship between Sally (Ellen Burstyn) and Jessica (Julia Anne Robinson)—mother-daughter or mentor-protégé?—is bizarrely physical, though it excuses Jason's sideways dalliances.

There is a key scene with Jessica as a beauty pageant contestant and David as the master of ceremonies that forces him into new territory. The man who normally hides behind the mic in radio anonymity becomes the

13. Misfits and Misanthropes 199

Look at David's discomfort with this big welcoming hug from his brother in Bob Rafelson's *The King of Marvin Gardens* (1972). When Bruce Dern (right), as brother Jason, embraces the radio monologist, Nicholson accentuates his character's uneasiness through this backward recoil.

focus, as host (albeit in rehearsal). Nicholson is this man, his character energy infusing a rough transition into the light. He appears natural in his unnaturalness, true in his discomfort, but trying his best to be the host with much less than the most as well as a reluctant ham.

Nicholson employs the perfect nuance of mocking sincerity during an obviously fictitious dolphin story to Asian investors. He adopts a rougher, rhythmic, staccato delivery when feigning tough talk with Lewis (Scatman Crothers), as his words get ahead of themselves to the degree that he eventually runs out of air in his attempt to match his brother's style with his own tremulous voice.

Getting such a penetrating performance wasn't without conflict, as actor Josh Mostel (who played the radio station engineer) recounted. "He complained [*doing an impression of Nicholson*]: 'It's not like acting. You're doing everything in groups of three.' It's like there were so many takes, with Bob Rafelson. So he just sort of complained about that a lot, you know. [*Impression of Nicholson:*] 'Oh gee, let's not.'"[5]

The production, though dealing with such a downbeat character, wasn't completely devoid of laughs. Mostel told me, "I forgot my line or something and I just sort of stood there with egg on my face, and [Nicholson] went, 'I tried to work with him, but I was getting nothin'.' It was funny."[6]

Nicholson may seem restrained or appear to underplay, but much goes into this portrayal. The subtleties of David's emergence are small to us, but large to David. That is what makes the role work as real.

David's last step in his advancement was a big blowup at Jason, pleading with his brother to open his eyes and his ears—for once—to reality. Even in this confrontation, the closest David could come to a Jacksplosion, Nicholson holds just enough back in order to be true to the man, keeping both hands in his pockets to stay small and constrained by his own inhibitions about emotion. While yelling at his brother, Nicholson's David only removes a hand from his pocket temporarily, a momentary expansion that he then reels back in. When David yells, he exposes his upper and lower teeth, perhaps holding in some sound as he always remains partially closed. This is Nicholson's loudest, most uncontrolled moment, yet he still confines his character within narrowly defined limits.

No matter, as Jason could never see the reality because he chose not to, and with good reason. The reality was always obvious: The dream was over, though it never truly began. A nightmare took over, violently ending the dream in the only way it could be made final. Dern's Jason would never see that the dream could never happen for them, for any or all of them, and so he had to go away in the only way that made sense, forever.

Nicholson historian Don Schiach classes *The King of Marvin Gardens* and *Five Easy Pieces* "as companion movies, variations on the theme of the fruitless chase after the American Dream of happiness, success, money, love and community."[7]

Later, as his murdered brother's body is being loaded for transport, David goes right back to being as dead as he had been at the beginning of the film. David Staebler's journey ended with his return to his original personality, to his former home, and to the only means of reaching out to others—as anonymous and unconnected as it was—over the radio. Like outsiders and misfits Warren Schmidt and Bobby Dupea, David can only weep to himself as he recounts his experiences as radio monologue. Schmidt pitied himself instead of Ndugu; Dupea broke down over his own misanthropic choices; Staebler shared his tragedy with a microphone. David could only bring his own experience to true emotion in story form, as an abstraction rather than an expression, after which he wrapped up the program almost as if it had been a fiction.

These characters don't think for the now, but lament the past. They do not act with intent, but react with impulse. They live mostly unnoticed, unless their antisocial tendency brings attention. Schmidt and Staebler are both weak, not so much wallflowers as wallpaper. Dupea minimizes himself, weakening his prospects and himself. Yet all three are among the strongest examples of rich and nuanced character energy in the career of Jack Nicholson. As Dick Summer put it, "I have a hunch that Nicholson really is as complicated, as humanly muddy, as the characters he played. And he let us see it."[8]

* * *

Jonathan in *Carnal Knowledge* and Francis Phelan in *Ironweed* both became broken men, Jonathan by slowly self-destructing and Francis through a single careless act. Jonathan comes to hate women, for reasons that are not exactly clear, though we can surmise it's grounded in competition with friend Sandy (Art Garfunkel) combined with a free-at-any-cost rebellion against female control. Francis is Jonathan's opposite. He genuinely loves the women in his life. He loves his wife Annie (Carroll Baker), despite having left her behind due to his shame about having dropped their baby to his death. He loves his fellow hobo-alcoholic-girlfriend Helen (Meryl Streep), living together as normally as Depression-era homeless and aimless souls can. Francis has devoted so much of himself to his women that he can give to the memory of his former life while simultaneously giving to his current companion. Jonathan instead has no devotion to give, nor any desire to try.

Nicholson takes quite a journey in his portrayal of Francis Phelan in William Kennedy's screenplay, based on his novel. Francis is lost, and then he's found. He finds his real family again, briefly, only to lose his later adopted family. Jack plays a caring friend, a tender lover, a besotted drunk, a clean visitor. He's fallen angel and killer dad, happy and remorseful and tormented and nostalgic. Nicholson's Phelan hallucinates with pleasure and with torture.

Director Hector Babenco struggled to understand giving three years of his life to the project. "There is something about the guilt of this character, something about establishing harmony with your past, something about having the courage to come back to the home base of your past and face it."[9]

When we first see Nicholson in the film, he is hardly recognizable. His voice is familiar when he yells while having imagined "arguments" with the ghost of Harold Allen (Nathan Lane) as he rides a streetcar together with excellent supporting player Tom Waits (as Rudy). After a bath at his former wife's home, he does finally look like Nicholson, and he and Carroll Baker are cute together—like on a first date—only thicker and grayer and older.

Nicholson's range in this role is as powerful as Francis' story. When he violently confronts a phantom group of dead people, his delivery, gestures, body language and even his speech pattern is suddenly (and for just a moment) like his Jimmy Hoffa at his most explosive.

Yet, in his attempt to reconcile with his family after so many lost years, Jack plays Francis so humble and soft-spoken and tentative, until he reads the heartbreaking little girl's letter to the same now-adult daughter. At this moment, he transitions to a real man, alive and in control, with confidence and memories, as he recounts playing baseball in Toronto.

There is a cemetery scene, no less striking than that in *The Crossing Guard*, during which he talks to his dead son, the son he drunkenly dropped; the son who died from a careless second in time. Nicholson's monologue reminds us of the one delivered by son Bobby Dupea to his immobile, wheelchair-bound father in *Five Easy Pieces*, as well as the closing radio speech in *Marvin Gardens*. All share a progression from composed to crying back to composed and back to crying, a human bounce from complex emotion toward reflection and from regret toward inconsolable guilt.

While *Carnal Knowledge*'s Jonathan cannot connect in any meaningful way with his parade of women, Francis remains committed to his pair of loves even after they are gone.

Upon discovering Meryl Streep's character dead in her rooming house, Francis sinks and slumps, as whatever life he had slips away. His defeat is real, yet he perseveres to compliment her on retrieving their possessions from a pawnbroker, making the room nice, and on her appearance—how she was "mighty pretty."

Nicholson is portraying true love, perhaps purer because Helen and Francis had no possessions aside from one another. Now, Francis is left with only memories. On his final train ride, he conjures the false image of Annie. When he realizes that what he sees cannot be real, Francis directs true hatred at his bottle of booze. We see a man who for the first time realizes and admits to himself the source of his pain and the waste of his life. We feel the tragedy of a good man. About Jonathan, in contrast, we merely gaze as voyeur toward a slump of a futile life. We have sympathy for Francis but no empathy for the pathetic Jonathan.

Nicholson called *Ironweed* "one of the best movies I've done, but was it a commercial success? Some movies are jazz, some are rock and roll."[10] The musical metaphor extended to his acting duet with Streep, "a dream" working in a manner that is "kind of like dancing with a partner where you don't have to do anything, you just get carried along by it and fascinated by it."[11]

To Babenco, the film served as "a collective soul" about anonymous vagabonds "showing the courage and beauty of people we don't usually think of as having deep and complex emotions."[12]

In *Ironweed*, Nicholson embodies his character in a *pas de deux* with Streep, far from movie stardom and closer to the bone and a reality that's too real, a loss that loses too much, and a life that wasn't quite lived, but sustained … barely sustained.

Francis is that fly, something hardly noticed, inconsequential in life and unmissed when dead. He's glimpsed in flashes, but mostly he's ignored and looked through as if nonexistent. He's swatted and cursed and waved away. That is, until he buzzes around the periphery before he finally disappears.

14

The Dicks Versus the Hoods

The place was filled with more suspicion than most places could contain. Their professions demand suspicion in order to be successful, if not to be successful at remaining alive. Honor amongst thieves was as much of a myth as an honest private eye.

Put some dicks in one place and put hoods together in that same place, and you're asking for trouble. You're also asking for acting worthy of Academy Awards. The only question is about who lies better. The detective trying to mete out a meager living or the career criminal grasping to gain the blessings of "the organization"?

The sleuth and the crook are archetypes of cinema and standards for any actor. Nicholson has played his share, often choosing the misfit over the genius, to show the struggle instead of the triumph.

The Joker was a freakish hood, bent more on revenge than fortune. The hapless brothers of *The Fortune* spend more time fighting than hustling. After all the planning, everything goes wrong for Alex Gates in *Blood and Wine* due to poor execution. Charley Partanna and Frank Chambers let women double-cross them, two victims of love's blindness in *Prizzi's Honor* and *The Postman Always Rings Twice*, respectively.

Watching them all is Jake. J.J. Gittes spends his time recording married infidelity, yet he too suffers a double-cross when he lowers his guard to a woman.

* * *

But no one loses more to a woman than *Postman*'s Frank Chambers. Chambers is the hood equivalent of the dick Gittes—small-time and struggling, aimless and distracted, superficial and vulnerable.

A remake of the John Garfield–Lana Turner noir classic, the film brought together a powerhouse combo of producer and director Bob Rafelson with director of photography Sven Nykvist; a David Mamet screenplay based on the James M. Cain novel; and Nicholson paired with sultry Jessica Lange,

14. The Dicks Versus the Hoods

who was completely credible in the role of a woman who could make a man do anything.

Author Douglas Brode called the story "a modern variation of Greek tragedy ... in which a man kills his adopted father figure to sleep with a substitute mother, setting a terrible fate into motion for himself."[1]

Nicholson convinces as a drifter and con man using faux mess-ups to give Christopher Lloyd the impression that the latter is duping the former, all the while continuing with compliments and warm conversation to complete his own set-up.

He's also believable as a woeful and down-on-his-luck auto mechanic who positions himself to make time with the boss' younger wife and connives himself a place to gain bit by bit. Nicholson advances Frank's nerve in a neatly transitional way, edging from admiring looks to little nothings to abandoned boldness, expanding the character with each step.

The initial sequence between Frank and Lange's Cora starts with what today would be considered sexual assault and turns into action reminiscent of the spinning and banging on the walls with Sally Struthers in *Five Easy Pieces*, which then escalates into a fairly explicit sexual representation (for a mainstream movie of the time). There is a lingering close-up of manual foreplay between her legs; a long and loose belt that suggests we are seeing more of Nicholson than we actually see; and prolonged pounding and plunging by the pair. The film's trailer spotlighted the frankness of the sex scenes, with a *Playboy* magazine quote calling it the hottest since *Last Tango in Paris* (yet another Brando connection for Nicholson). In a later scene, smart continuity shows Nicholson's belt end tucked around because it is too long.

The primal connection between the two actors and their two characters make the movie. Without it, there would be no motivation for desperate acts. With it, the audience is seduced, pulled in by passion and its blinded hope.

After their second kitchen scene, which is not fully sexual, Jack looks at Jessica as she walks up the stairs in a way that shows his animal power and betrays his own assumed prowess. Yet appropriate to the unfolding narrative, the actor hints at the false understanding, unaware that *he* is the prey. This adds another touch to Nicholson's nuanced journey with the character.

As they seemingly come closer through escape, Frank and Cora seem like newlyweds in Chicago's train station, but Chambers' questionable nature surfaces as he gambles and pushes Cora away. When Nicholson is in his gangsterish mode of a hood, he employs a clipped, down-gestured pattern that we occasionally see in Jimmy Hoffa and more directly in *Prizzi's Honor* mobster Charley Partanna, at the same time as his Italian dialect creeps up.

Everything turns when Cora's intension become clear, in a revealing scene in the diner backyard. Nicholson's close-up shows a man suddenly seeing reality with fear mixed with desire, and excitement with hesitancy, all accomplished in a few mostly wordless moments accented with slight eye widening and subtle expression.

Nicholson probed and prodded to find his way in the character, digging in with determination. Once in, he held on with possession and tenacity—just as Cora discovered the depths of Frank Chambers' being to control him with that insight. The actor owns his character just as her character owns her man. Nicholson is comfortable in his discomfort, while his false confidence and delusions of partnership with Cora never betrays the actor's knowledge of the truth behind the surface. We aren't seeing someone pretend to be in charge prior to the point in the script where he finally has to understand the truth. Instead, we see someone who lives the lie *because* he can't see that it is a lie; not acting, but spontaneously reacting. This is the "in the moment" creed mentioned so much but experienced too infrequently. Nicholson resides in his character. Therefore, he can only be "in the moment," because there is no other moment, no foreknowledge to suppress, no disbelief to suspend.

Desperation and hope and lust meet at a crossroads called Frank Chambers. We can tell that his character knows that his "way out" may not have a way out, yet Jessica Lange looks, acts and taunts to the degree that wishful plotting seems plausible enough to drag him along further and further. Cora delivers Frank to the ultimate point, when their plot to murder her husband moves from an idea to a deed, and when good and bad are no longer available choices.

As he waits for Lange to do the deed, Nicholson looks stunned and terrified, furthering the moment's truth with an overlaid impression that Frank is at the same time trying to hide his reaction while appearing in charge of the situation. He simultaneously exhibits both emotions to us, making the scene more powerful through the character's depth of dimension.

Frank's little childlike near-screams as he stands over her husband Nick's injured body represents a real reaction from someone not worried about how he looks or sounds to anyone else. Reaction just happens, naturally. Concern over appearances would instead have required detachment and considered thought.

When people who are not bad do bad things, they look different than when bad people do bad things. Both Nicholson and Lange convey this unnaturalness and unease, in the act, in the aftermath, and as they enter their next chapter together as premeditated murderers.

Frank is suitably disgusted with the visual result when he bashes in Nick's head, shocked at his own act and his own fall from con man to killer. After all, hustlers do no real harm, they rationalize to themselves, but murderers don't benefit from the same chance at justification to themselves, let alone to others.

Bob Rafelson said the prior adaptations missed the point. "What do they

14. The Dicks Versus the Hoods

know about making violent, dirty movies? This is why I made the movie—because they didn't do it. It's a book about sado-masochism."[2] Brode described this as "the intense bond that can grow between two people who despise each other, how such a relationship can prove more obsessive than one based on love."[3]

The Frank Chambers of *Postman* is not the broad Jack, but the understated and disciplined actor who helps the audience believe his is an unsuccessful and uncertain person. Bombast and outburst are not part of the character's makeup. Instead, Jack's character energy injects little pieces of action and reaction, motion and emotion, but only in small pieces until the point when Cora changes her plea in court.

Chambers and Cora must beat each other up to mask their staged car accident and manufacture injuries in order to advance its credibility. As they pick up enthusiasm for this depraved act, Nicholson and Lange mirror their first sex scene, while their erotic S&M romp—which proves to be their undoing—prefigured David Cronenberg's *Crash*.

After the heights of their murderous collusion and passionate concealment, the workaday lies and ongoing cover-up had to seem a letdown. Without the adrenaline and the thrill, unaided by the struggle for self-preservation, Frank and Cora must rely on their wits rather than instinct (not a particular strength for either).

They also retreat to their original selves. Interrogated by cops while in his hospital bed, Chambers returns to his bad lying and faux-innocent guise from the beginning of the movie. Later, when Cora leaves to check on her mother, he reverts to his old appearance (the backward cap), his old stance (hapless) and his old future (non-existent).

Nicholson unveils another side of the character in his light, but restrained, treatment of a comical brief interlude with Anjelica Huston, while yet another puts his savagery on display when he beats Kennedy (John P. Ryan) for attempting a shakedown, repeatedly banging a door against the man's head.

The latter part of the movie shows the couple's high-profile, sensational trial that lets them trade on their notoriety for self-promotion, which pays off after they return to their non-bustling diner, perhaps a warning premonition about today's obsession with uncelebrated celebrities and reality non-stars.

Frank and Cora's relationship becomes strained. How could it not when it was formed on duplicity and murder? Suspicion and tension grow, leading to the film's true climax, Frank's second moment of realization. The first was when he came to understand Cora's real intentions. Here, he comes to understand her real nature as well. When Lange discloses that she did not need his confession because she had already been tried for the crime—that double-jeopardy is "in the Constitution"—his eyes show the shock, the pain, the hurt and the worry, all in a mere few seconds. Those telling eyes get wider, in disbelief, and then narrow intently as if attempting to see inside his double-crosser, using the same look Nicholson employs in Freddy Gale's final confrontation with his daughter's killer in *The Crossing Guard*.

But *Postman* goes on too long, with a false happy ending unnecessarily destroyed with tin "irony" and ham-fisted dramatics. Cora informs Frank that she is pregnant. They narrowly avoid a serious auto accident. That death would have been more stunning and less contrived, if more sudden (like the ending of *Chinatown*). Instead, the audience is also double-crossed with an abrupt "Now it's for real" accident that kills the only thing that Chambers ever loved, though it was a deeply flawed love.

Cora and Frank would have deserved the first type of destruction, taken together just as they took from others together. Chambers did not deserve the destruction that actually happened, alone suffering the pain of solitude and regret. He wails at the end, as much for himself and his guilt-filled fate as for the death of Cora. She got off easy. That is his true suffering, through a typically bleak Rafelson ending, the kind characterized by Peter Tork as never allowing anyone to escape their particular "black box."[4]

Nicholson plays Frank Chambers as a lesser man than the original portrayed by John Garfield. Garfield is tougher, yet brought down through supplication and obeisance, in contrast to Nicholson's Chambers, who is raised up by desire for a woman and by the lure of twisted success. Cora's influence weakens the first Chambers' reserve and lowers his standards to become her conspirator, while the second is strengthened through Cora's attention and by how she lets him think he succeeded with her, a sick orchestrated pantomime of seduction.

* * *

The 1981 Frank Chambers enters the film a loser. In a succession of stages, he becomes more and more pathetic, culminating in the darkest loss of all, to be left alone with himself and his own failures. The J.J. Gittes of *Chinatown* had seemingly been a success of sorts, undefined but implied. He then lost what he had built, both in his career with the district attorney's office and with the love of his life.

This all happens before the film begins, so we are introduced to another loser, this time one who—unlike Chambers—knew some good times. Chambers had always been a drifter and undistinguished hustler, but Gittes became someone drifting through his second act as an undistinguished private eye and hustler of his own sort.

Nicholson bites into the *Chinatown* role with gusto, displaying so many facets of one man, with a depth of meaning rarely enjoyed in a Hollywood movie. He's catapulted through the combined strengths of the triumvirate of director Roman Polanski, producer and Paramount studio head Robert Evans and screenwriter Robert Towne.

Evans described Polanski as a martinet, yet on occasion the director allowed for the spontaneous to define character reality. One example was a scene in which Nicholson couldn't get his cigarette lighter to function. Always searching for the moment, Nicholson was "playing through," and kept the action going despite this accident, and incorporated the result into his portrayal. Polanski preserved the take "not only because it lends a quality of verisimilitude, but because it makes us vaguely aware of the actor behind the performance."[5]

Nicholson is obviously having fun with this part, sensing its scope if not its iconic proportions, his fully realized character energy the key to the success of this challenging and complex portrayal.

Despite the tension between the writer and director, Nicholson was fully ready for this chance at a romantic lead role. When Jack arrived on set, he was "getting his nuts off, his smile on full, sucking up the lunacy of his pals' mutual disdain," recalled Evans.[6]

Actor James Hong, whose 500 credits in a career of 64 years include *Blade Runner* and *Big Trouble in Little China*, called Polanski very detailed and precise in his quest to get exactly what he envisioned in a scene. Much rehearsal was invested by "the master director and the master actor ... trying as hard as they could to accomplish what the other one wants in the scene," shooting an average of 20 takes for each angle. Every scene had an underlying mood. Hong described filming as a learning experience for both men, as well as for himself. "These two creative people are geniuses. The way they can move a scene is brilliant."[7]

Gittes can't possibly care about petty matrimonial skirmishes, but he has to feign involvement to make a living. "There's nothing worse than sitting for ten hours and watching the side of a building that will never move," observed real-life high-profile Los Angeles private investigator Scott Ross. "You can never prove that someone isn't having an affair. You're seen together, there are photos, and even if it's two friends having dinner, you can't prove nothing is happening."[8]

As the third-rate dick provides proof of a wife's affair to husband Curly, deliciously played by Burt Young, Nicholson reacts with beautiful impatience, while Young parodies an escalating overreaction to pictures of his wife's infidelities. In establishing the Jake Gittes character, Nicholson plays against the other actors, responding to what happens in their lives and about their situations rather than acting in relation to his own. He remains detached from their circumstances and uninvolved beyond doing his job. Gittes is stickily insensitive and falsely caring toward former *Rebel Rousers* co-star Diane Ladd (as the phony Evelyn Mulwray).

When Nicholson tells a dirty joke to his operatives, he is blissfully unaware that they are trying to warn him that urbane client, the real Evelyn Mulwray (Faye Dunaway), is standing directly behind him. He takes such great delight and seems so natural in his camaraderie that we might think that this is what the actor is most like in real life. His broad laugh after the "screwin' just like a Chinaman" joke is the same, open-mouthed cackle not seen nor heard since his *Little Shop of Horrors* scene in the dentist's chair.

He continues to react to others in order to define his character, with flourishes like the hat-salute to Roy Jenson's Mulvihill that accompanies Gittes' mocking cracks. Nicholson emphatically pounds his cigarette on its case in a gesture to receptionists. He also has some playful business with Perry Lopez as Lieutenant Lou Escobar and Dick Bakalyan as Detective Loach.

Private investigator Scott Ross worked such infamous Hollywood cases as Robert Blake and Michael Jackson. He confirmed the enmity between the police and P.I.s depicted in the film. "If I get pulled over by a cop, I wouldn't show my private investigator's license, because they'd tear my car apart." Ross explained the source of the conflict as competing interests, noting, "All they want is to get a conviction. I'm here to help exonerate my client. Even if there is evidence that can prove innocence, they won't test that evidence and I can't force them to do it."[9]

Nicholson's characterization went beyond acting to include action more physical and dangerous. Because of the closeness of the shot, he even has to do his own stunt in rushing water that throws him against a fence, a scene that harkens back to his fight against the waves in *The Terror*.

Nicholson's sequence with Polanski is remembered for its realistic and stunning knife flick to the nosy "kitty cat," an attack by the director on his star. However, it is more than that, also capturing a classic meeting of two established actors. Remember that Roman's on-screen roles have spanned comedy, with wife Sharon Tate in *The Fearless Vampire Killers*; to voyeuristic weirdo in *The Tenant*; as well as a range of parts in his early films in Poland.

Polanski also chose to give the film itself an active role in Gittes' characterization, telling the story from the private eye's perspective by shooting from behind him or over his shoulder. The director explained that though he read and loved Raymond Chandler and Dashiell Hammett, the movies based on their works missed the main element: the first person.[10]

Much has been written about how a major star in a lead role could have much of his face covered with a face bandage for a sizable portion of the film. In *Acting Male: Masculinities in the Films of James Stewart, Jack Nicholson, and Clint Eastwood*, Dennis Bingham views the bandage as a more calculated effort to call attention to the actor behind the character, making the spectator think that this star does not care how *he* looks. He even dares to appear

14. The Dicks Versus the Hoods

Three legends in one study. Jack Nicholson, John Huston, and Roman Polanski prepare for the wrenching denouement of *Chinatown* (1974). The project suffered (or perhaps benefited) from friction between writer Robert Towne and director Polanski. Here, we witness some tension between star and director, natural for such a charged scene in such an intense film.

ridiculous, to the extent that "as soon as one is tempted to think of Nicholson, the actor-as-hero, one is reminded that it is a problematic hero who comes dressed in adhesive tape and gauze, dripping blood from a nearly surreal attack." Bingham is not the first acting scholar to label Nicholson's approach as "Brechtian." Here the actor telegraphs Jake's fragilities and undermines his facade by coming on screen "accompanied by a banner explaining his character's condition."[11]

As Roger Ebert proclaimed in his celebration of *Chinatown* as one of *The Great Movies*, "Great actors don't follow rules, they illustrate them." He summed up the character's importance by saying that Gittes "stepped into Bogart's shoes as a man attractive to audiences because he suggests both comfort and danger. Men see him as a pal; wise women find weary experience more attractive than untrained lust."[12]

He gives his character the kind of unparalleled range that helps make J.J. Gittes real and bring his story to life. Pretending to be a concerned son checking out a retirement home, Gittes is smarmy and disarming, hoping that the facility's staff looks out for Dad. The same Gittes is later charming in his flirtation with Mrs. Mulwray.

Ebert called Gittes "a nice, sad man."[13] And Jake only becomes alive when he cares about someone. He cares about Evelyn and he cares about her case, also something differing from his standard uninvolved manner. He is now a real person, perhaps for the first time since whatever took him from the D.A.'s office and did away with his former love. As a personality, J.J. Gittes was destroyed, with Nicholson perfectly setting up a jokester and P.I. hack to provide the later contrast to this man who reemerges because of an enigmatic woman and her strange mystery.

This is much more than being interested in the woman and intrigued by her case. He actually becomes a human being because of it, living and acting and thinking instead of merely sleepwalking through an empty existence. Jake looks fresh and innocent after making love with Evelyn for the first time, exposing yet another aspect of the character. When he comes to life through his involvement with Mulwray, Gittes becomes an authentic detective, likely for the first time since he left the district attorney's. He invests energy to uncover truths, using his wits to break through barriers and delve into the story behind the mystery.

Actor Ed Nelson, who appeared in *The Cry Baby Killer*, told me, "Yeah, *Chinatown* … he was wonderful. It didn't surprise me. There's a lot of keys that he followed to make these [acting] choices. The actor knows the lines, but the character doesn't. Now that's a subtle thing, but it's important. Kazan said the art of shooting films isn't the dialogue, it's the reactions."[14]

There exists the possibility that Nicholson based something in his portrayal on an admiration for antihero actor Jean-Paul Belmondo, best known for *Breathless*, whom Jack often discussed during the filming of *Back Door to Hell*, perhaps in the wish to "craft a persona like Belmondo's dapper, alienated scoundrel of a man."[15]

Unlike in *A Few Good Men*, Nicholson's character here demands the truth of Dunaway, slapping her to loosen away a truth that he cannot handle. The mother-sister revelation was given additional depth when a reporter uncovered the hidden truth in Nicholson's own life by informing the actor that the woman he believed to be his sister his entire life was in fact his mother, while his grandmother had been representing herself as his mother due to the mores of the time.

Noah Cross (John Huston) inhabits evil when he attempts to take his daughter Evelyn and his other daughter—by Evelyn—simply because he could. Cross carries himself throughout the film with assurance, which here escalates to a sick confidence. This sense of entitlement forces a chain of events that leave the daughter-mother dead and the remaining granddaughter-daughter as an assumed possession. The creepiest part is the way Huston envelopes Evelyn and Katherine in the car. He is the full embodiment of what was hinted at by Peter Lorre in *M*.

Bakalyan, who played Loach (the cop who shot Evelyn in the final scene), knew what would happen yet didn't know the type of horror to expect. "I tell you the special effects makeup was unbelievable. I had no idea what she was going to look like," adding to the dread of its discovery, as Jake looks at her and her eye is blown out. "They took the eggshell, the inside liner of an egg … then they put the blood and all the other stuff there. Unbelievable. It gave me a strange feeling, I must say. It helps the actor when they do that because you're really responding to that."[16]

That final scene "took one or two nights to shoot in the streets of Chinatown in Los Angeles, on Spring Street," recalled Hong. "As I remember, Polanski tried many ways of ending the scene. It was very important to the whole movie, that ending scene. At times, tempers began to flare."[17]

Producer Robert Evans recalled the deep dispute about the film's ending between Polanski and Towne. The writer had Jake rescuing Evelyn and her sister-daughter. "Roman saw it another way, an evil way, the unexpected." Polanski called his violent and tragic ending "memorable" while Towne countered with "demented … ruinous … immoral." Towne derisively referred to Polanski's vision as "the tunnel at the end of the light" and attributed it to the director's own personal tragedy of losing his wife and unborn child at the hands of the Manson Family. "'Roman's argument was: 'That's life…. Beautiful blondes die in Los Angeles. Sharon [Tate] had.' He didn't say that but that's what he felt."[18]

The ending still shocks and pummels the emotions. Nicholson's character is believable, a man left empty, cracked open to release his life's essence like the diverted water itself. *Chinatown* leaves the viewer exhausted, feeling just a little of what J.J. Gittes must feel. Lou Escobar and Jake's partners are tender with this damaged soul, but what consolation can there be for this sort of replay of whatever it was that broke him the first time? What solace can there be that these things can't matter as much because it's Chinatown?

This is where it is better not to act and much better not to know, according to Michael Eaton in the British Film Institute's study of the film. Towne called it "the futility of good intentions," because if you do attempt to act, action will result in tragic, unforeseen consequences.[19]

* * *

Nicholson's virtuoso performance, the embodiment of a man defeated and then reborn, only to be destroyed, is as far from his comedic turn in Mike Nichols' *The Fortune* as can be found.

The perhaps ironically named Oscar is the dimwitted brother of Warren

Beatty's Nicky, approaching a *Dumb and Dumber* caricature in spots, while sporting frizzed-up hair that's part Larry Fine and part Art Garfunkel. Beatty plays a scheming, fast-talking Bud Abbott–type in what's called a comedy more because of the necessity to assign a genre as a mere technicality than through any earned merit.

It's a farce that's supposed to harken back to 1930s classic comedy teams, about avoiding a Mann Act charge (surely comedy gold). Married man Nicky (Beatty) persuades brother Oscar to marry the underage Freddie, wonderfully played by Stockard Channing—all layered with an additional scheme to snatch her daddy's fortune.

Not until the second time watching this movie did I realize that Nicholson was impersonating pal Bruce Dern throughout, thus enhancing its enjoyment greatly. Nicholson's voice, expressions and gestures capture the man with whom he shares several film credits, particularly in a scene about buying a "mouse bed" (tampon) and talking about his character's mother. When I asked Dern what he thought of Nicholson playing him for the entire movie, he had not even been aware of it, replying, "I never saw it. That was with Warren Beatty?" After my endorsement of Nicholson's hilarious lampooning of his speech patterns and mannerisms, Dern proclaimed, "He's got Bruce Dern privileges."[20]

Nicholson uses an eye-popped focus, open mouth and jutted upper teeth to create Oscar. He's at his most hilarious in a breakfast scene in which he tells Beatty about his "foolproof scheme," expressive and "Dernsie"-like.

One of his smaller, finer moments is a great reaction close-up shot in bed in which Freddie falls in love with a baby chick, marveling, "It thinks I'm its mother" before crying.

For the most part, Bruce—no, Jack—and Warren quarrel and fight and roll around on the ground, more loud and raucous than fun and frolicsome. Beatty is too pushy to be likable, leaving Nicholson with greater empathy. Channing is the winner in this production; her fun, engaging and eminently zany portrayal earned her a Golden Globe nomination for best female acting debut in a motion picture. Small wonder that years later, the actress called it a life-changing project: "Despite the bad rap it got, I think *The Fortune* is a small gem—and I'm good in it."[21]

Considering the talent—Nichols as director and producer; writer Carole Eastman; actors Beatty, Nicholson, Channing, Dub Taylor, Christopher Guest and Scatman Crothers—no fortune was made on this picture (in an artistic or financial sense), which tellingly was not available for viewing until a 2015 limited release.

In this mostly laugh-free comedy, there is one strong sustained scene, with the brothers attempting to toss Freddie off a bridge to her death inside a trunk, after getting caught up in a traffic jam along the way.

Nothing, however, could save this bungled opportunity of a movie. *The Fortune* simply is not screwy enough to qualify as a screwball comedy, nor ballsy enough to push any limits. Beatty and Nicholson may be friends and six years later successfully collaborated on *Reds*, but a comedy duo they are not. Perhaps Dustin Hoffman might fare better...

* * *

Nicholson advanced immeasurably as hood Charley Partanna in the dark comedy *Prizzi's Honor*. This time he was directed by *Chinatown* co-star John Huston and played opposite Huston's daughter Anjelica, whose then-current relationship with Nicholson provides a juicy subtext. In *Watch Me: A Memoir*, Anjelica revealed, "Jack hadn't hitherto understood that *Prizzi's Honor* was a comedy ... until Dad suggested that perhaps he wear a toupee as the main character, which Jack confided he had no intention of doing."[22]

In this film, Nicholson's range is on display. His broad mannerisms and physical embellishments enliven the role without overtaking it. He wins by pushing the character instead of overtly pushing the comedy, allowing situation and exaggerated conflicts to create the humor and the humanity. Nicholson can be the hit man and the romantic; plays confused and in-command; romps and swings and bounces Kathleen Turner before conjugating with Anjelica "on the Oriental, with all the lights on" as her real-life father directs the proceedings.

Turner valued the freedom to trust her instincts while working with Nicholson, to commit to her choices without worrying about the other actor. "All I had to do was my role [because] Jack is one of the best actors I've ever worked with." She pointed out that though Huston was ill, on full-time oxygen, the director "wasn't mentally diminished in any way. His personality and his mind, his decision-making was as powerful as ever." Huston's frailty let the actors come up with ideas and block out scenes, saying "Work up something and then show it to me."[23]

Yet subtlety counts. Charley sits silent and motionless in a meeting with the Family, conveying a change of heart as he questions "the system" when faced with the prospects of kidnapping a child.

Partanna was an expansion upon and update of Nicholson's uncredited role as Gino, a *St. Valentine's Day Massacre* hit man. Like Charley, Gino is a pro, loading his garlic-dipped bullets into his Tommy Gun. The added ingredient is not for flavor, but a backup "so you die of the blood poison." This could very well be the guy in *Studs Lonigan* a bit down the line, with Weary Reilly hardened by his jail time and trading his earlier juvenile delinquent gang for a real one to become a professional who loves his work a little too much, and three decades later becoming the twisted danger known as Francis Costello in *The Departed*.

* * *

Private eyes develop an immunity to "the life" and shut off all feeling, too. The J.J. Gittes of *Chinatown* returns as another, more slight and more detached J.J. Gittes 16 years later in the letdown of a sequel called *The Two Jakes*.

Watching the two films back to back, it almost seems as if Nicholson is not playing Jake in the latter film, but rather a lighter, almost rom-com figure. In contrast, Perry Lopez's Lou Escobar is the same guy.

Film acting scholar Dennis Bingham called the film a sad failure sunk by the "confusion of middle-aged male fantasy with frankness about middle age," and blamed the sequel's weakness to Nicholson's having "lost his level of irony and his Brechtian edge."[24]

Nicholson attributed the smoothening of Gittes' character to America's collective World War II experience, labeling the earlier incarnation "full of piss and vinegar" and now "a little more laid-back.... He watches people being

James Hong reprised his role as Evelyn Mulwray's butler in *The Two Jakes* (1990), the Nicholson-directed sequel to *Chinatown* (1974). Hong explained, "I played the scene with Jack as though I was very happy to meet someone from the past; however, I think you caught the tension beneath the warm feeling."

immoral all day ... he doesn't believe marriage is an act of God, and he thinks he's helping people."[25]

James Hong reprised his role as Evelyn Mulwray's butler, Kahn. In *Chinatown*, he was very faithful to the Faye Dunaway character and treated Gittes "as someone who would harm the family I served." In the sequel, "I played the scene with Jack as though I was very happy to meet someone from the past; however, I think you caught the tension beneath the warm feeling. I can say this is one of Jack's favorite scenes in *The Two Jakes*."[26]

Gittes' first sign of life is his reaction to hearing the name Katherine Mulwray (Evelyn's daughter and sister) on a wireless recording. Nicholson does grow into the character as the film unfolds, as if needing to catch up to the past in order to become himself. The question remains whether this is intentional to the circumstance portrayed, with Jake requiring the Mulwray connection to garner any kind of emotional involvement, or whether this is simply a product of a less intense portrayal matching the inconsequential material. It could also be a function of the production's notorious troubles and Nicholson's overlapping responsibilities as actor and director.

The duel between Nicholson and co-star Harvey Keitel (earlier paired in *The Border*) provides a rare element of interest, with

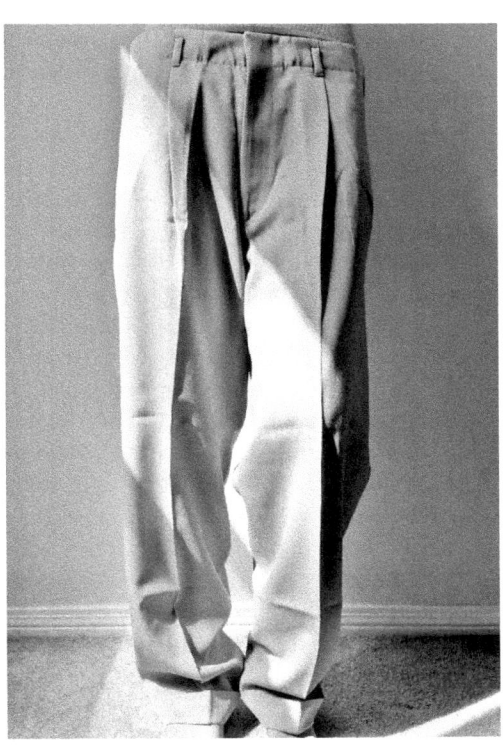

Western Costume Company is famous for its wardrobe work, including providing the reproduction period pants worn by Nicholson's character Jake Gittes in *The Two Jakes* (author's collection).

Nicholson convincingly playing the outclassed and the outsmarted. He gets into the character more deeply after being nearly blown up, suggesting that the messed, disheveled appearance and resulting injury were necessary to push him into a more engaged mode—a sort of character's muscle memory triggered by a dramatic, violent act that's associated with his knifed-nose trauma in *Chinatown*.

Keitel said the two rehearsed a lot. "We started by poring over the script together, by doing little improvisations together," for about three weeks prior to shooting, and that "it was a pleasure to work with another actor in this manner."[27]

Nicholson does have a funny sequence, one that relates to the effects of the passage of time since the first film, during a sexual encounter with Madeleine Stowe in Gittes' office. Jack denies his star glamour by humorously portraying vulnerability when he gets worn out through the lengthy undressing and coupling process, finally telling her to "take the rest of that goddamn thing off" and instructing her to get on her knees and raise her ass in the air.

His most rewarding scenes in the sequel do cover a broad range of characterization. Nicholson is explosive and intense when he flashes back to Evelyn Mulwray's shooting by Detective Loach and then returns to his current encounter with Loach's son. This culminates in Gittes pushing his barrel into Loach Jr.'s mouth and scathingly commanding the cop to "suck it."

In sharp contrast, Gittes tends to Evelyn's now adult daughter Katherine Mulwray (played by Meg Tilly) with sweetness and concern, almost like a father to a daughter in a protective and caring manner.

Later, we see a nice actor's courtship between Jack and Keitel (the other Jake), with the more celebrated veteran generously allowing his co-star to enjoy the greater dramatic turn. In the narrative set-up, there's a smart twist on how the detective usually shows compromising photos to his client, which inevitably leads to tears or some other histrionics. Here, the detective Jake Gittes returns X-rays to the client Jake Berman to let the realtor hide the fact that he is terminally ill. Now Berman's wife can collect on his insurance. All Berman needs to do is die accidentally on purpose.

Nicholson reacts to Keitel's tearful exposition, tamping his own part down as he watches the younger Jake's suicide in close-up, accomplished by lighting a cigarette in a highly gaseous environment during an earthquake on an oil-rich housing development.

Nicholson ends the film by encapsulating the two movies' journeys through tragedy and loss, age and loneliness, and the regrets over a meaningless career. His career's only flashes of positivity have been helping Jake Berman and Katherine Mulwray. Kitty had asked him if the past ever goes away, but he responds only by pushing her away, in the guise of the learned elder and while looking appropriately weary. He subsequently answers the

14. The Dicks Versus the Hoods

question to himself, imparting the message of the movie, and the two-part story, that the past itself never does go away.

Gittes claims he doesn't want to live in the past, but he does not know how to live in the present. Nicholson's characterization only comes to life when that life reflects the one behind him.

* * *

For the private dicks, their own pasts keep piling up, together with those from their cases. Some could not be solved. Others might better have remained unsolved. Each broken and lost life adds another past that can never go away.

For the hoods, they cannot escape their past. Perhaps they are paying for it in the pen. Maybe their own fellow gangsters will make them pay, so the constant vigilance and suspicion of everyone and everything makes their past everpresent. Then, that past can only truly go away if they fall victim to a hit. Otherwise, they flail around in a murky pool of memories they do not want to remember, treading in a fetid wave of those memories, sinking into the past ... because their future is all used up, as Marlene Dietrich told corrupt cop Orson Welles at the conclusion of *Touch of Evil*.

15

Head Trips

Everybody's a writer. Scribbling that novel everyone has inside. Pushing out that blog to a dedicated few. Tapping out posts and tweets and who knows what else. Oh yes, and writing that screenplay.

They all gather, informally and without being aware of their shared experience, at the local coffeehouse to grab the free Wi-Fi and stay caffeine-fortified. Perhaps it's the modern version of Schwab's Pharmacy, where actor wannabes wanted to be seen in order to be discovered. In a world where people seem more and more illiterate, there are (in seeming contradiction) more and more who believe they can write.

Writing a screenplay can be an artistic expression, or it can be a way to pay the bills, or it can be a means to advance a career toward directing. For Jack Nicholson, at one point or another, all three were true.

Nicholson drew upon this double life and captured the melancholy of creative weariness suffered by blocked writers more than a dozen years later on *The Shining*. "That's the one scene in the movie I wrote myself," said Nicholson. "That scene at the typewriter—that's what I was like when I got my divorce." A new wife, a new daughter, acting in the daytime, and writing a screenplay at night turned the frustrated and disillusioned actor into a proto–Jack Torrance. As he recounts the incident, one can hear the character emerge from the man: "I'm back in my little corner and my beloved wife Sandra walked in on what was, unbeknownst to her, this maniac." Nicholson confided, "I remember being at the desk and telling her, 'Even if you don't hear me typing, it doesn't mean I'm not writing. This is writing…'"[1]

It's natural for an actor to think they can deliver better lines if they wrote them. *The Rebel Rousers* actor Robert Dix mentioned how Nicholson and Bruce Dern "kind of rewrote the script because it wasn't much of a script in the first place." It also makes sense that, once in the movie business, one might hope to bring more serious, deeper, more introspective themes to the screen. Particularly if one can act in (or direct) them.

Actress Hazel Court, who worked with Nicholson in *The Raven*, related to me how he would go home after shooting every night to do scriptwriting. "He would write when he was on the film, and he kept saying 'I want to go to write.'"[2]

Nicholson has written or co-written six screenplays that have been produced as films, beginning with *Thunder Island* in 1963 and followed over the next couple of years with *Flight to Fury* and *Ride in the Whirlwind*. Two psychedelic, counterculture movies, *The Trip* and *Head*, preceded his collaborative adaptation of Jeremy Larner's novel *Drive, He Said*. That's six official credits in eight years, but none since 1971.

His writing reflects a dedication to message and theme, enlivened by an artistic style that reaches beyond the banal Hollywood toward the more ambitious foreign film sensibility admired by the actor.

His first screenplay was co-written with a Jeff Corey associate, actor-turned-producer Don Devlin. The title, *Thunder Island*, may or may not be a nod to then-wife Sandra Knight's film debut with Robert Mitchum in *Thunder Road*.

Like *Flight to Fury* from the following year, this story takes place in a foreign land (the Philippines in that case and the Caribbean here). This is one of only two directorial credits for Jack Leewood, otherwise used only in a production capacity. It was filmed in San Miguel, Puerto Rico. A strong Hispanic presence takes this beyond the typical location shoot where the locals are nothing more than props in the background.

Billy Poole (played by Gene Nelson) is a menacing figure who meets a contact woman named Anita (Miriam Colon), from whom he is given the assignment to assassinate former dictator Antonio Perez, a job to be "completed in six days." She hires a hit man from the U.S., and the plot is foiled by another American, who does so mainly to save the lives of his wife and daughter.

Poole is matter-of-fact, detached and flip—a typically cold, all-business gringo. She explains the reasoning for this political act and he lets her pontificate with no particular interest.

Anita makes a committed justification ("Do you have any idea what it's like to live under a terrible dictatorship?") and he blows it off sarcastically: "You should have known my old man." He minimizes her country's plight by declaring, "People get killed all the time. One pig is as good as another," and finally gets down to business by dismissively poking, "Let's skip the speeches, huh?"

In retrospect, Anita's quest to kill the dictator takes on greater interest upon learning the story of Marita Lorenz, who had an affair with Cuban President Fidel Castro and later attempted to help the CIA assassinate that dictator by delivering poison pills said to have been supplied by Bay of Pigs veteran Frank Sturgis.

Nicholson and Devlin's political thriller features a subplot about an ad man named Vince (Brian Kelly from *Flipper*), who brings his estranged wife (Fay Spain) and their daughter from the U.S. for a possible reconciliation.

Vince left Madison Avenue and "the gray flannel suit," he declares disparagingly, to become a commercial fisherman. Reflecting Peter Fonda's character of Paul Groves in Nicholson's script for *The Trip*, Vince needed to escape "the rat race" and "that whole New York advertising scene" because he hated "peddling soap and cigarettes."

Here, the screenwriters create a very effective and appealing plot device that combines two little girls, a friendship and zoo animals to make a father and her daughter potential accessories to an assassination.

Vince's daughter meets the ex-dictator's daughter and they become fast friends. This puts in motion a chain of events that intertwines the unwitting characters, the fisherman and his family, with the deadly plot. The concept that Vince's daughter becomes susceptible to luring her father into the plan due to her desire to see the island's zoo animals—collected, of course, by Perez—adds another offbeat twist.

Bad guy Poole's machinations to kidnap the girl were meant to serve as his way to get onto the island and be in position to make the hit. When the plan is undermined by Anita, Poole must have Vince's wife taken instead. In a light touch, Helen's kidnapping takes the form of a pleasant day of sightseeing and dining.

When Poole comes ashore and assembles his rifle, another interesting tactic takes advantage of the setting and its inclusion of the zoo animals as part of the earlier plot device. As the hit man prepares to make the kill, he is unaware that an increasingly agitated puma paces above him. This enriches the visual action with an additional dimension and multiplies the possibilities for the climax. Will non-human intervention save Perez, ascribing greater morals to the beast than to the man?

Instead, all elements come into play, ultimately allowing the movie's protagonist to become the hero. Kids get in the way; the puma gets more distressed; and Vince comes from out of nowhere to drive in front of the assassin to block his shot. Violence erupts and a chase ensues.

The final part of the chase inevitably reduces the conflict to Vince against Poole, similar to Nicholson's next screenwriting credit, *Flight to Fury*. As we might expect, Vince is somehow able to outshoot a professional hit man and kill the villain. In another precursor to *Flight*, the dying man's hand dangles into the water—in this instance continuing to hold his gun (thereby connecting him to his life's work even after his life is over) and in that case using a close-up that follows Nicholson's last defiant act when he drops stolen jewels into the current for a final "Fuck you" to society.

An abrupt happy ending between Vince and Helen belies a more serious, cynical message. After the initial stage of gunfire, Anita's cohorts force Helen into their car. But Helen belittles Anita's idealism, saying she is no different than the dictator she targets. When Anita counters that "sometimes an act of violence is needed to bring peace," Helen sums up the lie behind it all when she challenges Anita's notion that an act of violence can bring peace by countering: "There'll just be another Perez."

A bleak cynicism also becomes an unseen character in Nicholson's next screenplay, 1964's *Flight to Fury*, based on a story by director Monte Hellman and producer Fred Roos. Like the previous film, it takes place in an exotic locale, adding to the intrigue and atmosphere.

Flight to Fury is an homage to John Huston's *Beat the Devil*, a 1954 movie, featuring Humphrey Bogart and Nicholson's on-screen father (in the prior year's *The Raven*) Peter Lorre. It "satirized those kinds of genre movies," according to director and co-writer Hellman. "It's not a comedy but it has comic overtones."[3]

One significant advance since Nicholson's prior script was in its characterizations. Aside from the assassin's eating obsessions and repeated business with raisins, *Thunder Island* was thin in the development of the roles. Here, there are several interesting characters, the best of which Nicholson wrote for himself. Jay Wickham is a fun and frightening psychopath whose main joy derives from killing, with the threat of murder or painful physical harm coming a close second. Nicholson told Robert Crane and Christopher Fryer that it was "one of the best characters that I've gotten to play, and certainly one of the best ones that I've written."[4]

Hellman reminisced that he and Nicholson took a ship to the Philippines "and he wrote the script for *Flight to Fury* on the ship ... getting feedback and information from whatever passengers were kibitzing at the time [*laughs*]."[5]

Other worthwhile parts are played by Fay Spain as the progressive and aggressive (for the time) Destiny Cooper; Vic Diaz in the juicy role of the odd and inhumane diamond smuggler Lorgren; and Nicholson pal John Hackett as the rough and heroic pilot Al Ross. Unfortunately, the lead character Joe Gaines (Dewey Martin) does not match the eccentric flavor and depth of the other characters, with Martin giving a stiff portrayal in this generic role.

Things begin strangely, when lounge lizard Wickham sets up Gaines, more for the pleasure of it than any real benefit to himself. Nicholson, well-known for being very particular about his wardrobe, sports a white suit and narrow black tie and wears a mustache for the first time on-screen (he had a goatee in his recurring *Dr. Kildare* role). His appearance and manner should have been clues for Gaines, but free booze breaks down a lot of barriers.

Jay gets Joe involved with a local lady, hides in Joe's closet and kills her (thus leaving Gaines in a bit of a predicament). The highlight of this sequence is Nicholson's maniacal grin as he displays the ligature toward his victim. Nicholson here has twice the fun. He provides meat to the character, establishing the fact that Jay Wickham will do anything, making it possible for any number of scenarios and establishing a credible foundation for all acts and behaviors. This supplies incredible freedom to a screenwriter, putting the viewer on notice to expect the most unexpected and allowing himself the flexibility to break beyond narrative norms. In short, crazy is as crazy does.

Gaines lets himself be manipulated by Wickham again, to organize a flight out of Manila on which Wickham appears without warning.

In addition to the stronger characterization, *Flight to Fury* represents a progression in the young writer's dialogue. He treats a fellow passenger (Hellman's then-wife Jacqueline) to an odd sort of in-flight patter with an existential discourse about death that's highlighted by an idea about setting the age of 50 as the point to make a go/no-go decision (a concept relatively easy to float when in his mid-twenties).

He makes Destiny unpredictable and flirtatious, telling Joe he "has a nice mouth" and kissing him out of the blue before walking away because he "asks too many questions."

A plane crash in the jungle reveals the true plot motivation. Jay Wickham is after smuggled jewels and he will do whatever is necessary—even beyond what is necessary—to get them. This sets the conflict and the tone for the remainder of the film.

The crash landing provides well-directed tension, with the mortally wounded pilot giving Gaines the contraband. Hackett goes out with a laugh, encouraging Joe to "win one for the Gipper."

Naturally, many of the plane's passengers are fellow diamond smugglers. The Peter Lorre–esque Vic Diaz takes the jewels back at gunpoint, after which the group attempts to move *en masse* when locals show up out of nowhere to shoot an elderly Japanese man and take them all as prisoners.

When they try to escape, a gunfight breaks out. One nice notion was having a young Japanese man avenge his father's death by killing several with a Samurai sword, even after being mortally wounded himself. He then sacrifices himself to bring the leader out into the open to be shot.

Wickham subsequently shows just how coldblooded he could become, shooting partners Lorgren and Destiny before getting shot himself. As in *Thunder Island*, the good guy and the killer leave the scene of battle for a chase scene to conclude the movie. Just as in the previous film, the more experienced gunman is outgunned by the hero. Joe traps Wickham, but Wickham won't give him the satisfaction of winning. In another twist that shows Nicholson's potential as scenarist, Wickham throws away the jewels he has worked so hard to gain rather than let Gaines or anyone else get them. Now, the water owns them. And then, Wickham finishes himself off after taunting his rival—whom he has already set up in the hotel with the dead hostess and by involving him with the ill-fated flight—one last time by correctly predicting, "You can't shoot me, Joe!" Jay Wickham meets death his own way, with Nicholson's final line of dialogue serving as the character's own defiant "Made it, Ma. Top of the world!" and done well before his fiftieth birthday.

Flight to Fury is a tight, well-balanced and textured script with good action and interesting characters, rich beyond the small budget of this programmer. There's fiery interplay, noirish atmosphere and narrative tension.

Another quality delivered by Nicholson's second script is a similar sense of futility found in the first. *Thunder Island* represents a political futility, how blindly following a cause and justifying violence to end a larger violence becomes meaningless. In *Flight*, crime ultimately does not pay, yet justice is not possible. The hero is denied any reward by the final sick act of the twisted criminal mind who outwitted him time after time. The closest thing the movie had to a heroine, Fay Spain's Destiny, was killed by Wickham to thereby deny her to Joe. The film ends with Joe alone, as all of the other main characters are dead, leaving him stuck in a jungle and facing a future of having to stay ahead of any of the remaining locals who had imprisoned him with the gang of smugglers. A similar fate met Nicholson's Wes in his next script, *Ride in the Whirlwind*.

No jewels, no lover, no chance. And so the final shot fittingly focuses on the dirty shoes of the strange man in the white suit, ending Nicholson's second written work with a close-up of a wardrobe item of a dead man.

* * *

Nicholson's next script was another collaboration with Monte Hellman as part of a back-to-back, economical on-location shoot in Kanab and Paria, Utah, with *The Shooting*.

Nicholson and Hellman wrote *Ride in the Whirlwind* in a building called the Writer's Building, next door to Fred Astaire's office. Monte recalled, "We'd go there every day and I would pace and [Jack] would sit down and write the script out longhand."[6]

Whirlwind continued the bleak undertone of the prior two works, a pervasive sense that would inhabit his later projects with director Bob Rafelson, most notably *Five Easy Pieces* and *The King of Marvin Gardens*, but also reappear in *Head* and *Blood and Wine*. The Hellman-Nicholson and Rafelson-Nicholson collaborations share an overriding futility against existences outside the understanding or control of its characters. It's as if the people in these films can almost feel as if something is not quite right, nearly uncovering that they are in fact characters created by a dramatist who fully controls what they cannot.

A whirlwind is a small, spinning windstorm as well as a confused rush of events and feelings. Nicholson's script uses both meanings, with the two main characters Vern (Cameron Mitchell) and Wes (Nicholson) caught in a metaphorical cycle that whirls them around, effectively removing their free will and leaving them befuddled about what is happening to them or why. Perhaps Jack's line for himself, when Wes notes, "Lost my spurs," is meant to sum up their situation. And their fate. Having a western character lose his spurs removes the character from the genre orthodoxy. Writing and delivering the line, "lost my spurs" also shows Nicholson's taste for the unusual.

Hellman said, "If I had to say the theme in one phrase, I would say, 'Guilt by association.'"[7] They have no hope. It is not clear whether they understand this; whether they somehow sense it; or whether their "ride in the whirlwind" leaves them oblivious to their chances of escape or survival.

They begin their ride as a trio and soon become the victims of coincidences. They luck upon a cabin by coincidence and seek refuge for the night, but it's with a gang of outlaws led by Harry Dean Stanton as eye patch–wearing Blind Dick, who earlier held up a stagecoach.

By coincidence, they're assumed to be part of the gang by posse members who surround the cabin and start a fire to smoke them out. The posse now shoots to kill, and plans to clean up the remainders later, in a typically unrestrained example of frontier justice. Luck (of a sort) make Vern and Wes the only men who escape the attack, though they are now a duo and are forced to take their chances over the forbidding terrain on foot.

It was no coincidence that the outlaw Indian Joe, played by African American actor Rupert Crosse, was shown with a rope around his neck as part of that "justice" in action. This was written and filmed in 1965, during the height of the Civil Rights struggles. Nicholson commented upon the times by reflecting the horrid act of lynching. Yet, in the film, Crosse wasn't lynched because of his race.

Vern and Wes escape the fire. They escape the shootout. They escape the lynching of the leftovers. But just as coincidence after coincidence saves them, coincidence after coincidence brings them closer to their fate. It may even be crueler that they are allowed false hope and the illusion of escape.

Hellman called this "the consequences of not speaking out," explaining that the two "ride into an outlaw camp and they don't protest, they accept the responsibility of the outlaws." When they spend the night in the cabin with the gang, the pair thereafter suffers the penalties in "[a] kind of you-make-your-bed-you-lie-in-it kind of thing."[8]

Their story is a tough romantic ballad, a frontier poem of trapped men in unforgiving and hostile surroundings. Illustrated by stark imagery, the film takes on the appearance of a photo essay, a study of small men lost in a large landscape that is dotted by the rare sight of deserted cabins. In this small story in a large setting, mindless men watch a lynching as if staged for a sick postcard.

Their story is a narrative that teaches us the lesson of fatalism, a lesson that tastes like dust and leaves the marks of steep rocky struggles.

The pair's next coincidence brings them into view of a ramshackle farm in the middle of nowhere. On foot in an impossible land, Vern and Wes climb a rocky climb with a rocky partnership that strengthens by necessity with each difficult move up and along the punishing red-rock bluffs.

But why is this farmhouse here? Is it actually where it appears, or is it an elaborate desert mirage playing a perverse joke? Nicholson later wrote such an ambiguous possible hallucination for Micky Dolenz, who discovers a solitary Coca-Cola vending machine on a desert dune in *Head*.

More than mere isolation, the choice of location seems masochistic, as stubborn as the farmer who swings and strikes ... swings and strikes ... swings and strikes over and over again while getting nowhere slowly in his attempt to remove a tree stump.

This family farm of three—father, mother and daughter—is stuck there just as the stump is stuck there. And now Vern and Wes are stuck there. So much land, endless Utah miles of bluffs and canyons and skies, yet the two interior locations shown in the film are claustrophobic. The sequences in which the original trio stays with outlaws in the abandoned cabin, and when Vern and Wes stay with this family, feel both uncomfortable and stifling. Despite the great space outside, the atmosphere inside is oppressive.

Millie Perkins plays Abigail, the daughter who is trapped here away from any other part of civilization. She described her view of the character as someone who had no way of knowing how she was supposed to look or act: "She just was." She walks like she is one of her chickens, because that is what she knows best. Her downward look, her gait and movement mirror their motion. "I loved it that the chickens were her best friends. She spent more time around them than anything beside her parents."[9]

Every action is as small and contained as possible, with no room for sentiment or daydreams. A pair of strangers appear without notice and seemingly without any means to do so (remember that they no longer have horses), yet there is no panic.

Wes puts his hand over Abigail's mouth to stifle any scream, but she probably would not have needed the hand or the warning: "She just was." And it simply happened. The pervading impression is one of inevitability.

Vern and Wes seem likable enough and not particularly threatening. So they are fed, with Abigail spooning out the food with great attention to function over appearance. When she walks, she does so with her feet straight in the direction of travel, while those feet hardly leave the ground, with each action economical and without adornment or waste. Even when alone with

Wes outside, in what's as close to courting as she's likely ever experienced, nothing approaches showiness or affectation.

Perkins describes her reaction to this rare interaction of the opposite sexes, particularly near her own age, as instinctual about "a feeling she never had before, but she didn't know what to do with it. [Abigail was] not vulnerable on purpose, but it made her have a vulnerability, but she didn't understand it."[10]

The script carefully considers the time and place. Dialogue is simple and straightforward, as minimal as the settings and the range of their lives. Though a young and relatively inexperienced scenarist, Nicholson resists the urge to overwrite or use his character creations to pontificate or fill every moment with sparkling and inappropriately theatrical lines.

Once settled into the family's cabin, the main characters are allowed to relax, temporarily moving outside of their total concentration on survival. Vern and Wes are almost like father and son or older brother looking after a younger sibling. Nicholson plays boyish and for-the-moment against Cameron Mitchell's delusional longing and nostalgia for his homestead.

We get a glimpse of their real relationship in an extended scene in which the two play checkers while the father pointlessly works on the tree stump. Both acts, the board game inside the shack and the axe game outside it, appear to be more about amusement or passing the time than for any purpose. The checkers game serves as another example of Nicholson's feel for the unusual in his scriptwriting.

It was important that Nicholson use some screen time to humanize the pair, making the older man's ultimate sacrifice, made to allow his younger colleague to escape, that much more meaningful and poignant.

In the final coincidence, a posse member decides to give the tiny farm one more look despite having already checked the place and finding no signs of trouble. This time, escape cannot be possible for both. One partner was lost during the smoke-out and shoot-out at the outlaw's cabin. Now, a second partner must pay for a wrong never committed, while Abigail's father must also lose his life, to make her life even harder.

Kent felt that these realities made the story more authentic and honest. "I didn't know that Monte had an existential outlook on life or did he think that life was bleak," he reflected. "All I knew was ... that it was pretty bleak and hard during these times." Kent believed the fatalistic turn of the story was also a product of Nicholson's devotion to studying the era and to its truth over an idealized version of it.[11]

Wes does escape on horseback, with an ambiguous getaway ending the film, but we doubt that he makes it. It's more of the game, and it's likely that Wes realizes this at the same time as does the audience.

Ride in the Whirlwind may not be a classic, but it works as a departure

15. Head Trips   229

from the standard western. "I was amazed when I read the script," says Kent. "I thought, 'This is wonderful,' because it wasn't the usual John Wayne shoot-em-up, where a guy takes ten guys down at once. There actually was some feeling amongst the characters and I was shocked they got it going."[12]

Perkins also viewed the project as part of the Nicholson career plan. "I think it was just him doing everything he could do to be in the movie business.... I don't know if he had fantasies of doing one thing over the other. I think it was to be an actor, but he was certainly planning to write and direct, too."[13]

Hellman, who had experience with Nicholson twice as a writer, "thought he gave me good material for the job at hand, and I was able to shoot both scripts with very little modification on my part."[14] The director summed up Nicholson the screenwriter by saying, "I would characterize him as a good craftsman."[15]

* * *

Writing good roles for himself, as Jack did on *Flight to Fury* and *Whirlwind*, was certainly part of that process. The plan didn't always work out, as he learned when director Roger Corman cast Bruce Dern instead of Nicholson as the LSD guide in Nicholson's next produced script.

The Trip was a journey inside the mind, which as it turns out is a more accommodating space than the entirety of Utah. Largely an experimental script that's experiential in nature, Nicholson's journey takes us along with lead character Paul (Peter Fonda) and his self-exploring first LSD trip.

More subjective travelogue than objective narrative, the film was the first overground or mainstream movie directly dealing with the drug. Said to be substantially biographical (relating to the end of his crumbling marriage, as well as his own LSD and free love experiences), *The Trip* shows foreign film ambition within an exploitation ambiance.

I asked star Peter Fonda what he thought of the script the first time he saw it, and Fonda clarified that he was "with Jack a lot of times as we talked" about the work in progress. He then revealed what he felt was the real import of Nicholson's work: "When I first read it straight through as a full script, I thought, 'I'm gonna be in the first true American art film.' But of course Roger Corman was directing, so he didn't really do Jack's script. Which was a shame, I thought."[16]

Nicholson told Corman, who had also "tripped" under clinical conditions, that he did not want to treat the subject as exploitation. "He had higher aspirations this time," Nicholson observed. "He knew he couldn't get a writer as good as me through regular ways. I was happy to write it and make a more demanding picture out of it."[17]

Salli Sachse, a contract player for AIP, graduated from *Beach Party* and

Roger Corman meets acid. *The Trip* (1967) was Nicholson's fourth produced screenplay out of six during his career. Salli Sachse, shown here with star Peter Fonda, recounted how Fonda and Dennis Hopper began the production excited about its prospects, but became disillusioned at the watered-down results.

Dr. Goldfoot to the more adult biker and drug culture features. She portrayed Glenn, the girlfriend of drug dealer Max (Dennis Hopper), and a recurring lure for Fonda to leave the straight life to live with more feeling. Salli confirmed to me the gap between vision and outcome that Fonda mentioned. "I remember Peter and Dennis were so excited because they said, 'Oh wow, this is such a bitchin' movie, this is gonna be far-out.' Then, as filming continued, scenes were changed and I understand they became a little disillusioned that the original ideas that they thought had been lost."[18]

Paul is a director of television commercials, with TV and advertising again serving as Nicholson targets of vacuous pandering and the ugly style of capitalism. It makes sense then that Paul suffers disillusionment of his own, seeking enlightenment in the form of a psychedelic ride. He needs a world away from our sponsors as well as a break from his failing marriage.

In *The Films of Jack Nicholson*, Douglas Brode references a similarity to

15. Head Trips 231

Jean Cocteau's *Orpheus* (1949), "which likewise studied a frustrated, despairing would-be artist who fears he is a charlatan, his successful career merely satisfying the masses without saying anything of lasting significance." Paul and Orpheus are both obsessed with death; they both seek truth through a trip of an expressionistic nature; both are torn between two women, one representing safety and the other a more mysterious risk. "The external artist's tragedy is that he wants it both ways," Brode observed, "wanting to possess both the straight life and the dark side ... a double existence, as do so many Nicholson characters."[19]

Straight as he is, the ad man won't be dropping acid at some wild party, but under the controlled guidance of a possible psychologist or self-proclaimed LSD guru, Bruce Dern, as Paul's friend John.

Jack starts Paul's journey with John at (where else?) Dennis Hopper's pad. On the way into that first trip, a flirty blonde (Salli) wants to go along, but he declines. She then whispers something in his ear to which he reacts before pausing and saying, "Okay." What Salli said to Fonda was meant to elicit an embarrassed response, even to make him blush, but when I asked her to reveal that secret, she heartily laughed, "I can't say! I can't tell you."[20] It had to be good. It also reminds viewers of a scene in Nicholson's next screenplay, *Head*, in which Monkee Michael Nesmith whispers conspiratorially to Nicholson's real-life girlfriend I.J. Jefferson (aka Mimi Machu). Nesmith can be heard asking her to come back when the other guys aren't around. She responds, "Are you kidding?" before giving her trademark two-note lilting laugh.

In *The Trip*, Nicholson uses a sly pop culture reference to prepare Paul for his acid inauguration. Fonda had repeatedly informed John Lennon that he knew what it's like to be dead, inspiring the Beatles' *Revolver* track "She Said, She Said." Here, Dern (John!) quotes Lennon's album closer "Tomorrow Never Knows" to advise Fonda (Paul!) to turn off his mind, to relax and to float downstream.

Imagery and experience take over Nicholson's work at this point with editing and special effects playing as substantial a part as character or dialogue. Time and place become elastic and illusory. Sachse recalled that Nicholson's script "was a lot of visuals" and that "psychedelia was upon us, but I wasn't part of that because I hadn't been exposed to that yet."[21]

Nicholson described it as "very McLuhanesque. It was about the juxtapositions of reality ... to show how quickly things move. It was so dense with material you could see a one-frame cut."[22]

A flash-cut puts Paul on the rocky surf (which looks like the one in *The Terror*) in a white puffy shirt. Back with John, Paul studies an orange, proclaiming it "alive," foreshadowing William Tepper's similar exploration of himself in an orange as seen in Nicholson's *Drive, He Said*. Fonda caresses the fruit in wonderment and declares that he holds the "sun in my hands" as he displays it in front of himself as the foreground to his view of the ocean. Nicholson explained that the "idea of the whole script was seeing the objective camera-eye experience of the guy actually on the trip when he's got the orange. He can't believe it."[23]

There's a fantastic, psychedelic light projection lovemaking scene that switches back and forth, noticeably yet subtlety, between Fonda with Susan Strasberg (as Paul's wife Sally) and Fonda with Sachse, in an editing *ménage à trois*. Salli explained the transition, "rolling over and it's me ... and rolling back and it's Susan Strasberg. I remember Peter saying something about, 'Can you imagine Roger Corman editing a love scene?' Because he was such a cerebral person, Roger. He seemed very left-brained and analytical and not a real emotional person, so that was kind of a little joke between us all."

Yet it worked. The footage was sensual and artful. Flesh and special effects met for several groundbreaking moments of movie intimacy. "We had a set in the studio, where it was a bedroom made on the set," Sachse said. "It's something I certainly hadn't done before, and you know, you're on a movie set with the camera and the grips and I think I had little pasties on. There was some excitement there, but you can't get too intimate with 20 people watching."[24]

It's a very sexy film, with the lovemaking scenes close and personal, as the camera shares much stroking and multiple views of hands running down backs and much caressing of someone else's skin.

Things start to get intense for Paul, what with hooded riders on horses, a witch, a desert (*à la* Micky Dolenz in *Head*), and a haunted house (perhaps from Corman's *House of Usher*). Amongst all this, one disturbing image— aside from a crucifixion—shows Fonda and Strasberg, both with blood on their faces and Fonda's coming out of his eyes, while he holds a baby's severed hand.

Nicholson's highly visual script brings *Seventh Seal* references together with a dwarf on a less-than-merry merry-go-round. The dwarf joins Paul's tour guide of his dreams, Dennis Hopper, to tell the advertising producer that he hasn't "done anything" with his life, in conjunction with a *non sequitur* mention of the Bay of Pigs.

The screenwriter's disdain for advertising is underscored when Paul is challenged about the first word that comes to his mind about TV commercials, with the strong suggestion of "lies." Fonda's character defends with a weak, "What? It works." and "It's a living" in response to this Spanish Inquisition on acid.

It almost seems as if the worst part of Paul's trip occurs when he's assaulted with advertising, punished with his own creation through a rapid machine-gunning of billboards and signs promoting hotels and gas stations.

When Paul starts to have a bad trip, John pulls the fully nude Fonda out of a pool and drops him inside. Clearly, this is part of the intent, as Nicholson has shown that he likes to shock and break through with male nudity, most evidently on his direction of *Drive, He Said*.

Nicholson shows another example of his view of the ordinary as absurdity in a lengthy scene with Paul, who has escaped from John's guiding protection, inside a laundromat with Corman regular Barboura Morris. The sequence highlights a drug naiveté while the characters reflect a perfect combination of commercialism vs. hipsterism; a class chasm between the big-time TV ad director vs. the lower class woman left to do her laundry on a weekend evening; along with male vs. female politics. Fonda and Morris do not understand one another, and he lives up to her fears when he takes out her laundry and tosses it as if he is as suspicious of it as she is of him.

In contrast, a charming scenario between Fonda and a little girl (Caren Bernsen, daughter of soap opera star Jeanne Cooper and brother of Corbin) illustrates how even in the height of hippiedom there was still an openness and sensitivity, when everything wasn't seen as risk or a frontal attack. In Paul's altered state, he's been mentally reborn, so he can relate to a small child.

Here and there are countercultural messages, such as when Max (Hopper) calms Paul, assuring him that "there's nothing to be afraid of, man" or when Sachse tells him, "I don't believe in police" at a drive-in restaurant. But the main point of the movie is to serve as a detailed guide, or "Acid for Dummies," that throws in promises of uninhibited sex as further inducement.

A corporate hack, who makes "a living" but hasn't "done anything" of import, seeks enlightenment and freedom. Friends help him on his journey. Women love him. Strangers welcome him or fear him. He makes it through nightmarish visions and samples based on foreign art films. But "there's nothing to be afraid of, man." At least until AIP undermined the entire vision and intent by tacking on a near-parody spoken warning before the official beginning of the film and by editing on an abrupt, tacky, broken glass freeze frame at its conclusion. (Get it? Paul cracked up because of his bum trip!)

* * *

If you had been a member of the TV-band-that-became-a-real-band known as the Monkees, you could be forgiven if you retrospectively viewed Nicholson's next screenwriting credit (shared with director Bob Rafelson) as a bum trip. *Head* accomplished one of the goals of its filmmakers, to destroy the group. The other goal, to be responsible for an artistic and countercultural hit, was not realized.

Rafelson and Bert Schneider created the show as a television cash-in on the Beatles and *A Hard Day's Night* and cast the group as personalities who also happened to possess musical talent.

Cash in they did. The series, hit singles and albums, merchandising from dolls and novelizations to trading cards and posters, made these men wealthy. One of the odd characters in *Head*, Lord High'n'Low (played by Timothy Carey), valued these "byproducts" as worth "millions!"

Rafelson and Schneider made money. They did so for the wrong reasons (at least from their viewpoint). They felt guilty. They used *Head* in part to clear that guilt and to regain (or gain) some street cred. The TV show was a lampoon of movies and television shows and music, irreverent and formless, and on which they often broke the fourth wall.

Many have characterized *Head* as the Monkees committing suicide. But it's not suicide if you are forced into it. The four are driven to jump off a bridge, chased to its edge. Behind the script, the group's creators decided the band must end its own commercial life. Forced suicide is not a self-inflicted death. *Head* therefore stands as the creators' filicide, as well as its attempted entry into the world of serious, artistic cinema.

In filicide, they succeeded. The show had just been canceled and the group's recordings had ceased to be automatic top-sellers. The movie exposed their "manufactured image," though really to those who already knew about it. It depicted the group as a plastic and commercial venture, from the viewpoint of those who had the fortunate access to do so and benefitted the most from it.

In art, they also succeeded. The film may have flopped at the time and may have been inaccurately tossed together with other pop music exploitation flicks or unfairly tagged as uncool because of the Monkees, but the cult knew better, and today, more also know better.

Thanks to Nicholson's avant garde script; Rafelson's adventurous direction and risky view toward a more expansive and less commercial future; and the collective talents of Micky Dolenz, Michael Nesmith, Davy Jones and Peter Tork, this film remains a psychedelic treat filled with timely commentary, exploratory style and musical celebration. Take the six music video masterpieces and you have six testaments to the evolved Monkees maturity, deftly balancing their individual songwriting and performing strengths with the enhancement of outside tunesmiths Carole King and Harry Nilsson, alongside instrumental talents Neil Young, Ry Cooder, Jerry Scheff, Earl Palmer and Leon Russell.

Despite the powerful and often beautiful depiction of the music, the film destroys the group behind that music. It has to, in order for Rafelson and Nicholson to move forward toward *Five Easy Pieces* and Schneider to advance into serious endeavors such as *Hearts and Minds*, an Academy Award–winning documentary about the Vietnam War. Coincidentally (or not so coincidentally), Monkees money made *Easy Rider*, no doubt more hippie-palatable than its benefactor TV property.

15. Head Trips 235

Head is an exploration based around the art of the juxtaposition. Juxtaposing images, sounds, plot devices and archetypes turns the familiar into the new and the ordinary into the special. Using the modes of media to comment on his society while resolving the story of a media creation, elevates Nicholson's work beyond a trippy turn-on or merely a ride into the whirlwind within a pop phenomenon.

The film is a media manipulation. Fame is juxtaposed with oppression. The Monkees know they are owned and controlled by a corporate entity, and in the film we see and hear their controllers at points where the crew and their writers-producers-director Nicholson and Rafelson are visible or audible. This self-referential break with cinematic convention had already been established as a convention on their TV show, but with neither the malevolent undercurrent nor the identification of the four as human chattel.

Joy is juxtaposed with horror. We see the youthful, beloved group and the effect their mere presence has on its fans, the love pouring from teenyboppers during a staged concert in Salt Lake City. The band is tight. The group has never been captured as gloriously, their talent and charisma spotlighted by their cracking performance of the Nesmith composition "Circle Sky." Interspersed, we see disturbing images from the Vietnam War. Recall that this was a group whose main audience was teenagers or younger girls. Yes, the film was meant for an older, more mature audience, but fan magazine features and interviews about the movie talked about "the kids" and used words like "zany."

Here, Monkees concert material is intercut with a repeated view of the execution of a Viet Cong leader by a South Vietnamese major general. What other mainstream film, marketed as entertainment by a major studio, would show clear, close-up, complete footage of a man being shot in the head point-blank by another man? How's that for "zany?"

Freedom is juxtaposed with imprisonment. The boys are shown in a groovier update of their TV pad, often having a groovy time with groovy chicks, groovy music and groovy happenings. Ultimately, they come to the realization that they are trapped, having been led into a black box and escaping, only to be fooled back inside that prison. Peter Tork has commented that the black box represents Rafelson's bleak view of life and insensitivity to others, most notably the band.[25]

The utility of technology is juxtaposed with its futility. The film itself remains a tribute to moviemaking technology, with innovative special effects and inventive editing. Nevertheless, the frustration and failure associated with machines portends a future overreliance on fancy gadgets.

At the beginning of the film, a malfunctioning public address system ruins a local politician's repeated attempts to dedicate a new bridge, itself a "magnificent marvel of modern architecture." Comically, only the politician suffers this indignity. Elsewhere, Micky's confounded by an empty Coke machine, his only remaining form of thirst-quenching in the desert. A manufacturing plant responsible for producing the black boxes is beset by many hazards and unsafe conditions. Boxes fall, people slip, thirsty workers gratefully gulp sludge, one of a group of secretaries is revealed to be a mannequin whose head falls off, and the supervisor has his middle finger encased in a medical apparatus. All this happens while he takes the group on a tour of the facility, mechanically intoning about the wonders of automation and productivity toward a future in which all that matters will be finding new ways to amuse oneself (Nicholson at his most prescient!). This irony of mishaps in such a computer-controlled environment underscores the parallel message that the band's biggest tragedy (and by extension that of American society) will be to get exactly what they (and we) want.

That is the true prison, according to the filmmakers. Scriptwriters Nicholson and Rafelson, director Rafelson and the editors (Mike Pozen and an uncredited Monte Hellman) juxtapose old movie clips, snippets of television commercials, samples from cartoons and sound bites from man-on-the-street interviews to create new meanings. Media are manipulated to make new realities, new wholes from appropriated fragments. In one now-eerie example, a piece from the film *Salome* shows Charles Laughton (as King Herod) pointing camera left as he identifies the Messiah, only to cut to news footage of then Governor Ronald Reagan as this messianic prophecy. We hear about a powerful narcotic from Bela Lugosi; see one of the largest Ford dealerships from its huckster owners; witness a hapless hippie's lack of perception about the world; and get mini-sneak previews that foreshadow future scenes in the movie itself; all controlled by a literally larger-than-life Victor Mature. As Micky Dolenz put it, "The idea was that the movie was kind of circular. In fact, when we had this press opening screening in New York, it wasn't in a theater, it was in this weird warehouse and they set up all these Moviolas, old school editing machines."

Dolenz remembers the publicity events as a '60s happening of sorts:

> They had little rolls of film and little tiny screens and they set all these Moviolas up around the room. And it was totally psychedelic and out there, this party thing launch.
> They put one reel of the film on every Moviola and they just started running them, because the idea was, kinda weird and crazy....
> They played the movie, all the reels, and it could go on simultaneously. And you can, you can watch that movie from almost any part in the movie and it all just comes back around.[26]

Structurally, the circular nature of the action—another example of inevitability and futility at the core of Jack's scripts—plays against a salute of sorts for Hollywood forms, the signifiers of genre. The movie takes off on a cavalcade of motion picture varieties:

- The film's overall comedy format is undercut by message and atrocity through an intentionally uncomfortable mix of fiction with current event documentation;
- The war movie genre gets punctured by depicting confusion, non-heroic behavior, and showing a shell-shocked soldier in a football helmet;
- The desert epic, including a less-than-epic spat between the protagonist and his interior voice, climaxes with a tank attack on a soda machine and the less-than-politically correct surrender by cowardly Italian soldiers;
- The classic "cowboys and Indians" western is shown to be a sham, complete with obviously fake arrows and cavalry officer Micky unromantically kicking Teri Garr with a snotty, "Get up, lady. You're not dead!";
- The mythic rise of an unknown boxer lives up to all the expected clichés for exaggerated effect, as the diminutive Davy Jones plays a local tenement boy who leaves behind his musical ambitions to make quick money by taking a dive in the ring, much to the dismay of his family, "Father Duffy" and girlfriend Annette Funicello;
- Timothy Carey's deliciously over-the-top run-in with the boys turns the spaghetti western into a bizarre, otherworldly affair, summed up best when he gets trapped in his own cloak while exhibiting a little too much dramatic flair;
- Industrial spy movies like *In Like Flint* are pushed to another level of mystery and paranoia when the Monkees find the factory that produces the black box which imprisons them (a sewage treatment plant in real life);
- Dancing around in Victor Mature's hair, pretending to be dandruff, lets them take a poke at TV advertising and science fiction "incredible shrinking" and "attack of the giant" favorites at the same time;
- Mike's birthday takes the gang into a haunted house, where we get a few scares and learn that he does not like surprises;
- A lengthy scene excised from the original script worked the Samurai genre into the mix, centering its action around a character named Godzilla;
- Hippie flix like *The Trip*, the Hollywood musical, harem backlotters and pastoral love stories are touched upon in the music video segments;
- The Monkees themselves are the prime targets for parody, whether it's lampooning their assigned character traits from the TV show, their plastic phoniness or how helpless they'd be without their creators;
- We also sample prison melodrama and damsel-in-distress pastiches

in this journey through the commercial cinema factory—all the way through to the film burn over the Paramount logo at the movie's conclusion.

"The movie was essentially about the deconstruction of the film industry, the Hollywood corporate studio film industry, which was going on at that time," said Dolenz. "There was a movement to try and break through the Hollywood studio system and *Head* was one of the first films to try to do that." The former child star pinpointed a key point in the film that helped symbolize its meaning:

> The one scene that I think is the theme of what that movie is all about is the cavalry thing with Indians and Mike and I are in cavalry outfits. And Teri Garr, in maybe her first [film], was in that scene. And Mike and I am there and we're fighting off the Indians, and there's a big set with the landscape and the backdrops and I get hit with four or five arrows which are fake, obviously. And I go, "Bob (meaning Bob Rafelson), I don't wanna do this any more, it's just crap, it's just stupid" and I break the arrows and I walk through the backdrop and burst out of this fake Hollywood scene.[27]

Michael Nesmith explained the unusual genesis of the unusual film to me. "We all went up to Ojai, which is a little place with a country club, a golf club, and we'd sit around and told tales."[28] Reportedly copious quantities of the type of grass not found on that golf course opened up the four band members, along with Nicholson and Rafelson, for some mighty brainstorming. Dolenz explained,

> Jack spent months, actually, going around and meeting all of us, and hanging out, partying, just kind of getting a sense of us individually. And then we had this weekend in Ojai, sitting around this tape recorder sitting on the floor and just talking, just groovin' about what we wanted to do, what we didn't want to do.
> Jack, in his brilliance took away—and Bob Rafelson, it must be said—took away all of this Monkeeness, and Jack penned this incredible, weird, psychedelic movie. I have no friggin' idea what it is supposed to be about … but now I look back and see that was sort of the point of the whole movie, beyond the Monkees thing, beyond the whole Monkees paradigm. It was about breaking out of the traditional old school Hollywood and they did.

Ironically enough, particularly with a running theme about the dangers of machines, Nicholson enthusiastically embraced the technology as a way to capture the individual personalities and incorporate some of the many fragmented ideas, jokes and random streams of altered consciousness. "He had a really important part, but he didn't think it up, it was thought up by seven or eight of us who sat around,"[29] the singer explained.

Peter Tork credited the screenwriter for more than narrative, setting and character. "I know that he upped the level of energy and … just a little bit of vinegar to keep from getting too sweet. I know that was Jack's contribution."

15. Head Trips

Director Bob Rafelson prepares his co-creation, the pop/rock group The Monkees, for a scene in the movie *Head* (1968). Did they then know that one of the main purposes of the film was to destroy them? Shown left-to-right are Rafelson, Davy Jones, Michael Nesmith, Micky Dolenz, and Peter Tork.

Tork also explained the relationship between the writer and the director, while playacting one of Nesmith's scenes as the mob boss for a fixed boxing match between Davy Jones and ex-champ Sonny Liston—with the boss's style of speech based on Nicholson himself. "Jack brought an attitude and Bob fell in love with Jack, artistically speaking ... that was something special, extra energy, that we all liked.... And so we went for Jack in a big way."[30]

The completed story follows a loose circular narrative that chases the group toward their demise, settling in the end for trapping them and removing them from the movie studio. As in *Flight to Fury* and *Ride in the Whirlwind*, the motif of false escape that merely postpones the inevitable also ends this picture, albeit within a less threatening context.

The chase starts on a newly erected bridge, where the Monkees crash an official ribbon-cutting ceremony as Micky breaks through the ribbon like a victorious marathon runner rather than a man being pushed toward a suicidal leap from a bridge.

An honor guard is entirely black except for one stupidly grinning white guy. Audio problems with the mayor's microphone comment on technology with an anti-authority bent. The finish line meshes two disparate elements, sports and politics (which might not be too dissimilar after all) into one cohesive concept.

As Dolenz hits the water, an entrancing underwater scene featuring mermaids provides the foundation for a visual effects feast, using a new solarization imaging process to add further magic to the theme song music-video-within-a-movie. Gerry Goffin and Carole King's "Porpoise Song" remains a Monkees classic, one of their most accomplished recorded tracks, and a perfect psychedelic score.

We're then introduced to the guys at their home base, as they engage in a standard practice for any rock group. A kissing contest with Nicholson's then-current squeeze I.J. Jefferson makes sense, at least as a reflection of Nicholson's own Reichian openness about sex. As the glamorous hippie chick moves from Monkee to Monkee, the sequence exposes the benefits of stardom while parodying the Davy Jones character—through an exaggerated version of his typical "stars in the eyes" love-at-first-sight persona.

Head sports a unique musical montage that's part message machine, part summary of the movie, and part disclaimer for its lack of standard narrative structure and its circular mode. Nicholson and Rafelson rewrote the Tommy Boyce–Bobby Hart "(Theme from) The Monkees" specifically for this purpose. It's a cynical send-up that paints the band as pandering, manufactured, money-grabbing puppets. Performed in a mechanical singsong manner as directed in the recording studio by Nicholson himself, "Ditty Diego" works within the film as soundtrack to the TV screens montage that juxtaposes old movie and contemporary television clips against portions of the film itself. Interestingly, after deflating the group and their film, this blackout segues into the powerful concert footage that shows the band to its best advantage, for yet another example of juxtaposition (this time unintentionally).

The media serves as both reference point and recurring target for Nicholson and Rafelson. A battle scene is interrupted as an off-screen photographer's voice asks soldier Peter Tork to hold his pose ("This is for *Life*") and a car dealership television ad shows a "666" price tag. Victor Mature controls everything, in a god-like matter, through use of a remote control.

With dangerous irony, the teenyboppers' fave group leads a stadium's crowd in a chant in favor of war. By no means a Country Joe "Fish Cheer," each Monkee leaps and yells their respective part in "give me a.... W ... A ... R...!"—an odd chant that figuratively spells several more lost years in

15. Head Trips 241

Vietnam. In the battle scene, football star Ray Nitschke personifies the nation's stubborn and mindless continuation of that war by relentlessly ramming his helmeted head into the wall of a trench, further symbolizing the conflict by pummeling the much smaller Tork over and over again with his superior might. "We're number one!" he says. Peter eventually ends up with Nitschke's gold football helmet, which happens to be similar to that worn by Jack in *Easy Rider*, instead of his own government-issued model.

Consumerism takes a beating as Timothy Carey lectures the group on the millions to be had through merchandising, urging them to market their "byproducts" and that "the phallic thing is happening," the perfect business advice from an out-of-control, well-armed lunatic in a huge cape and Pilgrim's hat to a pop band marketed toward teenage girls. In the first draft of the script, Carey's character, Lord High'n'Low, was called "Dernsie," leading to some speculation that Bruce Dern was intended for the part. When I asked Dern, he responded perfectly, "Well, that's my name. Tim Carey was better nuts than I was. He was fabulous."[31]

Coca-Cola kept Micky going in the desert, but when he finds the soda machine empty, he responds in the most rational way by blowing it to smithereens with a tank. Again, consumerism and the urge to consume corporate goods becomes a driver, even in the middle of the desert. It's also a tip of the hat to a scene in Kubrick's *Dr. Strangelove* in which Colonel "Bat" Guano shoots a Coke machine to get change for an emergency phone call attempting to save the world, only to be thanked by getting squirted with a stream of the beverage.

The mechanism of society and its impersonal treatment of workers has a *Modern Times* feel to it, particularly the juxtaposition of the bucolic nature scenes in the "As We Go Along" musical interlude against a series of quick cuts of billboards with a harsh sound effect of an oil rig pump. In the manufacturing plant, everyone turns their backs on safety and ignores accidents. Dehumanizing through modern "advances" and technological progress seems to trouble Nicholson, for yet another variant on fatalism.

Making a joke out of it, a screaming jumper (June Fairchild) on a rooftop is reduced to entertainment and friendly wagers ("Ten dollars says she will"). Some of the contradictions and unexpected reveals are funny. A cop hassles the long-haired "weirdos" for no good reason, with the guys reacting with formal and respectful cooperation, only to be rebuffed and told to shut up and move along. Later, the same cop is shown to be a prancing aspiring stripper in the studio's rest room.

A swami speaks engagingly about conceptual belief, philosophizing that we cannot meaningfully distinguish between what's real and what's vividly imagined. He is framed in medium close-up and close-up, within a vague setting that's made more atmospheric by a hypnotic mist, perhaps rows of burning incense—only to find that he's just a guy in a towel in a sauna. Sonny Liston breaks the mood of enlightenment and serenity by asking if anyone wants more steam!

The swami's speech could be taken as an allegory suggesting there may be no difference between being inside or outside of the black box, so when the group is trapped again, Peter recreates the imparting of wisdom. However, when he gets to the sauna swami's self-effacing conclusion ("Why should anyone listen to me, as I know nothing?"), Davy does not take the question rhetorically and goes ape shit, comically demanding to know why they're sitting around, stuck in a box, listening to someone who admits he knows nothing. His rage manifests itself in attacking the box to help them escape ... for the time being.

Coming full circle, we traipse through all of the vignettes shown in screens at the beginning and relive the cycle of escape and capture, before ending up back in the desert where everyone in the film is lined up like having your life flash before your eyes. The Coke machine returns as well, standing tall like a Kubrick monolith to show the invincibility of corporate consumerism, before it's blown up again. And, in the end, the Monkees are given the choice-without-choice to commit suicide in order to get away, hereby committing career suicide to escape their plastic lives.

In Nicholson's script, time and space are somewhat fluid, taking the characters and the viewers through a trip in the whirlwind in which they move in circles, repeat and flash back and flash forward. At the time the film was made, there had been some controversy about the group members expecting—and never receiving—writing credit based on their contributions at Ojai.

However, in viewing the Criterion Collection's 2010 box set *America Lost and Found: The BBS Story* and its Blu-ray update of the film with participant commentaries, I noticed that any time a member of the group mentioned the script, particularly Micky Dolenz, they always mentioned Nicholson and never referred to Rafelson. When I asked Peter Tork about this, he diplomatically responded, "I have no information as to which part of the script was Bob's and which part was Jack's so I can't possibly comment."[32]

Nesmith was still circumspect, yet made the point: "Well, there may be some justice to that. What can I say?"[33] He further described what he felt was behind Nicholson's success with the project: "It was almost like he was immune in some sense to the proceedings and just took down certain ideas and he framed it. He really was the critical path of the whole thing, in my estimation. And he's a prince of a guy."[34]

Head stands as Nicholson's screenwriting masterwork, a time capsule of commentary which mirrors the culture within a musical presentation that delivers on multiple levels. There's surface entertainment and humor; social meaning that's pro-freedom, pro-sex, pro-drugs vs. anti-war, anti-consumerism, anti-establishment; a deconstruction of Hollywood prototypes and of a pop phenomenon; and a stylistic achievement that is impressionistic in nature, taking the audience between what's real and what's imagined in a mesmerizing trip that still keeps viewers—and the band members themselves—guessing and wondering.

Nicholson remains justly proud of his work, gushing, "I co-wrote *Head*. Nobody ever saw that, man, but I saw it. A hundred fifty-eight million times. I loved it. Filmically, it's the best rock'n'roll movie ever made. I mean, it's anti–rock'n'roll. Has no form. Unique in structure, which is very hard to do in movies."[35]

As a bonus, we also get a glimpse into the future of some then-unknowns. In a diner scene featuring female impersonator T.C. Jones as a waitress, the Monkees are treated as pariahs, much like the hippie bikers and their lawyer companion in the redneck diner in *Easy Rider*. When the scene breaks and the director yells "Cut," we see three figures representing the future of cinema (Rafelson, Nicholson and Dennis Hopper) interacting with the band, which at the time represented the superstars of pop culture.

Nicholson was also responsible for the film's wondrous soundtrack, in effect "writing" this counterculture tribute to all things McLuhan while employing the audio cut-up techniques of William S. Burroughs.

As Tork explained, "Jack arranged and assembled the album.... I thought Jack did a fabulous job putting the record together, because he was curious and he's an intense artist, as everybody knows."[36] Nesmith expanded on this: "[Nicholson] was fascinated by the technology. If you know Jack, he has a wicked sense ... and he's very, very fast. He contributed mightily to everything, but artistically wasn't the director or producer, but he led with so many important contributions."[37]

According to *Head* soundtrack compilation–producer and Monkees archivist Andrew Sandoval, "Jack went through the mag reels for the film and layered the audio in collage fashion. He had an interesting feel for stereo, and the overall concept of superimposing sounds over sounds was very fashion-forward." Sandoval called it "Pre-'Revolution #9' (referring to the Beatles' experimental track on their *White Album*) and many years before the mash-up."[38]

Tork commented on Nicholson's avant garde approach to creative juxtaposition on the album: "There's this wonderful little bit where [Frank] Zappa, in that one scene, says to Davy, 'You're pretty white.' And they've got Michael going, 'Yeah, the same thing goes for Christmas.' That's from a completely different place in the film. So creative, I thought, you know, and the stuff, the soundtrack, the effects."[39]

Nicholson took the music, the dialogue and a variety of sound bites from Hollywood oldies and horror flicks, to create a completely independent work of art. The soundtrack itself plays as its own movie, a continuous sonic montage broken only by the original LP's two-sided format. Though Sandoval reports that "there really aren't any other notes and sadly Jack has never fully gone on record about his process,"[40] we can still marvel at how he built this cryptic and multilayered work.

* * *

Following the breakthrough of *Easy Rider* and *Five Easy Pieces*, and three years after *Head*, Nicholson was able to parlay his newfound industry strength toward his directorial debut with *Drive, He Said*. He directed it. He co-produced with Steve Blauner and Harold Gittes. He co-wrote the screenplay with Jeremy Larner, an adaptation of Larner's 1964 novel, with uncredited assistance from Robert Towne and Terrence Malick.

The film follows familiar Nicholson themes of fatalism, featuring main characters trying to escape their trapped conditions. As with *The Trip* and *Head*, this work favors sexuality and personal freedom. Like the latter, authority and the Vietnam War are obvious targets.

A basketball player is disillusioned about playing a game and he wants out. His roommate has been called up for the draft, and definitely wants out. A professor's wife is having an affair with the basketball player, so she may want out of the marriage or the affair or both. Even she probably doesn't know, though she's more emotionally developed than the jock or the teach. They all feel trapped, experiencing a helplessness that views escape as difficult or doubtful; an oppression that causes rebellion as much out of frustration as out of a legitimate attempt to escape; and a malaise that's a natural reaction to their plight; as well as an underlying seeping away of hope. These are three characters in search of a future.

Hector, played by newcomer William Tepper (who was chosen due to his basketball skills), is the college team's star player. He's a celebrity on campus. The young coeds love him. He doesn't have to worry about the draft, it seems, because of his status.

Gabriel, portrayed by Michael Margotta (from the campus unrest classic *The Strawberry Statement*) is a protest leader. His theater group stages a theatrical stunt, commandeering one of the big games by turning off all the arena lights and taking over its public address system, convincing the teams, the school officials and the fans that they are all under siege by the police state. The public relations "happening" culminates in a mock execution of an Asian protestor by a fake soldier with a fake gun that shoots a flag instead of a bullet. The scene recreates documentary footage of a Viet Cong's point-blank execution used so shockingly in *Head*.

Olive, Karen Black from *Easy Rider* and *Five Easy Pieces*, is a professor's wife who carries on with Hector, more or less in the open. She may be doing so more out of boredom and dissatisfaction with her husband's weakness than seeking passion or attention. Richard, the professor, also has an odd relationship with Hector, based on the teacher admiring and envying the student as opposed to the student looking up to the teacher. This can only add to Olive's disgust toward her husband, who has been sufficiently effective at emasculating himself without requiring any cuckolding on her part.

Timeliness and relevance were the point. Social commentary had played an increasing role in Nicholson's career as a screenwriter, with *The Trip*, *Head* and *Drive, He Said* forming an effective cinematic trilogy, not because of any overt connection but due to a unity of theme and message. Narratives don't continue and characters don't resurface, yet a sympathetic fundament links the three scripts.

The risk was the transient consequence of timeliness and relevance. As Margotta explained to me, "I think everyone at the time knew that the film came late for the issues it embodied, with perhaps the one exception being Karen Black's character. But the issues of Vietnam, the draft, drugs, anti-establishment, counter-revolution themes, had already been played out in the collective. Maybe if it had been three years earlier, it would have been another story. It was 1971, and people wanted to move on."[41]

Nicholson and Larner weave together the worlds of college life, athleticism, political commitment and complex relationships with deftness and nuance. Though weighted with subjects of great import, the final product was not overwhelmed by topical content or finger-pointing, but instead energized by things that matter. Hector and Gabriel and Olive become real people because they care about issues worth caring about—whether the class politics of celebrity and the entitlement of stardom; the politics of a conflict in Southeast Asia and a generational conflict at home; or sexual freedom and gender politics that break the constraints of institutional hierarchy and marital roles.

They seek escape, but should they succeed? Of the three, Hector's case seems the most dubious. Without a future in hoops, what can Hector do? He has become accustomed to the coddling. He doesn't appear to have any other strengths or interests. Even he laughs when he tells a pro team's management that he's majoring in Greek. He's also immature and aimless. At the end of the film, his destiny is ambiguous, as he attempts to rejoin the team, but a gratuitous on-court fight during which he needlessly throws a punch won't help his prospects.

Olive escapes a rape attempt by Gabriel, but it's not known if she will decide to escape her marriage. Prior to the attack, she had already told her husband and Hector that they were "a couple of big babies" and commented, "You two are just right for each other." It's clear that she's through with Hector and that she should leave Richard. If she does, Olive gives the impression that she would build on the experience to become a consequential and liberated person. If not, she will still emerge as strong and vital within a newly defined relationship.

Gabriel's future is the most troubling. Margotta provided background about his character's actions: "I believe there had already been a number of draft board sequences done in Hollywood films and I think the idea was to push the envelope a little further on the subject. Or to put the final touch on the issue. It was pretty much a straightforward concept of taking the character to an inexcusable limit. Something that would create a lot of pressure and give the final snap."[42]

His heavy drug use in order to fail his induction examination backfired, because Gabriel took it too far and flipped out before breaking free to create more havoc—ultimately more on himself than on the system. Though Richard and Olive probably wouldn't have reported his break-in and attack, Gabriel's paranoid rampage made any such advantage moot. His final break from reality, running across campus completely nude and trapping himself inside a science lab where he lets trapped animals free, seals his fate. Michael does point out, however, "we were deviating from Larner's novel and the concern was for the big ending. I like the Larner ending more, but Jack brought it more down to earth. The character self-immolates at the end of the novel after doing some nasty things. There were many parts to the draft sequence that didn't make it in. We did a lot of coverage of me breaking into the draft board later and destroying it."[43]

Instead, the Nicholson-Larner Gabriel became the victim of the screenwriter's penchant for situations of futility and conditions of fatalism. This isn't to say that Nicholson himself carries that attitude, as it is always dangerous to confuse the art (and its message) with the artist. It's more likely a commentary on society, cleanly summed up by one line from the film, "We're living in a diseased culture," which comes across as a Nicholson statement or warning about the future.

Gabriel is caught and escorted, in a van, to a mental institution. He took his gambit too far, overindulging in chemicals and thoughts of conspiracy. He sought to escape the draft by playing it crazy, but he played it too convincingly, escaping his own reality in the process.

In another enigmatic Nicholson ending, Gabriel is pushed into the asylum van to the tune of music that makes it seem like he's going into an ice cream truck. While it drives away, the viewer's perspective is from inside the van, showing Hector jumping onto the back of the vehicle.

Adding a poignant touch, Nicholson has Hector yell to his roommate, "Your mother called." As if it matters.

This scene is reminiscent of Nicholson's conclusion of *Head*, in which the Monkees are trapped again, for the final time, driven away in a clear box on the back of a truck, all under the control of Victor Mature. Gabriel's van is shaped like the box, with a campus radical and the pop group both riding off to uncertain, scary futures.

* * *

Drive, He Said has remained the last of Nicholson's six produced scripts. Monte Hellman, who directed two of the titles, assessed, "I think writing was one of Jack's many talents, and I was very happy with the screenplays he wrote for me [*Flight to Fury* and *Ride in the Whirlwind*]."[44] As part of AFI's Life Achievement Award tribute to Nicholson, Roger Corman wrote, "I truly believe that he would have done equally well as a full-time writer or director if that were his desire."[45]

Nicholson's skills at storytelling and imagery advanced markedly with each work. The extant first draft written script for *Head* shows a facility for guiding the director; strong descriptive skills to establish setting, character and action; a balance of substantive and stylish dialogue; and particularly a feeling for the cinematic side of the cinema, creating many innovative and striking visual sequences.

When Hollywood gained a movie star, it lost a promising scenarist. Every scribbler in coffee shops here, there and elsewhere may not truly qualify as "writers," but six films remain that show that Nicholson certainly qualified as one.

16

The Occasional Filmmaker

The whir of the motor, the controlled click of the workprint reel, slowed down and stopped. Groans and a squashed "wup-wup-wup" from the soundtrack, advanced forward and stepped back. Then the slap and cut, like a stapler hit twice, followed by the crisp sound of plastic pulled off the sprockets.

We travel down the hall, again and again hearing the whirs and clicks, wups and slaps ... more whirs and clicks, more wups and slaps. These are the sounds of a filmmaker, unusual to us and unnoticed by them, as they concentrate on the images and sounds.

What we hear are Moviolas as we pass editing rooms. In the first is a young man working and reworking, obsessively perfecting an artistic statement; in the second, the director wants to bring out the laughs and accentuate the humanity; the third contains a more weary, middle-aged artist who's trying to salvage a seemingly ill-fated project.

It could be the BBS office on LaBrea, Columbia Pictures in Culver City, or Paramount Studios in Burbank. The filmmaker in each is the same man, but in different stages and under different conditions with different purposes, the director Jack Nicholson.

Because he is so strongly associated with acting and being a Hollywood movie star, most may not think of Nicholson as a director. Of course, he only has three official credits (as he's uncredited for some second unit work on *The Terror*—though Monte Hellman rejects any notion of Nicholson's directorial involvement as Corman mythmaking).

In 1971, Nicholson fulfilled a longtime ambition of filming *Drive, He Said*, a political, sociological, and artistic statement that went largely ignored. Seven years later, he helmed the western romantic comedy *Goin' South*. It was another 12 years before he had to step in to help save the *Chinatown* sequel *The Two Jakes*.

With sixty years in cinema, this serious and important actor directed but three films. He did not act in the first, but starred in the other two. The first was an independent production distributed by Columbia, while the latter

16. The Occasional Filmmaker 249

were both commercial productions for Paramount. First 1971 ... 1978 ... 1990 ... then over 25 with no signs of ever going back. This is interesting, because the developing artist acted, wrote and directed, appearing to be open to any of those eventualities. Had *Easy Rider* not been the success that it was, Nicholson may have taken a path similar to colleague and collaborator Henry Jaglom.

Stuntman-actor Gary Kent described a long drive during which a young Nicholson exposed his frustrations with his career. "I thought he wanted to go strictly acting and that he was producing [*Ride in the Whirlwind* and *The Shooting*], because he had to get it done. It was later, on *Hells Angels on Wheels*, that we drove together from Bakersfield back to L.A. And he told me that he wanted to direct.... I asked what he wanted to do with his life, and that's when he said, 'I want to do what Dick was doing [Richard Rush was directing the film].'"

Nicholson elaborated about "what a hard business film was and what a difficult thing it was." Kent felt the sentiment was important: "I'll never forget that drive because he really opened up. And I had the feeling that he really wanted to direct and that was going to be his goal."[1]

* * *

Drive, He Said was his official directorial debut. He was producer and he co-wrote the screenplay. This was a personal project, Nicholson having earmarked the book years before. And it had basketball as a central subject!

Thanks to Michael Margotta, who played campus revolutionary Gabriel in the film, this book may very well possess the most comprehensive study available on this work. He is also eminently qualified, both as participant and exponent of the acting craft, to offer his insights. He is Artistic Director of the Actor's Center–ROMA and former teacher at the Lee Strasberg Theatre Institute and the Academy of Music and Dramatic Art in New York City. He acted in the youth unrest classics *Wild in the Streets* and *The Strawberry Statement*, as well as in *9½ Weeks* and Jaglom's *Can She Bake a Cherry Pie?* with *Drive* co-star Karen Black.

From Rome, Margotta traveled back 40 years to a production as political as artistic. Even the pre-production work was more about issues than art: "We didn't have rehearsals or meetings regarding the script, except while we were shooting. We went up early—Jack, myself, maybe one or two others—to a demonstration in Oregon against the train shipment of nerve gas that the federal government was storing in the mountains."[2]

Back then, movies could be about something, something that examined current events and war and what matters vs. what doesn't. A basketball player has doubts about dedicating himself to what is only a game. His roommate has no doubts about dedicating everything he has to avoiding the draft. A professor's wife has doubts about her marriage and more doubts about her affair with his student, the basketball player with doubts about playing a game and taking it seriously.

The project was in no way a comfortable shoot on a Hollywood back lot. Margotta related that shooting at the University of Oregon (the school stood in for an unnamed institute of higher learning) "was a pretty radical situation. Just before we arrived in Eugene, students had already burned down the ROTC building on campus so there was this climate of tension in the place. The Feds were investigating…. [T]hen you had someone driving around supposedly in a green pickup truck shooting 'anyone with long hair for sport'"[3] (similar to the events depicted in *Easy Rider*).

Drive, He Said features a great opening shot that superbly frames lead actor William Tepper as basketball star Hector, taking a jump shot in slow motion straight on, his vertical jump in the frame as the camera remains static. We don't see teams, or the court, or a crowd, as expected to set the scene for a sporting event. Instead, this is a close-up, zoomed in enough to add heavy grain (thus enhancing its immediacy), before it pulls back slowly in order to work in other players vaguely, prior to very slowly going to black. As this sequence develops, we also see much-smaller-than-usual opening credits.

Margotta: "He had some first-timers on *Drive*. Bill Tepper was working for the first time and Michael Warren (later of *Hill Street Blues*) also." Nicholson, too, was a first-timer. "Jack's style was that he trusted his actors to get results. It was a very free process," with Margotta then expanding on what this sort of freedom meant:

> Ad lib, yes. And it gave me a chance to explore dimensions of working that I had not experienced before that. In one scene, for instance, I got up on an impulse and walked out of the shot and kept talking, off-camera, and then walked back in again and sat down. I had never done anything like this before…. Anywhere else, had I done something like that, you would have heard, "Cut." It was very freeing to know we could work this way. Hell, it was a revelation. Also, we invented a number of situations on the spot.[4]

The film intersects the worlds of college basketball with campus unrest; affairs of convenience with destruction of the mind; and the battle between order (represented by the basketball team and the military) and disorder (draft protests and a hapless attempt to beat the draft). Top-billed Tepper is a droopy-eyed Elliott Gould with a hook shot. Bruce Dern as his coach is perfectly cast due to his competitive intensity and personal background as a jock, having been a high school track star and runner at the University of Pennsylvania. Karen Black plays the wife of a professor portrayed by Robert Towne, the screenwriter of Nicholson's *The Last Detail*, *Chinatown*, *The Missouri Breaks* and *The Two Jakes*.

16. The Occasional Filmmaker

BBS

July 28, 1970

Miss Karen Black
8267 Hollywood Boulevard
Los Angeles, California

Dear Blackee:

Had to put it in writing. You are the greatness that is Black and the true wonder of it is the beauty of it. All this in addition to your great art and person.

Thanks for being in "Drive".

As always,

Jack Nicholson

JN/em

A personal letter from director Jack Nicholson thanking actress Karen Black for her work on his debut *Drive, He Said*.

Nicholson chose Black in part because of his comfort with the co-star of his own breakout feature *Five Easy Pieces*, as well as due to her command and versatility. The director thanked the actor in a note to "Blackee" after the production wrap, writing: "You are the greatness that is Black and the true wonder of it is the beauty of it. All this in addition to your great art and person."[5]

Michael Margotta portrays Hector's roommate Gabriel, who looks astonishingly like Dean Stockwell in Nicholson's *Psych-Out*, from hair to headscarf. It's almost as if Nicholson designed Margotta's appearance for this film as a younger version of Dave in the earlier hippie exploiter. Margotta considered the process organic, allowing for exploration. "Jack gave the feeling in general of being supportive and open and having a collaborative spirit."[6]

Though a film of import and message, the coverage of the games and scrimmages was deft, which could only be accomplished by someone who knew both the visual medium of cinema and the physical medium of the sport. It looks real, with energy that moves and propels, using angles, cuts and slow-motion effects to follow the action in smart, knowing ways. The game environment, complete with crowd, band, cheerleaders, concessions stand, National Anthem and even a pickpocket, makes the games feel real, as only a true fan of the game could.

The contrast between those serious about playing a game with those revolutionary students who turn a game into performance art as part of their deadly serious war against the war, is clear and sensible. These protestors, these guerrilla agitators create "happenings" that may have appeared dated by the time of the film's release. Hector's conflict with Dern, as his coach, and Coach Bullion's straight-laced reaction is interesting in light of Dern's later role as a returning Vietnam Marine captain who commits suicide in *Coming Home*.

Karen Black's ballet class is the third environment in which we travel. She seeks expression and the need to establish her own identity, entering into what she likely sees as a silly affair with campus darling, basketball star Hector, as a way to dance around the restrictive academic bureaucracy and try to wake up her clueless professor husband.

Could this teacher seem any more wimpy and insubstantial? If he were self-absorbed, that would have been understandable, but Richard is more wrapped up in Hector and his in-class and on-court performance than about his own wife. Towne is first seen at a car where Tepper and Black are clearly getting it on, yet he actually asks the younger man to take her home as a favor.

In the BBS *America Lost and Found* documentary, Nicholson points out that this scene, shot in enough dark to obscure any visual sexuality, broke through with Olive's "I'm coming!" and what he called "contra-nudity," as they appear fully dressed, almost resembling two bears.

16. The Occasional Filmmaker

To cement his emasculated impression, Richard is shown spending a good deal of time and effort blow-drying his hair. He's inarticulate when Hector visits his and Olive's home, actually sending his wife to her suitor. Finally, in a nice and fluffy bathrobe, Towne becomes this film's Jim Backus, the pathetic dad symbolically dressed in an apron like James Dean's dad in *Rebel Without a Cause*.

Drive, He Said has been a lost film, unseen and unappreciated, an oddity to many or a bit of trivia used to stump those unaware that Nicholson had ever directed a film. Included in the Criterion Collection's BBS Story Blu-ray box set, this obscurity can now be appreciated for its lyrical beauty and offbeat, suitably flawed storyline.

The editing is masterful, with Nicholson and a team of four editors creating a flow that doesn't rely on any need for completion in action, sentences or scenes. The structure instead is based around providing just enough material,

Jack Nicholson in control on his feature film debut, an adaptation of the Jeremy Larner novel *Drive, He Said* (1971) shown with UCLA champion Bill Sweek. Though much of the film involves a swirl of relationships amidst campus unrest about the Vietnam war, the director may have been drawn by the opportunity depict the energy and majesty of his beloved sport of basketball.

with what's sufficient becoming more effective than what everything would have been, so viewers travel through the narrative rather than being weighed down by it.

Nicholson directs with assurance and style. One transitional scene, which depicts the psychological warfare that Hector is experiencing, shows the player yelling on top of a concrete wall (complete with the requisite "HD Stanton" graffiti) as he holds a basketball, in a composition that is Antonioniesque in scope.

With director of photography Bill Butler, Nicholson shoots the first big game, focusing on a midair collision shot that's undercranked and grainy and has a striking verité effectiveness. Later, the beginning of another game is shown in poetic slow motion, with the game sequence carrying over a setup that captures the crowd during "The Star Spangled Banner." Slow motion then segues into standard speed and its actual synched sound to depict a fight scene and Hector's ejection.

A curious post-production touch occurs when Dern, off-screen, tells his players, "Don't want to see any bush behavior," to which Bucky responds, "We shoulda brought a cannon." Except that this most clearly is director Nicholson himself, via voiceover dub, an audio cameo *à la* Orson Welles (who looped many parts in his foreign productions).

The contrast between the world of the basketball team and that of the antiwar students, in particular Hector vs. Gabriel, supplies a recurring theme to the movie. Hector becomes so dissociated from playing a game as an honest pursuit that he cannot take a meeting with professional team officials seriously. As he interviews with David Ogden Stiers and B.J. Merholz, the team's star negotiates for better quality hot dogs at the games.

The protestor theater "class" seemed fittingly dazed out and incoherent, but they certainly took themselves seriously. Yes, their cause was important, but these students came off as self-important and humorless.

Gabriel will go to any length to avoid going to war, so he prepares for his military physical by chain-popping pills and depriving himself of any sleep. Margotta's draft test scene might seem somewhat over-the-top today, but it works both in terms of truth and in providing some comic relief to balance the bodily dramatics that the actor described as "taking the character to an inexcusable limit."

His induction sequence stands as a highlight of the film, pushing the boundary between commentary on the process shown and the comedic, immense reaction of the character in a way that would "create a lot of pressure and give the final snap." Margotta further related,

> There was a story behind the psychiatrist scene. In the middle of the scene, Jack sent in a guy from the crew to ask if he could install a phone. And he stays in the scene. I recognized him as a guy from the crew, and the phone routine harkened back to the

day I auditioned for the film. The casting director picked up a phone during the audition, and there were a lot of people in the room, and I stopped immediately even though I wasn't hearing the conversation and I was pissed that anyone would do such a thing. I think Jack remembered that, because that was the same scene I was doing.[7]

The adventurous nature of the shoot extended to the breakthrough depiction of male nudity, a message important to Nicholson. His full-frontal views are in no way fleeting. An early shower scene breaks the barrier, while Gabriel's full-on breakdown follows the character as he streaks across campus to break into a science lab and release test animals and reptiles.

According to Margotta, "We talked a great deal about that nudity sequence. Jack had a way of putting the contradictions into the ratings system: 'It's okay to shoot or stab a woman in the breast, but it's not okay to show male genitalia.'"[8]

Four years earlier, Nicholson wrote the screenplay for *The Trip*. Star Peter Fonda caresses and studies an orange. He extends it in front of himself and proclaims that he's holding the sun in his hands. He says it is "alive" and he believes it. In *Drive, He Said*, the co-screenwriter and director shows this film's protagonist, Hector, fondling an orange in evident connection to that earlier scene.

Hector visits Olive (Karen Black) and Richard (Robert Towne) in an effectively emotional scene with the participants in their love triangle that is nothing about their love triangle. Olive wears an olive green wool hat and Hector covers his view from the camera with an orange for a remarkable visual image that is spotlighted on the film's one-sheet poster graphic. In fact, the movie's trailer presents this shot as especially significant, cropping in on the image artificially through an optical effect at its conclusion.

At one time, the orange is like Hector's head, as he rolls the fruit back and forth in front of his face; it's like seeing a navel on a pregnant belly, perhaps giving birth to a more mature man beyond the limitations of a hoops star; and it's like a basketball itself, the tool by which Hector has gained identity and significance. He moves it to and fro as if pondering his future—with the ball as its center or as if exposing the real person behind it—continuing to play the game or to become manifest in a new and independent way.

This striking visual may reflect a similar impression as surrealist painter René Magritte's *The Son of Man*, which shows a self-portrait of the artist's face largely obscured by a green apple. Magritte explained, "Everything we see hides another thing, we always want to see what is hidden by what we see," creating an interest in what we cannot see.[9]

Oddly, certain conventions of the horror genre surfaced upon my subsequent re-watching of this film. After Gabriel flips out and escapes his home (but not until destroying Nicholson-nemesis, the television), he's shown as if frozen in place in a sand dune with his arms outstretched toward the sky ("a Christ-like image" as Margotta put it) in a way that's an eerily similar premonition to Nicholson's death in *The Shining*.

Upon Gabriel's recovery, he breaks into Richard and Olive's home. She is in the bathtub. Gabriel prowls around and eventually attacks her, with his bizarre appearance (combining a fur hat with stocking stretched over his face) a precursor to the horror-slasher mask or Leatherface/chainsaw attacker idiom. Having him release her pet birds and making the lights go on and off creates a beneficial hook device that's all the more scary because there is no reason or motivation for Gabriel's actions.

When Margotta chases Black and attempts to rape her, she fights back with a mannequin's head, as in Stanley Kubrick's *A Clockwork Orange*, making for another Jack connection.

The most memorable scene and climax of *Drive, He Said* occurs when Gabriel forces his way into the university lab and sets the collection of creatures free. Margotta points out, "It was originally very different. The character, fully dressed, breaks into the lab, they catch him, put him into a straitjacket, give him an injection, put him into a cage, and take him away. [Instead,] it was decided: no clothes, no injection, and I would go of my own volition."

Michael Margotta, as Gabriel, plays a man lost, just as devoid of personality or direction as he is of clothing or any other societal norms. Shooting this sequence turned out to be as histrionic and daring as anything Gabriel was doing. The actor explained how the streak across campus "was going to be the last shot. It was too risky," because it was going against the contract between Columbia and the University of Oregon.

The intrigue involved getting a secret phone call which came on a Sunday at six a.m. as go-ahead to drive to the site. Margotta remembered,

> I sat in the car with Jack and Fred [Roos, the casting director] while the other guys set the camera and tripod up. I took off my clothes and wrapped myself in a blanket. The idea was that as soon as the camera was ready, we would drive to another location, and when we received a signal, I would get out and run and Fred would get out and walk in the background as an extra and Jack would drive back, and we would scramble.

Margotta continued his play-by-play of nakedness by noting that it all had to be accomplished in one take. "I got the signal. I started running and when I reached the building, I bolted up the stairs, grabbed the handle on the glass door and it wouldn't open. Immediately, a guy on the inside rolled around in front of the door holding a walkie-talkie, and through the door said, 'Don't move. You are under arrest.' I turned and ran down the stairs, the car was back, they were rushing to get the camera, the tripod, the film into the car."[10]

Gabriel's lingering nude scene inside the laboratory disconcertingly juxtaposes weird snakes, bugs, centipedes, a mouse, a turtle and a lizard with a completely vulnerable man in a modernized Buñuelian-Daliesque waking nightmare. The snake-plus-penis imagery wasn't exactly subtle, though understandable given the importance to Nicholson of featuring male full-frontal nudity.

Margotta remembers that no preparation took place for that scene and that Nicholson asked him to say, "Too late, Kālī" (a reference to the Hindu goddess of time and change) when he picks up a human skull. "And with all these little guys running around, things easily became impromptu. The iguana had to be kept cold or otherwise he would be too frenetic. When they are kept at a cold temperature, they become immobile." He added a personal viewpoint that enriched the sequence, "I always hated zoos, so it fulfilled a fantasy of letting the little guys go free."[11]

My overall impression of the film has altered dramatically. Seeing the intended work by seeing the film in a higher resolution than my original bootleg revealed what the filmmaker intended, *Drive, He Said* somehow seemed like a much better piece of work that was more coherent and less flawed, less dated, and more relevant. Nicholson's direction came across with a greater emotional connection that's more immediate and meaningful.

This revelation formed an understandable hope for a further exploration into Nicholson's filmmaking, hope which *Goin' South* and *The Two Jakes* did not enliven. As Gary Kent put it, recalling Nicholson's confession about wanting to direct,

> I thought *Drive, He Said* was going to be his debut, and Jack was going to be off as director, but he wasn't. [*Drive, He Said*] sort of disappeared and is seldom mentioned in connection to Jack. I would venture that many of his fans don't even know that he directed it, or that that film was even made. I was surprised, because I heard he was directing it, and I thought, "Good for Jack. He's taken off and got his shot," and I thought we were going to see many more Jack Nicholson–directed films, and it just didn't happen.[12]

What did happen were two films, separated by a dozen years and a dozen roles, neither of which shared the exploratory magic, intensive artistry or singular thumbprint seen—though in imperfect form—in that debut. It could simply be that Nicholson put all of his energy into directing *Drive* rather than splitting it, as he did when both directing and starring in the latter two films.

Margotta related that Nicholson "understands the medium from both sides. He knows what it takes to do both, acting and directing, and how difficult it is to do both at the same time. Like John Huston and Roman Polanski (both of whom directed and acted with Nicholson)." Margotta then drew the key distinction between Nicholson's directorial efforts: "The industry itself defines some of the rules. And the public decides in the end. Jack has always had to add his name value as an actor to directing, with the exception of *Drive*. He has had to appear in what he directed. Not easy."[13]

* * *

Goin' South dramatically shows this difficulty. For an actor known for his research about and immersion into a role, how can it reasonably be expected to apply the same level of preparation to overseeing the entire movie—including directing a famous movie star by the name of Jack Nicholson?

The answer is, not well in either accounting. Dividing energies strained his efforts on both. Nicholson the director became less experimental and less experiential, turning in a product more serviceable than volatile. Nicholson the actor lost sight of self-restraint, as if rebelling from under the control of his executive alter ego.

Here, the director relies on a stock company of sorts, collecting *Cuckoo's Nest* patients Christopher Lloyd and Danny DeVito; friends Jeff Morris, B.J. Merholz and the criminally overlooked actress Luana Anders; as well as collaborators John Herman Shaner, Harry Gittes, Harold Schneider and Toby Carr Rafelson.

The crew under Nicholson's direction consisted of many veterans, some from the 1950s and even the '40s, along with natives from the Southwestern U.S.–Mexican geography. Meanwhile, both Mary Steenburgen and John Belushi were making their film debuts under a sophomore director.

The movie presents a rocky counterbalance between broad comedy and sentimental romance. Jack's Henry Moon is "Gabby" Hayes to his outlaw gang, much more in debt to the Bowery Boys and Abbott and Costello than Ernst Lubitsch or George Cukor.

As a lover of film, particularly foreign art-house cinema, Nicholson had the prescience to choose Néstor Almendros, known for Eric Rohmer's *Love in the Afternoon* and Francois Truffaut's *The Story of Adele H.* Almendros could have been recommended by Monte Hellman (who worked with Nicholson on several films and used Almendros as cinematographer on *Cockfighter*) and/or Terrence Malick (the lenser won the Best Cinematography Oscar for Malick's *Days of Heaven*, released the same year, though shot two years earlier under producers Bert and Harold Schneider). Hellman, however, told me that it was "probably neither. Jack would have been aware of Néstor from *Days of Heaven*, not so much because of Terry, but because of Bert Schneider. Of course, Jack was a fan of *Cockfighter* as well."[14]

Ed Begley Jr., who played Moon Gang member Whitey, called Nicholson a great actor-director. "He was a force to be reckoned with," elaborating that as director, Nicholson didn't see himself as the actor. "He was bright. He knew exactly what he wanted. He had his video playback, which was very unusual for that time, in 1977."[15]

Another gang member, Tracey Walter, said, "It was the first time I had seen the use of a monitor and playback. And so we were sitting around watching the monitor."[16]

Thirty-six years after the film's release, co-producer Harry Gittes' original *Goin' South* script was offered for sale without the knowledge of Nicholson's friend and colleague. At that time, the title on the bright red cover still read "THE CONJUGAL RIGHTS OF HENRY MOON/A Romantic Comedy/by John Shaner & Al Ramus" (two other screenwriters would do whatever they did after this draft). The title page includes alternate titles in Gittes' own hand, *The Ball and Chain of Henry Moon*, *Irreverent Moon* and *Going South, Going East*.[17]

In several instances throughout the script, the producer worried that Henry's gang was getting lost in the action. In the opening, he writes "INVOLVE GANG IN THIS,"[18] asking whether they are at the hanging "watching." He makes almost the same note in a later scene (page 104) when three ladies show up at Henry and Julia's home and interrupt their chicken dinner, asking, "Where did the gang go?"[19]

Gittes knew that the gang was a better source for humor than Moon alone, but that was not his sole area of concern. Showing a producer's keen eye for plot and continuity, he wonders about the motivation for Deputy Towfield (Christopher Lloyd), inquiring, "What has he got against Moon early in story?"[20]

As the film shifts toward the more personal romantic comedy, Gittes becomes more concerned about the strength of the narrative. His handwritten notes include: "NO THEMES," "MAGNIFY THE DIFFERENCES" and "Who are they? What do they want?"[21] Later, when the Henry and Julia marriage turns into an old-fashioned courtship, he remarks, "He thinks she's a virgin. She lets him."[22]

There are breakout moments here and there that connect to Jack as art film enthusiast. In an early scene featuring Henry and Moon's gang in jail, Nicholson and Almendros skillfully move the actors' faces in and out of the light for an effect of heightened reality.

The director appears to have learned from mentor Roger Corman, employing camera motion, plus tight shooting that's slightly out of focus, to enhance the immediacy of the action. As the movie shifts its focus from the caricatures of Moon and his gang to Moon and the wife he must win as his love, we see a pivotal transitional composition of Henry Lloyd Moon and Julia Tate Moon in which Nicholson rides on a porch swing, in side view from the perspective of Mary Steenburgen, moving toward and away from the camera as if on a pendulum. This perfectly represents the negotiation of love that takes place between the characters.

Henry is saved from hanging by Julia by a Civil War–era law that allows the condemned to be redeemed by an unmarried woman who claims the noose-naysayer as her own responsibility. Julia takes her awfully wedded husband merely as gold mine laborer, only to eventually swing toward affection, back toward boss, then toward suitor, and finally toward lover and true spouse—as both life partner and business partner.

Conflict during this emotional growth occurs when Hermine (Veronica Cartwright) from the old gang and the guys show up at his new homestead, blithely looking to pick up with Henry where they left off and jump Moon after howling at the moon (yes, that's what actually happens). It's shot with an out-of-focus sense of placing the viewer as intruder. As elsewhere, a narrow focus is chosen to capture the moment's intimacy.

Cartwright impressed the director enough to play key supporting roles both in *The Witches of Eastwick* and *Man Trouble*. The former child actress (*The Birds* and *The Twilight Zone*) related that Nicholson chose her for the role of his old flame:

> Actually it was funny, because my first interview for it, I went to Paramount Studios to meet Jack, and I had done a movie called *Inserts* with Richard Dreyfuss (originally X-rated, the film dealt with pornography and heroin addiction in the 1930s). So he comes out with this jean jacket on, and says, "Come back into my office," and of course we'd all heard stories. And as I'm walking, and he lets me lead the way, and he goes, "I just loved you in *Inserts*," at which point I turned beet red. He said, "I love a woman who blushes." And this was from behind! He's terrible, he's so great![23]

Tracey Walter had an equally unusual anecdote about how he landed his role as Coogan. "When I met Jack, he's sitting behind a desk at the height of his career. I'm sitting at the other side of the desk. I didn't plan if out, but we were talking about doing something like re-reading a book that you once loved and things are different and you dare read it again. You want to make sure you love it as much." Not at all calculated, Walter brought up Holden Caulfield in *The Catcher in the Rye*, and that "his most burning question was, 'Where do the ducks in the pond in Central Park go in the wintertime?' And with that, Jack leaned over the desk and said, 'Trace ... they're goin' south.'" A couple of days later, Tracey got his part in *Goin' South*. As a nice postscript, when his director found out what the actor was getting paid, he doubled his salary.[24]

When the married couple later become more engaged in their mining venture and a structural collapse separates husband from wife with tons of stone and miles of panic, Nicholson moves the camera with the character, handheld to search along with Moon as he looks for his trapped wife. Almendros' camera does not observe, but becomes part of the action.

These moments of cinematic mastery are fleeting, making *Goin' South* more workaday than wondrous. Scenes connect, lines touch, images shine and feelings move. But overall, the film falls in equal proportion to Nicholson's rambunctious overreach in his portrayal. He is over the Moon, too far over the top to overcome a slight but promising storyline typified by uneven and insubstantial storytelling.

16. The Occasional Filmmaker

The comedy was also shaky, as evidenced by several hand notations in the script of co-producer Harry Gittes, including "need punchline," "reprise joke," "never work" and "too *contrived*."[25]

However, he celebrates the climax of the film, explaining how Julia sacrifices the material for the sentimental: "[S]he gives up her gold to save his life."[26] That is a love story, though one the movie did not share as movingly as it could have.

It's no surprise that Nicholson would have a more positive view of the film, not unlike a parent seeing only the good in the child. "Before I directed *Two Jakes*, I thought I should watch the other ones I'd directed," he recalled. "It was good seeing *Goin' South* ... the movie wasn't very successful, but I love it. And I love people who love it."[27]

That sentiment is understandable. Nicholson put all he had into the movie, according to Ed Begley, Jr., pushing himself before, during and even after the production.[28] Barry Dennen, who worked with Nicholson on *The Shining*, talked about Nicholson's filmmaking multitasking. "When he was working, he was working. When he wasn't on camera, Jack was editing a movie down the hall—*Goin' South* with Mary Steenburgen, I believe."[29]

* * *

Between *Goin' South* and *The Two Jakes*, Nicholson won an Oscar (Best Actor in a Supporting Role) for *Terms of Endearment* and was Oscar-nominated for *Reds*; was nominated for Best Actor in a Leading Role for *Prizzi's Honor* and *Ironweed*; and starred in the classics *The Shining*, *The Postman Always Rings Twice*, *The Border* and *Batman*.

When Nicholson acted in his sequel to Polanski's *Chinatown*, as one of the two titular Jakes, his acting turned out to be less than memorable and his directing less than formidable. From an observer's standpoint, attempting to follow up a work as monumental as *Chinatown* can only be seen as a frustrating folly.

The crazy history of the making of this film might be more interesting and entertaining than the movie itself. A conflict between three important colleagues—Nicholson (the original Gittes), Towne (the writer) and Robert Evans (the studio wunderkind who was originally slated to make his acting comeback as the second Jake, only to be replaced by Harvey Keitel)—becomes a center to the story that's stranger and more intriguing than that of J.J. Gittes and his search for the daughter of Evelyn Mulwray.

Nicholson took the job as director, not as champion of his vision like with *Drive, He Said*, nor as the center of the action, as in *Goin' South*. Here, it's as if he loses a bet or draws the shortest straw, taking the gig as a contractual obligation or to repay a financial debt. He's stuck, and the movie looks it.

Goin' South (1978) was Jack's second directorial effort, but his first in the dual role as star. A monitor system helped him navigate his split duties. Looking back, Nicholson said, "The movie wasn't very successful, but I love it. And I love people who love it."

The Two Jakes presents a sadly slight treatment of the original character and a disappointingly bland neutralization of the inspiration for the original story. Evans was uncharacteristically understated when offering, "Robert [Towne] didn't quite keep up his end of the bargain, because the script was 80 percent complete," and that at the time of the release of his autobiography *The Kid Stays in the Picture*, "it remains 80 percent complete!"[30]

Voiceover narration is part of the film noir convention, but here it's a bad sign, not spicing up the story or providing a spoken form of potboiler literature as complement to its pulp fiction narrative. No, the Jake Gittes voiceover is a stagnant yet overwritten cue that the story's not clear enough, for a string of self-conscious lines of puffery that exists solely for cleaning up and for adding clarity.

What happens to an interesting character first woven into an absorbing plot with the intensity of a classic? Reduced to a tired sequel, executed more because too much time and money had already been invested to abandon the project—not much.

Quick: Mention the movie *Chinatown* to someone and you get a visceral response. Mention *The Two Jakes*, and even bolster its aided awareness by adding that it's the motion picture follow-up to *Chinatown*, and you get as much of a response as the movie itself did in comparison to its antecedent.

Nicholson always cared about the visuals, always understanding that the shooter makes the film, having learned the beauty and lyricism that the "motion" and the "pictures" which define motion pictures come from master cinematographers such as Gregory Sandor, László Kovacs, Haskell Wexler, Sven Nykvist, Andrzej Bartkowiak and Néstor Almendros. He chose Vilmos Zsigmond, best known for Robert Altman's *McCabe & Mrs. Miller*; Peter Fonda's *The Hired Hand*; John Boorman's *Deliverance*; Steven Spielberg's *Close Encounters of the Third Kind*; and Michael Cimino's *The Deer Hunter*; along with George Miller's *The Witches of Eastwick* that of course featured Nicholson.

Tracey Walter called working with Nicholson again a great experience, "because I continued my relationship with Jack. I worked in two films on which he acted and directed," *Goin' South* and this film, adding that Nicholson did not show any difficulty dividing his attention between acting and directing as "it's not that hard to do with playback, using a monitor."[31]

"I think he went from actor to director and back and forth very well," agrees James Hong. "I felt very comfortable with him in both roles. Knowing that he is also the director, I had to bring something extra to the scenes, and I think he saw that in the scene I did with him in the greenhouse with the plants." Hong considered this one of the director's favorite scenes because Nicholson showed it as part of an interview, "a great compliment to my achievement as an actor."[32]

Nicholson's acting in *The Two Jakes* appears tired at points, though there still is some directorial magic in his work with Zsigmond. Striking instances of attention to visual style include an array of tracking shots, interesting angles, a reflection shot with the Moon shown on a desk, a slow-motion explosion, a *Psych-Out* type of spin when his character is knocked out, and a multi-image view of Rubén Blades. There's also a framing of Richard

Farnsworth, this movie's John Huston, that's a sly reminder of *Five Easy Pieces'* oil field scene.

Though the story doesn't add up to much, the more discerning viewer might recognize that the director knows his stuff and has studied the filmmakers from around the world and around the Roger Corman universe (including the influential moving camera as practiced by Corman). Nicholson's active camerawork is not overdone, but is more outwardly "directed" than originator Roman Polanski and his intrinsically immersed style.

No matter the added strain, he gave his full attention to the actors. Co-lead Harvey Keitel addressed the split focus as actor-director by acknowledging the difficulty of participating in a scene and setting up that scene, while emphasizing that he received all the attention that he needed, "because he's an actor's actor. Anyone who is an actor's actor will give you full attention in a scene, even if they're acting opposite you, because they have deep respect and awe and value of acting."[33]

The actor's interplay with Keitel provides most of Gittes' highlights in the sequel. Nicholson the director's most effective use of Nicholson the actor occurs when Gittes' vulnerability is exposed, capturing how Jake handles the emotions and the pressure. This is a man who has become successful, but within the world of matrimonial betrayals and shady dealings. The war's over, but everyone's still a little on edge. They see things differently and Gittes sees things differently. Not better. Just different.

He's older and slower, but not much wiser. His past clings to him and weighs every step and slackens every word. He is prosperous, yet his "future is all used up," as Dietrich warned Welles in *Touch of Evil*.

Nicholson's strongest, most impactful direction is also Nicholson's most raw and emotional acting in the film, the unflinching close-up that records Jake as he looks through the Evelyn Mulwray file. Camera and editing restraint intensifies the pain, because like with pain in real life—looking away will not diminish it. One cannot be distracted from a pain this deep and a loss this true.

This pain triggers an explosive attack by Gittes on Detective Loach's son, when the cop won't let up. He tears at Jake's wound until Jake flashes back to the Mulwray shooting and then forces Loach Jr. to suck the barrel of his gun until the errant policeman wets himself in fear. In these two scenes, we're reminded of the masterful Nicholson, who can nimbly walk a high wire between tenderness and violence, exploring a character as frankly as the private eye explores Evelyn's file.

A symbolic director's touch concludes the film. Jake number one lets Jake number two commit suicide without seeming to commit suicide (protecting his wife's insurance) when Keitel lights a cigarette to ignite a gas explosion. This takes place in a pleasant housing development meant for returning veterans, who survived World War II only to witness a fatal firebomb on Main Street. Nicholson ends *The Two Jakes* with a huge blast that resolves itself into a sundown in the background and an American flag in the foreground. The sequence looked like a war scene about two vets, but sets up the theme of the movie—that the past and its pain never go away.

* * *

Nicholson understood that film was a visual medium. He chose the best visual artists for his three directorial efforts: Bill Butler for *Drive, He Said*, Néstor Almendros for *Goin' South* and Vilmos Zsigmond for *The Two Jakes*.

He called himself "very radical as a director," explaining, "I have a lousy narrative sense and feel like I'm more of a poetic director." Quoting French New Wave director Jean-Luc Godard, he added: "Of course film should have a beginning, middle and end, but not necessarily in that order."[34]

In an interview with Beverly Walker, he said that he loved directing because the "imagery of a movie is where it's at, and that is based on the director's vision." Nicholson pointed out that, despite the unbalanced attention to script in the importance of filmmaking, "in actuality, cinema is that 'other thing'; and unless you're after that, I'd just as soon be in another medium."[35]

He cared about making a statement, addressing the Vietnam War, social shifts and sexual freedom in *Drive*; women's liberation and the encroachment of predatory land-grabbing industrialists in *Goin' South*; and a similar cautionary focus on land development and the assumed entitlement held by large corporate entities in their quest for natural resources and its valuable preserves (oil and gas in place of the gold of *Goin' South*) in *The Two Jakes*.

His directorial career lasted only three films, yet spanned nearly 20 years. From a crackling debut to the thud of his finale, Nicholson showed he very well could have comfortably switched from acting to directing. Instead, he made meaning even out of the most limiting roles rather than fighting studios and poor storylines to take his chances as a director.

The final walk down the hall revealed the key visuals in this visual medium. Hector manipulates an orange, holding the Sun in his hands. Henry Moon grins broadly as he appeals to the townswomen to spare his life. The movie star saves a studio from disaster by starring as his noir detective one more time and directing the ill-fated sequel in his final such project. The Sun … the Moon … and the star all flicker with the whir and the wup-wup-wup, groaning slowly to a distorted, haunted sound until the last image of the last Moviola comes to a complete stop. The foot leaves the pedal and the director leaves the editing room. Forever.

Chapter Notes

Preface

1. Sandy Bressler, telephone conversation with the author, 2003.

Chapter 1

1. Millie Perkins, telephone interview with the author, February 20, 2011.
2. Beverly Walker, "Interview: Jack Nicholson," *Film Comment*, May/June 1985, 9.
3. Cynthia Baron and Sharon Marie Carnicke, *Reframing Screen Performance* (Ann Arbor: University of Michigan, 2008), 5.
4. Dennis Bingham, *Acting Male: Masculinities in the Films of James Stewart, Jack Nicholson, and Clint Eastwood* (New Brunswick, NJ: Rutgers University Press, 1994), 143.
5. Eric Morris and Joan Hotchkis, *No Acting, Please* (Los Angeles: Ermor Enterprises Publishing, 2002), 4.
6. Perkins interview.
7. Gary Kent, telephone interview with the author, May 19, 2005.
8. Robert Vaughn, *A Fortunate Life* (New York: Thomas Dunne, 2008), 72.
9. Rainer Knepperges, "The Monologist and the Fighter: An Interview with Bob Rafelson," *Senses of Cinema*, April 2009, 8.
10. Bruce Dern, comment to the author, April 28, 2007.
11. Martin Landau, comment to the author, April 25, 2015.
12. Jeff Corey, "The Jeff Corey Collection" (The Thompson Library Special Collection, The Jerome Lawrence and Robert E. Lee Theatre Research Institute of The Ohio State University Libraries).
13. *Ibid.*
14. *Ibid.*
15. Kent interview.
16. Shirley Knight, telephone interview with the author, October 17, 2010.
17. Perkins interview.
18. Salli Sachse, telephone interview with the author, May 12, 2011.
19. Perkins interview.
20. David Mamet, "Tell the Truth," in *The Twenty-Second Annual American Film Institute Life Achievement Award, March 3, 1994* (Los Angeles: American Film Institute, 1994), 13.
21. Ron Rosenbaum, "The Creative Mind; Acting: The Method and Mystique of Jack Nicholson," *The New York Times Magazine*, July 13, 1986, 2.
22. Joseph Turkel, comment to the author, February 16, 2007.
23. Kent interview.
24. Perkins interview.
25. Kent interview.
26. Richard Kaufman, telephone interview with the author, December 21, 2013.
27. *Ibid.*
28. Barry Dennen, Skype interview with the author, January 19, 2016.
29. Sonny Barger, interview with the author, May 5, 2002.
30. Kent interview.
31. Noah Wyle, comment to the author, April 11, 2015.
32. Nancy Allen, telephone interview with the author, March 27, 2011.
33. Dern comment, 2007.
34. Robert Dix, interview with the author, June 25, 2011.

35. Allen interview.
36. Rita Moreno, comment to the author, October 19, 2003.
37. James Hong, written interview with the author, November 7, 2016.
38. Kent interview.
39. Perkins interview.
40. Knight interview.
41. Dern comment, 2007.
42. Mews Small, telephone interview with the author, October 1, 2015.
43. Michael Margotta, interview with the author via email, September 3, 2011.
44. Ed Nelson, interview with the author, June 25, 2011.
45. Allen interview.
46. Kent interview.
47. Bert Cardullo, *Playing to the Camera: Film Actors Discuss Their Craft* (New Haven, CT: Yale University Press, 1998), 25.
48. Barney Hoskyns, *Lowside of the Road: A Life of Tom Waits* (New York: Broadway, 2009), 344.
49. Margotta interview.
50. James Naramore, *Acting in the Cinema* (Berkeley: University of California Press, 1988), 122–23.
51. Nelson interview.
52. Monte Hellman, response to the author via Facebook Messenger, December 31, 2013.
53. Patrick McGilligan, *Jack's Life: A Biography of Jack Nicholson* (New York: W.W. Norton, 1994), 222.
54. Milos Forman, "He Called Me Meatloaf" in *The Twenty-Second Annual American Film Institute Life Achievement Award, March 3, 1994*, 12.
55. Meryl Streep, "The Outlaw Icon" in *ibid.*, 9.
56. Jack Nicholson, "I Go the Hard Way Every Time" in *ibid.*, 17.
57. Beverly Walker, *Jack Nicholson: Anatomy of an Actor* (London: Phaidon Press, 2013), 65.
58. Fred Schruers, "Jack Nicholson: The Badass Hollywood Star," *Rolling Stone*, March 19, 1998, 3.
59. Dern comment, 2007.
60. Nelson interview.
61. Michael Caine, *Acting in Film: An Actor's Take on Movie Making* (New York: Applause, 1990), 6.
62. Morris and Hotchkis, 1.
63. *Ibid.*, p. 4.
64. Baron and Carnicke, 44–45.
65. *Ibid.*, 186.
66. *Ibid.*, 98.
67. Kent interview.
68. Shaun R. Karli, *Becoming Jack Nicholson: The Masculine Persona from Easy Rider to The Shining* (Lanham, MD: Scarecrow, 2013), 9.
69. Kent interview.
70. Dennen interview.
71. Perkins interview.
72. John Farr, "Tough Guy: The Best of James Cagney," *The Huffington Post*, huffingtonpost.com, July 17, 2012.
73. Naramore, 159.
74. *Ibid.*, 220.
75. Peter Bogdanovich, *Who the Hell's In It: Portraits and Conversations* (New York: Alfred A. Knopf, 2004), 99.
76. Naramore, 235.
77. Knight interview.
78. Perkins interview.
79. Corey Collection.

Chapter 2

1. Arlen Schumer, telephone interview with the author, January 25, 2016.
2. *Ibid.*
3. Ve Neill, comment to the author, May 13, 2016.
4. Mike Sager, "What I've Learned: Jack Nicholson," *Esquire*, Volume 141, Number 1, 2007, 66.
5. Schumer interview.
6. *Ibid.*
7. Jack Douglas, *Jack, The Great Seducer: The Life and Many Loves of Jack Nicholson* (New York: HarperEntertainment, 2004 [Uncorrected Proof]), 256.
8. Schumer interview.
9. *Ibid.*
10. Adam West, comment to the author, October 8, 2011.
11. David Boeri, telephone interview with the author, December 8, 2014.
12. *Ibid.*
13. *Ibid.*
14. *Ibid.*
15. *Ibid.*
16. Rusty Schweickart, comment to the author, June 5, 2011.

17. Michael Collins, comment to the author, June 11, 2016.
18. Cindy Lee Berryhill, email response to the author, December 8, 2011.
19. Schweickart comment.
20. Alan Bean, comment to the author, June 5, 2011.
21. Al Worden, interview with the author, June 2, 2012.
22. Cardullo, 257.
23. Dave Scott, interview with the author, June 4, 2011.
24. Dick Gordon, comment to the author, June 5, 2011.
25. Bean comment.
26. Jim Lovell, comment to the author, June 5, 2011.
27. Worden interview.
28. Scott interview.
29. Worden interview.
30. Collins comment.
31. Marion Ross, comment to the author, April 9, 2016.
32. *Ibid.*
33. Perkins interview.
34. Kent interview.
35. Perkins interview.
36. Monte Hellman, response to the author via Facebook Messenger, May 9, 2016.
37. Peter Tork, comment to the author, March 2, 2013.
38. Elisa Leonelli, "The Visionary Journey of Bob Rafelson," *Los Angeles Arts and Entertainment Magazine*, February 1997, 34.
39. Caine, *Acting in Film: An Actor's Take on Movie Making*, 68, 43.
40. Michael Caine, *Michael Caine: The Elephant to Hollywood* (London: Hodder & Stoughton, 2010), 206.

Chapter 3

1. FeatsPress, "The Pledge: Interview with Jack Nicholson," Cinema.com. http://cinema.comarticles/601/pledge-the-interview-with-jack-nicholson.phtml (2001), 1.
2. *Ibid.*
3. Tom Noonan, comment to the author, October 26, 2013.
4. John Savage, comment to the author, October 25, 2013.
5. Anjelica Huston, *Watch Me: A Memoir* (New York: Simon & Schuster, 2014), 268.

6. Graham Fuller, "New Again: Sean Penn," *Interview Magazine*, October 1995, 3.
7. Kari Wuhrer, comment to the author, April 24, 2014.
8. Fuller, 4–5.
9. Cardullo, 291.
10. Jimmie Rodgers, telephone interview with the author, February 17, 2014.
11. *Ibid.*
12. *Ibid.*
13. *Ibid.*

Chapter 4

1. Adrien Joyce and Bob Rafelson, *Five Easy Pieces* (Los Angeles: BBS Productions, 1969; Original Revised Script 12/4/69 #8974 with Excised Content, Annotated by Karen Black), 132.
2. Don Schiach, *Jack Nicholson: The Complete Film Guide* (London: B.T. Batsford Ltd., 1999), 54.
3. Walker, *Jack Nicholson: Anatomy of an Actor*, 30.
4. Joyce and Rafelson, 131.
5. Schiach, 52.
6. Robert Crane and Christopher Fryer, *Jack Nicholson: The Early Years* (Lexington: University Press of Kentucky, 2012), 168, 25.
7. David Toussaint, "The Color of Hollywood: Karen Black's History of Might," *New York Guyd*. http://www.guyspy.com/the-color-of-hollywood-karen-blacks-history-of-might/, April 19, 2012, 5.
8. Sally Struthers, comment to the author, October 2006.
9. Crane and Fryer, 88.
10. Morris and Hotchkis, 44.
11. Joyce and Rafelson.
12. Jordan Riefe, "Jack's Back: Hollywood Rogue or Hollywood Royalty? Jack Nicholson Returns Enigmatic as Ever," *Gene Simmons Tongue*, Spring 2003, 43.
13. Riefe, 41.
14. Rebecca Murray and Fred Topel, "Jack Nicholson Talks About *About Schmidt*," *About.com Hollywood Movies*, http://movies.about.com/library/weekly/aaaboutschmidtinta.htm, 2002.
15. Leo Adam Biga, "Alexander Payne Discusses *About Schmidt* Starring Jack Nicholson, Working with the Iconic Actor, Past Projects and Future Plans," *Leo Adam Biga's My Inside*

Stories, https://leoadambiga.com/2011/12/06/from-the-archives-alexander-payne-discusses-his-new-feature-about-schmidt-starring-jack-nicholson-working-with-the-star-past-projects-and-future-plans/, December 6, 2011 (originally published in the *Omaha Weekly*), 4.

Chapter 5

1. Noah Wyle, comment to the author, April 11, 2015.
2. Bingham, 157–158.
3. James Marshall, comment to the author, October 9, 2010.
4. Ve Neill, comment to the author, May 13, 2016.
5. Dan Moldea, email response to the author, April 3, 2012.
6. Neill, comment to the author.
7. Mamet, 15.
8. Nelson interview.
9. Dern comment, 2007.
10. Kent interview.
11. Knight interview.
12. Jay Parini, email correspondence with the author, January 9, 2016.
13. Walker, *Jack Nicholson: Anatomy of an Actor*, 30.
14. Peter Fonda, *Don't Tell Dad: A Memoir* (New York: Hyperion, 1998), 268–69.
15. Bingham, 125.
16. Schiach, 66.
17. Bingham, 106.
18. *Ibid.*, 122.
19. Allen interview.
20. *Ibid.*
21. McGilligan, 243.
22. Allen interview.
23. Bingham, 125.
24. Schiach, 65–66.

Chapter 6

1. Dern comment, 2007.
2. Roger Corman and Jim Jerome, *How I Made a Hundred Movies in Hollywood and Never Lost a Dime* (New York: Random House, 1990), 67.
3. Ed Nelson, interview with the author, June 25, 2011.
4. Sam Tweedle, Pop Culture Renaissance Man: A Conversation with Brett Halsey, *Confessions of a Pop Culture Addict*, http://popcultureaddict.com/interviews/bretthalsey/, April 2010, 1.
5. Dern comment, 2007.
6. Crane and Fryer, 10.
7. Roger Corman, comment to the author, July 29, 2000.
8. Charles B. Griffith, comment to the author, March 31, 2007.
9. Jonathan Haze, comment to the author, March 31, 2007.
10. Griffith comment.
11. Haze comment.
12. *Ibid.*
13. Corman and Jerome.
14. Hazel Court, interview with the author, September 27, 2003.
15. Corman and Jerome, 86.
16. Court interview.
17. *Ibid.*
18. Victoria Price, comment to the author, October 24, 2015.
19. Victoria Price, *Vincent Price: A Daughter's Biography* (New York: St Martin's, 1999), 338.
20. Bogdanovich, 323.
21. Jack Hill, comment to the author, September 22, 2008.
22. McGilligan, 110.
23. Salli Sachse, telephone interview with the author, May 12, 2011.
24. *Ibid.*
25. *Ibid.*

Chapter 7

1. Dr. Brooke Cannon, email interview with the author, February 9, 2014.
2. *Ibid.*
3. Schruers, 11.
4. Knight interview.
5. *Ibid.*
6. Cannon interview.
7. *Ibid.*
8. *Ibid.*
9. Michael Berryman, comment to the author, October 5, 2013.
10. Small interview.
11. Berryman comment.
12. Zane Kesey, Facebook Messenger response to the author, January 8, 2015.
13. Small interview.
14. Berryman comment.

15. Walker, *Jack Nicholson: Anatomy of an Actor*, 71.
16. Anthony Petkovich, "Vincent Schiavelli—Have a Heart," *Psychotronic Magazine*, Number 37, 2002, 56.
17. Josip Elic, comment to the author, October 26, 2012.
18. Small interview.
19. Berryman comment.
20. Cannon interview.
21. Berryman comment.
22. Small interview.
23. *Ibid.*
24. Cannon interview.
25. Small comment, 2008.
26. Small interview.
27. *Ibid.*
28. *Ibid.*
29. Berryman comment.
30. Small interview.
31. Cannon interview.
32. *Ibid.*
33. *Ibid.*
34. *Ibid.*
35. *Ibid.*
36. *Ibid.*
37. *Ibid.*
38. Peter Tork, comment to the author, March 2, 2013.
39. Danel Olson, Justin Bozung, Catriona McAvoy, and Lee Unkrich, *Stanley Kubrick's The Shining: Studies in the Horror Film* (Lakewood, CO: Centipede Press, 2015), 34.
40. Olson, Bozung, McAvoy and Unkrich, 32.
41. Cannon interview.
42. Michel Ciment, *Kubrick: The Definitive Edition* (New York: Faber and Faber, 2001), 81.
43. Cannon interview.
44. *Ibid.*
45. Perkins interview.
46. Cannon interview.
47. David Boeri, telephone interview with the author, December 8, 2014.

Chapter 8

1. Noel Murray, "Richard Rush: Interview," *The AV Club*, http://www.avclub.com/article/richard-rush-57414 (June 13, 2011), 7.
2. Justin Bozung, "Henry Jaglom Interview," *Justin Bozung Blog*, http://justinbozung.net/henry-jaglom-interview, December 1, 2014, 5.
3. Kent interview.
4. Garry Marshall, comment to the author, April 21, 2012.
5. Miles Kreuger, telephone interview with the author, January 24, 2013.
6. *Ibid.*
7. Fonda, 68.
8. Sonny Barger, interview with the author, May 5, 2002.
9. TCM, "Motorcycle Gangs, Hippies and Stunt Men: An Interview with Richard Rush," *Movie Morlocks.com*, http://moviemorlocks.com/2010/04/17/motorcycle-gangs-hippies-and-stunt-men-an-interview-with-richard-rush/, April 17, 2010, 8.
10. Gary Kent, telephone interview with the author, May 19, 2005.
11. Murray, 6.
12. Barger interview.
13. *Ibid.*
14. Kent interview.
15. *Ibid.*
16. Dix interview.
17. Dern comment, 2007.
18. Dix interview.
19. Perkins interview.
20. Kent interview.
21. Millie Perkins, telephone interview with the author, February 20, 2011.
22. *Ibid.*
23. Kent interview.
24. Perkins interview.
25. Kent interview.
26. *Ibid.*
27. Perkins interview.
28. Cardullo, 25.
29. Randy Quaid, Twitter response to the author, December 17, 2014.
30. Damien Love, "The Miracle Worker: An Interview with Arthur Penn," *Bright Lights Film Journal*, http://brightlightsfilm.com/the-miracle-worker-an-interview-with-arthur-penn/#.VmnJT9Z8vcM, July 31, 2009, 27.
31. Douglas Brode, *The Films of Jack Nicholson* (Secaucus, NJ: Citadel, 1996), 191.
32. McGilligan, 279.
33. Richard Schickel, *Brando: A Life in Our Times* (New York: Athenaeum, 1991), 193.
34. Love, 25.

Chapter 9

1. Douglas, 115.
2. Chris Nashawaty, "An Intimate Conversation with Mike Nichols," *Entertainment Weekly*, November 20, 2014, 7.
3. Ann-Margret and Todd Gold. *Ann-Margret: My Story* (New York: Putnam, 1994), 208.
4. Rita Moreno, comment to the author, October 19, 2003.
5. Gavin Smith, "Of Metaphors and Purpose," *Film Comment*, May/June 1999, 5.

Chapter 10

1. Nelson interview.
2. Knight interview.
3. Perkins interview.
4. TCM, 7–8.
5. Frank Gorshin, comment to the author, April 24, 2004.
6. Kent interview.
7. *Ibid.*
8. James M. Tate, "The Nurse and Beyond: An Interview with Louise Fletcher," *Cult Film Freak*, http://www.cultfilmfreaks.com/2012/12/louisefletcher.html, December 2012, 15.
9. Rosenbaum, 3.
10. Tate.

Chapter 11

1. Olson, Bozung, McAvoy and Unkrich, 57–58.
2. Joseph Turkel, comment to the author, February 16, 2007.
3. Joseph Turkel, comment to the author, April 25, 2015.
4. Dennen interview.
5. Shane Rimmer, comment to the author, April 9, 2016.
6. Olson, Bozung, McAvoy and Unkrich, 372.
7. *Ibid.*, 653.
8. Dennen interview.
9. Ciment, 194.
10. *Ibid.*, 188.
11. Dennen interview.
12. Danny Lloyd, comment to the author, March 19, 2016.
13. Ciment, 298.
14. Turkel, 2007.
15. Douglas, 166.
16. Smith, 4.
17. Paul Sorvino, comment to the author, October 23, 2015.
18. Professor Robert M. Dowling, email response to the author, July 23, 2014.
19. *Ibid.*
20. Rosenbaum, 3.
21. Streep.
22. Carlo di Carlo and Giorgio Tinazzi, *Antonioni Discusses* The Passenger—*The Architecture of Vision: Writings and Interviews on Cinema* (Chicago: University of Chicago Press, 2007), 4.
23. *Ibid.*, 6.
24. Karli, 52–53.
25. di Carlo and Tinazzi, 9.
26. Shirley Knight, comment to the author, October 9, 2010.
27. Knight interview.

Chapter 12

1. The Editors of *Playboy*, "Playboy Interview: Jack Nicholson," *Playboy 50th Anniversary Collector's Edition*, January 2004, 87.
2. Alana Lee, "Peter Segal: Anger Management," *BBC Movies*, http://www.bbc.co.uk/films/2003/05/30/peter_segal_anger_management_interview.shtml, May 30, 2003, 1.
3. Roundtable of Writers, "Q&A with Nancy Meyers," MovieFreak.com, http://www.moviefreak.com/features/interviews/nancymeyers.htm, 5.
4. Rebecca Murray, "*Something's Gotta Give*: Diane Keaton Interview," Movies.About.com, http://movies.about.com/cs/somethingsgotto/a/smtgdk120703.htm (Retrieved 2-09-2011), 2.
5. Ed Begley Jr., comment to the author, January 9, 2016.
6. Tracey Walter, comment to the author, April 25, 2015.
7. Begley Jr. comment.
8. Adam Begley, Twitter responses to the author, January 13, 2015.
9. Kaufman interview.
10. *Ibid.*
11. Rosenbaum,, 1.
12. Adam Begley.
13. *Ibid.*
14. Bozung, 5.

15. Ann-Margret and Gold, 269.
16. Pete Townshend, *Pete Townshend: Who I Am* (London: Harper Perennial, 2013), 262–63.
17. Perkins interview.
18. Kent and Nelson interviews.
19. Dick Gautier, comment to the author, July 13, 2013.
20. Perkins interview.
21. Veronica Cartwright, comment to the author, April 12, 2014.

Chapter 13

1. Joyce and Rafelson, 8.
2. *Ibid.*, 126.
3. Crane and Fryer, 15.
4. Dick Summer, email response to the author, April 16, 2012.
5. Josh Mostel, comment to the author, October 26, 2013.
6. *Ibid.*
7. Schiach,, 60.
8. Summer response.
9. Thomas O'Connor, "Hector Babenco Harvests *Ironweed*," *The New York Times*, December 13, 1987, 2–3.
10. The Editors of *Playboy*, 87.
11. Riefe, 43.
12. Hoskyns, 342–43.

Chapter 14

1. Brode, 216.
2. Knepperges, 6–7.
3. Brode, 217.
4. Tork comment.
5. Naramore, 45.
6. Robert Evans, *The Kid Stays in the Picture* (New York: Hyperion, 1994), 270.
7. Hong interview.
8. Scott Ross, telephone interview with the author, May 11, 2016.
9. *Ibid.*
10. Walker, *Jack Nicholson: Anatomy of an Actor*, 51–53.
11. Bingham, 130.
12. Roger Ebert, *The Great Movies* (New York: Broadway, 2002), 104–06.
13. *Ibid.*, 104.
14. Nelson interview.
15. McGilligan, 147.
16. Justin Humphreys, "Dick Bakalyan Interview," *Psychotronic Magazine*, Number 25, 1997, 64.
17. Hong interview.
18. Michael Eaton, *Chinatown* (London: British Film Institute, 1997), 65.
19. *Ibid.*, 55.
20. Dern comment, 2011.
21. *Movieline* Staff, "Stockard Channing: Great Dame," *Movieline*, http://movieline.com/1998/01/01/great-dame-stockard-channing/, January 1, 1998, 1.
22. Huston, 146.
23. Nathan Rabin, "Kathleen Turner talks *The Perfect Family*, *Body Heat*, and her return to cinema," *The AV Club*, http://www.avclub.com/article/Kathleen-turner-talks-emtheperfect-familyem-embod-73499, May 4, 2012, 7–8.
24. Bingham, 153.
25. *Ibid.*, 153–154.
26. Hong interview.
27. Ethan Silverman, "Harvey Keitel," *Bomb*, Fall 1990, 6–7.

Chapter 15

1. Rosenbaum, 5.
2. Court interview.
3. Kris Gilpin, "Monte Hellman: The Lost Interview," *Cinema Retro*, http://www.cinemaretro.com/index.php?/archives/4107-CINEMA-RETRO-PRESENTS-MONTE-HELLMAN-THE-LOST-INTERVIEW.html, December 28, 2009, 8.
4. Crane and Fryer, 167.
5. Matthew Thrift, "Interview: Monte Hellman," *Cinephile*, http://www.cinephile-uk.com/2011/05/monte-hellman-is-nothing-short-of_2049.html, May 9, 2011, 4.
6. *Ibid.*
7. Gilpin, 9.
8. *Ibid.*
9. Perkins interview.
10. *Ibid.*
11. Kent interview.
12. *Ibid.*
13. Perkins interview.
14. Mike White, "Monte Hellman: An Interview," *Cashiers du Cinemart*, Issue 7, Article 122, 2.
15. *Ibid.*
16. Peter Fonda, comment to the author, October 25, 2013.

17. Corman and Jerome, 147–148.
18. Sachse interview.
19. Brode, 89.
20. Sachse interview.
21. *Ibid.*
22. Corman and Jerome, 147–148.
23. Crane and Fryer, 16.
24. Sachse interview.
25. Tork comment.
26. Micky Dolenz, comment to the author, March 15, 2014.
27. *Ibid.*
28. Michael Nesmith, interview with the author, April 9, 2013.
29. Dolenz comment.
30. Tork comment.
31. Dern comment, 2011.
32. Tork comment.
33. Nesmith interview.
34. *Ibid.*
35. Andrew Sandoval, *The Monkees: The Day-by-Day Story of the '60s TV Pop Sensation* (San Francisco: Thunder Bay, 2005), 265.
36. Tork comment.
37. Nesmith interview.
38. Andrew Sandoval, Facebook Messenger response to the author, January 24, 2012.
39. Tork comment.
40. Sandoval response.
41. Margotta interview.
42. *Ibid.*
43. *Ibid.*
44. Hellman, 2013.
45. Corman. "Whose Trip Is This, Anyway?" in *The Twenty-Second Annual American Film Institute Life Achievement Award*, March 3, 1994, 11.

Chapter 16

1. Kent interview.
2. Margotta interview.
3. *Ibid.*
4. *Ibid.*
5. Jack Nicholson, "Letter to Karen Black," Los Angeles: BBS Productions, 1970.
6. Margotta interview.
7. *Ibid.*
8. *Ibid.*
9. Harry Torczyner, trans. Richard Millen *Magritte: Ideas and Images* (New York: Harry W. Abrams, 1977), 172.
10. Margotta interview.
11. *Ibid.*
12. Kent interview.
13. Margotta interview.
14. Monte Hellman, Facebook Messenger response to the author, March 31, 2014.
15. Begley Jr. comment.
16. Walter comment.
17. Harry Gittes, "The Conjugal Rights of Henry Moon," Original *Goin' South* script by John Shaner and Al Ramus, annotated by the producer. (Undated), title page.
18. *Ibid.*, 1.
19. *Ibid.*, 104.
20. *Ibid.*, 2.
21. *Ibid.*, note inside p. 18.
22. *Ibid.*, 20.
23. Veronica Cartwright, comment to the author, April 12, 2014.
24. Walter comment.
25. Gittes, 5, 36, 9, 68.
26. *Ibid.*, 102.
27. The Editors of *Playboy*, 87.
28. Begley Jr. comment.
29. Dennen interview.
30. Evans, 362.
31. Walter comment.
32. Hong interview.
33. Silverman, 6.
34. Nicholson, 16.
35. Walker, *Interview: Jack Nicholson*, 7.

Bibliography

Primary Sources

Interviews, Comments and Correspondences

Allen, Nancy. Actress. March 27, 2011, via telephone.
Barger, Sonny. Motorcycle club leader/actor. May 5, 2002, at the Louie Run at the Lake County Fairgrounds, Painesville, OH.
Bean, Alan. Astronaut. June 5, 2011, during Apollo Panel moderated by Andy Chaikin at Spacefest, Tucson, AZ.
Begley, Adam. Author. January 13, 2015 via Twitter messages.
Begley Jr., Ed. Actor. January 9, 2016, at The Hollywood Show, Los Angeles, CA.
Berryhill, Cindy Lee. Singer/songwriter. December 8, 2011, via email.
Berryman, Michael. Actor. October 5, 2013, at Cinema Wasteland, Strongsville, OH.
Black, Karen. Actress. May 30, 2004, via telephone.
Boeri, David. Reporter. December 8, 2014, via telephone.
Bressler, Sandy. Agent. 2003, via telephone.
Cannon, Brooke. Professor. February 9, 2014, via email.
Cartwright, Veronica. Actress. April 12, 2014, at The Hollywood Show, Los Angeles, CA.
Collins, Michael. Astronaut. June 11, 2016, at Spacefest, Tucson, AZ.
Corman, Roger. Director. July 29, 2000, at Classic Film Fest, Arlington, VA.
Court, Hazel. Actress. September 27, 2003, at Monster Mania, Cherry Hill, NJ.
Dennen, Barry. Actor. January 19, 2016, via Skype.
Dern, Bruce. Actor. April 28, 2007 at *Los Angeles Times* Festival of Books and July 16, 2011, at the Hollywood Show, Burbank, CA.
Dix, Robert. Actor. June 25, 2011, at Monster Bash, Butler, PA.
Dolenz, Micky. Musician/actor. March 15, 2014, at Monkees Convention, Secaucus, NJ.
Dowling, Professor Robert M. Author. July 23 and 26, 2014, via email.
Elic, Josip. Actor. October 26, 2012, at Chiller Theatre, Parsippany, NJ.
Fonda, Peter. Actor. October 25, 2013, at Chiller Theatre, Parsippany, NJ.
Gautier, Dick. Actor. July 13, 2013, at The Hollywood Show, Los Angeles, CA.
Gordon, Dick. Astronaut. June 5, 2011, during Apollo Panel moderated by Andy Chaikin at Spacefest, Tucson, AZ.
Gorshin, Frank. Actor. April 24, 2004, at Chiller Theatre, Secaucus, NJ.
Griffith, Charles B. Screenwriter. March 31, 2007, during *Little Shop of Horrors* Panel at Cinema Wasteland, Strongsville, OH.
Haze, Jonathan. Actor. March 31, 2007, during *Little Shop of Horrors* Panel at Cinema Wasteland, Strongsville, OH.

Hellman, Monte. Director. December 31, 2013; March 31, 2014; and May 9, 2016; via Facebook Messenger.
Hill, Jack. Director. March 31, 2007, during *Little Shop of Horrors* Panel and September 22, 2008, both at Cinema Wasteland, Strongsville, OH.
Hong, James. Actor. November 7, 2016, via Facebook Messenger.
Kaufman, Richard. Violinist/film music supervisor. December 21, 2013, via telephone.
Kent, Gary. Actor/stuntman. May 19, 2005, via telephone.
Kesey, Zane. Furthur bus leader and son of author Ken Kesey. January 8, 2015, via Facebook Messenger.
Knight, Shirley. Actress. October 9, 2010, at The Hollywood Show, Burbank, CA, and October 17, 2010, via telephone.
Kreuger, Miles. President and founder of The Institute of the American Musical. January 24, 2013, via telephone.
Landau, Martin. Actor. April 25, 2015, at The Hollywood Show, Los Angeles, CA.
Lloyd, Danny. Actor. March 19, 2016, at HorrorHound Cincinnati, Sharonville, OH.
Lovell, Jim. Astronaut. June 5, 2011, during Apollo Panel moderated by Andy Chaikin at Spacefest, Tucson, AZ.
Margotta, Michael. Actor. September 3, 2011, via email.
Marshall, Garry. Writer/producer/director/actor. April 21, 2012, at The Hollywood Show, Los Angeles, CA.
Marshall, James. Actor. October 9, 2010, at Hollywood Collectors Show, Burbank, CA.
Moldea, Dan. Author. April 3, 2012, via email.
Moreno, Rita. Actress. October 19, 2003, at Cleveland Public Library, Cleveland, OH.
Mostel, Josh. Actor. October 26, 2013, at Chiller Theatre, Parsippany, NJ.
Nelson, Ed. Actor. June 25, 2011, at Monster Bash, Butler, PA.
Neill, Ve. Makeup artist. May 13, 2016, at Motor City Con, Novi, MI.
Nesmith, Michael. Musician/actor. April 9, 2013, at Carnegie Library Music Hall, Pittsburgh, PA.
Noonan, Tom. Actor. October 26, 2013, at Chiller Theatre, Parsippany, NJ.
Parini, Jay. January 9, 2016, via email.
Perkins, Millie. Actress. October 21, 2010, and February 20, 2011, via telephone.
Price, Victoria. Author and daughter of actor Vincent Price. October 24, 2015, at Chiller Theatre, Parsippany, NJ.
Quaid, Randy. Actor. December 17, 2014, via Twitter.
Rimmer, Shane. Actor. April 9, 2016, at The Hollywood Show, Los Angeles, CA.
Rodgers, Jimmie. Singer/actor. February 17, 2014, via telephone.
Ross, Marion. Actress. April 9, 2016, at The Hollywood Show, Los Angeles, CA.
Ross, Scott. Private investigator. May 11, 2016, via telephone.
Sachse, Salli. Actress/model. May 12, 2011, via telephone.
Sandoval, Andrew. Music reissue producer/author/musician. January 23 and 24, 2012, via Facebook Messenger.
Savage, John. Actor. October 25, 2013, at Chiller Theatre, Parsippany, NJ.
Schumer, Arlen. Author. January 25, 2016, via telephone.
Schweickart, Rusty. Astronaut. June 5, 2011, at Spacefest, Tucson, AZ.
Scott, Dave. Astronaut. June 4, 2011 at Spacefest, Tucson, AZ.
Small, Mews. Actress/singer. July 2008 at Hollywood Collectors Show, Burbank, CA, and October 1, 2015, via telephone.
Sorvino, Paul. Actor. October 23, 2015, at Chiller Theatre, Parsippany, NJ.
Struthers, Sally. Actress. October 2006 at Hollywood Collectors Show, Burbank, CA.
Summer, Dick. Radio personality. April 16, 2012, via email.
Tork, Peter. Musician/actor. March 2, 2013 at Monkees Convention, Secaucus NJ.
Turkel, Joseph. Actor. February 16, 2007 at Hollywood Collectors Show, Burbank, CA, and April 25, 2015, at The Hollywood Show, Los Angeles, CA.

Walter, Tracey. Actor. April 25, 2015, at The Hollywood Show, Los Angeles, CA.
West, Adam. Actor. October 8, 2011, during *Batman* Panel at The Hollywood Show, Burbank, CA.
Worden, Al. Astronaut. June 5, 2011 during Apollo Panel moderated by Andy Chaikin and June 2, 2012, both at Spacefest, Tucson, AZ.
Wuhrer, Kari. Actress. April 24, 2014, at Chiller Theater, Parsippany, NJ.
Wyle, Noah. Actor. April 11, 2015, at Steel City Con, Pittsburgh, PA.

Film and Television Resources

About Schmidt. Directed by Alexander Payne. 2002. USA: New Line Cinema Home Entertainment, Inc., 2002. DVD.
The Andy Griffith Show. "Opie Finds a Baby" and "Aunt Bee the Juror" episodes directed by Lee Philips, 1966 and 1967, respectively. USA: Paramount, 2006. DVD Box Sets.
Anger Management. Directed by Peter Segal. 2003. USA: Revolution Studios Distribution Company, LLC, 2003. Widescreen Special Edition DVD.
As Good as It Gets. Directed by James L. Brooks. 1997. USA: Columbia TriStar Home Video, 1998. DVD.
Back Door to Hell. Directed by Monte Hellman. 1964. USA/Philippines: Twentieth Century Fox Home Entertainment LLC, 2006. DVD.
Batman. Directed by Tim Burton. 1989. USA: Warner Bros. Entertainment Inc., 2010. Blu-ray Disc.
Blood and Wine. Directed by Bob Rafelson, 1996. USA: Twentieth Century Fox Home Entertainment LLC, 2006. DVD.
The Border. Directed by Tony Richardson, 1982. USA: Universal Studios, 2004. DVD.
Broadcast News. Directed by James L. Brooks, 1987. USA: The Criterion Collection, under exclusive license from Twentieth Century Fox Home Entertainment, Inc., 2010. Blu-ray Disc.
The Broken Land. Directed by John Bushelman, 1962. USA: American International. DVD unofficial release.
Bronco. "The Equalizer" episode directed by Marc Lawrence, 1961. USA: American Broadcasting Company/Warner Bros. Television. DVD unofficial release.
The Bucket List. Directed by Rob Reiner, 2007. USA: Warner Bros. Entertainment Inc., 2007. Blu-ray Disc.
Carnal Knowledge. Directed by Mike Nichols, 1971. USA: MGM Home Entertainment Inc., 1999. DVD.
Chinatown. Directed by Roman Polanski, 1974. USA: Paramount Pictures, 1999. DVD.
The Crossing Guard. Directed by Sean Penn, 1995. USA: Buena Vista Home Entertainment, Inc., 1999. DVD.
The Cry Baby Killer. Directed by Jus Addiss, 1958. USA: Buena Vista Home Entertainment/Hollywood Pictures, 2006. DVD.
The Departed. Directed by Martin Scorsese, 2006. USA: Warner Bros. Entertainment Inc., 2007. Blu-ray Disc.
Dr. Kildare. "A Patient Lost," "Whatever Happened to All the Sunshine and Roses?," "Out of a Concrete Tower," "A Taste of Crow," episodes directed by Alf Kjellin, 1966. National Broadcasting Company/MGM Television/Arena Productions. DVD unofficial release.
Drive, He Said. Directed by Jack Nicholson, 1971. USA: The Criterion Collection under exclusive license from Sony Pictures Home Entertainment in *America Lost and Found: The BBS Story*, 2010. Blu-ray Disc Box Set.
Easy Rider. Directed by Dennis Hopper, 1969. USA: The Criterion Collection under exclusive license from Sony Pictures Home Entertainment in *America Lost and Found: The BBS Story*, 2010. Blu-ray Disc Box Set.

The Elephant's Child. Directed by Mark Sottnick, 1986. USA: Rabbit Ear Entertainment, 2012. DVD.
Ensign Pulver. Directed by Joshua Logan, 1964. USA: Warner Bros. Entertainment, Inc., 2010. DVD download.
The Evening Star. Directed by Robert Harling, 1996. USA: Paramount Pictures, 2000. DVD.
A Few Good Men. Directed by Rob Reiner, 1992. USA: Columbia TriStar Entertainment, 2001. DVD.
Five Easy Pieces. Directed by Bob Rafelson, 1970. USA: The Criterion Collection under exclusive license from Sony Pictures Home Entertainment in *America Lost and Found: The BBS Story*, 2010. Blu-ray Disc Box Set.
Flight to Fury. Directed by Monte Hellman, 1964. USA: Warner Home Video, 1990. VHS.
The Fortune. Directed by Mike Nichols, 1975. USA: Twilight Time, 2014. Blu-ray Disc.
Goin' South. Directed by Jack Nicholson, 1978. USA: Paramount Pictures, 2002. DVD.
The Guns of Will Sonnett. "A Son for a Son," episode directed by Richard Sarafian, 1967. USA: Shout Factory/Timeless Media, 2008. DVD.
Hawaiian Eye. "Total Eclipse" episode directed by Robert Douglas, 1962. USA: American Broadcasting Company/Warner Bros. Television. DVD unofficial release.
Head. Directed by Bob Rafelson, 1968. USA: The Criterion Collection under exclusive license from Sony Pictures Home Entertainment in *America Lost and Found: The BBS Story*, 2010. Blu-ray Disc Box Set.
Heartburn. Directed by Mike Nichols, 1986. USA: Paramount Pictures, 2004. DVD.
Hells Angels on Wheels. Directed by Richard Rush, 1967. USA: Castle Hills Productions, 1986. DVD.
Hoffa. Directed by Danny DeVito, 1992. USA: Twentieth Century Fox Home Entertainment Inc., 2003. DVD.
The Hour of St. Francis. "The Challenge!" episode directed by Joseph Santley, 1962. USA: Franciscan Communications Center. Unofficial release on YouTube.
How Do You Know. Directed by James L. Brooks, 2010. USA: Columbia Pictures Industries, Inc., 2010. Blu-ray Disc.
Ironweed. Directed by Hector Babenco, 1987. USA: Lionsgate Home Entertainment, 2009. DVD.
The King of Marvin Gardens. Directed by Bob Rafelson, 1972. USA: The Criterion Collection under exclusive license from Sony Pictures Home Entertainment in *America Lost and Found: The BBS Story*, 2010. Blu-ray Disc Box Set.
The Last Detail. Directed by Hal Ashby, 1973. USA: Columbia TriStar Home Video, 1999. DVD.
The Last Tycoon. Directed by Elia Kazan, 1976. USA: Paramount Pictures, 2003. DVD.
Little Amy. TV pilot directed by Sidney Lanfield, 1962. USA: Columbia Broadcast System. Public domain file via Internet Archives on archive.org.
The Little Shop of Horrors. Directed by Roger Corman, 1960. USA: BCI in *Classic Jack 4-Movie Pack*, 2004. DVD Box Set.
Man Trouble. Directed by Bob Rafelson, 1992. USA: Twentieth Century Fox Home Entertainment, Inc., 2004. DVD.
Mars Attacks! Directed by Tim Burton, 1996. USA: Warner Home Video, 1997. DVD.
The Missouri Breaks. Directed by Arthur Penn, 1976. USA: Sony Pictures Home Entertainment Inc., 2005. DVD.
Mr. Lucky. "Operation Fortuna," episode directed by Jack Arnold, 1960. USA: CBS Television Network. Unofficial release.
On a Clear Day You Can See Forever. Directed by Vincente Minnelli, 1970. USA: Paramount Pictures, 2005. DVD.
One Flew Over the Cuckoo's Nest. Directed by Milos Forman, 1975. USA: Warner Bros. Home Entertainment Inc., 2010. Blu-ray Disc Special Edition Box Set.

The Passenger. Directed by Michelangelo Antonioni, 1975. USA: Sony Pictures Home Entertainment Inc., 2006. DVD.
The Pledge. Directed by Sean Penn, 2001. USA: Warner Home Video, 2001. DVD.
The Postman Always Rings Twice. Directed by Bob Rafelson, 1981. USA: Warner Home Video, 1997. DVD.
Prizzi's Honor. Directed by John Huston, 1985. USA: MGM Home Entertainment LLC, 2003. DVD.
Psych-Out. Directed by Richard Rush, 1968. USA: MGM Home Entertainment LLC in *Midnight Movies Double Feature*, 2003. DVD.
Ragtime. Directed by Milos Forman, 1981. USA: Paramount Pictures, 2004. DVD.
The Raven. Directed by Roger Corman, 1963. USA: MGM Home Entertainment LLC, 2003. DVD.
Rebel Rousers. Directed by Martin B. Cohen, 1970. USA: Rhino Entertainment Company, 1995. DVD.
Reds. Directed by Warren Beatty, 1981. USA: Paramount Pictures, 2006. 25th Anniversary Edition DVD.
Ride in the Whirlwind. Directed by Monte Hellman, 1966. USA: VCI Home Video, 2000. DVD.
A Safe Place. Directed by Henry Jaglom, 1971. USA: The Criterion Collection under exclusive license from Sony Pictures Home Entertainment in *America Lost and Found: The BBS Story*, 2010. Blu-ray Disc Box Set.
The St. Valentine's Day Massacre. Directed by Roger Corman, 1967. USA: Twentieth Century Fox Home Entertainment LLC, 2006. DVD.
Sea Hunt. "Round Up," episode directed by Leon Benson, 1961. USA: ZIV Television Programs/United Artists Television. DVD unofficial release.
The Shining. Directed by Stanley Kubrick, 1980. USA: Warner Bros. Entertainment Inc., 2007. DVD.
The Shooting. Directed by Monte Hellman, 1966. USA: VCI Home Video, 2000. DVD.
Something's Gotta Give. Directed by Nancy Meyers, 2003. USA: Columbia Pictures Industries, Inc. and Warner Bros. Entertainment, Inc., 2003. DVD.
Studs Lonigan. Directed by Irving Lerner, 1960. USA: BCI in *Classic Jack 4-Movie Pack*, 2004. DVD Box Set.
Tales of Wells Fargo. "That Washburn Girl," episode directed by William Witney, 1961. USA: Shout Factory, Timeless Media, 2009. DVD Box Set.
Terms of Endearment. Directed by James L. Brooks, 1983. USA: Paramount Pictures, 2000. DVD.
The Terror. Directed by Roger Corman, 1963. USA: BCI in *Classic Jack 4-Movie Pack*, 2004. DVD Box Set.
Thunder Island. Directed by Jack Leewood, 1963. USA: DVD archives courtesy of www.movielead.com.
Tommy. Directed by Ken Russell, 1975. USA: Sony Pictures Home Entertainment Inc., 2010. Blu-ray Disc.
Too Soon to Love. Directed by Richard Rush, 1960. USA: Blair & Associates, Ltd. in *Youth Run Wild* Kit Parker Double Features, 2006. DVD.
The Trip. Directed by Roger Corman, 1967. USA: MGM Home Entertainment LLC in *Midnight Movies Double Feature*, 2003. DVD.
The Two Jakes. Directed by Jack Nicholson, 1990. USA: Paramount Pictures, 1999. DVD.
The Wild Ride. Directed by Harvey Berman, 1960. USA: BCI in *Classic Jack 4-Movie Pack*, 2004. DVD Box Set.
The Witches of Eastwick. Directed by George Miller, 1987. USA: Warner Home Video, 1997. DVD.
Wolf. Directed by Mike Nichols, 1994. USA: Sony Pictures Home Entertainment Inc., 2009. Blu-ray Disc.

Secondary Source Material
Books

American Film Institute. *The Twenty-Second Annual American Film Institute Life Achievement Award, March 3, 1994*. Los Angeles: Institute, 1994:
    Corman, Roger. "Whose Trip Is This, Anyway?" (pp. 10–11);
    Forman, Milos. "He Called Me Meatloaf" (p. 12);
    Mamet, David. "Tell the Truth" (p. 13);
    Nicholson, Jack. "I Go the Hard Way Every Time" (article adapted from published interviews from 1974 to 1992) (pp. 16–17);
    Streep, Meryl. "The Outlaw Icon" (pp. 8–9).
Ann-Margret, and Todd Gold. *Ann-Margret: My Story*. New York: Putnam, 1994.
Baron, Cynthia, Diane Carson, and Frank P. Tomasulo. *More Than a Method: Trends and Traditions in Contemporary Film Performance*. Detroit: Wayne State University Press, 2004.
Baron, Cynthia, and Sharon Marie Carnicke. *Reframing Screen Performance*. Ann Arbor: University of Michigan, 2008.
Bingham, Dennis. *Acting Male: Masculinities in the Films of James Stewart, Jack Nicholson, and Clint Eastwood*. New Brunswick, NJ. Rutgers University Press, 1994.
Bogdanovich, Peter. *Who the Hell's In It: Portraits and Conversations*. New York: Alfred A. Knopf, 2004.
Brode, Douglas. *The Films of Jack Nicholson*. Secaucus, NJ: Citadel, 1996.
Caine, Michael. *Acting in Film: An Actor's Take on Movie Making*. New York, NY: Applause, 1990.
_____. *Michael Caine: The Elephant to Hollywood*. London: Hodder & Stoughton, 2010.
Cardullo, Bert. *Playing to the Camera: Film Actors Discuss Their Craft*. New Haven, CT: Yale University Press, 1998.
Ciment, Michael. *Kubrick: The Definitive Edition*. New York: Faber and Faber, 2001.
Corman, Roger, and Jim Jerome. *How I Made a Hundred Movies in Hollywood and Never Lost a Dime*. New York: Random House, 1990.
Crane, Robert, and Christopher Fryer. *Jack Nicholson: The Early Years*. Lexington: University Press of Kentucky, 2012. (Originally published as *Jack Nicholson: Face to Face*. New York: M. Evans and Co., 1975.)
di Carlo, Carlo, and Giorgio Tinazzi, editors. *Antonioni Discusses* The Passenger—*The Architecture of Vision: Writings and Interviews on Cinema*. Chicago: University of Chicago Press, 2007.
Douglas, Edward. *Jack, The Great Seducer: The Life and Many Loves of Jack Nicholson*. New York: HarperEntertainment, 2004 (uncorrected proof).
Eaton, Michael. *Chinatown*. London: British Film Institute, 1997.
Ebert, Roger. *The Great Movies*. New York: Broadway, 2002.
Evans, Robert. *The Kid Stays in the Picture*. New York: Hyperion, 1994.
Fonda, Peter. *Don't Tell Dad: A Memoir*. New York: Hyperion, 1998.
Hoskyns, Barney. *Lowside of the Road: A Life of Tom Waits*. New York: Broadway, 2009.
Huston, Anjelica. *Watch Me: A Memoir*. New York: Simon & Schuster, 2014.
Karli, Shaun R. *Becoming Jack Nicholson: The Masculine Persona from Easy Rider to The Shining*. Lanham, MD: Scarecrow, 2013.
McGilligan, Patrick. *Jack's Life: A Biography of Jack Nicholson*. New York: W.W. Norton, 1994.
Morris, Eric, and Joan Hotchkis. Foreword by Jack Nicholson. *No Acting, Please*. Los Angeles: Ermor Enterprises Publishing, 2002.
Naramore, James. *Acting in the Cinema*. Berkeley: University of California Press, 1988.
Olson, Danel, Justin Bozung, Catriona McAvoy, and Lee Unkrich. *Stanley Kubrick's* The Shining: *Studies in the Horror Film*. Lakewood, CO: Centipede Press, 2015.

Price, Victoria. *Vincent Price: A Daughter's Biography*. New York: St. Martin's, 1999.
Sandoval, Andrew. *The Monkees: The Day-by-Day Story of the '60s TV Pop Sensation*. San Francisco: Thunder Bay, 2005.
Schiach, Don. *Jack Nicholson: The Complete Film Guide*. London: B.T. Batsford Ltd., 1999.
Schickel, Richard. *Brando: A Life in Our Times*. New York: Athenaeum, 1991.
Torczyner, Harry. *Magritte: Ideas and Images*, trans. Richard Millen. New York: Harry W. Abrams, 1977.
Townshend, Pete. *Pete Townshend: Who I Am*. London: Harper Perennial, 2013.
Vaughn, Robert. *A Fortunate Life*. New York: Thomas Dunne, 2008.
Walker, Beverly. *Jack Nicholson: Anatomy of an Actor*. London: Phaidon Press, 2013.

Periodical Articles, Web Articles, Blogs

Biga, Leo Adam. "Alexander Payne Discusses 'About Schmidt' Starring Jack Nicholson, Working with the Iconic Actor, Past Projects and Future Plans." Leo Adam Biga's My Inside Stories. https://leoadambiga.com/2011/12/06/from-the-archives-alexander-payne-discusses-his-new-feature-about-schmidt-starring-jack-nicholson-working-with-the-star-past-projects-and-future-plans/. (December 6, 2011; Originally published in the *Omaha Weekly*).
Bozung, Justin. "Henry Jaglom Interview." Justin Bozung Blog. http://justinbozung.net/henry-jaglom-interview. (December 1, 2014).
The Editors of *Playboy*. "*Playboy* Interview: Jack Nicholson." *Playboy 50th Anniversary Collector's Edition*, Volume 51, No. 1 (January 2004).
Farr, John. "Tough Guy: The Best of James Cagney." *The Huffington Post*. huffingtonpost.com. July 17, 2012.
FeatsPress. "The Pledge: Interview with Jack Nicholson." Cinema.com. http://cinema.com/articles/601/pledge-the-interview-with-jack-nicholson.phtml. (2001).
Fuller, Graham. "New Again: Sean Penn." *Interview Magazine* (October 1995).
Gilpin, Kris. "Monte Hellman: The Lost Interview." *Cinema Retro*. http://www.cinemaretro.com/index.php?/archives/4107-CINEMA-RETRO-PRESENTS-MONTE-HELLMAN-THE-LOST-INTERVIEW.html (December 28 2009; Original Interview in 1988).
Humphreys, Justin, "Dick Bakalyan Interview." *Psychotronic Magazine*. Number 25, 1997.
Knepperges, Rainer. "The Monologist and the Fighter: An Interview with Bob Rafelson." *Senses of Cinema*, Issue 50 (April 2009).
Lee, Alana. "Peter Segal: Anger Management." BBC Movies. http://www.bbc.co.uk/films/2003/05/30/peter_segal_anger_management_interview.shtml. (May 30, 2003).
Leonelli, Elisa. "The Visionary Journey of Bob Rafelson." *Los Angeles Arts and Entertainment Magazine*, pp. 34–26 (February 1997).
Love, Damien. "The Miracle Worker: An Interview with Arthur Penn." *Bright Lights Film Journal*. http://brightlightsfilm.com/the-miracle-worker-an-interview-with-arthur-penn/#.VmnJT9Z8vcM. (July 31, 2009).
Movieline Staff. "Stockard Channing: Great Dame." *Movieline*. http://movieline.com/1998/01/01/great-dame-stockard-channing/. (January 1, 1998).
Murray, Noel. "Richard Rush: Interview." *The AV Club*. http://www.avclub.com/article/richard-rush-57414. (June 13, 2011).
Murray, Rebecca. "Something's Gotta Give: Diane Keaton Interview." Movies.About.com http://movies.about.com/cs/somethingsgotto/a/smtgdk120703.htm. (Retrieved 2-09-2011).
Murray, Rebecca, and Fred Topel. "Jack Nicholson Talks About 'About Schmidt.'" About.com Hollywood Movies. http://movies.about.com/library/weekly/aaaboutschmidtinta.htm. (2002).
Nashawaty, Chris. "An Intimate Conversation with Mike Nichols." *Entertainment Weekly*. (November 20, 2014).

O'Connor, Thomas. "Film: Hector Babenco Harvests "Ironweed." *The New York Times* (December 13, 1987).
Petkovich, Anthony. "Vincent Schiavelli—Have a Heart." *Psychotronic Magazine*. Number 37, 2002.
Rabin, Nathan. "Kathleen Turner talks The Perfect Family, Body Heat, and her return to cinema." *The AV Club*. http://www.avclub.com/article/Kathleen-turner-talks-emthe-perfect-familyem-embod-73499. (May 4, 2012).
Riefe, Jordan. "Jack's Back: Hollywood Rogue or Hollywood Royalty? Jack Nicholson Returns Enigmatic as Ever." *Gene Simmons Tongue*, Volume 1, No. 4. (Spring 2003).
Rosenbaum, Ron. *The Creative Mind; Acting: The Method and Mystique of Jack Nicholson*. The New York Times Magazine. (July 13, 1986).
Roundtable of Writers. "Q&A with Nancy Meyers." MovieFreak.com. http://www.moviefreak.com/features/interviews/nancymeyers.htm.
Sager, Mike, "What I've Learned: Jack Nicholson." *Esquire*. Volume 141, Number 1, 2007.
Schruers, Fred. "Jack Nicholson: The Badass Hollywood Star." *Rolling Stone*, Issue 782 (March 19, 1998).
Silverman, Ethan. "Harvey Keitel." *Bomb*. Issue 33 (Fall 1990).
Smith, Gavin. "Of Metaphors and Purpose." *Film Comment*. (May/June 1999).
Tate, James M. "The Nurse and Beyond: An Interview with Louise Fletcher." *Cult Film Freak*. http://www.cultfilmfreaks.com/2012/12/louisefletcher.html. (December 3, 2012).
TCM. "Motorcycle Gangs, Hippies and Stunt Men: An Interview with Richard Rush." Movie Morlocks.com. http://moviemorlocks.com/2010/04/17/motorcycle-gangs-hippies-and-stunt-men-an-interview-with-richard-rush/. (April 17, 2010).
Thrift, Matthew. "Interview: Monte Hellman." *Cinephile*. http://www.cinephile-uk.com/2011/05/monte-hellman-is-nothing-short-of_2049.html. (May 9, 2011).
Toussaint, David. "The Color of Hollywood: Karen Black's History of Might." *New York Guyd*. http://www.guyspy.com/the-color-of-hollywood-karen-blacks-history-of-might/. (April 19, 2012).
Tweedle, Sam. "Pop Culture Renaissance Man: A Conversation with Brett Halsey." *Confessions of a Pop Culture Addict*. http://popcultureaddict.com/interviews/bretthalsey/. (April 2010).
Walker, Beverly. "Interview: Jack Nicholson." *Film Comment* (May/June 1985).
White, Mike. "Monte Hellman: An Interview." *Cashiers du Cinemart*. Michigan: Issue 7, Article 122.

Annotated Scripts, Personal Letters, Private Papers

Corey, Jeff. The Jeff Corey Collection. The Thompson Library Special Collection. The Jerome Lawrence and Robert E. Lee Theatre Research Institute of The Ohio State University Libraries.
Joyce, Adrien, and Bob Rafelson. *Five Easy Pieces*. Los Angeles: BBS Productions, 1969. Original script with excised content, annotated by actress Karen Black, formally in the author's personal collection.
Shaner, John, and Al Ramus. *The Conjugal Rights of Henry Moon*. Los Angeles: Paramount Pictures. Original early script for *Goin' South*, annotated by co-producer Harry Gittes. Undated. Anonymous private collection.

Index

Numbers in **_bold italics_** indicate pages with illustrations

About Schmidt (2002) 11, 21, 23, 51, 53, 65–74, **_72_**, 100, 112–3, 158, 164, 172, 177, 194
Academy Award (Oscar) 75, 80, 88, 99, 100, 129, 153, 165–6, 171, 204, 234, 258, 261
acting class 8–9, **_9–10_**, 27–8, 82, 92, 131, 147, 249
actor as auteur, application of theory 5, 6–7, 23
Actors Studio 8, 130
advertising, disdain for 98, 222, 230, 232, 237
Allen, Nancy 2, 14, 15, 16, 86–8
Almendros, Néstor 166, 258, 259, 263, 265
Anders, Luana 86, 97, 181, 258
The Andy Griffith Show (1966, 1967) 6, 125, 138
Anger Management (2003) 12, 25, 100, 111–2, 177–8, 194
Ann-Margret 20, 139, **_140_**, 141, 188–9
antihero, character exhibiting alienation 20, 23, 24, **_67_**, 68–9, 71, 78–9, 90, 126, 176, 194–6, **_195_**, 197, 201, 212, 240
Antonioni, Michelangelo 43, 254; *The Passenger* 23, 84, 167, 169–71
appearance, lack of concern 53, 73, 79, 141–2, 186–7, 206, 210, 218
As Good as It Gets (1997) 9, 11, 12, 24, 27, 82, 100, 101–3, 112, 127, 156, 171–5, 176–7, **_173_**, 180, 191, 192
Ashby, Hal 86, **_88_**

Babenco, Hector 202, 203
Back Door to Hell (1964) 59–62, **_61_**, 212
Bakalyan, Dick 210, 213
Baker, Carroll 201–2
Barger, Sonny 13, 126, 127, 130
Barkin, Ellen 24, 190
Batman (1989) 11, 12, 21, 30, 31, 32–3, 48, 100, 116–7, 118, 176, 181, 194, 261
Bean, Alan 38, 40
Beatty, Warren 213–5; *Reds* 164–5

Begley, Adam 185, 186
Begley, Ed, Jr. 2, 181, 258, 261
Bergen, Candice 18, 138–9, 141
Bernstein, Carl 164, 166, 175, 176, 181
Berryman, Michael 103–5, 107, 111
biker exploitation, experience in film genre 23, 99, 120, 124–5, 126–30
Bingham, Dennis 7, 78, 84, 85–6, 87, 210–1, 216
Black, Karen 56, 65–7, **_67_**, 69, **_70_**, 71, 245, 249, **_251_**, 252, 255–6
black box, symbolism of being trapped inside 46–7, 114, 208, 235–6, 237, 242, 244, 247
Blake, Robert 80, 147, 210
Blood and Wine (1996) 24, 30, 45–8, 194, 204, 225
Boeri, David 33, **_34_**, 35–6, 118
The Border (1982) 6, 21, 51, 55–8, **_57_**, 168, 172, 217, 261
Brando, Marlon 39, 69, 98, 120, 129, **_129_**, 130, 134–6, **_135_**, 142, 183, 205
breakthrough, struggle in achieving 6, 7–9, **_24–5_**, 28, 65, 68, 81–2, 126, 130, 175, 197, 229, 244
Brechtian performance style 87, 211, 216
Bressler, Sandy 1, 3
Broadcast News (1987) 11, 22, 31, 41–2, 191
The Broken Land (1962) 96–7, 136–7
Brooks, Dr. Dean 104–5
Brooks, James L.: *As Good as It Gets* 102, 171, 191; *Broadcast News* 41–2, 191; *How Do You Know* 191–2; *Terms of Endearment* 39, **_39_**, 191
The Bucket List (2007) 21, 62–3, 177
Bulger, James "Whitey" 3, 33, **_34_**, 35–6, 117, 118, 164
Burton, Tim 189; *Batman* 30–1, 116; *Mars Attacks!* 30
"business," physical acting device 82, 92, 93, 134, 142, 149, 173, 174, 191
Butler, Bill 108, 254, 265

283

Index

Cagney, James 26, 160
Caine, Michael 21, 46, 47
camera awareness, artful use of 15, 17, 68, 170, 232, 247, 250, 252, 255, 257, 259, 260, 263–4, 265
Cannon, Dr. Brooke 101–3, 107, 108, 112–3, 114–5, 116–7, 118
Carnal Knowledge (1971) 6, 15, 18, 20, 21, 24, 115, 138–145, *140*, 166, 201, 202
Cartwright, Veronica 2, 134, 181, 182, 190, 260
Channing, Stockard 166, 214
character energy 15, 16, 17, 20, 32, 51, 55, 63, 69, 71, 77, 85, 92, 102, 133, 143, 159, 160, 161, 166, 175, 177, 180, 184, 187, 200, 201, 207, 209
Cher 25, 185, 187
Chinatown (1974) 11, 15, 22, 23, 128, 166, 171, 183, 194, 208–13, *211*, 215, 216–8, *216*, 248, 250, 261, 263
A Clockwork Orange (film) 141, 186, 256
Cohen, Martin B. *129*, 130
Collins, Michael 37, 40
consumerism, thematic targeting 1, 6, 56, 58, 121, 125, 230, 232–3, 235–6, 237, 241, 243
Corey, Jeff (Jeff Corey Collection) 8–9, *9–10*, 28, 82, 131, 147, 82, 221
Corman, Roger 15, 23, 82, 90–9, 131, 138, 146, 247, 259, 264; *The Little Shop of Horrors* 25, 92–3, 95, 99; *The Raven* 25, 92–3, *94*, 97; *The St. Valentine's Day Massacre* 97–8; *The Terror* 95, *96*, 97, 248; *The Trip* 11, 98–9, 229, *230*, 232–3
counterculture, themes of 23, 78–9, 98, 120, 123, 124, 146, 221, 233, 243, 245
courage, fearlessness as actor 13, 16–17, 88, 127
Court, Hazel 2, 93–4, 220
Crosse, Rupert 97, 131, 226
The Crossing Guard (1995) 6, 50, 53–5, *54*, 194, 202, 208
Cruise, Tom 17, 75–7, 78
The Cry Baby Killer (1958) 16, 23, 45, 81, 90–1, 98, 146–7, 154, 190, 194, 212

Daniels, Jeff 16, 39–40, 166
Davis, Hope 67, 72
DeNiro, Robert 58–9, 90
Dennen, Barry 2, 13, 26, 158, 161, 261
The Departed (2006) 11, 24, 30, 33–6, *34*, 45, 48, 58, 100, 117–8, 164, 194, 215
Dern, Bruce 2, 8, 15, 20, 31, 46, 81, 90, 91, 97, 99, 122, 129–30, *129*, 157, 159, 161, 198, *199*, 200, 214, 220, 229, 231, 241, 250, 252, 254
DeVito, Danny 1, 80, *110*, 134, 181, 258
dialogue, expressive delivery 17, 20–21, 22, 32, 44, 60, 92, 97, 166, 174, 179, 181, 187, 192
diCaprio, Leonardo 33, *34*, 35, 117, 170
direction, aspiration 94, 125, 188, 220, 229, 249; experience 16, 23, 106, 170, 181–2, 194, 216–8, *216*, 221, 233, 244, 248–65, *253*, *262*
Dix, Robert 15, 130, 220

Dolenz, Micky 2, 168, 227, 232, 234, 236–42, *239*
Douglas, Michael 104, 110, *110*
Dourif, Brad 109–10, 154
Drive, He Said (1971) 16, 23, 84, 106, 156, 170, 181, 188, 194, 221, 231, 233, 244–7, 248, 249–57, *251*, *253*, 261, 265
drug use, depiction as cultural subject 6, 23, 33, 98, 120, 122, 129, 194, 229–30, 232–3, 243, 245–6
Dunaway, Faye 210, 212, 217
Duvall, Shelley 158–9, *161*

Eastman, Carole (Joyce, Adrian) 68, 131, 190, 214
Easy Rider (1969) 1, 6, 7, 11, 25, 38, *39*, 63, 68, 69, 81–4, *83*, 86, 97, 99, 115, 120, 124–6, 128, 131, 137, 170, 194, 196, 234, 241, 243, 244, 245, 249, 250
editing proficiency 13, 16, 231–2, 244, 253–4, 261, 264
Ensign Pulver (1964) 125, 189–90
Ephron, Nora 166, 176, 181
Evans, Robert 209, 213, 261–2
The Evening Star (1996) 3, 41, 180, 181
eyes, expressive use 11–2, 19, 26, 33, 43, 50, 52, 62, 65, 66, 77, 79–80, 92, 107, 121, 148, 157, 174, 180, 182, 184, 196, 208

fatalism, bleak outlook as theme 223, 225, 227, 228, 235–6, 239, 241, 244, 246
Feiffer, Jules 140–1, 143
A Few Good Men (1992) 1, 12, 14, 31, 75–9, *77*, 176, 184, 212
Five Easy Pieces (1970) 6, 7, 11, 12, 17, 20, 22, 23, 46, 47, 56, 60, 63, 65–74, *67*, 112, 122, 130, 139, 158, 167, 168, 169, 175, 190, 195–7, *195*, 200, 202, 205, 225, 234, 244, 245, 252, 264
Fletcher, Louise 106–7, 109–10, *109*, 153
Flight to Fury (1964) 24, 30, 44–6, 48, 60, 155, 194, 221–5, 229, 239, 247
Fonda, Peter 2, 55, 81, 82–4, *83*, 90, 97, 98, 99, 125, 127, 222, 229–33, *230*, 255, 263
Forman, Milos 18; *One Flew Over the Cuckoo's Nest* 105, 108–9, *110*, 152, 166
The Fortune (1975) 21, 25, 31, 166, 177, 194, 204, 213–5
Freeman, Morgan 62–3

Garfunkel, Art 19–20, 138, 141, 201, 214
Garr, Teri 237, 238
Gittes, Harold 181, 244, 258, 259, 261
Goin' South (1978) 11, 21, 22, 25, 134, 135, 166, 177, 181–3, 194, 248, 257, 258–61, *262*, 263, 265
Gorshin, Frank 150, *151*
Grant, Cary 26–7

Hackett, John 59–60, *61*, 223, 224
Haze, Jonathan 92–3, 98

Index

Head (1968) 8, 45, 46, 66, 84, 114, 156, 168, 194, 221, 225, 227, 231, 232, 233–43, *239*, 244, 245, 246, 247
Heartburn (1986) 156, 164, 166–7, 180–1, 194
Hellman, Monte 225–6, 236, 248, 258; *Back Door to Hell* 59–62, *61*; *Flight to Fury* 44, 46, 223–5, 247; *Ride in the Whirlwind* 7, 17, 43–4, 97, 130–2, 225, 228–9, 247; *The Shooting* 7, 13, 17, 42–4, 97, 117, 130–1, 225
Hells Angels on Wheels (1967) 13, 23, 81, 122, 126–8, 130, 137, 150, 194, 249
hero, portrayal of characters 1, 11, 23, 29–49, 211
Hill, Jack 2, 95
Hoffa (1992) 1, 6, 22, 26, 75, 79–81
Hoffa, James R. ("Jimmy") 1, 11, 12, 17, 21, 33, 63, 75, 79–80, 81, 89, 164, 183, 184, 202, 205
Hong, James 2, 15, 209, 213, *216*, 217, 263
Hopper, Dennis 90, 97, 98, 130, 230, *230*, 231, 232, 243; *Easy Rider* 81, 82–4, 99, 125
How Do You Know (2010) 6, 21, 176, 190, 191–2, 194
Hunt, Helen 9, 24, 27, 82, 102, 171–2, 174, 176, 180, 192
Hurt, William 41–2
Huston, Anjelica 53–54, *54*, 184, 207, 215
Huston, John *211*, 212–3, 223, 257, 264; *Prizzi's Honor* 183, *183*, 215

improvisation, use of ad lib method 33, 58, 86, 87, 94, 95, 105, 126, 128, 130, 133, 164, 170, 187, 218, 250
Ironweed (1987) 6, 11, 16, 21, 24, 115, 118, 166, 167, 201–3, 261
It's a Wonderful Life (film) 156–7, 163

"Jacksplosion(s)" 3, 17, 20, 57, 65, 69, 85, 91, 106, 139, 167–8, 191, 200
Jaglom, Henry 82, 122, 249; *A Safe Place* 187–8
juvenile delinquent, characters portrayed 23, 63, 91, 103–4, 106, 109, 146–54, *148*, 194, 215
juxtaposition, device employed 231, 235–7, 240, 241

Karloff, Boris 93, 94–5, 189
Kaufman, Richard 2, 13, *185*, 186
Kazan, Elia 212; *The Last Tycoon* 58
Keaton, Diane 24, 142–4, *144*, 165, 176, 178–9, 180, 192
Keitel, Harvey *57*, 58, 217–8, 261, 264
Kent, Gary 2, 7–8, 9, 12–14, 15, 16, 22, 25, 43, 81, 122, 127–8, 131–3, 151–2, *151*, 190, 228–9, 249, 257
Kesey, Ken 103–4
The King of Marvin Gardens (1972) 6, 11, 21, 23, 31, 38, 46, 100, 113–4, 118, 172, 197–201, *199*, 202, 225
Kinnear, Greg 102, 172
Knight, Christopher 150–1, *151*
Knight, Sandra 95–6, *96*, 147, 171, 220, 221

Knight, Shirley 2, 9, 15, 27, 82, 102, 147–8, 171–2
Kovács, László (Leslie) 121, 126, 128, 129, 263
Kreuger, Miles 123–4
Kubrick, Stanley 141, 241, 242, 256; *The Shining* 114–5, 157–62, *161*, 196

Ladd, Diane 129–30, *129*, 209
Landau, Martin 2, 8
Lange, Jessica 149, 204–8
Larner, Jeremy 221, 244, 246, *253*
The Last Detail (1973) 6, 14, 16, 17, 21, 81, 84–9, *88*, 128, 171, 176, 194, 250
The Last Tycoon (1976) 58–9
The Little Shop of Horrors (1960) 12, 21, 25, 36, 60, 82, 85, 92–3, 95, 99, 152, 194, 210
Lloyd, Christopher 108, 111, 134, 181, 205, 258–9
Lloyd, Danny 159, 162
Lloyd, Kathleen 135–6
Lorre, Peter 92, 93, 94, *94*, 213, 223, 224
love for movie business, acting 20, 25–6, 209

MacLaine, Shirley 36, 38, *39*, 41, 181, 196
"Maid in the Ozarks" *24*, 25
Mamet, David 11, 80–1, 204
Man Trouble (1992) 6, 24, 176, 190–1, 192, 260
Manasquan, New Jersey 36, *37*
Margotta, Michael 2, 16–17, 244–6, 249–57
Mars Attacks! (1996) 11, 25, 30, 177
McGilligan, Patrick 86, 190
mental illness, characters with 1, 3, 7, 24, 50, 52, 100–119, 156–7, 171, 175, 177, 246
Merholz, B.J. 97, 181, 254, 258
Method acting, employment of theory 8, 12, 15, 19, 21, 22, 81, 93, 101, 118, 130, 131, 186
Meyers, Nancy 138, *144*, 178
Miller, Dick 95–6
Miller, George *185*, 263
Minnelli, Vincente 123–4
The Missouri Breaks (1976) 130–1, 134–6, *135*
Mitchell, Cameron 97, 129–30, 131, 133, 137, 226, 228
Mitchum, Robert 26, 59, 221
The Monkees 2, 8, 45, 46, 66, 168, 233–43, *239*, 247
Moreno, Rita 15, 142

Neill, Ve 2, 31, 80
Nelson, Ed 2, 16, 17, 21, 81, 91, 147, 190, 212, 268
Nesmith, Michael 2, 129, 231, 234–5, 238–9, *239*, 242, 243
Nichols, Mike 67; *Carnal Knowledge* 138, 166; *The Fortune* 166, 213–4; *Heartburn* 164, 166; *Wolf* 113, 163–4, 166
Nicholson, Jack: characters (Rexford Bedlo 93, *94*; Jerry Black 51–3, 115, *116*, 118; Harry Bliss 190–1; Garrett Breedlove (*The Evening Star*) 3, 41, 181; Garrett Breedlove (*Terms of*

Endearment) 3, 19, 30, 36, *37*, 38–41, *39*, 99; Brimmer 58–9; Will Brocious 136–7; Billy "Badass" Buddusky 14, 17, 21, 24, 81, 84–8, *88*; Buddy 149–50; Bunny *129*, 130; Burnett 60–2, *61*; Frank Chambers 149, 204–8; Charles 191; Edward Cole 62–3; Francis/Frank Costello 17, 21, 30, 33–6, *34*, 45, 117, 164, 194, 215; President James Dale/Art Land 30–1, 177; Yeoman Dolan 189; Robert Eroica Dupea 11, 65–74, *67*, *72*, 193–7, *195*, 201, 202; Lt. Andre Duvalier 21, 95; Wilbur Force 21, 36, 60, 82, 90, 92, 99, 193, 194; Mark Forman 155, 164, 166–7, 181; Freddy Gale 53–5, *54*, 208; Alex Gates 30, 45, 47–8, 193, 204; Gino, Hit Man 97–8, 215; J.J. "Jake" Gittes (*Chinatown*) 11, 19, 22, 23, 128, 171, 204, 208–13, *211*, 216–7, *216*; J.J. "Jake" Gittes (*The Two Jakes*) 11, 22, 23, 217–8, *216*, *217*, 261–5; George Hanson 1, 19, 81–2, *83*, 84, 86, 89, 125, 137; James R. "Jimmy" Hoffa 1, 11, 12, 17, 21, 33, 63, 75, 79–81, 89, 164, 183, 184, 202, 205; Col. Nathan R. Jessep 1, 12, 14, 17, 19, 21, 75–9 *77*, 81, 84, 89, 184; The Joker/Jack Napier 17, 30, 31–3, *34*, 116–7, 118, 150–1, 157, 193, 194, 204; Jonathan 24, 138–45, *140*, 193–4, 201, 202, 203; David Locke 155, 167–71, 175; Tom Logan 134, 136, *135*; R.P. McMurphy 17, 19, *110*, 152–4; Mitch 187; Henry Lloyd Moon 19, 21, 177, 181–2, 258–60, 265; Eugene O'Neill 11, 155, 164–6, 175; Oscar 21, 177, 213–4; Charley Partanna 17, 21, 175, 177, 183–4, *183*, 204, 205, 215; Francis Phelan 19, 24, 115, 118, 193, 194, 201–3; Poet 126–8; Tad Pringle 123–4, *124*; Will Randall 113, 155, 163–4, 175; Weary Reilly 7, 25, 82, 146, 149, 150, *151*, 152, 154, 215; Bill Rorish 30–1, 41–2; Dr. Buddy Rydell 177; Harry Sanborn 19, 138, 139, 141–5, *144*, 176, 178–80, 181, 192; Warren Schmidt 65–6, 68, 72–4, *72*, 112–3, 118, 139, 160, 193, 201; Charlie Smith 17, 23, 55–8, *57*; Billy Spear 21, 30, 42–3, 117; The Specialist 189; David Staebler 38, 113–4, 118, 193, 194, 197–201, *199*; Stoney 120–3, *121*; Jack Torrance 17, 19, 22, 26, 44, 66, 114–5, 118, 142, 155, 156–7, 159–63, *161*, 175, 187, 194, 196, 197, 220; Melvin Udall 11, 12, 20–1, 101–3, 106, 118, 155, 171–5, *173*, 176, 177, 178, 180–1, 192, 193, 194; Daryl Van Horne 13, 38, 177, 184–7, *185*, 193, 194; Johnny Varron 146, 147–9, *148*, 152, 154; Jimmy Wallace 90–1, 146–7, 154; Wes 226–9; Jay Wickham 30, 44–6, 48, 223–5); direction (*Drive, He Said* 16, 23, 84, 106, 170, 181, 188, 194, 231, 233, 244, 248, 249–57, *251*, *253*, 261, 265; *Goin' South* 181–3, 248, 257, 258–61, *262*, 263, 265; *The Two Jakes* 217–8, 261–5)

Nixon, Richard M. 32, 162

nudity (male) 233, 246, 255, 256–7

Nykvist, Sven 204, 263

Oates, Warren 43, 58, 97

On a Clear Day You Can See Forever (1970) 123–4, *124*, 188

One Flew Over the Cuckoo's Nest (1975) *2*, 11, 12, 15, 19, 21, 23, 24, 52, 100, 103–11, *110*, 141, 152–4, 158, 166, 176, 177, 181, 258

orange, symbol utilized 84, 170, 231–2, 255, 265

overaction, criticism as over-the-top 21, 22, 33, *34*, 91, 158, 160, 162, 182, 187, 190, 260

The Passenger (1975) 6, 23, 84, 156, 167–71, *168*, 175, 194

Payne, Alexander 65, 73

Peet, Amanda 139, 142, 178

Penn, Arthur 134–6, *135*

Penn, Robin Wright 52, 116

Penn, Sean 115; *The Crossing Guard* 50, 53, *54*, 55; *The Pledge* 50–1, *116*

Perkins, Millie 2, 5, 7, 9, 11, 13, 15, 17, 26, 27, 43–4, 97, 117, 131, 132–3, 137, 147–8, 189–90, 227–9, 267

Pfeiffer, Michelle 25, 113, 164, 176, 185

physicality, body as instrument of nonverbal language 3, 9, 13, 17, 19, 22, 26–7, 32, 47, 54, 55, 63, 66, 69, 70, 71, 73, 74, 79, 85, 86, 93, 122, 141–2, 144, 148, 157, 159, 161, 162, 163, 165, 169, 172, 174, 177, 179, 180, 182, 184, 187, 188, 198, 200, 202, 210, 215

The Pledge (2001) 6, 12, 24, 50–4, 100, 115–6, *116*, 194

Polanski, Roman 171, 209–10, *211*, 213, 257, 261, 264

The Postman Always Rings Twice (1981) 24, 149, 171, 194, 204–8

preparation and research, dedication toward 5, 12–15, 16, 22, 27, 47, 97, 101, 125, 127, 128, 132, 133, 163, 186, 228, 258

Price, Vincent 94–95, *94*, 98

Prizzi's Honor (1985) 21, 24, 175, 176, 177, 181, 183–4, *183*, 194, 204, 205, 215, 261

production, role in 8, 125, 131

Psych-Out (1968) 23, 120–3, *121*, 137, 150, 252, 263

Quaid, Randy 85, 87–8, *88*, 134, 136

Rafelson, Bob: *Blood and Wine* 46–7, 225; *Five Easy Pieces* 46, 65–7, 197, 225; *Head* 8, 46, 66, 144, 225, 233–6, 238–40, *239*, 242–3; *The King of Marvin Gardens* 46, 197, 114, 197, *199*, 200, 225; *Man Trouble* 190; *The Postman Always Rings Twice* 204, 206–8

The Raven (1963) 25, 93–5, *94*, 97, 138, 220, 223

Rebel Rousers (1970) 15, 23, 126, 128–30, *129*, 137, 209, 220

Reds (1981) 6, 156, 164–6, 215, 261

Reeves, Keanu 143, 145

Reiner, Rob 63, 75

Richardson, Tony 56, *57*, 168

Index

Ride in the Whirlwind (1966) 7, 12, 17–18, 21, 43, 44, 81, 97, 131–3, 137, 155, 194, 221, 225–9, 247, 249
Roarke, Adam 123, 126
Rodgers, Jimmie 2, 59–62, **61**
Roos, Fred 223, 256
Ross, Marion 2, 41
Ross, Scott 209–10
Rush, Richard: *Hells Angels on Wheels* 126–8, 130, 150, 249; *Psych-Out* 120, **121**, 123, 150; *Too Soon to Love* 150
Russell, Ken 188–9
Ryan, John P. 65, 207

Sachse, Salli 2, 11, 98, 229–33, **230**
A Safe Place (1971) 25, 187–8
The St. Valentine's Day Massacre (1967) 24, 97–8, 194, 215
Sandler, Adam 111–2, 177
Sandoval, Andrew 243–4
Sarandon, Susan 25, 176, 185–6
Scharf, Sabrina 126–7, 128
Schneider, Maria 84, 169–70
Schumer, Arlen 30, 31–2
Schweickart, Rusty 36–8, **37**
Scorsese, Martin 90; *The Departed* 33, 35, 117
screenwriting 6, 7, 11, 15, 24, 44–5, 46, 55, 66, 94, 98–9, 125, 131–2, 155–6, 194, 220–247, 249, 255
Segal, Peter 177–8
sexual liberation, depiction 1, 6, 23, 97, 98, 122, 205, 207, 218, 231–2, 240, 243, 244, 245, 252, 265
The Shining (1980) 12, 13, 17, 22, 24, 26, 32, 36, 44, 66, 100, 114–5, 156–63, **161**, 175, 176, 187, 194, 195, 196, 197, 220, 256, 261
The Shooting (1966) 7, 11, 13, 17–8, 21, 24, 30, 42–4, 48, 81, 97, 117, 118, 131, 133, 137, 194, 225, 249
Small, Mews 2, **2**, 15, 103–5, 107–11, **110**, 154
social commentary, message conveyed 1, 6, 56, 98, 103, 107, 121, 131, 226, 236–7, 240, 242–3, 245, 246, 249, 250, 252, 254, 265
Something's Gotta Give (2003) 24, 127, 138–45, **144**, 176, 177, 178–80, 192
Spader, James 66, 113, 164, 172
Spain, Faye 45, 222, 223, 225
Stanton, Harry Dean 9, 129, 135, 190, 226, 254
Steenburgen, Mary 24, 135, 182, 258–9, 261
Stockwell, Dean 120, **121**, 122, 147, 252
Strasberg, Susan 19, 120, 122, 232
Streep, Meryl 19, 118, 166–7, 181, 201–3
Streisand, Barbra 123, **124**
Struthers, Sally 69, 205
Studs Lonigan (1960) 7, 23, 25, 82, 97, 115, 150–2, **151**, 183, 194, 215
Summer, Dick 197–8, 201

television, antipathy toward 125, 149, 159, 230, 232, 255
Tepper, William 84, 231, 244, 250, 252
Terms of Endearment (1983) 3, 11, 16, 21, 23, 30, 36–41, **39**, 73, 84, 85, 99, 115, 166, 181, 191, 196, 261
The Terror (1963) 95–6, **96**, 97, 98, 210, 231, 248
Thunder Island (1963) 155, 221–3, 224, 225
Tommy (1975) 188–9
Too Soon to Love (1960) 23, 149–50
Tork, Peter 2, 46, 114, 208, 234–5, 238–43, **239**
Touch of Evil (film) 93, 170, 219, 264
Towne, Robert 209, **211**, 213, 244, 250, 252, 253, 255, 261, 262
The Trip (1967) 11, 24, 55, 97, 98–9, 156, 170, 194, 221, 222, 229–33, **230**, 237, 244, 245, 255
Turkel, Joseph 2, 12, 157–8, 162–3
Turner, Kathleen 176, 183–4, **183**, 215
The Two Jakes (1990) 11, 15, 22, 23, 58, 181, 194, 216–9, **216**, **217**, 248, 250, 257, 261–5

underplay, aptitude for nuance 53, 62, 69, 71–3, **72**, 80, 95, 134, 167, 169–70, 176–7, 178–9, 184, 200, 207
Updike, John 185–6

video playback and monitor, use of in directing 258, **262**, 263
Vietnam War 6, 23, 235, 237, 240–1, 244, 245, 252, 253, **253**, 254, 265
villain, villainous character 1, 11, 24, 29–49, 117, 150, 194

Waits, Tom 16, 202
Walter, Tracey 32, 181, 258, 260, 263
wardrobe and costume, importance of 13, 15, 35, 121, 133–4, 174, 179, **217**, 223, 225
Weld, Tuesday 25, 187–8
Welles, Orson 66, 93, 169, 170, 188, 219, 254, 264
West, Adam 3, 33
Wexler, Haskell 108–9, 263
The Wild Ride (1960) 23, 63, 91, 147–9 **148**, 152, 154, 194
The Witches of Eastwick (1987) 12, 13, 22, 25, 31, 38, 73, 122, 176, 177, 181, 184–7, **185**, 260, 263
Wolf (1994) 66, 113, 156, 163–4, 166, 172, 175
Worden, Al 38, 40
Wyle, Noah 2, 14, 76

"yes" and "no," care employed in vocalizing 22–3, 172
Young, Otis 85, 87, **88**

Zsigmond, Vilmos 263, 265

www.ingramcontent.com/pod-product-compliance
Ingram Content Group UK Ltd.
Pitfield, Milton Keynes, MK11 3LW, UK
UKHW041928140426
5217IPUK00014B/364